The Persian Empire

J.M. Cook

Schocken Books · New York

First American edition published by Schocken Books 1983
10 9 8 7 6 5 4 3 2 1   83 84 85 86
Copyright © Text, J.M. Cook 1983
Published by agreement with J.M. Dent & Sons Ltd London

Library of Congress Cataloging in Publication Data

Cook, J.M. (John Manuel)
    The Persian Empire.
    Bibliography: p.
    Includes index.
    1. Achaemenid dynasty, 559–330 B.C.   2. Iran—History
    —To 640 A.D. I.   Title.
    DS281.C66   1983   935'.05   82–10382

Manufactured in the United States of America
ISBN 0–8052–3846–8

Preface

This book is intended to fill a gap. It does not compete with A.T. Olmstead's posthumous *History of the Persian Empire* (1948) in either length or scope. But many new discoveries have been made since Olmstead died, and many new ideas have been put forward; the matter I have omitted is mainly what in Olmstead was not strictly relevant to Persian history, and a great deal that Olmstead seemed to present as fact is now dubious or must be discarded. Valuable, but no less speculative, are R. Ghirshman's *Iran from the Earliest Times to the Islamic Conquest* (1954) and *Persia from the Origins to Alexander the Great* (1964). As far as possible I have tried to distinguish between conjecture and fact so that the reader may not mistake the one for the other. In matters closely related to the Achaemenid realm – the Achaemenids being the dynasty that ruled the Persian Empire from 550 to 330 B.C. – I have tried to include in the notes the most essential references to recent writings; but I could not attempt to do the same for outlying regions and peripheral topics.

In the last ten years or so, thanks partly to the interest aroused by the 2,500-year anniversary of Cyrus the Great and the publication of the Persepolis Fortification tablets, the modern literature on the Achaemenids has doubled itself. Two important new books on the early period are M.A. Dandamaev, *Persien unter den Ersten Achämeniden* (1976), and W. Hinz, *Darius und die Perser* (1976). For the Iranian background R.N. Frye, *Heritage of Persia* (1962, 1976) remains indispensable.

My ignorance of the relevant languages has compelled me to take at second hand the information from Babylonian and Egyptian sources, Aramaic documents, and Elamite tablets; the same applies to the work of Soviet archaeologists in Russian. I am specially indebted to D.M. Lewis for pointing out many errors in my drafts, making valuable suggestions, and informing me about books and articles that were unknown or inaccessible to me; also to D.M. Stronach and Michael Cook at a number of points. Finally also to Simon Hornblower, who has put me further in debt to him by reading the proofs, and to Julia Kellerman who conjured up photographs and turned my unsightly copy into a book.

In this book the homeland of the Persians is spoken of as Persis; they themselves called it Parsa, and it corresponds very roughly to the modern province of Fars. On the rare occasions when I speak of Persia – a name that has come to us from Latin – it is the geopolitical entity or great power that is referred to. Iran (Ariana), the land of the Iranians whom the Persians called Ariya, had no very definite geographical boundaries in ancient times. Media and Persis formed its western flank towards Mesopotamia. On the east it may be thought of as stopping short of the Indus basin, though perhaps reaching to the Jaxartes (Syr Darya) in the north-east. In the south what is now known as Baluchistan should probably not be counted to ancient Iran; and strictly the same might be said of the land of the Khuzis (Ahwaz in Arabic) which was generally known as Elam and included the Achaemenid capital of Susa.

My spelling of ancient names conforms to common English phonetic rendering except in Greek names (where by established convention ch represents the letter chi, as in Chios, and not the sound ch as in church).

Edinburgh   July 1982

Contents

List of Plates

Between pages 164 and 165

List of Figures

Abbreviations

AA	Archäologischer Anzeiger
AJA	American Journal of Archaeology
AJP	American Journal of Philology
AJSL	American Journal of Semitic Languages
AMI	Archäologische Mitteilungen aus Iran
Anz. Öst. Akad.	Anzeiger der österreichischen Akademie der Wissenschaften
BSOAS	Bulletin of the School of Oriental and African Studies
CHI	Cambridge History of Iran
CRAI	Comptes rendus de l'Académie des inscriptions et belles-lettres
DAFI	Délégation archéologique française en Iran
FGH	F. Jacoby, Die Fragmente der griechischen Historiker
IsMEO	Istituto italiano per il Medio ed Estremo Oriente
Ist. Mitt.	Istanbuler Mitteilungen
JAOS	Journal of the American Oriental Society
JdI	Jahrbuch des deutschen archäologischen Instituts
JEA	Journal of Egyptian Archaeology
JHS	Journal of Hellenic Studies
JNES	Journal of Near Eastern Studies
JRAS	Journal of the Royal Asiatic Society
JRGS	Journal of the Royal Geographical Society
NH	Pliny, Natural History
OLZ	Orientalistische Literaturzeitung
Proc. RGS	Proceedings of the Royal Geographical Society
Rev. arch.	Revue archéologique
SB Berl.	Sitzungsberichte der deutschen Akademie der Wissenschaften zu Berlin
SB Öst. Akad.	Sitzungsberichte der österreichischen Akademie der Wissenschaften
ZDMG	Zeitschrift der deutschen morgenländischen Gesellschaft
ZfA	Zeitschrift für Assyriologie
Vth Int. Congress	Vth International Congress of Iranian Art and Archaeology, 1968

DB, XPh, etc. connote royal inscriptions, the first letter indicating the king (e.g. Darius, Xerxes), the second the site (e.g. Behistun, Persepolis), and small letters being serial figures. Cf. R. G. Kent, Old Persian.

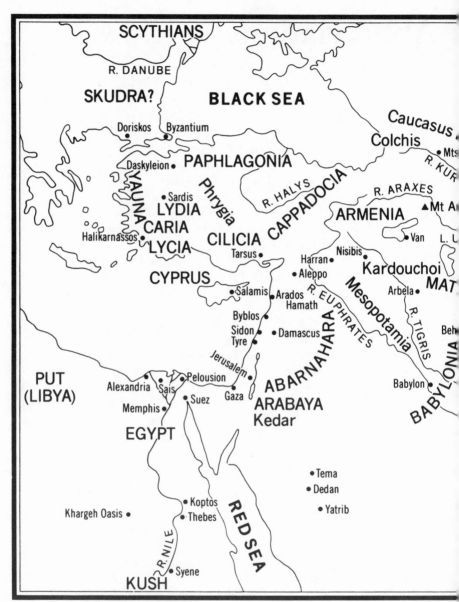

Fig. 1   The Persian Empire

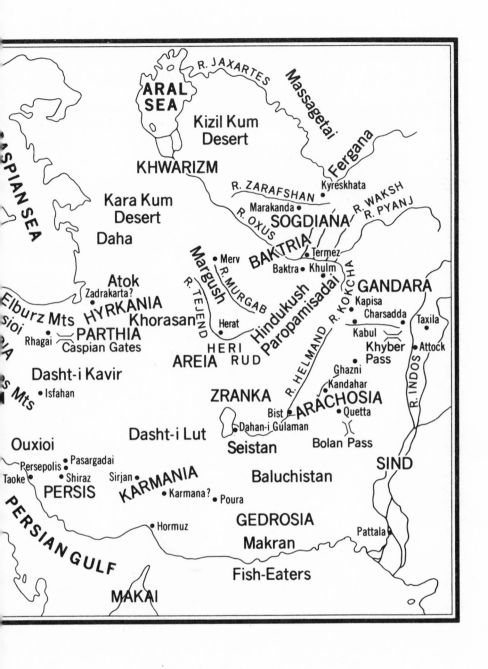

Enid's book, for which she did so much

I The Emergence of Medes and Persians

Parsua, a land of Persians, is first mentioned on the Black Obelisk of the Assyrian Shalmaneser III in the record of his campaign of about 843 B.C., and the Mada (Medes) are first mentioned eight years later. Their positions are not precisely fixed. But Parsua certainly lay in what we call Persian Kurdistan somewhere well south of Lake Urmia and well north of the valleys which the Great Khorasan Road traverses.[1] The Mada were encountered in the central Zagros; but in general they were both more numerous and more distant, stretching back as far as Mt Bikni (the 'lapis lazuli mountain') which most scholars have taken to be Demavend in the Elburz,[2] and to the edges of the salt desert – in fact as far as Assyrian troops ever to our knowledge penetrated the interior of Iran. The questions when these Iranian peoples arrived in the Zagros and where they came from are at present unanswerable. It has been claimed that the forms of their names in Greek (Mēdoi and Pĕrsai for Iranian Māda and Pārsa) prove on linguistic grounds that they were known to the Greeks by the tenth century B.C. at latest, in which case they must have been well to the west.[3] But it is difficult to believe that the Greeks knew of them before they entered the horizon of the Assyrians. It is curious that Mēdea and Pĕrseus were figures of the Greek legends who had Oriental connections. But granted that they were, it was natural that when word of the Mada and Parsa reached them the Greeks should tie them in to their own mythology, making Medea travel to Media and claiming Perseus as the progenitor of the Persians and in due course the father of Achaemenes (whose name suggested Achaean ancestry).

Archaeological investigation of the Zagros is still at an early stage. It would be hazardous to associate any known culture there with the people of Parsua, especially when their situation in Kurdistan is so ill defined; and in the central Zagros the Iron Age cultures from about 1250 B.C. till the seventh century show no obvious break in pottery or settlement pattern that can be associated with an Iranian immigration in the period. What can be said is that from the time of Shalmaneser III the position of Parsua seems to have remained constant in Persian Kurdistan for several generations. Though limited in extent, it nevertheless housed twenty-seven 'kings' about 835 B.C. who could pay tribute if the Assyrian appeared to exact it from them. Under Tiglath-Pileser III and Sargon II, between 745 and 705 B.C., the people of Parsua are mentioned in close association with the Medes, but also with the Mannaeans, so they must still have been well north of the Great Khorasan Road.

The Medes were an altogether more formidable proposition. They are mentioned almost constantly in the annals of every warlike Assyrian king from Shalmaneser III down to Ashurbanipal (668–627). They were firmly established in the western part of the Iranian plateau and were evidently infiltrating the highlands and upper valleys of the Zagros where they would seem to have been absorbing an existing non-Iranian population. In 713 B.C. Sargon II received the submission of forty-five Median city chiefs, and he claimed to have incorporated thirty-four districts of the Medes in his realm. By the time of Esarhaddon (680–669 B.C.) the familiar non-Iranian states of the central Zagros, Ellipi and Harhar, were disappearing from the records, and the Medes were becoming the dominant power on the Assyrians' mountainous east flank. Close study of the names of petty local rulers in the Assyrian texts seems to show that a process of medization was taking place; names appear that will be familiar later, as Shidirparna (in its Persian form known to us as Tissaphernes).

If the Parsua in Persian Kurdistan were the only place of that name known, it would be natural to think in terms of immigrants who had squeezed past the Caucasus, and in fact most scholars do so. But the Assyrian king Sennacherib in his eighth campaign (692/91 B.C.) was confronted with a Parsua or Parsuash which took part, along with Ellipi and Anshan, in an alliance with Elam against him, and he was unable to gain a decisive victory over the confederates in the battle of Halule on the Tigris. Ellipi, which was a buffer between the Assyrian and Elamite spheres of domination, should correspond to what is now northern Luristan in the valleys around and south-east of the Great Khorasan Road, but Anshan is far to the south-east and it looks as though this Parsua should be placed somewhere towards Elam and a long distance from Shalmaneser's Parsua in Kurdistan. Finally we learn from the Babylonian titulature of Cyrus the Great, who reigned from 560/59 to 530, that his Achaemenid forbears for three generations had been kings of Anshan, which we now know to have been situated in Persis (modern Fars). There is at least a *prima facie* presumption that a Cyrus (Kurash), who is called king of Parsua in Assyrian texts and sent his eldest son with tribute to Ashurbanipal when Elam had been crushed about 640 B.C., was ruler of Anshan and therefore already settled in Persis. We thus seem to have three different locations for people with the Persian name: (i) in Persian Kurdistan between the 840s and 714 B.C., (ii) in all probability in the Zagros towards Elam but not yet in Anshan (beginning of the seventh century), and (iii) in Persis where the Achaemenid dynasty established its rule and gave the name Parsa to the land – this should have happened after 692 B.C. when the Elamite king in Susa, Kudur-Nahunte, was still calling himself king of Anshan.

At first sight it would appear that we are dealing with one lot of people who more than once migrated south-eastward to new lands; and the great majority of scholars have taken this to be the case. Certainly the Persians cannot have been in control of Fars (Persis) before the seventh century. But free movement of a large body of people along the length of the Zagros does present problems: for there were normally states or confederations who were sufficiently organized to provide an obstacle. Ellipi disappeared from the record in the time of Sennacherib's son Esarhaddon (about 670 B.C.), and about the same time Scythian (Asgusu) intruders began to be a nuisance to the Assyrians in the north. Later the Scythians ran loose and seem to have caused considerable disruption to the growing power of the Medes; but if the people of the original Parsua leapfrogged the Medes, it must have happened earlier than this, and similarly by the time that the powerful kingdom of Elam was devastated by Ashurbanipal and resistance in its hinterland would have been weakened (about 640 B.C.) it is supposed that the Achaemenids had already reached their final destination.[4] Most recently, therefore, some scholars have inclined to assume that there were two, if not even three groups of Persians occupying lands called Parsua or Parsuash in the Zagros, and it has been suggested that the reason why the Parsua in Kurdistan drops out of the record is not that they had emigrated but that the Assyrians had given up campaigning in the northern area in the seventh century. Young in fact has called the supposed migration 'an artifact of the sources'.

With this belief goes the corresponding one that the Persians entered Iran from Turkestan and not by way of the Caucasus, and – reverting to the nineteenth-century hypothesis of H. Kiepert and Tomaschek – that they reached their situations in the Zagros from the East not only by crossing the Iranian plateau north of the great central deserts but by working round to the south of them and entering Fars (Persis) through Karmania. This northeastern origin has some support from similarity of names east of the Caspian (as Parthia) and the resemblance noted between the Old Persian and Sogdian languages. But it is a long hop from Turkestan without any sign of their passage in the archaeological record up to the present, and Ghirshman has produced arguments for the Caucasus route based on recent Russian researches.[5] One thing at least is clear, that the Persians did not reach Persis through the plain of Elam, and that the so-called 'Achaemenian Village' by Susa can no longer be claimed as a sign that they were dominant in Elam before Cyrus' capture of Babylon in 539 B.C.[6] The proof of this is that (the city of) Anshan – long considered to be in the foothill country of Elam – has now been placed exactly on the map by the discovery in 1972 of inscriptions naming it at Malian in the high basin of Fars, a long day's walk north of Shiraz. Once again, unfortunately, archaeology has not advanced far enough to enable scholars to choose with any certainty between the different views that are currently held.

By the middle of the seventh century things were running for the Medes. The Assyrians, whose systematically trained and equipped armies had proved almost irresistible in the ninth century and again from the middle of the eighth, were finally wearing themselves out by their constant wars of aggression, including Esarhaddon's conquest of Egypt; Babylon as a protectorate was a running sore, and Ashurbanipal's best efforts from a military angle were spent in subduing the revolt there under his brother and annihilating Elam. The time had passed when they could mount a major offensive in the Zagros. And the Medes, who by 735 B.C. at latest seem to have had a sort of capital called Zakruti, were forming themselves into a confederation, if not a kingdom.

The only consecutive sketch of Median history that we have is that in

Herodotus (I 95–130), which shows every sign of having stemmed, whether directly or indirectly, from a Median oral source in the fifth century. He names four kings who reigned in succession father to son, until the last of them was overthrown by Cyrus the Great; and he gives some account of their doings mixed up with folklore elements. He tells us the length of their reigns; and if we count back from 550 B.C. – the year in which the Babylonian Nabunaid Chronicle appears to record Cyrus' victory (below, p. 27) – and not (as Herodotus would do) from Cyrus' accession-year (560/59), we reach the following sequence:

Deiokes	(53 years)	about 700–647
Phraortes	(22 years)	about 647–625
Kyaxares	(40 years)	about 625–585
Astyages	(35 years)	about 585–550.

We have some check on the last two reigns. The Babylonian Nabunaid chronicle names Ishtumegu (i.e. -wegu) as the Median king overthrown by Cyrus.[7] A war between Kyaxares and the Lydian king Alyattes is described by Herodotus (I 73–74), who says it terminated in the sixth year after a battle between them was spoiled by an eclipse of the sun, the ensuing peace being cemented by the marriage of Alyattes' daughter to Astyages; whether or not Kyaxares was still alive, the eclipse was rightly identified by ancient chronographers, as transmitted to us by Pliny and Jerome, being that of 28 May 585 B.C.[8] From the Babylonian side again we know that it was Kyaxares who captured Nineveh, thus destroying for ever the power of Assyria, that he achieved this in 612 B.C., and that he had been manoeuvring for at least three years previously.[9] It was Kyaxares, Herodotus tells us, who remodelled the Median army, brigading the different units and separating the three arms (spearmen, archers, and cavalry) which had previously been jumbled together. But when he says that having first set out to conquer Nineveh with his model army Kyaxares was headed off by a great host of Scythians who overran Asia as far as the Egyptian border and that it was only after twenty-eight years of Scythian domination that he was at last able to return to the assault on Nineveh, we find ourselves in serious chronological trouble. Scythians, who according to Herodotus were led by Madyes, son of Protothyes (doubtless the Scythian chief Bartatua whom Esarhaddon named as an ally of his against the Medes), evidently did create a diversion and compel Kyaxares to postpone his assault. But – formidable though they were – the Scythians' twenty-eight-year domination of Asia is not reflected in Assyrian and Babylonian texts and must be an overstatement.

Deiokes and Phraortes are figures whose actions are known to us only through Herodotus. Deiokes, we are told, was a son of an older Phraortes; he lived at a time when the Medes were village-dwellers, and as a man of repute he subtly persuaded his fellow villagers to make him their justice of the peace; as his reputation for incorruptibility spread he was invited in the prevailing lawlessness of the times to become ruler of the Medes, and on being made king he had a stronghold built for himself with seven concentric rings of fortifications and founded the capital city of Agbatana around it; in this way

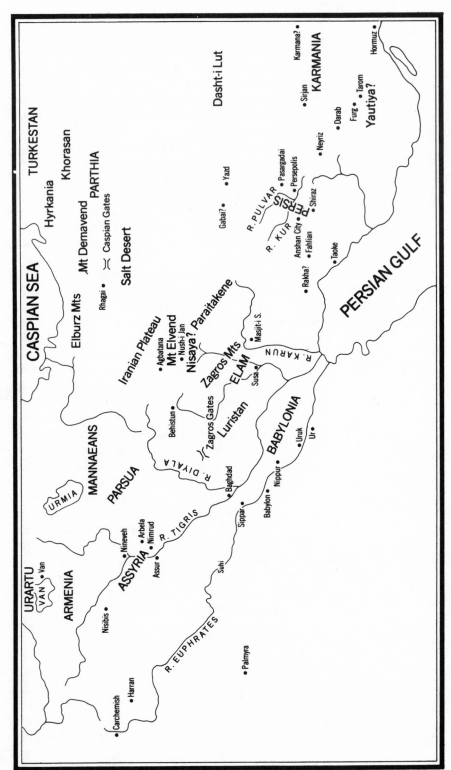

Fig. 2   Mesopotamia and western Iran

Media was united, and Deiokes stayed in his kremlin thereafter for the fifty-three years of his reign, unseen by his subjects, but with messages going in and out and a special branch to keep him informed. Phraortes was more energetic. According to Herodotus he made the Persians subject to the Medes, and then in conjunction with them he proceeded to conquer Asia, going from one nation to the next, until after twenty-two years he lost his life and the greater part of his army in an attack on Assyria.

The name Deiokes corresponds to that of Daiaukku who offended Sargon II by betraying Mannaean territory to Rusas of Urartu and was deported with his family to Hamath in Syria in 715 B.C.; though he appears merely as one of many local chieftains and to have been a Mannaean rather than a Mede, scholars seem generally to accept that he was Herodotus' Deiokes and the first king to rule over the Medes as a whole. But the Assyrian texts lend no further support, and it would be frivolous to suggest that the reason he was invisible in Agbatana is that he was living under duress 650 miles away in Syria. The person who seems to have impressed the Assyrians as being a chief capable of uniting the Medes in alliance with Mannaeans and intrusive Cimmerians to form an anti-Assyrian block was Kashtariti of Kar-Kashshi in the central Zagros, who makes his first appearance in omen texts in 674 B.C. (two years after the great drive on to the Iranian plateau which brought Esarhaddon in sight of Mt Bikni); and the name Kashtariti (in Median Khshathrita) does not occur in Herodotus or fit with his chronology of the Median kings. The names in themselves are all good. Deiokes fits with Daiaukku, and two lines of Darius' Behistun inscription referring to a claimant to the Median throne in 522–521 B.C. give us the rest: 'one Frawartish (i.e. Phraortes) by name, a Mede, he lied, he said "I am Khshathrita of the lineage of Huwakhshatra (i.e. Kyaxares)" '. He may well have been so, and certainly we seem to be dealing with a single dynastic family in the seventh century.

Different scholars play it differently. Olmstead and Ghirshman seem to understand Herodotus as meaning that Kyaxares reigned for forty years *plus* the twenty-eight years of Scythian domination, thus bringing him to the throne before 650 B.C. (an alternative view that has been put forward is that there was an interregnum of twenty-eight years between Phraortes and Kyaxares); and though some scholars believe that Khshathrita was the predecessor of Phraortes, it is now a fairly common belief that they are the same person, Khshathrita being the throne name. There is also mention of a chieftain of the river (country) called Uksatar in a list of twenty-seven chiefs (many with Iranian-sounding names) who came to Parsua to pay homage to Sargon II in 714 B.C., and he is said to appear also a dozen years later when Sennacherib was attacking Harhar in the central Zagros. On the strength of this evidently identical name a Kyaxares I is now coming to be recognized as the successor of Deiokes, followed by Khshathrita. Thus either one or two kings are now commonly inserted after Deiokes in the list given by Herodotus. At the same time we must not forget that the Babylonian chronicles prove that Herodotus had no workable Median chronology.

The Persians did not have to carve out an empire for themselves from scratch. Cyrus the Great took over one ready-made from the Medes. The unifying of the Medes, which Herodotus attributes to Deiokes, may have been largely the work of Khshathrita in the second quarter of the seventh century. This would not conflict with the archaeological evidence; Moorey in fact has gone so far as to remark that after the middle years of the century pottery taken to be typical of the Iranian-speaking intruders is for the first time found widely distributed in Luristan;[10] and it would provide a suitable context for Herodotus' statement that, having subjected the Persians, Phraortes went on to conquer the peoples of Asia (in the middle and third quarter of the century by his reckoning). The new conquests at that time were not in the west, because the Assyrians still stood firm and the Mannaeans towards Lake Urmia held out as long as the Assyrians did. After the fall of Nineveh in 612 B.C. of course Kyaxares' model army must have been active. Harran in High Mesopotamia was sacked by the Medes in 610, and they must have brought the Mannaeans and the declining power of Urartu in Armenia under their control before they could come to grips with the Lydian kingdom in the east of the Anatolian plateau – a concurrence that, thanks to the total eclipse, we can date exactly to 590 B.C. Consequently if Herodotus is right about them, Phraortes' conquests must have been in the east and it was peoples of the Iranian lands who formed the original nucleus of the Median empire. Consideration of its extent can be left until we come to Cyrus the Great's career of conquest (see below, p. 29f.).

Media as we know it under Achaemenid rule was a large province which took in the central Zagros and the highland country northward as far as Azerbaijan and eastward as far as the salt desert and the 'Caspian Gates'. Conquered peoples such as Ellipi and Harhar must have been absorbed with a resulting mixture of population and culture. Herodotus speaks of six Median peoples or 'clans' (I 101). One is the Magi, who normally functioned as priests, and not only for the Medes but for the Iranians generally. This has led scholars to assume that these 'clans' were really castes or classes (or at least that they developed into such). Another of the six, the Paretakenoi, can be placed geographically in what the Greeks called Median Paraitakene between the Zagros and the central deserts, and they have in the past been claimed as nomads; Partakka seems to have been a people of Iran in eighth-century Assyrian annals. The Boudioi, Stroukhates, and Bousai have been explained as, for instance, cultivators of the soil, tent-dwellers, and aborigines, while the remaining 'clan', the Arizantoi, is often taken to be the 'Aryan' (that is to say, Iranian) aristocracy. This has given rise to a fairly common notion that the Magi and others were non-Aryan, but it is only right to point out that the Paraitakene was in Median hands before the Zagros valleys were taken over. In fact we can place no confidence in these explanations, and Herodotus' 'clans' remain obscure. At all events the Medes declared themselves to be 'Aryans', and the Iranian element was certainly dominant enough to impose its own language and institutions.

According to Herodotus, the Persians, whom he knew no reason to place anywhere save in Persis (Fars), were subjected by Phraortes, and then joined the Medes in their career of conquest. This must have happened, if happen it did, later than the 640s when Kurash of Parsua paid homage to Ashurbanipal – in fact it has been claimed that documents of Susa show Kurash as tributary to Elam. The ruling Persian dynasty in Persis was Achaemenid, that is to say they claimed descent from an ancestor call Achaemenes (Hakhamanish) who was said in a late Greek source to have been reputedly nurtured by an eagle. He is commonly thought by modern scholars to have led the Persians on the trek that ended in Persis. But his semi-mythical origin does not prove that he was founder of a realm as well as of a lineage (Romulus, who was nurtured by a wolf, founded Rome, but Moses, who was a foundling with a better start, did not reach the promised land). The date assigned to Achaemenes by modern scholars is about 700 B.C., and this could fit. But the family tree is not as simple as it looks.

We can certainly trust the titulature of Cyrus the Great as set down by Babylonian scribes on the Cyrus cylinder of 539/8 B.C., though we must bear in mind that the name Anshan is probably an anachronism and Cyrus himself would perhaps have spoken of his kingdom as Parsa rather than Anshan: 'son of Cambyses, Great King, King of Anshan, grandson of Cyrus, Great King, King of Anshan, great-grandson of Teispes, Great King, King of Anshan.' At Pasargadai he calls himself an Achaemenid in his Akkadian cuneiform. Darius however, who won the throne on the death of Cyrus' son Cambyses, complicates the issue when he gives his own ancestry in his royal texts. At Behistun when he begins his Res Gestae with a statement of his royal descent he declares that his father was Hystaspes (Wishtaspa), Hystaspes' father was Arsames (Arshama), Arsames' father was Ariaramnes (Ariyaramna), Ariaramnes' father was Teispes (Chishpish),[11] and Teispes' father was Achaemenes; and he goes on to tell us that eight of his family had been kings before him. His eight kings would thus seem to be Achaemenes, Teispes, Cyrus I and Cambyses I, Cyrus II (the Great) and his son Cambyses II, Ariaramnes and Arsames. To this may be added the testimony of two gold tablets said to have been discovered on separate occasions a generation or two ago at Hamadan (Agbatana) and bearing texts in Old Persian that purport to be prayers on the part of Ariaramnes and Arsames, each of them being given the title of 'Great King, King of Kings, King in Parsa'. But happily for once there is agreement among the specialists that the writing dates to the fourth century, so they do not provide evidence independently of Darius.

Anshan (or Anzhan or Anchan), commonly denoted as a city, is a name that had meant something in its day; and the Great Kings who ruled in Elam had for a millennium or two included it in their titulature. On the assumption that it could not be the same as Parsa, scholars have supposed that Teispes' kingdom was divided between his two sons Cyrus and Ariaramnes, and that the latter reigned in Persis (Fars) while the former ruled territory (Anshan) that the Persians had occupied in eastern Elam. But in 1972 inscribed bricks excavated in Fars on a great Bronze Age site at Malian fixed the old city of Anshan in the heart of Persis, and consequently the notion of two separate Achaemenid kingdoms has ceased to be plausible. In fact everything points to Darius having falsified the record when he left it to be inferred that his grandfather and great-grandfather were kings. But we need not necessarily assume that he also falsified his lineage. The difficulty comes when we try to place Cyrus' and Darius' ancestors in a chronological context.

It is generally assumed that the Cyrus (Kurash) who was involved in the ruin of Elam about 640 B.C. was the grandfather of Cyrus the Great (who reigned from 560–559 to 530). This gives us a minimum of over eighty years for the reigns of the elder Cyrus and his son, and Cyrus the Great was probably still a young man when he came to the throne (see below, p. 25); Cavaignac and others have felt some uneasiness about the identification.[12] But Darius' ancestry is even more difficult. If Ariaramnes was the brother of this elder Cyrus, his son Arsames would be in the same generation as Arukku who was handed over to Ashurbanipal about 640 B.C.; and chronological tables in recent books, where two collateral royal lines are shown, bring Arsames to the throne about 615 B.C.[13] But a small point has too often been overlooked: in his Susa building inscriptions Darius expressly informs the reader that by the grace of Ahuramazda both his father Hystaspes and his grandfather Arsames were alive when he became King (522 B.C.). Here we are dealing with a matter of public knowledge that Darius would not falsify; and in the reconstruction of the Achaemenid line we have now passed the limits of credibility.

There is one further testimony that can be brought into play. At the beginning of his seventh book Herodotus brings Xerxes on to the stage of history holding a council to decide whether to make war against Athens. Herodotus is concerned to show the grand manner of the new King and puts into his mouth these words (VII 11): 'if I do not punish the Athenians, may I not be the son of Darius, son of Hystaspes, son of Arsames, son of Ariaramnes, son of Teispes, son of Cyrus, son of Cambyses, son of Teispes, son of Achaemenes'. This would certainly have raised a smile when he recited it; it is natural to suppose that he deliberately inserted Cyrus' ancestors for good measure, and as Kent remarked 'surely Darius knew his own genealogy better than did Herodotus'.[14] But as we shall see, for all his protestations in his royal inscriptions Darius did not have a bias in favour of telling the truth, and the genealogy he does give verges on the incredible. If we were to take Herodotus seriously at this point and reckon that Cyrus the Great was a young man when he came to the throne, we should be able to assume that the Cyrus who reigned till at least 640 B.C. was the grandfather of Cyrus the Great's grandfather, and that he was succeeded by a second Teispes who is the first of his line to be attested as king of Anshan (in the titulature of the Cyrus cylinder). Our Cyrus I is spoken of as a king by Ashurbanipal, but in Parsua (i.e. wherever his Persians were settled at the time), whereas it is Anshan, and not Parsua, which gives a definite location in Persis (Fars).[15] As regards chronology, we are told by Herodotus (VII 2) that Darius had three sons by his first wife before 522 B.C. and he is supposed to have been under thirty then; if we assumed twenty-five as a mean age for an early Achaemenid to beget his successor and followed Herodotus, we should find that Cyrus I was probably elderly in 640 B.C. and Achaemenes in his prime in the later years of the eighth century.

Fig.3   Composite impression from the Seal of Cyrus of Anshan. (From W. Hinz, *Darius und die Perser*. Courtesy of Hölle Verlag, Baden-Baden.)

Fig. 3   At the present time the question must be left open. Either Darius was right and these Achaemenids were extraordinarily dilatory in starting their families, or Herodotus knew better than we thought and the Achaemenids were fast breeders. In the latter event it would be unlikely that Achaemenes saw the promised land, and not certain that Cyrus I did.[16] A relic of a Cyrus has survived in the form of impressions of a seal showing a horseman in battle which was still being used in the chancery of Persis in the time of Darius, with the legend in Elamite reading 'Kurash of Anshan, son of Chishpish'. This would have to be Cyrus II, son of Teispes II and grandfather of Cyrus the Great (who would then be Cyrus III).

II The Sources

To people born in the Near East in the early sixth century before Christ, as to those born in what, to be insular, we might call mid-Victorian Europe, the known world must have appeared a very stable place. Not only had the redoubtable Assyrian realm fallen to pieces, but after the destruction of Nineveh in 612 B.C. the Assyrians themselves had quickly disappeared from view. The Medes had gone on to extend their rule westwards across Armenia until they met firm resistance in eastern Anatolia, and then in 585 B.C. came to an amicable settlement with the kingdom of Lydia which was already dominant in peninsular Asia Minor. The marriage of the crown prince of the Medes, Astyages, to the Lydian king's daughter guaranteed peace in the north-west. In Mesopotamia a Chaldaean commander in the Assyrian service, Nabopolassar, had raised the standard of revolt and made himself king of Babylon in 626/25 B.C.; his alliance with the Medes had been consolidated not only by their collaboration in overthrowing the Assyrians but by another dynastic marriage between his son Nebuchadnezzar and a Median princess. Egypt had attempted to intervene in the Levant in the years after the fall of Nineveh. But Pharaoh Necho was defeated at Carchemish on the Euphrates in 605 B.C.; and after that the Egyptians confined their aggression to the odd foray into Palestine. Babylon was left as the principal heir to the Assyrian empire.

Nebuchadnezzar, who reigned from 605 to 561 B.C., was concerned to enlarge his territory at the expense of weaker neighbours. Elam in the south-east, unable to recover from the terrible devastation that Ashurbanipal's army had wrought about 640 B.C., was evidently under his control; and the kingdoms and principalities west of the Euphrates were brought into subjection, though he had to work hard year after year for his conquests in Palestine and Phoenicia. But in general the major powers were at peace with one another. By the 560s the three Great Kings in Asia were growing old; and the ancient civilizations had become set in their ways. Turbulence such as had followed the Cimmerian and Scythian incursions was forgotten. The ruthless aggression that sustained Assyrian rule had happily disappeared, and military efficiency seems to have declined. Traditional forms were sought after, and old models and precedents were imitated with antiquarian zeal. In Jerusalem the 'discovery' of an antique law-book had brought a Deuteronomic code into force again under Josiah. Babylonia looked back to her Sumerian past and Egypt to the Old Kingdom – both then 1500 years away in time. It had become an international age with conservative attitudes and wide-ranging commerce that is well reflected in Chapter XXVII of Ezekiel on the merchandise of Tyre. It was a world that must have begun to seem eternal. Yet in a quarter of a century (550–525 B.C. exactly) each of the four great powers was to collapse in turn under the onslaught of the remote and little-known Persians.

Even more important than the commerce in goods was that in ideas and accumulated knowledge. In this world where Babylonians and Egyptians were so proud of their antiquity and conscious of their cultural heritage, the Greeks were new-comers. They were not enveloped in an illusion of impeccability. They were aware how much they had to learn, and at the same time they were endowed with the gift of observing, enquiring, and proceeding to rational explanations. They were the gainers then; and we are gainers now because we are heirs to the tradition that started with them. From the middle of the sixth century the Greeks, and especially the Eastern Greeks, were developing prose writing as a literary medium in a way that no other ancient people had thought of doing; and one of the branches of literary activity that they made their own was the writing of history. That is why most of this chapter is devoted to Greek writers.

There are of course other written sources for ancient Persian history. As we have seen, the exploits of the Assyrian kings were recorded in more or less contemporary annals and omen texts, which can be taken as factually correct so long as allowance is made for royal vanity and the axiom that any battle is a victory; it is mainly the Assyrian texts that provide the information about the Persians down to the time of Cyrus I. The neo-Babylonian texts – to leave aside private transactions and correspondence – are mainly scribal exercises in a tradition that had become standardized many centuries earlier. Apart from the sphere of divination and exorcism, texts connected with contemporary matters are rare, and the royal ones mostly relate to rituals and public works that would win the approval of the gods – even the Cyrus Cylinder, which was recently being acclaimed as a unique charter of human rights and religious tolerance, was essentially a propaganda exercise for the god's benefit, vilifying Nabunaid and proclaiming the restoration of religious orthodoxy and the reconditioning of fortifications, gates, sanctuaries and quaysides in Babylon. But relics have come to light of a unique chronicle-series recounting important events in the neo-Babylonian era; and for the brief periods covered by extant fragments the information is priceless. In fact it is from the Nabunaid Chronicle that we have the three fixed points in Cyrus' career as a Great King down to the fall of Babylon.

The carved inscriptions of the Kings of Persia are generally formal. Most commonly they were records of palace construction or undertakings like the cutting of the Suez canal or bridging of the Bosporus, and occasionally monuments to the triumphal progress of the King. A number of them give the names of two dozen and more subject peoples of the empire which can be matched against figures in their sculptured reliefs. Darius I used inscriptions as a medium of self-expression; but there is only one inscription of his which constitutes a historical narrative, that accompanying the Behistun relief which relates in detail his struggles to secure the crown (522–519 B.C.). This unique document will be discussed later. Since the Achaemenids used Elamite as a chancery language and invented a new script for their own language also, their official inscriptions from about 519 B.C. were trilingual, being written in three different cuneiform scripts – Elamite (the language and script that centred on Susa), Akkadian (the common language and script of Babylonians and Assyrians), and Old Persian in the new script. Egyptian and no doubt Greek were added when appropriate (and Aramaic is found on Darius I's tomb).

These cuneiform scripts were, however, inconvenient. Aramaic had been increasingly establishing itself as the spoken language of Babylonia and Syria; and its alphabetic script was both simpler and more adaptable than cuneiform. For official correspondence in the Persian empire the lingua franca more or less from the outset was Aramaic; and as this was written on perishable materials such as parchment and papyrus, excavators tend to find only the clay sealings that had once secured the documents. Egypt with its dry climate has produced a couple of important dossiers which cast an occasional gleam of light on imperial affairs.[1] Fortunately in Babylonia Akkadian continued to be inscribed on clay tablets; and there is a wealth of more or less private documents, business transactions, and contracts including records of a banking house in Babylon that continued to operate in Achaemenid times[2] and a firm (that of Murashu) based on Nippur during the second half of the fifth century (see below, p. 202f.). Private correspondence is said to have declined under Persian rule, but the many thousands of tablets that have been recovered are proving a never-ending source of information for the social and economic history of Babylonia. At times precise historical detail can be gleaned from them. For instance, we could make a strong case from the Greek sources for placing Cyrus the Great's death in the summer of 530 B.C., but from the dating of cuneiform tablets it is now known that news of it reached Babylonia between 12 and 31 August of that year; and in general it is the Babylonian tablets that give the most precise dating for the accession of the Achaemenid Kings for over a hundred years.

The main palaces of the Persian Kings can yield documents. Ctesias and the book of Esther speak of royal records of deeds. But they would have been written on perishable materials; and in any case Darius' great inscription at Behistun serves as a warning that a narrative of historical events was only recounted for purposes of self-justification and establishing the claim to rule.[3] Cuneiform tablets that have come to light are concerned only with the palace economy. Those found at Susa are unfortunately in the main of pre-Achaemenid times (certainly earlier than Darius I); and Agbatana still awaits serious exploration. Persepolis has yielded two dumps of tablets in Elamite which range from 509 to 494 and from 492 to 457 B.C. (when the cuneiform was presumably abandoned in favour of Aramaic for this purpose). These are records of the supply centres and the treasury in Persis and show the administration at work (see below, p. 85ff.). They give information about a number of building operations and the workers from different parts of the empire employed on them; and they name a large number of places, of which a few can be identified. Occasionally they link up with historical personages who are known from Greek sources and the Behistun inscription; but the sort of facts that they disclose about them is that Gobryas had a bigger drink ration than any other official and made a journey with his new daughter-in-law, who was daughter of Darius, and that the princess Artystone, whom we know in Herodotus as Darius' favourite wife, seems to have entertained her husband at her residence in Persis about New Year 503, when she was supplied with 200 sheep and and 1940 litres of wine, and in 498 B.C., when the quittance bore the King's own seal. Similarly it can be inferred that the harvest failed in 467 B.C. In the texture of history the cuneiform tablets of Persepolis and Achaemenid Babylonia provide numerous stitches; but if we wish to see the overall pattern we must turn to literary sources, which, with the exception of a few books of the Old Testament which bear on national and religious aspirations in Judah, mean the Greek writers and (in a very limited degree) Latin authors who drew on the Greek sources.

Of the predecessors of Herodotus the most important from our point of view is Hecataeus of Miletus, who was active around the end of the sixth century. He was not a historian. But he constructed a map of the known world, with many hundreds of names of peoples and places forming a sort of gazetteer; and while we have very little knowledge of his map apart from the fact that it showed a circular land-mass divided between Europe on the north and Asia (with Libya) on the south and bounded by a circumambient Ocean, we know hundreds of names from Greek writers who drew on his gazetteer (especially Stephanus of Byzantium 1,000 years later). It was probably at this time, and as a result of the extension of knowledge of the East which was due to the Persians, that the concept of the two continents with their curiously localized names became current in Greek thought. Hecataeus and Herodotus between them had a far-reaching, if vague knowledge of peoples of what we call Central Asia acquired from Greeks of the Black Sea colonies who were in contact with the steppe folk; and this links up with Chinese sources of a later date to provide a sort of picture of the confederations of peoples who lived in Kazakhstan and Mongolia. Curiously, the Persians had little knowledge of what lay north of their empire in the East, with the result that Alexander the Great was less well-informed than the early Ionians had been. This also applies in a different way to the eastern and southern bounds of the Persian empire. Darius I had sent a flotilla to cruise down the Indus to the sea and round the Arabian peninsula to Suez; and a Greek-speaking Carian, Skylax of Karyanda, who went on the voyage, compiled a detailed list of regions and places traversed. This accounts for an important section of Hecataeus' gazetteer. When Herodotus tells us that Darius discovered the greater part of Asia (IV 44) we may feel a bit dubious because he has already told us that the Medes under Phraortes conquered all Asia (I 102) and that Cyrus reduced every people of Upper Asia (I 177). But as regards Darius it is fair to assume that it was the Indus valley and the north coasts of the Arabian Sea that Herodotus had in mind; and here again Alexander was less well-informed until he sent his own flotilla under Nearchus round from the Indus mouths to the Persian Gulf.

To the Greeks the 'Persian Wars' (that is to say, the unsuccessful expeditions of Darius I and his son Xerxes against Greece in 492–90 and 481–79) were the great event. They provided a unique topic to make history of, not forgetting of course the earlier encounters that started with the conquest of the Greeks of Asia under Cyrus. Dionysios of Miletus wrote a *Persika* that may have been known to Herodotus, though it is not at all clear what it covered; Charon of Lampsakos wrote one that may possibly have preceded Herodotus' work; and some scholars have claimed that Hellanicus of Lesbos, who was probably a few years younger than Herodotus, was the first of the two to publish his *Persika*. Thus Herodotus, to whom we now turn, may occasionally have been indebted to an Eastern Greek predecessor for specific information (about the parade state of the Persian army for instance). It would not necessarily be any the less reliable if that were so. What we can say is that in the few instances where citations from these other fifth-century authors occur in later Greek writers and allow a comparison with Herodotus, they appear unimpressive.[4]

What seems to have distinguished Herodotus from these writers of *Persika* was the breadth of his conception of history. But he was also humane. He lived in the age of Attic tragedy. He recognized that the god will not allow any man to enjoy unbroken success to the end, and with his generous nature he could sympathize with the mighty when they were humbled. To some extent he applied this notion of what we call 'nemesis' to the Persian kingdom, whose victorious career was ended by a handful of Greek cities. But he had a general interest in the contrasts of different peoples and polities; and he was free from racial prejudice. Certainly he probed far back, and he was not a man to leave out a good yarn that came his way; and few ancient writers were more conscious of the multiplicity and interdependence of human actions and contingencies. He is sometimes spoken of as discursive. In fact few great historical works have been more systematically arranged than his, and none with greater artistry. The last three books are devoted to Xerxes' attempt to conquer the Greeks. The first six fill in the background and of course cover the wars of aggression that preceded the Great Invasion. Starting near home, Herodotus begins his narrative with the Lydian kingdom of Croesus, and so we are a third of the way through book I before Cyrus the Great takes the centre of the stage. But thereafter it is the doings of Cyrus and his successors that in their chronological order dictate the sequence, and each time that the spotlight is turned on a new kingdom or people whose path is crossed Herodotus pauses to tell us what he has found out about its past history, its geographical setting, its curiosities, and the customs of its various inhabitants. In the course of these six books all the peoples with whom the Persians had contact are made known to us. In fact, by subtle manipulation he contrives to unfold before our eyes a panorama of almost the entire known world.

Born probably about 490–485 B.C. at Halikarnassos in Caria on the west coast of Asia Minor (and so nominally a Persian subject), he spent the later part of his youth as a refugee on the island of Samos, and then became a wanderer. He travelled extensively in Egypt, visited Gaza and Tyre, and went down the Euphrates to Babylon. He may possibly have been as far as Susa. Besides Greece and the Aegean he must have been familiar with parts of Asia

Minor, and he visited Greek colonies on the coasts of the Black Sea and even the Scythians. He is said to have given readings in Athens, which he left to join the new Athenian colony at Thourioi in Southern Italy. Much has been written about him in modern times, and with such ingenuity that there is hardly a single statement about his life that has not been contested; but the general impression of a well-educated and well-travelled man must stand.

His information varies greatly in quality, though with his own eyes he was a keen and accurate observer. There is little doubt that in Egypt, where there were many Greek and Carian mercenaries and traders from the seventh century on, he acquired much of his information from compatriots, while his contacts with the personnel of Egyptian temples gave him access to native oral traditions which defied systematic co-ordination. Thus he gives a full and mainly accurate account of the processes of embalming but loses his bearings in the long stretch of history of the Pharaohs and their spectacular creations before Saite times. In Babylon he describes the wall circuit and riverside in detail and seems to have ascended the Tower of Babel with its hostelry halfway up. But there does not seem to have been a Greek community in Babylon like those he met in Egypt; and though he picked up a good deal of legend about the famous Semiramis and a mystifying queen whom he calls Nitokris, his text does not include the account of the Babylonian kings and their works that he promised in book I 184 (or for that matter the description of the fall of Nineveh that he promised in I 106). It is possible that a chunk of his work has been lost; but more probably he never managed to acquire the coherent information required for a satisfactory narrative.[5] Any contacts he may have had with the priesthood cannot have been at a high level. The lack of Greeks in Babylon in the mid fifth century may at first sight seem surprising. But it is reflected in business documents (where people called Greeks in fact have Anatolian names) and also in nomenclature; for instance, the two great rivers of Babylonia were not known to the Greeks by their universal Near Eastern names, Purat and Deklath, but from the Medo-Persian corruptions of them (Ufratush and Tigra).

This is symptomatic. Herodotus is on firmer ground in treating the history of the Medes and Persians than he is with Egyptians and Babylonians. He can never have been to Persis; in any case the Persepolis tablets make it plain that official authorization would have been needed for travel beyond Susa. Indeed he can hardly have been in any genuinely Iranian land, though he speaks as though he had witnessed the exposure of the dead by Magi. But on Persian history and affairs he commands a surprising amount of hard detail. For instance, he can tell us the names and lineage of the five wives that Darius took after he became King, and he names twelve sons of his and distributes them all but one among their mothers. In mentioning individuals he distinguishes carefully between Persians and Medes and often gives the parentage of Persian nobles and notables. His account of the Persians, both at home and abroad, is full of incident throughout, and in general it carries conviction. In his preface he mentions Persian 'logioi' (men of learning or story-tellers) as an authority, but in a context so mythical that he can hardly have been speaking seriously – if he was, it is an instructive example of the danger of asking leading questions. Occasionally he reports that the Persians say one thing but others something else. He makes two bad errors, taking Mithra to be a goddess and the word arta – (justice) to mean 'great'; we may therefore doubt whether he had much more than a smattering of Persian. But this did not prevent him from pursuing his enquiries with diligence.

Much of Herodotus' information will naturally have come from the Greek side. The organization of Xerxes' army and navy in 480 B.C., with the different contingents and their equipment and commanders, was material for military intelligence; Xerxes showed that he was not hiding anything when he released the spies caught in his camp at Sardis. On Persian deliberations at the councils of war and Xerxes' behaviour in the field Herodotus could have had more than one source. Artemisia, the despot of his own native city, was in high esteem with Xerxes and present at the councils. Though his family belonged to the political opposition, Herodotus admired her; and the tale that she had to tell on her return to Halikarnassos comes through triumphantly in his narrative – most of all when Xerxes saw her galley ram another one at Salamis and exclaimed 'My men have become women and my women men!' while at the same time we hear the muted voice of her opponents claiming that she had rammed the galley of a friend and neighbour in order to escape pursuit. Another Greek who was in Xerxes' suite is Demaratos, the exiled Spartan king, who later had a fief near Pergamon. Herodotus relates a story told by Demaratos' companion Dikaios about the eve of the battle at Salamis, which Demaratos was called upon to confirm; and it is so vividly told that we might think the young Herodotus was present and heard the 'vox viva'. They seem both to have been living at the Persian court for some years before coming west with Xerxes, so they could have had inside information.[6]

Herodotus tells us at length about the wonders of Samos and its history. When he was living there he could have talked to people who knew Syloson, the 'benefactor' of Darius, who had been to the Persian court and was restored to Samos by a task force under Otanes (see below, p. 60); there could well have been a stock of oral information there. Information about the Persian court and harem could well have come also from Demokedes of Kroton, the doctor who was captured with Polycrates and sent up to the court, where he won acclaim and riches by successfully treating Darius' dislocated ankle. Having succeeded where the King's Egyptian doctors had failed, he had everything he could wish for except liberty to return home. But presently he had occasion to cure Queen Atossa of mastitis; and by her intercession he was sent with a Persian reconnaissance mission, from which he was able to escape in Southern Italy and return to Kroton. Herodotus' tale of her putting pressure on her husband in bed (the 'curtain lecture' as it has been irreverently called) has been received by scholars with varying degrees of scepticism; but Demokedes was better acquainted with harem routine than they, and Herodotus is likely to have had the story from his descendants when he was living in the neighbouring city of Thourioi.

Before leaving Herodotus' Greek sources we may note a small point that shows how conscientious he was. From the stage in the autumn of 481 when

Xerxes' army left the Anatolian plateau to enter Lydia he is fully in the picture. But before that he knows nothing of the march except that the marshalling point for the army was Kritalla in Cappadocia; and he frankly admits that he cannot say who won the prizes for the best turn-out there because he had no one who could inform him. One obvious source that seems curiously missing is Persian and other prisoners taken by the Greeks (Herodotus mentions naval commanders who fell into Greek hands and were taken to Corinth for interrogation and bakers, kitchen staff, and womenfolk at Plataea after the battle, and Plutarch names a number of prisoners of war including a eunuch; but there should have been Magi and well-informed secretarial staff).

There are two great bodies of consecutive historical narrative presented by Herodotus which must stem from Iranian sources. The first (book I 95–106, 73–74, 107–30) is the history of the Median kings from Deiokes down to the overthrow of Astyages, including the story of Cyrus' origins. The account of the Lydo-Median war had been given earlier in connection with the Lydian kingdom (in 73–74), but it is linked to the main Median narrative by the recurrence of a macabre folk tale of young children served up to their parents. There is some sound history in this narrative, as the later Median kings and the naming of Madyes' father show (see above, p. 4); and the story runs smoothly on, though that of Cyrus' origins is not to be believed. We may perhaps also sense a Zoroastrian flavour when Deiokes is spoken of as understanding that Right is at war with Wrong. The key figure in the Cyrus story is the Mede Harpagos, who was the trusty counsellor of Astyages, was wronged by him, and betrayed his army to Cyrus (below, p. 25f.). It was Harpagos who later was given the task of reducing the cities of western Asia Minor in the years following Cyrus' capture of Sardis. He was consequently a familiar figure to the Eastern Greeks; and he bulks so large in Herodotus book I that it is tempting to suppose that the long Median narrative emanated from his entourage. There was a Harpagos with a household brigade in the plain below Pergamon in 493 B.C.[7]

The other long consecutive narrative is in Herodotus book III (30, 61–88). This covers King Cambyses in Egypt having his brother Smerdis put to death, the revolt of the 'Magi' at home in the name of Smerdis, Cambyses' death by accident as he was returning to quell it, the seven-month rule of the 'Magi', the conspiracy of the Seven Persians and killing of the 'Magi', the discussion of the Seven on the form of constitution to be set up, and the trick by which Darius obtained the kingship (in detail below in Chapter V). Here we at last have a countercheck on Herodotus. In his Behistun inscription Darius gives his account of the sequence of events before coming on to the rebellions he had to crush after his accession. The central claim is the same in both: Cambyses had had his brother killed and it was a pretender that the Seven conspired to assassinate. There are some minor discrepancies; for instance, Herodotus did not know that the 'Magi' were on summer vacation up in Media at the time, and he has the name of one of the Seven different. But the real difference is one of view-point. Herodotus names Otanes as the discoverer of the fraud and originator of the plot, Darius being the last to be brought into it, whereas Darius claims the initiative as his own. And Herodotus' account makes it absolutely clear that Darius had no better claim to the throne than the others – a question that Darius evades by concentrating on the first person singular and not mentioning his fellow-conspirators until 300 lines later.

Darius not only had his huge inscription – his 'Res Gestae' – carved on the rock in Elamite, Akkadian, and Old Persian but he tells us it was circulated to all the provinces in the appropriate languages; and parts of copies have been found in Akkadian at Babylon and in Aramaic in Egypt. Dandamayev has claimed that it must therefore have been translated into Greek also. But no Greek writer ever showed the slightest acquaintance with it; and it is certain that Herodotus did not know of it.[8] The one mistake that Herodotus made in the names of the Seven is illuminating. In place of Ardumanish (or whatever name is to be read at Behistun for the son of Wahauka) he gives Aspathines. Now Aspathines is shown by his seal to be the son of Prexaspes, who in the story was Cambyses' right-hand man and did the killing of the true Smerdis; so though he was not one of the Seven, Aspathines could have been the key witness to what his father had done or said, and he became Darius' bow-case and battle-axe bearer. His testimony was even more important to the Seven if it was in fact not a pretender that they killed. The naming of Aspathines as one of the Seven was surely not an error of misreading but a lapse of memory on the part of someone who knew of the events from the inside. Herodotus has precise information about the fight in the palace chambers and the deliberations of the Seven before and after the coup. It is clear that somehow he heard an account of the events that had originally been transmitted orally from one of the Seven; it is equally clear that that one was not Darius.

There are two members of the Seven to whom, with Darius, Herodotus assigns speaking parts in the discussion after the coup, and it is to them that we naturally look. They are Otanes and Megabyxos. The latter had a son Zopyros, of whom Herodotus tells a long and historically improbable story of his recapture of Babylon for Darius after deliberately mutilating himself. This Zopyros' son was the heroic and headstrong Megabyxos who was a marshal in 480 B.C. and later reconquered Egypt (see below, p. 168f.); and one of his sons, also Zopyros, became an exile in Athens, where Herodotus could have known him and talked to him in Greek. The two points in favour of a connection here are the speaking part assigned to the elder Megabyxos and the extraordinary story of his son's capture of Babylon; but Herodotus makes the original Megabyxos one of the 'seconds' (the first three conspirators each introducing a second before Darius appeared). As regards Otanes, who re-instated Syloson in Samos, there is the aura of grandeur that seems to attach to him in Herodotus (where he appears to be brother of Cyrus' wife), his leading part as discoverer of the fraud and initiator of the conspiracy, his speaking part in the deliberations, and the mention of the special privileges his family enjoyed of receiving gifts from the King and not prostrating themselves before him.

Another name frequently put forward as an informant is Artabazos, who was a commander in Greece in 480–79 and afterwards satrap at Daskyleion.

Information may have come through him; but if, as is now thought, his father Pharnakes was the brother of Hystaspes (Darius' father), his account of the coup should have agreed with Darius'. As between Otanes and Megabyxos there is no need to choose; Herodotus could have had information descending from both sources. K. Reinhardt claimed a generation ago that these Persian stories belong to a developed novelistic tradition whose conceptual milieu is that of the Persian court-aristocracy; and if that were true we must allow time for them to have been worked up orally before they came to Greek ears. But the argument is an intangible one.

The last thing that must be mentioned in Herodotus is his list of the twenty 'nomoi' (satrapies) into which Darius divided the empire (III 89–97). This will be considered in detail later (Chapter VIII). But with some seventy peoples and communities named and exact figures given for the tribute payable by each satrapy, this list goes beyond the limits of what could have been orally acquired through casual enquiries; and there are indications that the source of his information was Iranian and not Near Eastern because it is the Persian names that he reproduces where the two differ (e.g. Sakai and Armenia).

Thucydides had little concern with the Persians except for their intervention in the war between Athens and Sparta in the late fifth century (the Peloponnesian War). Apart from that he is a source of confusion rather than enlightenment.[9] He was a short generation later than Herodotus. The following generation produced two men who wrote copiously on Persian affairs. Of the two, Ctesias may have been slightly the older; but it is convenient to take Xenophon first. As a young man with an upper-class background he cleared out of Athens in 401 B.C. to join the Greek mercenary corps which Cyrus, the younger brother of Artaxerxes II, was secretly assembling in western Asia Minor for the long march to contest the throne (see below, p. 211ff.). They went by the Cilician and Syrian Gates and down the Euphrates nearly to Babylon. In the ensuing battle they routed the opposing line, only to discover that Cyrus had been killed; and after the senior officers had been invited to a parley and murdered, the Greek corps (the 'Ten Thousand') had to make its way back unaided. Xenophon commanded the rearguard on the 2,000 mile march up the Tigris and across Armenia to the Black Sea coast. In 399 B.C. a need arose for these seasoned troops, and Xenophon spent the next five years fighting the Persians in western Asia Minor under Spartan command.

The narrative of these campaigns is related in two of his works (the *Anabasis* or *Expeditio Cyri*, and the *Hellenica* or *Historia Graeca*); they are especially informative about the Persian presence in the western part of the empire. Xenophon's views on the Persians and their imperial administration occasionally obtrude in an idealized form in some of his minor works. What he, however, set most store by was his *Cyropaedia* or *Institutio Cyri*, which he penned in his later years. This purports to be a life of Cyrus the Great, and it contains many references to still surviving Persian institutions, customs, ceremonial, and the like which are sometimes valuable. But though he has some knowledge of Herodotus' history and does probably draw a couple of times on Ctesias, his narrative of events is almost entirely fictitious. The *Cyropaedia* is really intended as an essay in statecraft written by one who in his youth had admired Cyrus the Younger and then idealized the Spartan king Agesilaos under whom he served in Asia Minor; and what it amounts to is Xenophon's conception of an ideal benevolent despotism with Cyrus and his nobles behaving and moralizing like cultured Greek landed gentry. In one matter his desire to glorify his subject did lead him to what is now known to be the truth; he made Cyrus' father Cambyses king of the Persians.

Xenophon does not present a problem for us. Though he was not a highly critical historian, nobody can seriously dispute the plain factual record of campaigns as far as he took part in them. Some scholars have tried to find history in the *Cyropaedia*. But it is always a losing battle; and the proof that there is none there is the extremes to which scholars have gone in the attempt to find it.

Ctesias was a doctor trained in the famous medical school of Knidos. Like Demokedes of Kroton he was sent up to the Persian court as a prisoner; and like Xenophon he was present at the battle of what he calls Kounaxa (in 401 B.C.) but on the opposite side. He treated Artaxerxes II for the wound inflicted by Cyrus, and he claimed that he spent seventeen years with the Persians. Modern scholars are not certain whether his sojourn there ended in 397, when his Persian history seems to finish, or in 393–92, when he had information about the palm trees growing on the grave of Cyrus' Greek mercenary leader.[10] Like Xenophon, Ctesias was a prolific writer, and apparently on medical topics among others. What concerns us is his *Persika* in twenty-three books. Though much used by later Greek writers (not least among whom was Plutarch), his original work has not been preserved. His first six books were on 'Assyrian' history, and an abridged version of them is incorporated in a surviving part of Diodorus Siculus' universal history compiled in the middle of the first century B.C. A complete text of Ctesias' *Persika* and *Indika* was found in Constantinople by the eminent Byzantine scholar and patriarch Photios in the mid ninth century; and noting that the author claimed to have witnessed much that he related or at least heard it from the Persians themselves and to be better informed than Herodotus, Photios had abbreviated extracts made from book VII onward. This is really a chrestomathy rather than the epitome that scholars call it; and it is so selective that we have little idea what the original may not have contained; besides which, there are errors and inconsistencies which can hardly be Ctesias' own. For the early history of Cyrus the Great we have a much fuller abridgement preserved in another Byzantine compilation from the 144-book universal history of Herod the Great's court historian, Nicholas of Damascus.

Ctesias claimed that he had studied royal Achaemenid 'hides' (strictly parchments, but in Ionic the word had come to mean simply books) and extracted information from the royal archives. In the event, we find that what he got out of them was a deheroized incident of the Trojan War in which Memnon, son of Tithonus and king of Susa, was killed in a Thessalian ambush – this could as plausibly be sought in the Ottoman imperial archives. As regards the oral information from high Persian sources, the one informant he names is Parysatis, the wife of Darius II. Ctesias says he had it from her lips that she had thirteen children, eleven of them being born after she became queen (in fact 424–23 b.c.); in Photios' text there is some confusion about her, so it may not have been Ctesias' error when she is called a daughter of Xerxes (who had in fact been dead over forty years when she became queen). But details like that would not have worried Ctesias. He must have been at the court under Darius II, who was King from 424–23 to 405–04; but he assigns him a reign of thirty-five years, which with the forty-two he assigns to Artaxerxes I would make Xerxes dead before his invasion of Greece took place. If his dating is often false (as can be proved from cuneiform tablets), his rendering of Persian names is little better.[11] As regards matters of fact, where we can compare both Ctesias and Herodotus with Darius at Behistun, Ctesias' fraudulence stands revealed in half a dozen cases. The one instance to the contrary that apologists for Ctesias have found, that Cambyses had his brother killed before he left for Egypt, is almost certainly the great non-event of early Achaemenid history (see below, p. 52). Ctesias' account of Xerxes' invasion of Greece is recognized to be a travesty of the facts: if it were not, what sort of reception would Herodotus have received from his hearers in Athens, some of whom had been in the wars? And generally speaking, much the same can be said of his account of historical events down to the second quarter of the fifth century. Even if we were to disregard Herodotus, we should still frequently be able to prove Ctesias wrong from Old Persian and Babylonian texts and even the Egyptian Demotic Chronicle. When he comes down into what in his time was living memory we can only hope he is not just inventing. But what he recorded – or at least the Byzantine scribe picked out from him – is mainly the scandals of the court, the machinations of eunuch chamberlains, unspeakable tortures, vicious harem intrigues, the gamut of 'petite histoire'. People that he names do turn up in Babylonian tablets; there will be some truth mixed up with the tittle-tattle, but at best we should expect the description of events to be sensationalized.

There is no actual mention of Ctesias travelling in Iran. But there are pointers to two journeys: one up the Great Khorasan road to Agbatana when he passed the Behistun relief and took it to be a monument of Semiramis, and the other to Persepolis when he saw the inaccesibility of Darius I's tomb at the 'double mountain'.[12] Much of his time may have been spent elsewhere than at Susa, where the royal palace had been burned down. Darius II was in Babylon towards the end of his reign at least, and Artaxerxes II was there around 401 b.c. After this Ctesias was, as he reveals, the queen-mother's doctor when she was detained in Babylon for poisoning her son's wife. So it looks as though much of his time was spent there. Drews has recently argued that what we might call the conceptual milieu of Ctesias' tales is not so much Persian as Babylonian;[13] and when it comes to stories such as those about Cyrus the Great it could well be that he picked up more in the bazaars of Babylon than in the archive rooms of the court. This would to some extent clear him of the charge of having himself invented many of the falsehoods that he narrates.

Ctesias seems to have left a successor as King's physician in Polykritos of Mende. He also had a literary successor in Dinon of Kolophon, who aspired to write an oriental history but in particular took on the story of the Persian court from where Ctesias left off and carried it down to 343 B.C. He too was used by Plutarch. With all the missions that were travelling up to the Persian court from contending Greek states, there was an increasing interest among the Greeks in the person of the King and the pomp and ceremony that surrounded him. Many scraps of information culled from Greek writers on Persian matters are to be found in the miscellany of erudite dinner-table conversation composed about A.D. 200 by Athenaeus of Naukratis, of which fifteen books survive. For the skeleton historical narrative within the Greeks' purview Diodorus is the staple (Chapter XVIII).

We at last get a first-hand conspectus of virtually the whole Persian empire in its death-throes from the narrative of Alexander the Great's career of conquest (334–323 B.C.). Our authorities for this are secondary, consisting generally of writers of a much later date who abridged original sources now lost. These sources were diverse, being composed of the court journals and the writings of a number of members of Alexander's staff (including top-ranking commanders), some of them with an inclination towards the sensational or romantic, and not all of them entirely in sympathy with Alexander. For the present purpose it is simpler to name our surviving authorities: Arrian, who has provided the most 'official' version of the Alexander history and also the fullest account of Nearchus' voyage from the Indus, Diodorus again (here using a range of more and less reputable sources), and the Latin writer Quintus Curtius Rufus who, despite his love of rhetoric and pedagogic moralizing, sometimes provides information not to be found elsewhere.

With Alexander's conquests the East as far as the Indus became known territory to the Greeks. We possess a mine of information about the Iranian lands in the *Geographika* of Strabo, who was indebted to many sources including the Alexander historians, but especially to the great all-round scholar and keeper of the royal library at Alexandria in the third century B.C., Eratosthenes. By the second century B.C. fresh information was ceasing to come through; and the only original sources of a later date to concern us are the description of main routes in Parthia by Isidorus of Charax on the Persian Gulf[14] and the derivative and badly corrupted, but surprisingly detailed later Roman itineraries. Ammianus Marcellinus, who came from Antioch and was with Julian the Apostate on his Persian expedition, ranks as a major historian; but unfortunately his information about Iran is garbled.

One non-Greek writer in Greek deserves a mention here. Berossos, priest of Bel, wrote a history of the Babylonians in three books for Antiochus I in Baghdad (Seleucia on the Tigris). It is of course lost. From the citations in later writers he appears to have had firmer knowledge than Herodotus of the late Assyrian and neo-Babylonian kings; and it is he who tells us that the Hanging Paradise (or Gardens) was constructed by Nebuchadnezzar for the Median princess whom he married. But what most of the writers who made excerpts from him sought was references to the Old Testament; and while he no doubt did say that the Ark came to rest on the mountains of the Kurds (the Flood being an age-old Babylonian legend), we can hardly join with Flavius Josephus in believing that his history included Abraham as a great and just man acquainted with celestial phenomena. It is difficult to judge how far Berossos had cuneiform texts at his disposal. But since his third book covered over 400 years down to Alexander the Great, the historical material must have been spread thin, and Drews in fact reckons that the main focus of his interest was astrological;[15] so the probability is that we have not lost much. Josephus in the late first century after Christ covered Jewish affairs in Achaemenid times in his *Antiquitates Judaicae*; he had the advantage of some knowledge of the Persian regnal sequence from earlier Greek writers; but his sources were the scriptural ones familiar to us, which are not internally reconcilable; and the effect of his work was to expand the fictional content of the Biblical tradition.

III The Deeds of Cyrus the Great

To begin at the end, Cyrus was killed in war in Central Asia in a year that can be fixed with virtual certainty as 530 B.C. News of his death reached Babylonia between 12 and 31 August. Persian couriers travelled fast (see below, p. 108); so it will have been July or early August when he met his end. According to Herodotus he reigned twenty-nine years, according to Ctesias and Dinon thirty. Babylonian texts referring to him do not carry back further than 556 B.C. But it is generally assumed that he came to the throne in Persis in either 560 or 559 and Diodorus concurs in this date. Cicero tells us that Dinon made him forty years old when he became King; this is found also in Justin and may have originated with Ctesias. Further support has been sought in the Biblical book of Daniel (vi. 1) where the conqueror of Belshazzar's Babylon (whose fall dates to autumn 539) is said to have been sixty-two years old at the time; but since he is there called 'Darius the Mede' and distinguished from Cyrus, the whole historical basis is false.[1] It is not impossible that Cyrus was seventy at the time of his last campaign. But his children were still young eight years later. Cambyses had no issue yet and Bardiya only a single daughter. Of Cyrus' three daughters two were married by Cambyses; the second one became pregnant by him and died about 524/23 B.C., Atossa, the eldest, was in the harem and her four sons were born to Darius after 522/21 B.C., while Artystone, who later bore Darius two sons, was still a virgin then. So it seems more likely that Cyrus came to the throne as a young man.

Herodotus tells one story of Cyrus' origins (I 107–130), but remarks that he knows of three others which he considers less probable (I 95). The one he tells is, he says, that which is related by certain Persians who do not wish to 'solemnify' Cyrus. It is, however, part of his long Median narrative (see above, p. 18). Briefly it is as follows. After the battle of the eclipse the Lydians and Medes made peace, and Astyages married the Lydian princess Aryenis. She bore him a daughter, Mandane, whom – as a result of a dream which portended that her offspring would supplant him – he married off to a respectable Persian named Cambyses. But warned by a second dream, he brought Mandane back to his court and handed over her infant son to his right-hand man Harpagos to dispose of.[2] The child was then presumed to be dead; but it had by chance been substituted for a still-born one, and Cyrus was brought up by a herdsman and his wife in the north of Media. At the age of ten his fearless behaviour brought him to the notice of Astyages, who recognized him as his own grandson and sent him back to his parents but punished Harpagos by serving up his own son to him at table. After this Harpagos began tampering with the loyalty of the leading Medes and in due course sent a message stitched up in a hare to Cyrus, urging him to revolt. Cyrus produced a fake order appointing himself commander of the Persians, and, summoning the principal clans, he demonstrated to them how much preferable mastery is to servitude. He then mustered for war. Astyages imprudently sent out his army under Harpagos' command; many of the contingents went over to the Persians and the rest fled. Astyages thereupon mustered the youths and old men of Agbatana and led them against Cyrus; but he was defeated and captured.

This story has a strong Median bias, for it both legitimizes Cyrus' rule over the Medes and denies the Persians a royal line of their own. It also makes Cyrus young when he overthrew Astyages and dates the beginning of his kingship from then. His father may of course have been married to a Median princess. But it is clear from cuneiform texts that Cyrus inherited a vassal-kingship of Persis (Anshan) in his own right and that Astyages was not overthrown until later. If Cyrus were to be the grandson of a marriage that followed the end of the five-year Lydo-Median war, the date of the battle of the eclipse would have to be pushed back to 603 B.C. But the 585 date has strong support, and it barely seems possible that the Medes could have mastered Armenia much before 590 B.C., both from the internal Urartian evidence and from the fact – for what it is worth – that Chapter li of the book of Jeremiah speaks of a time when Assyria was no more but Minni (the Mannaeans) and Ararat (Urartu) were extant as nations.[3] A Median campaign in Cappadocia would be unthinkable without control of central Armenia.

For Ctesias' story of Cyrus' origins Diodorus fails us, but Nicholas of Damascus is preserved here and we have a very detailed account.[4] Cyrus was the son of a poor Persian of the ill-famed Mardian clan. His father, Atradates, turned to banditry for a living, and his mother herded goats. In accordance with a common custom Cyrus attached himself for a livelihood to a Median palace groundsman, and thence by stages he raised himself to the position of King's cup-bearer. A dream which his mother had had, similar to Astyages' first one in Herodotus, now revealed to him that he would be master of Asia. Having become the King's right-hand man he had his father made satrap of Persis – such transitions from highwayman to governor are typical of Iran and Anatolia throughout the ages; and then with the help of another Persian adventurer named Hoibares he set off to join the troops his father had been instructed to raise. The resulting war will be described presently. Justin has the same story in a shorter form, though he also brings in Harpagos as a secondary figure.

Drews has remarked on the Babylonian character of Ctesias' story of Cyrus and claimed that the long-recognized resemblance to the old legend of Sargon of Akkad, which starts with the infant set adrift in a bulrush cradle and proceeds to make him in turn gardener, cup-bearer, and finally king, has been transferred to Cyrus.[5] The resemblance in the sequence from waif to king is undeniable; and though it is not difficult to find close parallels to the Sargon story elsewhere, the general milieu of the success story is clear. As history it can be disregarded. We also know two other bits of stories of Cyrus.

Herodotus mentions that the herdsman's wife was called Spako (the Median for dog) and that this had given rise to a false tale that he had been exposed and nurtured by a bitch; this presumably was sufficiently different to form another of the three stories that Herodotus rejected. Dinon had Astyages warned by a court minstrel who sang of a fierce beast let into the marsh, but this is probably no more than a variation on Ctesias at this point (a concubine singing about a boar getting the better of a lion in its lair). If Ctesias' story and that of the bitch are two of those rejected by Herodotus, the third could be the historical fact, that Cyrus came of a royal line and inherited the kingship in Persis before he went to war with Astyages.

The war against Astyages was described in detail by Ctesias, and most of it can be found in Nicholas of Damascus. Though braver, the Persians had more than once to yield to superior numbers. Eventually they concentrated their women and children on the mountain of Pasargadai, which was the highest in the region. Astyages encircled it, and the Persians moved to a second, lower summit girt with cliffs and forest, which they defended desperately. At this point, with omens favourable to Cyrus and the Medes for the moment repelled, the extract from Nicholas ends, and when it resumes Cyrus is seated on Astyages' throne. But Justin's abridgement covers the gap, so that we know that Nicholas was in fact coming to the final battle. On the throne at last, Cyrus received deputations from peoples who had taken the opportunity to revolt from Astyages. Only a few followers remained with the old king, and he was brought to Cyrus as a prisoner when he went after him. Possibly Ctesias had Astyages effect a temporary escape because at the beginning of Photios' epitome he is found hiding among the column capitals.

Long though Nicholas' account is, there is no suggestion of more than a single campaign. But there are two Babylonian texts which bear on this war. The Chronicle of Nabunaid is ostensibly a contemporary record. In the entry preceding Nabunaid's seventh year (before the vernal equinox of 549, so for campaigning purposes 550 B.C.) what survives of the entry reads: [Astyages collected his army] 'and marched against Cyrus king of Anshan to [conquer him] and . . . The army of Ishtumegu [Astyages] mutinied and he was captured, and they gave him up to Cyrus. In Agamtanu [Agbatana] Cyrus carried off the silver, gold, chattels, and possessions . . . of the land of Agamtanu, and took them to Anshan. The goods and chattels . . .' This presumably gives 550 B.C. for Astyages' fall. But the other text, the Abu Habba cylinder, which purports to give a dream that Nabunaid dreamed at the beginning of his reign (about 555), has the god Marduk order Nabunaid to go and restore the temple of the moon-god Sin at Harran, assuring him in what is said to be a 'prophetic perfect' that the Mede is no more: in the third year the god has caused Cyrus, the king of Anshan, his young (or little) servant, to advance against him with his small army, overthrow Astyages and take him captive to his own land. This should refer to 554 or 553 B.C. and makes a *prima facie* case, which most scholars accept, for a war lasting four years. This is a puzzle, because both texts seem to refer to the same event (the overthrow of Astyages).[6]

To Cyrus after his victory over Astyages Babylonia presented no threat.

Nabunaid, formerly a general and now king, was not of the Chaldaean dynasty, and Babylonia was not near to his heart; if we can believe the propagandist Verse Chronicle, he was insensitive enough to declare openly that he didn't know cuneiform. At the earliest opportunity, when Babylon seems to have been smitten by plague and galloping inflation, he had taken off for Harran to restore the temple of Sin where his redoubtable old mother was priestess before the Medes (and perhaps Babylonians) wrecked the place fifty-five years earlier; and after that he went with his army into western Arabia to conquer and colonize a string of oases between Tema (Taima) and Yatrib (Medina).[7] It has been suggested that he foresaw the danger from Cyrus and hoped to build up a fighting force in the desert. But if so, nothing came of it; and Babylon was becoming increasingly antagonized as year after year for a whole decade the king was not present for the New Year Festival.

In the north-west the R. Halys formed the boundary between the old Median empire and the Lydian kingdom under Croesus. The Lydian cavalry was formidable, and Croesus had no reason to love the Persian vassal who had overthrown his brother-in-law. Herodotus says that Croesus began the war by crossing the Halys and capturing Pteria, but he also speaks of Cyrus making overtures to the Ionians behind Croesus' back; so perhaps both of them were on the make. The battle lasted till nightfall and was indecisive; but seeing that his army was outnumbered and the season was advanced, Croesus returned to Sardis and dismissed his mercenaries for the winter, intending to assemble a larger army the next spring. Unexpectedly Cyrus followed on his heels. When Croesus opposed him in the Lydian plain Cyrus threw his cavalry into disarray by putting his camels up front – a trick that finds its counterpart in Ctesias when in his last battle Cyrus' own cavalry was confronted by

Plate 13   elephants. After his victory over Croesus Cyrus captured the citadel of Sardis in fourteen days (Hdt I 73–90).[8] According to Herodotus he did not stay long because he had other conquests in mind, but set off for home with Croesus and his treasure, leaving the Mede Mazares and, after he died, the trusty Harpagos to reduce the Greek cities and other peoples of the coast.

The Nabunaid Chronicle is tantalizing here. It records that in April 547 Cyrus, king now of Parsa, mustered his army and reached the Tigris below Arbela, the next month he marched against the land of Lu (?)–, he killed (?) its king, took its booty, and set a garrison there; after which the king and his garrison remained on the spot. It is unfortunate that the name of the land is not quite legible; experts vary between allowing the reading Lu- to be probable or possible with a trend towards the latter. Before the Chronicle was known the date most commonly arrived at from Greek sources was 546 B.C. and Lydia must have been Cyrus' main objective at this time. So the reading of Lu- would be most acceptable on general historical grounds. The fact that the notice in the Chronicle does not fit too well with Herodotus in regard to the duration of the campaign and Cyrus' subsequent action is not very significant since the Babylonian scribes will not have had the benefit of inside information and Herodotus had too much. But with a gap in the Chronicle for the next seven years it is not certain that Cyrus got as far as the River Halys in his campaign of 547 B.C. Any objection to reading Lydia must apply *a fortiori* to Lycia, which has been proposed as an alternative by Mallowan; Cyrus had no fleet then, and Lycia could not have been attacked without involving Lydia. Hinz has most recently read Su- instead of Lu- and claimed the name as Suhi on the middle Euphrates. Topographically this would fit admirably; but Suhi, which does not even seem to have had a king in 616–13 B.C., would have been a puny objective, and an improbable one while the important centres of Harran and Aleppo were still in Babylonian hands. If the reading Lu- is rejected, some principality in eastern Anatolia might be envisaged. With the Lydian and Median empires meeting on the Halys and the adjoining kingdom of Cilicia friendly to Cyrus, there is no room for an independent state; but the revolt of a former vassal of the Medes is not out of the question.

As regards Median rule in the East, we are told by Arrian at the beginning of his account of Nearchus' voyage that the Medes had ruled as far as the Indus before the time of Cyrus; but as they are said to have been successors to the Assyrians there, we are evidently following in the wake of the great legendary conqueror Semiramis.[9] In fact very little is known, and that little is conflicting. The key province in the East is Baktria. Ctesias seems to have it rise in arms against Cyrus but submit on learning that he was the accredited successor of Astyages. Herodotus, on the other hand, speaks of Cyrus being in a hurry to leave Sardis because Babylon was an obstacle to him, along with the Baktrian nation and the Sakai and Egyptians (I 153); but since he makes Cyrus proceed next against the Massagetai after the capture of Babylon (I 201), we cannot claim that he had reason to believe that Baktria had not been subjected by the Medes. The word for satrap (see Chap. VIII n.1) is from its form a Median title, and the names Bakhtrish and Zra(n)ka used in the Old Persian inscriptions for Baktria and Drangiana have also been claimed as Median forms. On balance we may prefer to think of Median rule as having extended to Baktria and the Oxus at least, though not (as Herzfeld supposed) to the Punjab. What can be ruled out is the notion, based on reading what is not there into Herodotus III 117, that the peoples of central Iran, including Hyrkania, Parthia, and Zranka (Seistan), were united in a Chorasmian empire or federation until the time of Cyrus (see below, p. 195); it persists in the writings of those who study Zoroaster.

The natural route eastward from the Median capital of Agbatana would be the 'militaris via' by Rhagai to Parthia, and the Medes could more easily have extended on the north side of the Hindukush than on the south.[10] Cyrus did take the southern route at some stage. The evidence for this is first the information in the Alexander historians that he had been succoured by the Ariaspai on the R. Helmand, and secondly Pliny's statement that Capisa was destroyed by Cyrus. The second is an isolated statement of fact whose authenticity we cannot judge; presumably it refers to the Kapisa in the Koh Daman plain north of Kabul (at Begram, which at the time of writing is reported to be the principal military base of the Russians in Afghanistan), whether or not this Kapisa is the same as the Kapishakanish named at Behistun as a fortress in Arachosia. As regards the Ariaspai, whose position up the Helmand from Seistan is fixed by Arrian, the fullest statement is in

Diodorus, who says that Cyrus and his army would have perished in the desert if they had not brought him supplies (hence the name Benefactors (Greek Euergetai) that he conferred on them).[11] Armies have suffered crippling losses in crossing the wilderness between there and Karmania; since the route east by Bost to Kandahar, Ghazni, and Kabul has no perils, it would appear that Cyrus was travelling eastward from Karmania. A similar story is told of the Khan of Kelat, who crossed the sand desert on the east with his force in the late eighteenth century and was succoured by the people of Noshki, whom he afterwards named the 'Open-hearted'.[12]

There thus seems to be evidence of an expedition by Cyrus which involved an insufficiently reconnoitred route to the Helmand and then perhaps resistance further eastward; and we may therefore doubt whether the Median empire had extended south of the Hindukush. Cyrus in that case will have added Arachosia, Gandara, and Sattagydia to the empire. If he did in fact make new conquests, it can hardly have been before 546 B.C., and the assumption (which is an explicit statement in Berossos) that he conquered the rest of Asia before descending on Babylon could have some authority. Since it seems to have been only in early 530 B.C. that he re-appointed his son Cambyses as king of Babylon to ensure the succession, the expedition to the far north-east that summer was probably a new and perilous venture and not just one in a series of eastern campaigns.

Xenophon in his *Cyropaedia* produces one fact which is not found in Herodotus and might stem from Ctesias, that Gobryas, the 'Assyrian' (i.e. Babylonian) governor east of the Tigris, defected to Cyrus with his forces and was the first to break into the palace at Babylon and overpower the king. Though wrapped up in fiction there is history here. The Nabunaid Chronicle comes to life again in the year 539 with the king back from Arabia and images of the gods being brought for protection into the capital from different parts of the realm. Probably about the end of September Cyrus won a battle at Opis against the people of the ancient capital Akkad, whom he destroyed with fire and slaughter. On 10 October Sippar, the old centre in the north which the sheep-raising nomads frequented, fell without a struggle. Nabunaid fled; and on the 16th, with Persian troops under his command, Ugbaru,[13] the rebel governor of Gutium, entered Babylon without a battle. Returning to Babylon Nabunaid was taken prisoner; and business and religious ceremonies were resumed in the normal way. On 29 October Cyrus entered the city. Branches were spread before him. He proclaimed peace to the city and all men. Gubaru (not Ugbaru), his governor, appointed officials in Babylonia, and the gods that Nabunaid had brought in were sent back to their cities.

Gutium is an anachronistic name in keeping with the conservatism of priests who were trying to keep their old language and cuneiform script alive – thus in the Akkadian texts of the Achaemenid trilinguals Scythians (Saka) are called Gimirri (Cimmerians) and Armenia continues to be called Urashtu (i.e. Urartu). It is not really possible to say more than that Gutium at this time meant a region east of the Tigris. As regards Elam, it seems likely that after Cyrus' ancestors had taken possession of the plateau of Persis (Anshan) which had belonged to the Elamites, there was considerable penetration by Persians into the hill country of Elam, as well as considerable cultural influence of Elam on the Persians. But Susa was part of the neo-Babylonian empire (as is shown by stamped bricks of Nebuchadnezzar found there), and with Assur and Akkad it was one of the places to which Cyrus returned the statues that Nabunaid had called in and which sent deputations to pay homage to their new master. This seems to put paid to the persistent belief that the Persians were already in possession of Elam before Babylon was attacked.

The reader may ask why Cyrus hung about so long before breaking into Babylon. There was of course good sense in having Ugbaru capture the city first so that he himself could enter it in peace and festivity as the chosen servant of Marduk. But Herodotus makes the delay much greater. He has a quaint story of Cyrus losing his temper with the River Gyndes (the Diyala) when one of his sacred white horses was drowned in it, and leaving Babylon alone so as to spend the summer splitting the river into 360 canals (I 189–90); according to this version he turned against Babylon the following spring, and finding the fortifications impregnable he diverted the flow of the Euphrates till it could be forded at the water gates. This pre-occupation with canals is peculiar. Cameron has pointed to the recent archaeological survey of the shelf east of the Tigris here and noted that the number of settlements and the area covered by them increased in Achaemenid times; and he suggests that Cyrus was undertaking a great irrigation project while waiting for Babylon to fall into his grasp.[14] We may also note that the elder Pliny speaks of an artificial arm of the Euphrates flowing across Mesopotamia to the Tigris at Seleucia (Baghdad), which he attributes to a governor named Gobar(es). This would seem to be Gobryas who was governor immediately after Babylon fell and then satrap under Cyrus and Cambyses (535–522 B.C.).[15]

Cyrus may well have been expecting Babylon to fall without a struggle; the one demonstration of frightfulness at Akkad was all the warning that was needed. He had no doubt been in touch with Babylonian priests, to whom Nabunaid had caused grave offence; and his propaganda showed him as the elect of Marduk – we must bear in mind that Babylon had a long history of alien dynasties whose rule was accepted as legitimate. It is astonishing too how he was hailed in Jerusalem as nothing short of the Messiah; possibly he had used the Jews of Mesopotamia as a fifth column. Dandamayev further suggests that the merchants of Babylon were disgruntled by the blocking of their trade routes, and believes that the forces of resistance were sapped by social conflict between the peasants and artisans on the one hand and the priesthood and merchants on the other.[16] When it comes to incentive we can certainly say that, apart from the Persians, the priesthood stood to gain both in Babylon itself and throughout Babylonia. In fact it was not only they who were gratified by the works of restoration carried out at Cyrus' behest in important sanctuaries; a document found at Uruk shows the guild of crafts-men at the temple of Eanna there giving its allegiance to Cyrus in return for the right to a closed shop.[17]

The conquest of Babylon gave Cyrus yet another empire. From Assur in the north to Susa and the Persian Gulf in the south the neo-Babylonian kings had held sway. But Nebuchadnezzar had also conquered the lands between the Euphrates and the Mediterranean, and Nabunaid had added to this Harran in High Mesopotamia and the oases of the Nejd-Hejaz borderland. It is quite possible that Cyrus had made contact with some of these peoples before the capture of Babylon. But he had no need to conquer any of them, and documents found at Nerab near Aleppo show that Syria still belonged to the Babylonians.[18] North of this, Cilicia had struggled to retain its independence; it had been invaded again by Nabunaid at the beginning of his reign, and its ruler must have been glad to ally himself with Cyrus when he marched against Croesus.

With Babylon, then, the whole of Abarnahara ('across the River', i.e. west of the Euphrates) fell to Cyrus by right of conquest, so he ruled from the Syrian Gates on the Cilician border to Gaza. The Cyrus Cylinder is a creation of the Babylonian priesthood, harking back (as Nabunaid had done) to precedents set by Ashurbanipal; and it has been well remarked by Berger that it tells us nothing of the personality of Cyrus except how much he was willing to put up with.[19] But it declares that the princes from sea to sea, even those of the West who dwelt in tents, came with heavy tribute and kissed the conqueror's feet. His titulature now was 'Cyrus, King of the All, Great King, mighty King, King of Babylon, King of the Land of Sumer and Akkad, King of the Four Rims (of the Earth), the son of Cambyses the Great King, King of Anshan,' and with the same titles back to his great-grandfather Teispes.

To call Cyrus' ancestors Great Kings was an exaggeration. But the kingship of Babylon was another matter because it involved religious duties at the Esagila and Borsippa which ought not to be neglected as Nabunaid had done. Cyrus' elder son Cambyses was now of an age to be named along with his father on the Cylinder, and Cyrus turned the kingship of Babylon over to him. At New Year 538 for the first and possibly almost the last time a Persian held the hands of Marduk. The festival was an eleven-day one, and on the evening of the fourth day (27 March in 538) the king was due to don a special robe and wig and receive his sceptre in a ceremony which a noble Persian must have found degrading. Cambyses refused to change his costume or lay down his arms. Finally he agreed to the latter. But Cyrus' desire to gratify priests and public had misfired;[20] next year Cambyses was no longer called king of Babylon, and documents were again dated by Cyrus alone until 530 B.C. when he was setting out for his last campaign.[21]

We do not hear of Cyrus showing himself in Abarnahara. The book of Ezra seems to leave us in no doubt that in 538 B.C. he gave instructions for the rebuilding of the temple in Jerusalem and the return of the sacred utensils that Nebuchadnezzar had removed fifty years before. And contrary to Assyrian and Babylonian practice he gave permission for deportees to return to their homelands, though few of the Jews availed themselves of it and little progress was made with the temple. There was not necessarily anything very unusual in his decree for Jerusalem to judge by a tablet which shows him making provision for the return of the Lady of Uruk. But Cyrus may have felt a special interest in having the peoples of Abarnahara in good humour before his next conquest, that of Egypt which in the event was left to his son Cambyses. It may have been in these years that a story was put about that Cambyses had an Egyptian mother (Hdt III 1–3), similar to the tale that made Cyrus heir to the Lydian and Median thrones. In this connection Herodotus names Cyrus' wife Kassandane, calls her the mother of his children, and says that when she died Cyrus enjoined mourning on all the subject peoples (II 1). Ctesias makes Cyrus' wife and mother of his children Amytis, daughter of Astyages, and he says that she survived him. This is a point on which the Nabunaid Chronicle is decisive. It almost certainly records that before the vernal equinox of 538 B.C. the King's wife died and there was public mourning in Babylon. The King at this juncture can only be Cyrus. Perhaps Kassandane pined for the Zagros and a fresher air, like the Median princess for whom Nebuchadnezzar built the artificial mountain with hanging gardens. After this some of the fire may have gone out of Cyrus because we hear of no action on his part in the next eight years. At the same time we must grant that after all these conquests a breathing space was needed for consolidating the empire. It has recently been claimed that a chain of defensive positions along the Syro-Phoenician coast owe their construction or repair to Cyrus. It is not easy to see whom he had to fear there. But certainly at the opposite end of his empire he had forts built close to the Jaxartes to protect the settled lands against the nomadic peoples (see below, p. 37).

Meanwhile Cyrus was building palaces for himself on no mean scale. The Nabunaid Chronicle spoke of him carrying off Astyages' treasure from Agbatana. But the Median fortress continued in use, for Herodotus made him return there from Sardis, he was there in September 537 (see below, p. 89), and it was there that his edict about the Jerusalem temple, sought for in vain at Babylon (Ezra vi), was finally run to earth. Herodotus and some Old Testament writers took it for granted that the Persian Kings thereafter resided in Susa. But there is no certainty that it became a Persian royal seat before the reign of Darius.[22] There is talk in the Behistun inscription of royal troops having come in 522 B.C. from a palace named Yada in the Old Persian but rendered as Anshan in the Elamite text; no trace of Achaemenid building has come to light at the known site of the city of Anshan at Malian. Remains of a palatial building were uncovered in 1971 at Borazjan inland from Bushire. This must be the palace mentioned by Nearchus as a dozen miles up-river from Taoke, which continued in use as a port into early Islamic times (Tawwaj); Junge assumed that this palace was erected by Darius I in the vicinity of his fleet station.[23] But from the preliminary notices of the excavation scholars have concluded that the use of different-coloured stonework and the oblong (as opposed to square) plan indicate the time of Cyrus.

The well-known fortification with the massive terrace on which stand the palatial buildings which we call Persepolis is generally agreed to date from the reign of Darius I (see below, p. 158); there does not seem to be evidence to support Godard's contention that work on the substructure went back to the time of Cyrus.[24] It is no longer possible to be sure that the palaces of which traces have been found on the level ground below the terrace go back no

Plate 16

earlier, but Darius did affirm in an Elamite text at Persepolis (DPf) that no previous fortification had been built there. Across the Pulvar stream four miles to the north is an inclined escarpment more than a mile long (Hussain Kuh), against whose lower end, facing the plain, the tombs of Darius I and three successors are sculptured in the cliff at Naksh-i Rustam. In the plain it seems that relics of structures are coming to light which, from the absence of claw-chisel marks, are assumed to be of a date earlier than Darius – in particular the discovery in 1973 of a palatial building with facades 160 feet long and with the same oblong plan and use of contrasting colours. This is about 200 yards east of the building on the left bank of the Pulvar which goes by the name of Takht-i Rustam. Of the latter only the huge blocks of the bottom courses survive, and they have not all been completely smoothed off. But it seems clear that a monument of similar form and dimensions to the Tomb of Cyrus at Murgab was intended to sit on this base. Since Herzfeld the Takht-i Rustam has been widely recognized as the tomb, perhaps unfinished, of Cambyses (see Chap. III, n.30). This is a conjecture; but it can be said that important structures seem to have been erected here before 522 B.C.

The rock face at Naksh-i Rustam was presumably a sacred spot before Darius I had his tomb cut there. The Persepolis tablets speak of an orchard and of Egyptian stone-masons at work at a place named Nupishtash; and the name, which means '[mountain] with writing' fits this cliff because several centuries earlier an Elamite relief had been carved there.[25] Work was proceeding at Nupishtash between 497 and 489 B.C.

The tombs of Darius and his effective successors down to Darius II are carved in the L-shaped cliff with a smooth perpendicular rock face underneath. They could only be reached with lifting tackle. Ctesias knew that the royal tombs were up at Parsa ('Persians'). He has a story that Darius' parents desired to see the tomb he had prepared for himself and were hauled up on ropes but let fall because the gang lifting them panicked when they saw (them).[26] Ctesias is the only writer to speak of this tomb at Naksh-i Rustam, and he speaks of it as at the 'double mountain'. His story, like the one in which he attributed the Behistun relief to Semiramis' campaign, is the sort of talk that would be picked up on the spot. And while the long ridge is quite continuous, a mile or so away in the plain there rises a hill with two cliff-girt flat crowns which belongs to a group of hills called the 'Three Domes' but dominates the view from the ground in front of Naksh-i Rustam. This should be Ctesias' double mountain; and it is difficult to resist the temptation to make it the twin summits where Ctesias envisaged Cyrus repelling the Medes. But in that case Ctesias must have thought of the inhabited centre here as Pasargadai.

The name Pasargadai has fascinated scholars in the last century or two. We may dismiss the more extravagant conjectures about its meaning, such as 'Before Surgadia' (a town which Sargon II added to the province of Parsua!), 'Behind Mt Arakadrish', and the equation with Strabo's tribe name Pateis-choreis. Paishiyauwada, mentioned twice in the Behistun text as what in effect could be a royal seat in Persis in 522–21 B.C., is a less fanciful conjecture. But the most obvious identification, that we find for instance in Sir

Plate 4

Plate 2

Plate 5

Plate 4

W. Ouseley, Canon G. Rawlinson, and Olmstead, is Parsaga(r)da. This precise form occurs in no ancient writer except Curtius Rufus, though Parsargadai is found in Appian's Mithridatic War, and the spelling Passargadai has rather better authority, being cited from an Anaximenes, presumably the one who wrote histories of Philip II and Alexander (about 380–320 B.C.).[27] The meaning then would be the 'City (or, as understood by Anaximenes, Camp) of the Persians' on the site of Cyrus' victory over Astyages. The difficulty with this is that we can not take Pasargadai to be the same place as Persepolis (the Greek name meaning 'City of the Persians') because the Alexander historians knew Pasargadai and Persepolis as two distinct places, both having a treasure, treasury, and royal tomb or tombs (that of Cyrus being in a paradise at Pasargadai). The distance between them is not indicated, and the uncertainty whether the lake of Neyriz existed then makes any inference from Alexander's return route unusable. There is now a further complication. In the Fortification tablets of Persepolis of 509–494 B.C. one of the places with a treasury is named (in Elamite) Badrakatash. If this were the name of the place that the Greeks knew as Pasargadai, the derivation from Parsa would seem less likely. The name Badrakatash is claimed as Median (and therefore indicating the presence of a Median garrison-post there before Cyrus' revolt!). This is one of a number of very plausible identifications which appear at the moment to conflict with one another.

Strabo mentions one other palace of the Achaemenid Kings, that of Gabai in the upper or inland parts of Persis. This is conventionally placed at Isfahan. It is no very serious objection that Isfahan is a good ancient Median name, Aspadana, and that sources of Roman date confirm this. It is, however, unlikely that Persis stretched so far north. The only known remains of palatial buildings on the route to Media are those at Murgab, fifty miles north-east of Persepolis. The problem of the region called Gabiene in the account of Antigonus' campaign against Eumenes in 317–16 B.C. is too complicated to be discussed here;[28] but it certainly could not have centred on Murgab, so Gabai could not have been there if it was the centre of Gabiene. Other places in Persis named in the Behistun inscription where we might expect remains of a palatial character are Paishiyauwada and Yada (City of Anshan), both mentioned above.

The site at Murgab, now admirably published in David Stronach, *Pasargadae* (1978), has in fact for some decades been almost universally recognized as Pasargadai. It is extensive, with clusters of buildings of palatial type that go back to Cyrus and evidently received finishing touches from Darius after 522 B.C. And the almost completely preserved gabled chamber set on six stepped courses of blocks (the so-called Qabr or Meshed of Solomon's Mother) has long been accepted as the Tomb of Cyrus the Great, which the *Plate 1* Greek writers tell us was a roofed chamber on top of a square ashlar foundation. There are two minor objections to placing Pasargadai at Murgab. The one, which is only serious if we take Ctesias seriously, is the situation in flat ground which does not fit with his description of Pasargadai. The other is that two rivers join in front of Persepolis to form the Araxes and Strabo tells us that it is the Kuros which flows past Pasargadai (XV 729), whereas at the present day the one that has the name Kur traverses the plain from the north-west past the 'Three Domes', while the river that flows from the north-east down the valley from Murgab is the Pulvar. It is also the R. Kuros that one ancient tradition associated with Cyrus, claiming that he changed his name to it from Agradates.[29] But Strabo is a bit muddled about the rivers of central Persis.

Fig. 9

As regards the historical tomb of Cyrus, which Alexander visited at Pasargadai, there are three possible candidates. First, the tower called the Zendan at Murgab, which is very ruined but closely resembles the more complete Kaaba of Zardusht at Naksh-i Rustam. Demandt has claimed that these two tower-like constructions had doors let in from above that could not be opened when the building was completed; he therefore rejects the explanation of them as fire-towers, treasuries, or other repositories, and claims them as the tombs of Cyrus and Cambyses respectively, the Kaaba being the later because it shows claw-chisel marks.[30] There are in fact serious difficulties in reconciling the Zendan with the descriptions of Cyrus' tomb in Strabo and Arrian, who were using the first-hand accounts written by members of Alexander's staff; and Demandt's argument is not helped by the fact that Alexander and his companions were able to enter the tomb chamber on their first visit when it was still unviolated.[31] The second candidate is the Meshed at Murgab – that is, the chamber on the stepped foundation which is generally

Plate 1

known as the Tomb of Cyrus. Demandt would make this the tomb of a predecessor of Cyrus; but the Greek-type cyma-moulding that crowns the walls can hardly date earlier than Cyrus' conquest of Lydia. The Meshed has two disadvantages: Onesikritos said the tomb of Cyrus had ten storeys (i.e. courses?) and we cannot reckon ten stages in the Meshed; and – more serious – there is no sign of or place for the inscription that both he and Aristoboulos saw and made little sense of. The third candidate is the very similar Takht-i

Plate 2

Rustam, which would have to be seriously considered if it ever were to turn out that Pasargadai was in the plain by the 'Three Domes'. But with the dating that is now firmly assigned to it, there is really nothing else that the Meshed can be but the tomb of Cyrus. So the identification of Pasargadai with Murgab seems the most acceptable. With the open lay-out of the 'pleasance', with its pylon, bridge, and high-halled buildings set in their gardens, and its

Plate 3

superb Lydo-Ionian stone-masonry, Pasargadai can be thought of as an imaginative creation reflecting Cyrus' taste and expansive attitudes.

For himself then Cyrus constructed handsome palaces in Persis in addition to those that he took possession of at Agbatana and Babylon. Xenophon may well not be wrong in saying that he expected his satraps also to have palaces and courts of their own so that they could live in a style befitting their rank; and in fact we hear in the ancient authors of many palaces (basileia) and places named Apad(a)na in different parts of the empire.

Cyrus' final campaign was in 530 B.C. According to Herodotus (I 201–end) this was against the Massagetai beyond the river that he calls Araxes, which was not only broad but contained many large islands (see below, p. 194). Ctesias and Berossos give other names for the steppe folk who were Cyrus'

1 Tomb of Cyrus at Murgab (Flandin and Coste)

2 Takht-i Rustam ('Tomb of Cambyses')

3 Tall-i Takht (citadel) at Murgab (west corner)

4 The 'Three Domes' and Naksh-i Rustam

5 Tomb of Darius I at Naksh-i Rustam

6 The 'Paradise' at Behistun

7 Relief of Darius I at Behistun

8 Darius I on Behistun relief

9 Part of Persepolis Treasury relief

10 The Ahuramazda symbol
(Hall of 100 Columns at Persepolis)

11 Guardsmen on glazed tile
relief from Susa

12 Detail of column base at Jin Jan, near Fahlian

13 Citadel of Sardis from Temple

14 The Rock of Van (south face)

objective, and the latter's (Daai) might suggest a position between the Caspian and what is now the lower course of the Oxus. Ctesias' story involves a Saka King Amorges or Homarges, who was allied to Cyrus; but the king's name is probably fictitious (see Chap. XVII n. 17). Herodotus was inclined to the belief that the Massagetai were not Scythians (Saka). The name of their queen, Tomyris, could of course be Turcic (the 'Iron Maiden', as in Timur), but her son Spargapises has an Iranian-sounding name.[32] The Massagetai later occupied a large area embracing the then very extensive delta-lands of the Jaxartes (Syr Darya); and though the Oxus as the only possible alternative can not be ruled out completely, it is generally believed that the river Herodotus is speaking of is the Jaxartes (his mention of the islands fits best with this). In any case Cyrus at some time reached the upper Jaxartes, because he is said to have built a line of seven forts to protect his frontier in Sogdiana, and the strongest of them, known to the Greeks as Kyra or Kyreskhata, was able to offer resistance to Alexander the Great. There is a linguistic coincidence here. Alexander in 329 B.C. founded a city in this corner of the empire at the Fergana Gate, and it was called Alexandria Eskhata (the Furthest). But Kyreskhata in fact had a quite different etymology: not Cyrus' Furthest but Kurushkat(h)a, i.e. fortress of Cyrus. Benveniste has noted that the name Kurkath was current there in Arab times (with Gaza, the treasury fort, nearby), and suggested that Kyreskhata was at Ura-Tübe some thirty miles south of the Jaxartes bend.[33] This gives us Cyrus' frontier in the north-east, Sogdiana being the most distant province.

Cambyses seems to have been re-instated as king of Babylon in the spring of 530 B.C., presumably before Cyrus marched east. According to Herodotus he accompanied his father as far as the Jaxartes and was then sent home as regent and successor-designate. This might sound pointless; but there would be sense in Cyrus' exhibiting his heir to his distant subjects to convince them that they would not lack for a master after him.[34] No doubt the northern nomads could be troublesome neighbours. But the Greek sources all show Cyrus as the aggressor, and Herodotus makes him out to be insatiable of conquest. In his account Cyrus crossed the river into Tomyris' territory and then set a trap by leaving his camp full of victuals and wine and withdrawing his fighting troops. One of the three divisions of the enemy under the queen's son Spargapises overran the camp and consumed the food and drink, with the result that they were unable to fight when the Persians returned. Spargapises in shame killed himself and Tomyris then committed herself to combat. The battle was fought first at bowshot, and then at close quarters. Neither side would yield, but finally the Massagetai prevailed and Cyrus perished together with the greater part of his army. The story ends with Tomyris taking Cyrus' head and saturating the 'insatiate of blood' – a detail that is not far-fetched because these were people who, like the Gepids, reckoned to know the history of each skull at their drinking-bouts.

At the end of the narrative Herodotus tells us that he knew many stories of Cyrus' death, but that the one he related was the most probable (I 214). Presumably he would have remarked this earlier if he had known an alternative to his death in Central Asia. We can ignore Xenophon when he makes

Cyrus die peacefully in the fulness of years; the historical tradition of his death in a war in the East would not have been unanimous if the Persians had known otherwise. We need not believe Ctesias' tale that Amorges avenged Cyrus' death by defeating his enemies and adding their land to the Persian empire. But it does appear that Cyrus' defeat did not lead to any loss of territory.

IV Cyrus' Rule

Cyrus had evidently inherited a rule in Persis that the Assyrians and Babylonians recognized as a kingship. But it can only have been in retrospect that
his predecessors were styled Great Kings. The land which the Greeks called
Persis was the homeland of the Persians, who alone of all the peoples of the
Achaemenid empire did not rank as conquered; and so it is said not to have
been a tribute-paying province or satrapy. In Old Persian it is called Pārsa; the
same word applied to the people, and also to the capital in central Persis
which we call Persepolis (the Greeks before Alexander the Great knew it only
as 'to (or from) Persians'). Since the Persians seem to have occupied land in
central and north-western Persis that had in the past been Elamite, we should
expect some racial mixture, but there is no evidence of a suppressed native
population, and Persian proper names seem to be in a majority in Persis, to
judge by Persepolis tablets (see Chap. VIII n. 22). The pre-Achaemenid
tablets found at the Elamite capital of Susa are said to show Persians and
people with Persian-sounding names going in and out, and particularly as
suppliers of textiles and equipment.[1] As they become better known it may
appear that the high level of production and manufacture revealed in the
Persepolis tablets from 509 B.C. on has a longer history than had been
supposed. In fact we seem from these sources to be dealing with a land that
had some sort of organized economy; the Persepolis tablets show officials of
different grades responsible to a high controller in Persis appointed by the
King. If there was a tribal structure, the tablets and royal inscriptions give no
hint of it. As regards population, Xenophon in his *Cyropaedia* (I 2, 15) speaks
of 120,000 adult male Persians; he gives no clue to the source of this
information, but the Persians were presumably less numerous than the Medes
and the estimate could be a fair one.

Herodotus has some detailed knowledge that we find in no other source
(I 125). He says that when Cyrus first mustered his subjects for war against
the Medes only three of the ten 'clans' (gene) which constituted the Persians
assembled.[2] These were the Maraphioi, the Maspioi, and – noblest of all – the
clan of Pasargadai in which the Achaemenid lineage was included. The other
'clans', he says, were dependent on the prime three. Four of them were
nomads (i.e. pastoralists). They were the Daoi, Mardoi, Dropikoi, and Sagartioi. Two of these are known from other sources. The Mardians had a bad
reputation as predatory folk; Ctesias' story made Cyrus' father a Mardian
bandit, it was a Mardian who scaled the citadel wall at Sardis, and they
re-appear in an Alexander historian as unkempt cave-dwellers in the mountainous western border of Persis. The Sagartians were more substantial.
Darius I could speak of a region Asagarta from which a Median pretender

arose in 522–21 B.C. and for a brief moment mentions it among the ethnic groupings over which he ruled (DPe); and 'gentlemen' (hunters ?) appear in a Persepolis tablet as travelling to Ashshakurda. Herodotus tells us that the Sagartians, who spoke Persian, provided a lassoo-throwing force of 8,000 cavalry in 481 B.C. and were included in the southerly 14th satrapy for tribute purposes (VII 85, III 93). If the sources are to be believed they would seem to have been semi-nomads with a regular annual migration (see below, p. 184f.).

The other three Persian 'clans' were sedentary cultivators: the Germanioi, Panthialaioi, and Derousiaioi. The first name is obviously Karmanians, so that from Herodotus' point of view Persis extended further to the east than the modern province of Fars; Karmania later was a satrapy and not part of Persis, but its status in early Achaemenid times is undefined. Tomaschek in his basic study of Iran in the Roman itineraries noted Pantyene/Pathienas as the first station (at sixty parasangs or 200 miles) on the route from Persepolis to the Fish-eaters, and he convincingly fixed it at Sirjan on the western border of Karmania.[3] His identification of this name with the Panthialaioi of Herodotus would give another territorial siting on the east flank of Fars, and we begin to get some idea of the spread of the different divisions of people who had come to be recognized as Persians. Presumably they were united in Persis after Cyrus conquered Astyages. With such a spread it becomes difficult to imagine them all as being a single stock which made the trek along the Zagros with Achaemenes.

Von Gall believes that three distinct types of Persians can be recognized in the files of guardsmen on the reliefs of Persepolis and relates them to Herodotus' three principal clans. His argument is based on differences of headgear or hair-style and of equipment, and those who in his view most resemble Elamites would be Maspians, while the Pasargadai would be those nearest to the King. It is difficult to judge the significance of artistic variations of this sort.[4] What does appear from the texts is that to be an Achaemenid counted for a great deal; Darius I declared himself in ascending order an Achaemenid, a Persian, and an Aryan, but he did not name his 'clan'. The Persepolis tablets once mention a Marappiyash, which could be Maraphian; and Herodotus knew of two commanders of an expedition to Libya about 512 B.C., of whom one was a Pasargadan and the other a Maraphian – a peculiar piece of information which might suggest that Aryandes, who was appointed satrap of Egypt by Cambyses, had his own adherents outside the Achaemenid lineage. But it would seem that these distinctions were becoming almost obsolete. It is uncertain whether the 'clan' name Pasargadai had any connection with the place that the Greeks knew by that name (see above, p. 34f.).

Cyrus was a great conqueror; and unlike Alexander he seems to have begun with no trained fighting force of his own. Xenophon tells us that at the outset Cyrus' Persians were not mounted and so he had to train his own cavalry. This is in the *Cyropaedia* and is one of the statements that have not been believed. It is true that the seal attributed to Cyrus' grandfather depicted a mounted spearman and the Persepolis tablets show that horses were main-

Fig. 3

tained in the time of Darius I. Indeed Darius speaks of Parsa as having good horses (and even good chariots) as well as good men. But the plateau lands of southern Iran are not good horse country, and we learn from Strabo that the Karmanians later used donkeys and not horses in war; in fact it is the donkey, with its greater endurance in steppe country, that transports the sedentary population of the uplands of Fars and Kerman. Once Cyrus gained control of the long Zagros valleys his supply of good mounts and suitable pasturage was *Plate 3* assured; in particular, as the Assyrians had known, Media was unmatched as a mother of horses, surpassing even Armenia and the grasslands of the Cilician-Cappadocian interior. But we cannot take it for granted that Cyrus had an effective cavalry arm when he first mustered the three central 'clans'.

Before the reign of Cyrus the main cultural influence on the Persians probably came from Elam. This may possibly be detected to a small extent in dress, and perhaps more so in military accoutrement including the use of the chariot. But it appears most clearly in the use of the Elamite script and language for administrative purposes in Persis under the early Achaemenids and its prominence as the initial key-language in their royal inscriptions.[5] After the capture of Babylon in 539 B.C. Akkadian too became a language of the royal inscriptions, translated, as it would seem, not from the Elamite but from a parallel Aramaic written text. In fact there seems to be little direct influence from Babylon on early Achaemenid culture, for few Iranians had settled in that most cosmopolitan of cities before 550 B.C. With his conquest of Astyages Cyrus became a Great King, and he must have been confronted with problems of kingship, court, and government on a far grander scale than before. As regards kingship, the impression given is that he preferred to set up his own governors in the realms that he conquered rather than ruling through vassal-kings as the Assyrians had done in the outlying parts of their empire. Thus he was not a true King of Kings as the Mede, or at least the Urartian Great King had been.[6] His court and transmission of royal authority was presumably modelled on the Median; and the structure and titulature from the word for King downward, together with the institutions governing the army, treasury, and religious formulae, are claimed as borrowings from that source.[7]

Cyrus, like Darius I after him, set great store by winning the goodwill of the priesthoods in the lands he conquered. And where evidence is available, this conservative policy, which under Cyrus involved the minimum of change in the conditions of rule, made the transition to provincial status in the Persian empire relatively easy. The empire was not highly organized before Darius; tribute of some sort must have been paid (see below, p. 82), but presumably in accordance with existing local practices. While he preferred to appoint his own governors in the conquered lands, Cyrus was by no means committed to the belief that they need be Persians. In Sardis he put a Lydian in charge of the treasury (and had a revolt to cope with in consequence). To Jerusalem he seems to have sent Sheshbazzar as governor with the store of gold and silver vessels that Nebuchadnezzar had removed and instructions for the rebuilding of the temple. In Babylon he at first tried a native satrap, though after three or four years the Persian Gobryas was appointed instead.

For some reason the Lydian kingdom was divided between two satrapies, but virtually the whole neo-Babylonian empire was incorporated as a single administrative unit.

In the same way Cyrus and his son Cambyses did not consider that only Persians were fit to be army commanders. Of the three generals of Cyrus that we know, two were Medes (Harpagos and Mazares), and Ugbaru, who commanded the assault force in 539 B.C., was the Babylonian governor of Gutium. No doubt at that time the Persian nobles had a good deal to learn about the handling of armies on the Median pattern. Under Darius, who came to the throne as the champion of the Persian nobility, all this changed; but in the revolts of his accession year, when experienced commanders were needed, the men he sent out to assume commands were three of his fellow conspirators, and one Persian, one Mede, and one Armenian – these last three were presumably officers accustomed to command under Cambyses.

Few great rulers have left so good an impression with posterity as Cyrus. Herodotus tells us that the Persians themselves spoke of him as a father who was kind and contrived everything good for them (III 89). He was undoubtedly generous towards them, giving his nobles estates as satraps and grandees in the provinces and expecting them to live in state as he did, while the apportionment of fiefs in Babylonia to Persian and allied soldiers with the obligation of providing a bowman, cavalryman, or chariot according to the recipient's status has been shown to go back to Cambyses' (and so presumably Cyrus') time.[8]

This generosity must to some extent have been at the expense of the natives, since lucrative appointments were no doubt being taken up by Persians and other Iranians as the result of royal and noble patronage. But Cyrus seems to have had what is now spoken of as charisma. His public relations work was throughout excellent, so that Medes and other Iranian peoples, Babylonians, Elamites, Jews, and perhaps even Lydians seem to have accepted him as their legitimate ruler. If it were not for the mention of his destroying Akkad with fire and slaughter, we should have no ground for qualifying the reputation for clemency that attached to him. And though Herodotus a number of times depicts him as quick-tempered, he certainly regarded him as humane. Aeschylus in his *Persae* of 472 B.C. makes the ghost of Darius single out Cyrus for special praise as fortunate and well disposed, bringing peace to all his friends and enjoying the favour of the god – a generous tribute to the conqueror of the Eastern Greeks. It is ironical that the name of Cyrus had no place in Iranian legendary history in Parthian and Sassanid times, and only among Greeks and Jews did his memory survive.

One sign of Cyrus' ability to accommodate himself to the conditions of the time is to be seen in the attitude of the outer world. He had conquered the Mede, and now his empire was undoubtedly Persian. But while Herodotus is careful in distinguishing individual Medes and Persians, the Greeks generally continued to know the great power in Asia as the Medes; and Herodotus himself often speaks of the Medes when he is referring to 'the enemy' or putting words into the mouths of other people such as the queen of the

Massagetai. And it is not only the Greeks; Jews, Egyptians (who also used the word Mede as a term of abuse), and even Minaeans from southern Arabia continued almost indefinitely to speak of the Medes and not of the Persians.

As regards Cyrus' personal religious beliefs, the twin stone altars in the sacred precinct at Pasargadai have later counterparts; and the Zendan there, *Fig. 9* which may or may not have been a house for the sacred fire, was the model for the Kaaba at Naksh-i Rustam (see below, p. 151ff.). Stronach found traces of a carved solar disk in the gable of the Tomb of Cyrus, but the Ahuramazda symbol (below, p. 149) has not yet made an appearance earlier than on Darius' relief at Behistun.[9] Cyrus may well have been a worshipper of *Plate 7* Ahuramazda. But if so, he did not stress the fact as Darius does; and his policy of religious tolerance allowed him to figure as the ruler selected by Marduk and Yahweh, or no doubt Baal and Apollo if it served his purpose. This universality was already making its presence felt in the palatial buildings on the Pasargadai site. Elam may have contributed its quota to the architectural design.[10] Stone dressing and the use of clamps show Ionic or Greco-Lydian masons at work. The reliefs on the door-jambs are the work of sculptors from different milieus. The four-winged deity with the high head-dress has been recognized by Barnett as a Syrian Baal; Hinz claims that the models for other reliefs are to be sought in Sennacherib's palace at Nineveh and (less convincingly) the Ishtar Gate at Babylon. It is as though Cyrus recognized the importance of the older civilizations and wished to unite them in a world empire.[11] Inevitably Cyrus' empire depended on the personality and demeanour of its founder. Dangers lay ahead – that of exploitation leading to revolts of the subject peoples and the struggle of the Persian feudal nobility to maintain its primacy in a state that needed to have a professional army and bureaucracy. In effect it could be that there was nothing new in this, and that the forces of dissidence that were to beset Cyrus' sons were the same as had brought down Astyages when the Median nobles went over to Cyrus a generation earlier.[12] The ten years after Cyrus' death were crucial to the survival of the empire.

V The Critical Decade

Cyrus' own name in the Old Persian script was Kurush (Elamite and Akkadian Kurash, Greek Kuros). Unlike most Persian names, which are compounded of two words and, as Herodotus seems to put it, conform to their physique and grandeur, Kurush has no self-evident meaning in Iranian. Eilers has surprisingly claimed that the first vowel is short; Aeschylus in his *Persae* (472 B.C.) made it long.[1] In the normal transcription of Old Persian the names of Cyrus' two sons are rendered at Behistun as Kabujiya and Bardiya (more properly perhaps Brdiya[2]). In classical usage we know them as Cambyses and Smerdis. In some such cases the Greek and Latinized forms that we use seem so different from the Persian that the reader might question their identity; and a few words of explanation may therefore be helpful. The main factors involved are the peculiarities of Old Persian utterance, the idiosyncrasies of the Ionic Greek dialect, and the inadequacy of the Greek alphabet for conveying unfamiliar sounds.

Cyrus the Great was griffin-nosed, and because of their admiration of him the Persians were enamoured of such noses. So Plutarch says.[3] But the Persepolis reliefs show that Cyrus may not have been exceptional, because a longish, slightly aquiline nose seems to have been the norm. This might perhaps account for some of the peculiarities of their speech, such as the nasalization which caused Greeks to hear Mega- and a Lycian to write Maga- when a Persian pronounced what his script renders Baga- in compound names like Bagabukhsha (= 'god-serving', Greek Megabuxos); Ctesias, who spent sixteen years with the Persians, plays it both ways (Megabuzos and Megabernes, but Bagapates and Bagorazos).[4] There are also latent nasals in the Persian script which the accompanying cuneiform scripts and Greek renderings show up as (Ka(m)bujiya, Wi(n)dafarna (Greek Intaphernes), Hi(n)dush, and Ga(n)dara. Major changes from original Indo-European in Old Persian are the loss of the vowels e and o, though the diphthong au was rendered in Greek as omega, and the degrading of s to h (Hi(n)du = Sanscrit Sindhu). Difficulties also arise in giving the proper sound values to some of the Old Persian signs (e.g. the j in Ka(m)bujiya) and ambiguities in the supplying of vowels (see below, Chap. VII n.7).

The Ionic dialect had long since dropped the aspirate, so that the Persian name Hakhamanish was rendered Akhaimenes and Hi(n)duya Indos. It had also long since lost the digamma (the w sound), so that Wi(n)dafarna was rendered Intaphernes, though the frequent use of initial upsilon in such cases in Greek has resulted in Persian Wishtaspa and Widarna being transmitted to us as Hystaspes and Hydarnes. The old Ionic habit of transforming ā into closed ē (eta) has given us Mēde and the numerous Persian names which end in -ês (as Hystaspes); in almost all such cases the final vowel in the Old Persian script is unemphatic (i.e. only inherent), but the Greeks received it as long. Greek in general had no sign for sh, so Wishtaspa becomes Hystaspes. Finally Herodotus insists that all proper names of male Persians end in 's' (i.e. a sibilant). He labours the point, saying that though the Persians themselves are unaware of it, it is a fact and not a matter of some names doing so and others not, but of all without exception (I 139). He is of course speaking of the nominative, which was the dominating case; and he is right about the u-stems and i-stems (as Kurush and Hakhamanish). But the numerous names that are shown as ending in 'a' constitute a problem. They belong to the old Indo-European -os declension (e.g. Greek theos, Latin deivos and deus, Old Persian daiwa). The Achaemenid texts give no hint of either sibilant or aspirate at the end. But not only is Herodotus insistent but Ctesias in his practice supports him; so some sort of emission of breath may have been audible. In general, when their limitations are recognized, the Greek renderings of Persian names are reasonably faithful. They compare fairly with other renderings, as Akkadian Gubaru (Gobryas, Old Persian Gaubaruwa), Aramaic Tadanmu (Datames), Hebrew Ahashverosh (Xerxes), and Lycian Ñtariyeus (Dareios).

Names coming through Greek have sometimes been Latinized and become familiar in those forms (e.g. Cyrus and Darius). Owing to the paucity of Old Persian texts the majority of Persian names are known to us only as they have been transcribed in Persepolis Elamite or in Greek (and to a lesser extent in other languages); so the Persian forms cannot always be determined. In conformity with our sources for Achaemenid history Greek or Latinized forms have become established, so that Xerxes for instance is more readily recognized than Khshay(a)rshā; but at the same time the Persepolis tablets are yielding an ever increasing number of Persian names for which no Greek rendering exists, so consistency is unattainable.

Most Persian names can be assigned meanings. Thus Achaemenes comes from two roots denoting friend and mind. In his study of names in Elamite in the Persepolis tablets Gershevitch has offered a remarkable range of meanings, some of which are perhaps rather recherché.[5] Among the commonest components of Old Persian names that are well attested are aspa (Greek Aspa- and -aspes) = horse; ariya (Ari-) = Aryan; arta (Art-) = justice, order; baga (Bag- and Mega-) = god; the god's name Mithra (Mit(h)r- and -mit(h)res); farna (Pharn- and -phernes) = glory, fortune; mana, manish (Meno- and -menes or -manes) = mind; patish (Pati-, -bates or -pates) = master; data (Dat- and -dates) = law or gift; bazu (-bazos?) = arm. There are also diminutives, as Datames from something like data-mithra. Darius (Darayawaush or -wush) seems to mean 'he who holds firm the good' (Kent), and Xerxes perhaps 'hero (arsha) among kings'; in its second component Artaxerxes has a root (= kingdom) similar to the first in Xerxes, the assimilation to Xerxes being a Greek blunder. If we add that the first component in the names Tritantaikhmes, Tissaphernes, and Tithraustes means lineage and 'takhma' means brave, a considerable proportion of the names we encounter explain themselves. Unfortunately the first component in Hystaspes escapes solution.

Bardiya, or in Herodotus Smerdis[6] (Aeschylus' Mardos), was the proper name of the younger son of Cyrus. Ctesias calls him Tanuoxarkes, which has been accepted as a good formation (tanu = body and wazraka = strong). Smerdis is said to have been the one person who could draw the Ethiopian bow,[7] and – to anticipate – it was only after a tough struggle that the seven conspirators won through. So it is possible that Bardiya was possessed of bodily strength which earned him this nickname. Ctesias says that Cyrus put his younger son in charge of the eastern satrapies. There is no word of this in Herodotus, who had him accompany Cambyses to Egypt. But at all events Cambyses did not have to spend much time settling the affairs of the upper satrapies, because in the autumn of 528 he is found living with his court in Babylonia – not at Sippar, where he had had his establishment in the 530s with a royal steward and officials, but in a palace at Abanu near Uruk in the South. Three tablets of the temple of Eanna at Uruk concern the requisitioning of supplies for the 'King's dinner', with the temple called upon to deliver sheep and goats. Gobryas, for some years satrap of Babylon, was probably in attendance at the court because he is named (Gubaru) as issuing a requisition order; and (to follow Hinz) a word in an obscure context, parnakka, could be the name (Pharnakes) that was borne by Darius' high controller in Persis from after 509 B.C. when the Persepolis tablets begin until 498 or later (see below, p. 89).[8]

Herodotus says (I 209) that Darius was barely twenty when Cyrus went on his last campaign (530 B.C.) and so not of an age for military service (the context is admittedly one of a dream in which Cyrus saw Hystaspes' eldest son (Darius) with wings overshadowing Asia and Europe). When Cambyses was in Egypt, Darius was a spear-bearer of his ('doryphoros' in Greek). Herodotus, who tells us this, understood that he was one of the guardsmen and, he adds, of no particular importance at the time (III 139).[9] But some scholars have assumed that Darius in fact held the post of King's spear-bearer (arshtibara) and was thus one of the high dignitaries at the court. It is tempting to believe that Herodotus misunderstood and that Darius was already moving in the highest circles in the winter of 528–27 – his first wife was a daughter of the satrap Gobryas, and according to Herodotus he had three sons by her before he became King in 522 (VII 2). In all probability Prexaspes was at court as Cambyses' right-hand man; and he is found in a key role in the coup of 522, while his son Aspathines was to become one of the principal dignitaries under Darius. So Darius was perhaps building up contacts that would stand him in good stead later. If he really was King's spear-bearer, he would have gained an insight into imperial and military affairs; Hinz has suggested that the quality on which he so prided himself in his tomb inscription, his ability to keep his temper when provoked (DNb lines 12–15), was acquired in serving the despotic Cambyses.

In 526 Cambyses completed his preparations for invading Egypt. His luck was in. The once resourceful old Pharaoh Amasis died while the expedition was on its way. The commander of the Greek mercenary corps, Phanes, had defected to Cambyses and informed him of the Egyptians' military dispositions. An agreement had been reached with the Arab king to provide

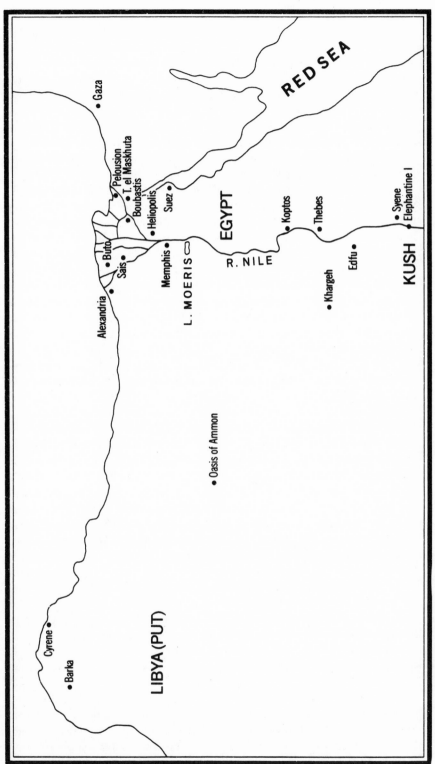

Fig. 4 Libya-Egypt

camel trains of water-skins on the desert crossing beyond Gaza (Esarhaddon the Assyrian had done likewise a century and a half earlier). The Phoenicians were providing a fleet which could help to provision the army and penetrate the Nile mouths; and Ujahorresne, priest of Neith and commander of the Egyptian high-sea fleet, whose naophoric statue inscription is a valuable source for what followed the Persian conquest, remains judiciously silent about his part in the war but emerged from it with titles that under Cambyses and Darius he built up into chancellor, companion of honour, secretary-general, major domo and generally chief of protocol in Egypt, and court physician as well as chief of the Egyptian marine.[10]

At the Pelousiac mouth of the Nile Psammetichus III, the new Pharaoh, was defeated in a hard-fought battle; and instead of regrouping and making the enemy fight at every dyke until the inundation came (as Nektanebo I did in 373 B.C.) he retreated to Memphis, where he was quickly overcome.[11] By mid summer 525 Cambyses had become King of Upper and Lower Egypt. From Egyptian sources we learn that troubles occurred and temples suffered; but this may have been no more than a matter of plundering and occupation of sacred premises by the victorious troops and camp followers. So far as can be judged, Cambyses brought things under control and did his utmost to conform to Egyptian traditions as his father had done with Babylon. Ujahorresne drew up a royal titulature for him, and he was duly crowned as a legitimate Pharaoh, whereas Esarhaddon had been an alien King of the Kings.

The conquest of Egypt gave the Persians Cyprus, which seems to have been under Egyptian control for the previous half century; and in fact Herodotus speaks of the Cypriots submitting voluntarily and sending ships to Cambyses. The Libyans sent gifts in token of submission, and so did the Greek cities of Barka and Cyrene (though their gifts were considered derisory and thrown as largesse to the troops). Psammetichus was given his liberty and might have been allowed to rule Egypt as a vassal if he had not meddled in political intrigue; after he had attempted to revolt and been put to death a Persian, Aryandes, was appointed satrap. Meanwhile Cambyses had sent spies into Ethiopia and he proceeded to advance up the Nile. A contingent was despatched to the oasis of Ammon. But with his main force he continued southward, presumably with Meroe as his objective. It was until recently thought that the inscription of an Ethiopian king Nastasen, recording the defeat of Kmbswdn somewhere north of Meroe, referred to Cambyses. But the experts insist on a fourth-century date (see below, p. 207), and it is true that Nastasen talks of his enemy as someone whose territory could be overrun, while according to Herodotus the Persian losses were due not to defeat in battle but to starvation with cannibalism resulting. Unfortunately the Eastern Greek levies in Cambyses' army were not taken on the Ethiopian campaign (III 25), and consequently Herodotus had to rely on Egyptian sources which consistently denigrated Cambyses. So we cannot with any certainty write the campaign off as a disaster. The one thing we can say is that after Cambyses, as before him, the military outposts of Egypt were at the First Cataract (Elephantine and Syene). But a few years later people of Kush (Ethiopia) were included among the subject peoples listed by Darius and

depicted on the Persepolis Apadana reliefs as negroes bringing gifts of Plate 29
elephant tusk, an okapi (or, we are now told, nilgai), and perhaps incense;
these Ethiopians who acknowledged Persian rule, Herodotus says, were the
ones bordering on Egypt whom Cambyses overran, and they brought bien-
nially gifts of specified amounts of gold, ebony, boys, and elephant tusks, but
were not actually subject (III, 97).

Apparently it was shortly after Cambyses captured Memphis, in August
525, that the sacred Apis bull died and according to custom was mourned for
seventy days. The Memphis Serapeum stelae show that it was subsequently
given sumptuous burial, and its handsome granite sarcophagus was dedicated by Cambyses himself. Its successor, apparently born on 25 August 525,
is recorded as having died in Darius I's fourth year after a life of eight years,
three months, and five days. The Egyptian stories about Cambyses that
Herodotus retails speak of atrocities, and not least that having gone mad after
his Ethiopian campaign he killed the Apis bull, which was then buried secretly
by the priests without his knowing. Here at least we can pin the story down as
a malicious invention. From the point of view of religious observances
Cambyses seems to have behaved with propriety, more so in fact than Darius
was to do.[12] To Ujahorresne's temple, that of Neith at Sais, which had been
the dynastic centre and cult sanctuary of his Saite predecessors, Cambyses
seems to have been generous; and three leading temples were from the outset
allowed to retain all their privileges. But in general he disapproved of the
enormous revenues that went to the priesthood in Egypt – far greater in fact
than the tribute exacted by the Persians. The Demotic Chronicle of two
centuries later quotes him as commanding: 'of the livestock which was
formerly given to the temples of the gods let them be given half', and of the
poultry 'give it them no longer; the priests should raise geese themselves and
bring them to the gods.' We need ask no further why Cambyses' memory was
damned. A few years later Darius restored the privileges and was conciliatory
towards the priesthood. His memory was greatly honoured by them, though
that did not prevent the people from rising in revolt before he died.

Not all that we hear about Cambyses' intolerance, however, comes from
the Egyptian side. The wilful shooting of Prexaspes' son the cup-bearer and
the burial alive of twelve noble Persians seem to be part of Herodotus' long
Persian narrative; and he also says that the Persians called Cambyses a
'despot' as compared with Cyrus the 'father', because he was harsh-natured
and contemptuous (III 89). Presumably Smerdis would not have usurped the
throne in Persis if Cambyses had not made himself disliked among the
Persians.

Cambyses had stayed too long away. According to Herodotus he was in Syria
on his way back when a messenger arrived with the announcement of the
usurpation; and the story continues that leaping on to his horse in a hurry he
accidentally stabbed himself in the thigh. He had received a prophecy at Buto
that he would end his life in Agbatana; and now, hearing that the city where
he lay was called by that name, he knew that he was to die. Three weeks later
he summoned the noblest of his Persians to hear his last instructions, and then

expired. If the place where he died did have a name resembling Ha(n)gmatana to prompt a post-eventum prophecy, it could be Hamath on the Orontes some days' journey from the Euphrates near Aleppo – otherwise it must be much further to the south.[13] Ctesias has Cambyses die from an accident sustained while working wood at home in Babylon, but the Egyptian Demotic Chronicle confirms that he died on the journey. Darius in his Behistun inscription says that Cambyses died by 'own-death'. Frye and others assure us that this means a natural death; and on balance it would not seem to mean suicide. Some scholars have thought of a conspiracy of Persian nobles in the army, in which Darius could have been involved. The stress laid on 'own-death' might then be intended by Darius as a rebuttal of rumours that Cambyses had been murdered. But there is no evidence to base theories on; and Herodotus' story of the accident, in which the chape of his sheath came off, agrees with the Persian wearing of daggers.

The dating of the events is given in Darius' Behistun inscription. The usurper, whom Darius calls a Magus named Gaumata, rose in revolt in Persis on 11 March 522 B.C., claiming to be Bardiya. He seized the Kingship on 1 July, and he was killed by Darius on 29 September, after which Darius became King. Cambyses' death occurred after the seizure of the Kingship on 1 July. Herodotus assigns a reign of seven years and five months to Cambyses and eight years altogether for him and Smerdis. The latter is correct enough, the former too short because the overlap has not been allowed for. It is not clear what Darius meant by the seizure of the Kingship on July 1, because Bardiya seems to have been recognized as King in Babylonian documents of a month or two earlier.[14]

Darius' account of the events is brief (DB col. I). After becoming King Cambyses killed Bardiya but the fact was kept secret: 'Afterwards Cambyses went to Egypt; and the people became evil, so that the Lie waxed great in the country, both in Persis and in Media and in the other provinces' (Kent's translation). Afterwards, he continues, a Magus named Gaumata rose up at Paishiyauwada[15] (in Persis) claiming to be Bardiya, son of Cyrus; he took the Kingdom away from Cambyses, and all the people rebelled against Cambyses, and went over to Gaumata in Persis and Media and the other provinces. Nobody dared oppose him until Darius arrived.

Herodotus gives a more circumstantial account. Smerdis (Bardiya) went to Egypt with Cambyses but was presently sent back home. Then as the result of a dream in which a message was brought that Smerdis was seated on his throne, Cambyses sent his most trusty counsellor Prexaspes to kill him. The deed was done secretly; and when the Magus who had been left in charge of the palace conspired with this brother to seize the throne people had no idea that Smerdis (Bardiya) was dead. The brother was the living image of the true Smerdis and he happened also to be named Smerdis (Herodotus did not know the name Gaumata that Darius gives him); but presently the high noble Otanes became suspicious and began the investigations which resulted in the conspiracy of the Seven. There is some good Oriental story-telling in Herodotus here: the Magus Smerdis had had his ears cut off by Cyrus, and Otanes sent messages to his own daughter in the harem so that when her turn

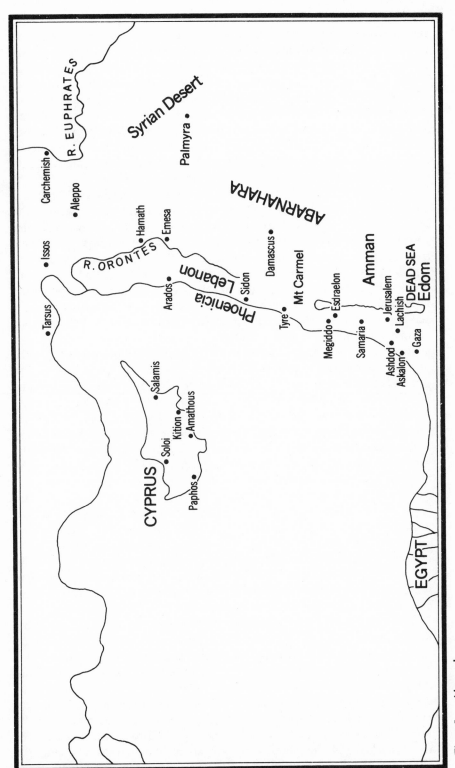

Fig. 5   Abarnahara

came round she felt his head while he slept (Demandt has claimed that this must be a Greek embellishment because Persians are shown with their ears covered in Greek art but not on the Persian reliefs!). The one person who of course knew the truth was Prexaspes, who had carried out the King's instructions. But after Cambyses' death he did not dare to admit that he had killed the son of Cyrus until the two Magi summoned the Persians together and had Prexaspes address them from the battlement; whereupon Prexaspes recounted the history of the dynasty from Achaemenes onward, then contrary to their intent he confessed the truth and dived to his death from the tower. By this time the seven conspirators were on their way.

Herodotus' story is certainly more than the truth. The lugless Magus is a fine touch, and the concourse of Persians below the battlements goes with the false assumption that the Magi were in the palace at Susa. Darius is briefer and more factual. But there are things that are misleading in his account of his rise to power. He doesn't positively declare that his grandfather and great-grandfather were kings, but he leaves it to be necessarily inferred. He doesn't say that he alone killed the Magus, but the six paladins are only mentioned four columns later, and there he speaks of them as his followers. He doesn't actually tell us that the Persians and Medes and others all believed that Gaumata was the true Bardiya, but the imposture is essential to his story; and in effect we are being asked to believe that Bardiya had been dead for three or four years without anyone becoming aware of it. The impersonation demands explanation, and the version of one of the Seven which Herodotus was following arouses suspicion in a generation like ours which is accustomed to detective fiction and official versions of political coups. In addition Prexaspes was Cambyses' right-hand man and he knew the truth; according to Herodotus' account he consistently denied that Smerdis was dead until the very moment when he was extinguished; after this he was not within the reach of questioning, but his son Aspathines became a high functionary at court. Finally we may consider Darius' integrity among a people who set great store by telling the truth. In the deliberations of the Seven Herodotus attributes to him a casuistical defence of lying to achieve one's ends (III 72); and in his Res Gestae at Behistun Darius constantly adjures the reader to believe *him* – Dandamayev has counted thirty-four instances of the use of the words Lie (noun and verb) and Liar in this text. The story smells, and few scholars now seem prepared to believe that it really was a pretender that the Seven killed.

It is impossible then to clear Bardiya of the charge of revolting against his brother; but since he had the immediate support of Persians, Medes, and the rest, there must have been something in the nature of a rising against Cambyses, and the interval of more than three months before he ascended the throne could even imply some reluctance on his part. Darius speaks of Gaumata destroying sanctuaries as well as confiscating property, and Herodotus understood that the new regime was more favourable to the Medes and less so towards the Persian nobility. He also says that Smerdis sent word round the provinces remitting obligations of military service and (like Shah Abbas in a similar situation) of tribute for three years, in consequence of which all the peoples of Asia felt his death as a loss. Herodotus only knows that 'things were swelling up' when Darius came to the throne and that at some unspecified time the Medes rose in revolt against him (III 76, 126–27, I 130). But the Behistun text makes it clear that Darius' seizure of the throne was immediately followed by risings in Mesopotamia, Armenia, and the Iranian lands, while the outlying satraps in Asia Minor, Egypt, and probably at first Baktria, sat tight and watched events take their course. There does not seem to have been popular support for Darius.

The Persian high nobility had co-operated with Cyrus, who seems to have treated them generously. But circumstances had been changing. The King was no longer so dependent on nobles bringing their feudal levies to form an army when he needed one. He had built up a standing army of professional soldiers, of which the core by this time was probably the 10,000 Persian infantry (the Immortals), 10,000 Persian cavalry, and perhaps similar forces of Medes. The allegiance of this army was to the King; and similarly the government of the provinces was probably becoming linked to the central administration under the King's jurisdiction, so that rule will have been passing into the hands of crown officers. As the structure of empire became more bureaucratic and less feudal, the Persian nobility was no doubt beginning to lose its dominant position; and Bardiya at least may have been thinking more in terms of a commonwealth of peoples with Medes and others having their place in the sun. The Seven were concerned to re-establish the dominance of the high Persian nobles. It was not popular support but good organization that was to see them through to victory. We must now turn back to the situation when Cambyses died.

Foreigners from all foreign countries, Ujahorresne said, had come to Egypt with Cambyses.[16] It was a motley army like that of Xerxes in 481–80. But we hear from Herodotus that on his return from Ethiopia Cambyses dismissed his Eastern Greek levies who had remained in Egypt (III 1 and 25); and others were no doubt sent home like Iddin-Nabu, who sold an Egyptian slave-woman and her three-month old daughter in Babylon on the last day of the year 524. So probably it was mainly with the Iranian core of his army that Cambyses was returning home, and later in the year we find Darius using what he called 'the Persian and Median army that was by me'. If Darius really is correct in not having Gaumata proclaimed as King until 1 July and making Cambyses die after that, the messenger would have reached the army in Syria before the middle of the month and Cambyses would have died perhaps early in August. The troops were well disciplined, and from the position he occupied beside Cambyses we may hazard the guess that Prexaspes took command and marched the army back to Babylonia. Aleppo-Baghdad used to be reckoned twenty-four daily stages (Curzon). Herodotus says that Darius came 'from Persians' because his father was governor in Persis. But the Behistun inscription shows that Darius' father was stationed in Parthia; and Darius should have been returning with the army from Egypt. His father-in-law, Gobryas, was on the spot as satrap of Babylon and Abarnahara; and if Darius really was the King's spear-bearer, his influence with the army officers would have made it worth while for Gobryas to draw him into the plot. Those already in, according to Herodotus, were Otanes, Ardumanish (?) (Herodotus' Aspathines, (see above, p. 19)), and Gobryas, with their seconds Intaphernes, Hydarnes, and Megabyxos. By this time we could be well into September.

Bardiya was in Media at what may have been a summer residence; Darius names the place Sikayauwatish ('Fort Rubble') in the district of Nisaya. It is not known where this was. But the probability is that the breeding grounds of the Nesaean chargers, which were five to six days' journey from Agbatana and visited by Alexander on his way to Agbatana after making a detour to see

Plate 37   Behistun,[17] were several days' riding beyond Behistun, which itself ranked as twelve daily stages from Baghdad (fifteen to sixteen from Babylon, though mounted men without baggage could travel further in a day). Herodotus says that Otanes was for proceeding with caution, but Darius insisted on immediate action for fear of a leak and forced Otanes' hand. The time-schedule is in fact tight enough to show that there was no delay. It has been suggested that the day the Seven came to the court (29 September) was that of the Mithra festival (at the autumnal equinox) when the King was more accessible than usual. At all events – to follow Herodotus now – they were such high-ranking nobles that the guards let them pass and the two 'Magi' were caught unprepared.

In the fight that ensued one of the Seven ('Aspathines') suffered a thigh wound and Intaphernes lost an eye. But while five of the paladins were struggling with the one 'Magus' Gobryas succeeded in pinning the other down until Darius could stab him. Whether it was Smerdis that Darius killed does not appear in Herodotus' story. Marquart has made a case that it was Intaphernes who killed him; and it is true that he is named first by Darius at

Plate 7   Behistun, which lends colour to the claim that it is he who stands next to Darius as King's bow-bearer in the relief.[18] Ctesias' account of these events seems worthless;[19] but from some source Justin had the name Cometes (i.e. Gaumata?) though he applies it to the other Magus. Apart from Aeschylus, all ancient accounts seem to accept the usurping Magi; and the feast of Magophonia (slaughter of the Magi) which Herodotus was the first to mention does not cease to bedevil scholarship. But if we believe that it was the true Bardiya that the Seven killed, the ghosts of the 'wicked heathen Magi' can be laid to rest.

Herodotus has the seven paladins display the heads of the 'Magi' publicly, and then five days later, when the uproar had subsided, discuss the future form of government. As we can see, the fate of the Persian nobility was at stake. Otanes, the initiator of the plot, favoured putting the power directly in the hands of the Persian people. Megabyxos was for setting up an aristocratic council. Darius, however, urged the advantages of monarchy and persuaded the uncommitted ones to agree with him. Otanes then withdrew on condition that he and his descendants should not be subject to any man; this was accepted, and special rights were accorded to all the Seven. The remaining six rode out at dawn on the understanding that whoever's horse was the first to whinny after sunrise should become King; and Darius' groom saw to the outcome. The story is a classic of one-upmanship. But scholars are inclined to believe in the compact itself. In Mesopotamian terms the Kingship had re-ascended into heaven, and, as von Osten maintained, a sign was needed from the god to assure the Persians of his will. Widengren sees it as an omen given by the Sun-god through the animal appropriate to him, and Dandamayev as hippomancy, while Gnoli seeks parallels in India.[20] Thus Darius became King about 5 October 522, and his reign lasted until November 486. Working from Herodotus, he will have been about sixty-four when he died. Ctesias, however, says he lived to seventy-two, which would make him thirty-six when he came to the throne. In some ways this might fit better with his early career because for four years after reaching the age of military service he might be expected to be one of the 'kardakes' (young Persians under training) and so too young to be the King's spear-bearer; and we could argue that in Herodotus' story of Cyrus' dream Darius had to be under age because otherwise there would be no reason for him not to be with Cyrus in the field and so put to death on the spot. But we should not forget that Darius avers that his grandfather Arsames was still alive when he became King,[21] and Ctesias' figures are for the most part totally irresponsible.

The troubles started almost at once. Unfortunately Herodotus' long and entertaining Persian narrative ended with Darius gaining the kingship, and the sum of his knowledge of what followed was that things flared up. So the Behistun text is our sole authority here. A rising in Elam was quelled by threats. But Babylon was up in arms under a claimant to the name Nebuchadnezzar. Darius led his army down to the Tigris, on 13 December he forced a crossing on camels, horses, and stuffed or inflated skins; and he won a second and decisive battle on the 18th, after which he entered Babylon. But by this time the outbreaks had become widespread; and they were not only nationalist risings aimed at liberation from Persian rule, but in Persis and in Media-Armenia they were inspired by rival claimants to the throne. Darius had not enough troops to cope with all fronts simultaneously. 'The Persian and Median army that was with me (he says), this was a small one. Thereupon I sent forth the (Median) army' under Hydarnes to Media. The pattern emerges. Hydarnes fought an engagement on 12 January 521 against that Frawartish who called himself Khshathrita of the seed of Kyaxares (above, p. 6); and then he held a defensive position until Darius could come up with his main force. Meanwhile Darius was near enough to Elam to nip another rising in the bud; troops were sent to Armenia to hold the enemy at bay as in Media, and similarly on other fronts.

Darius' success in holding enemies on so many fronts could hardly have been achieved unless he had crack troops at his disposal, in fact unless he had the nucleus of Cambyses' Africa corps under his command. This will have given him a great advantage against untrained levies.[22] Supplies no doubt were requisitioned or seized in the theatres of war. But gold and silver could be used in buying allegiance and good will and seducing the supporters of rival claimants to the throne. The royal treasuries in Agbatana and Persis were lost to Darius; but that at Babylon will have been available to him, together with Cambyses' war-chest and the riches of the great temples of

Babylonia. His relatively central position also made it more difficult for his enemies to combine – if they would have wished to;[23] so he was able to deal with them one by one.

Darius' fronts held; and by the spring he was able to start his great counter-offensive with his Persian troops to clear the way through Media. He won a decisive victory at Kundurush on 8 May and could then follow through to Rhagai, whence one contingent could turn and help to roll up Armenia, while another force was detached to enable his father to subdue the Parthian and Hyrkanian rebels. The Median bid for empire was thus at an end. Concurrently with his great Median drive Darius sent an army of Persian and Median troops under Artawardiya to Persis, which had been in the hands of a Persian named Wahyazdata who claimed to be Bardiya. Having risen up in the east of Fars at Tarawa (modern Tarom?), this pretender had taken over the Persian guard that had been at the palace and sent an army eastward into Arachosia (as far as Kandahar at least); the Persian satrap of Arachosia had fought three engagements with them between the end of December and March 521, when the revolt in the East was quelled. The army sent under Artawardiya now defeated Wahyazdata at Rakha on the Susa-Persepolis road on 25 May and finished the campaign off with a decisive victory on 15 July at Mt Parga (Furg in the east of Fars?).

By this time all the original rebels had been subdued. There were further revolts in Babylon and the following year in Elam, which were dealt with by two of the paladins (Gobryas and Intaphernes). But there was one major rebellion which has not been mentioned. 'A land by name Margush (Margiana round the oasis of Merv on the edge of Turkestan), it became rebellious to me. A man by name Frada, a Margian, him they made king. Thereupon I sent forth against him a Persian by name Dadarshish, my slave, satrap in Baktria. Thus I said to him "Go forth, smite that army which does not call itself mine". After that Dadarshish marched out with the army', and he duly smote them. This was in December, but scholars are not agreed whether 522 or 521 B.C.

Darius laid great stress on the fact that he fought nineteen battles and took captive nine kings in one and the same year. It was his 'annus mirabilis'. This will not work out exactly if the battle in Margush was on 28 December 521 unless we take the battle on the Tigris on 13 December 522 (or the capture of the Elamite Assina possibly a day or two earlier) as the beginning of the year, which would then with the intercalary month run until the end of December 521; and many eminent scholars maintain that the year must begin with Gaumata's death at the end of September 522. So the majority has been in favour of December 522 for the battle in Margush. But Frada stands last in *Plate 7* the line of 'kings of the Lie' on the Behistun relief, where the figures seem to be in chronological order with Gaumata first, followed by the first Elamite and the Nebuchadnezzar. We also have some idea of the scale of the rebellions from such enemy casualty figures as Darius gave in his first dictated text but omitted when he came to revise it.[24] The totals of enemy killed and captured generally range between something over 1,000 in the first Armenian engagements and 10,700 in Hystaspes' final battle. Only two battles exceed this. In his victory over Frawartish on the Agbatana road Darius recorded an uncertain number of dead (perhaps 34,425) and over 18,000 captured (but 108,010 captured in the Aramaic copy from Elephantine!). This was evidently a great battle to decide which of the two peoples was to rule the empire. In Margush the figures were only 6,972 captured, but no less than 55,243 killed. It is difficult to believe that in the anarchy of December 522 the satrap of Baktria could or would have fought such a battle of annihilation. A year later the eastern provinces were pacified, Hystaspes had received reinforcements in neighbouring Parthia, the resources of empire had been brought to bear, and above all there was no doubt in the satrap's mind who had won. So it seems easier to date this battle in Margush in 521. It is also difficult to see how Margush itself could have put so large an army in the field. Darius' first expedition after his accession wars was against the Pointed-cap Saka somewhere east of the Caspian in 519 B.C. (see below, p. 59); and it is an obvious conjecture that they had played a major part in the Margian attempt to throw off Persian rule. Another possibility has, however, now been suggested by von Voigtlander, that the high figure of dead represents the slaughter of the population of the city at Merv. The desolation of the fertile oasis resulting from this disaster has been said by Soviet scholars to be reflected in the archaeological record; it also perhaps accounts for the name not appearing in Herodotus and other classical writers.

Along with the other conspirators Darius had pledged himself to preserve the status and rights of the Seven. It is disconcerting to find him two years later speaking in his Behistun inscription of Hydarnes and Intaphernes as his 'slaves' (even if we soften it to 'subjects').[25] Intaphernes, who had lost an eye at Sikayauwatish and cleared up the last revolt in Babylon, insisted on his agreed right of direct access to the King; and in Herodotus' story he chopped off the ears of the palace servants who blocked his way, for which he and his household were destroyed by Darius on suspicion of rebellion. Herodotus speaks as though this happened immediately after the coup (III 118–19); but Intaphernes was still in favour in 519 B.C. when Darius revised his text at Behistun. The other paladins served Darius well and their families were revered – or at least the four consisting of Otanes, Gobryas, Hydarnes, and Megabyxos (see below, p. 167ff.). Under Darius the administration became more bureaucratic, the King's army dominant, and the distance between King and subjects increased.[26] But with the four great nobles and Prexaspes' son Darius kept faith.

VI Darius' Conquests

Darius I was justifiably proud of what he achieved with his Persian army; and it is possible to begin with the sequence of his military activities as they appear in his own inscriptions. After the revolts of his first year and the suppression of another pretender in Elam by Gobryas the following year, he proceeded in his third year against the Sakai; this expedition finished in time for him to have the Saka chief Sku(n)kha with his high pointed cap carved at the end of *Plate 7* the line of false kings on the relief at Behistun, and the record of the campaign included in the revised version of his text there. After Behistun we have only his lists of lands – or effectively peoples – whom he claimed as subject to him.[1] But these visibly grew over the years; so we may try to extract what hard information we can from them before starting to fill in from the Greek sources.

In the Behistun list twenty-two subject lands are named (excluding Persis); these were already in the empire when Darius became King in 522 B.C. (see below, p. 77f.). The Egyptian lists, known from the four frag-*Plate 15* mentary Suez canal stelae and the base of the Egyptian statue of Darius found in 1973, which had been transported from Heliopolis by Xerxes to adorn his new pylon at Susa, are now agreed to belong to the early 490s. They are elegantly drawn up, Gandara being omitted (perhaps to avoid asymmetry); and if the entry Saka of the Marshlands and Plains is counted as two peoples, the total excluding Persis is twenty-four. On Darius I's tomb at Naksh-i Rustam (DNa) there are no less than twenty-nine, and this should date somewhere about the end of the 490s after work there had reached its climax.[2] In both the Egyptian and Naksh-i Rustam lists there appear Hindush (Sind), Kush (Ethiopia), Put (Libya), and Skudra (apparently on European soil). The principal difference is that Yauna does not appear in the Egyptian lists at all, while Naksh-i Rustam has not only a people Yauna takabara ('bearing shields' on their heads, i.e sun-hatted) in addition to the land Yauna, but a new people called Karka. Yauna had been in the empire since the time of Cyrus, so a reason must be sought for the discrepancies. In 499 B.C. the Greeks under Persian rule rose in what is called the Ionian Revolt and were not reconquered until 494. At this time the Egyptian secretariat could well have felt that the less said about those turbulent Yauna the better. After 494, however, the Greeks were subjects again, together with the Carians in south-west Asia Minor who had been partners in the revolt and caused the Persians heavy losses; and the Naksh-i Rustam list contains not only two categories of Greeks but the reconquered Carians (Karka).[3]

The Egyptian royal inscriptions of Darius had their own peculiar nomenclature for Saka (Scythians). In other Old Persian inscriptions two Saka peoples are regularly distinguished – the Tigrakhauda ('Pointed-cap') ones and the Haumawarga (below, p. 195f.). Yet a third Saka people, 'Beyond the Sea', is named in Darius' list at Naksh-i Rustam; and though Struve recently proposed an equation with Xerxes' Daha, it is generally agreed to refer to the Scythians in Europe north of the Danube. Darius' campaign against these Scythians can not be dated precisely from the Greek sources; but 513 or 512 should be correct to within a year.[4] If now we take the list of peoples in the royal inscription on the south retaining wall of Darius' palace at Persepolis (DPe), we find twenty-four peoples. Hindush has already made its appearance, but Asagarta is there as a hang-over from Darius' campaign of 521 B.C. and the Saka are still single; Kush and Put have not yet entered the lists, there is of course no Karka and – more significant – there is no Skudra (let alone Saka Beyond the Sea). But there are Yauna both of the Dry Land and In the Sea (i.e. the Greeks of Asia Minor who were conquered under Cyrus, and Greek islanders who are new), and there is an entry of undefined people 'Beyond the Sea'. This seems to be a moment in time when some Greek islands were already subjected and the preparation for the Scythian expedition had involved a crossing of the Straits into Europe. So the inscription DPe should be of the eve of Darius' Scythian expedition and date within a year or two of 513 B.C.[5]

We thus have from Darius himself a sequence as follows: (i) Skunkha the Saka (519 B.C.),[6] (ii) India, Greek islands, and a foothold in Europe, (iii) the Scythian expedition (giving rise to the inclusion of Skudra) and the confines of Egypt (Kush and Put), (iv) probably the temporary occlusion of Yauna (during the Ionian Revolt of 499–494), and (v) the recognition of the Carians as a people (after 494 B.C.). The inclusion of sun-hatted Yauna (presumably in Northern Greece or Macedonia) could date after 494, but their appearance on glazed bricks of the Susa palace (DSm) might suggest an earlier date.

The insurrections of 522–21 B.C. have been described in the previous chapter. But Darius' original narrative left three revolting peoples in suspense. We are not told what happened to Thatagush in the far East or to Egypt; but we do hear about the Saka.

The supplementary fifth column at Behistun describes (in Old Persian only) Darius' campaign against the Saka with pointed caps under Skunkha. Kent's translation reads 'These Scythians went from me. When I arrived at the sea, beyond it then with all my army I crossed. Afterwards I smote the Scythians exceedingly.'[7] It was assumed that Darius ferried troops across the south-east corner of the Caspian. But Hinz maintains that 'went from me' is not correctly restored: they mustered against Darius. And secondly he claims that the word translated 'sea' means river here, and in effect that Darius crossed the Oxus, which then flowed along the Uzboy channel to the Caspian, on timber or brushwood floats.[8] In the event Skunkha was captured; Darius chose another chief to replace him, and the land became his. We must now use non-Persian sources.

Asia Minor remained quiet. But there was smiting to be done there too, and probably before 519 B.C.[9] Cyrus' satrap of Sardis, a Persian named Oroites, did nothing to help Darius at the time of the revolts, but he took the opportunity to avenge an insult on Mitrobates the satrap of Daskyleion and so make himself master of peninsular Asia Minor north of the Taurus. When Darius sent him orders he killed the messenger. So Darius summoned his principal nobles in council and asked for one to go and despatch the offending satrap. Bagaios, on whom out of thirty volunteers the lot fell, arrived in Sardis with a batch of missives bearing the King's seal and gave them one by one for the royal secretary to read out. This enabled him to watch the reaction of the Persian guardsmen until he felt confident enough to hand over the order to kill Oroites.

Before his death Oroites had lured Polycrates, the Greek tyrant of the island of Samos, to a rendezvous on the mainland and impaled him. One of Polycrates' brothers, Syloson, had been exiled and, according to Herodotus, gone sight-seeing in Egypt; and when a young Persian guardsman in the bazaar at Memphis wanted to buy his scarlet cloak Syloson by an act of inspiration gave it him for nothing. But later, when he discovered what had become of the guardsman, he travelled to Susa and sat at the palace gate claiming to be a benefactor of the King. Darius remembered him and undertook to restore him to Samos. We may smile at the story of the cloak and doubt whether a Greek could have travelled so freely to Susa without authorisation. At all events Syloson returned to Samos escorted by Otanes of the Seven and a contingent of Persian troops; and he was re-instated, though in the event not without considerable bloodshed.[10] Samos thus became subject to the Persians; and the two other large Greek islands of Lesbos and Chios also submitted to them. This no doubt gave Darius his 'Yauna in the Sea' of DPe.

The Sardis or Lydian satrapy (Sparda in the Old Persian) was not named at Behistun as having revolted. So the revolt in Egypt should mean more than that the satrap there sat on the fence like Oroites; and in fact, to follow Herodotus, Cambyses' satrap Aryandes continued in office for at least ten years under Darius. There is some evidence that could point to a visit by Darius to Egypt about 517 B.C. Not only is he shown to have taken a keen interest in its affairs and gratified the priests by restoring their privileges, but he was said to have loved the Apis more than any other Pharaoh had done; and a late writer Polyaenus, author of a miscellany of ingenious stratagems which commands little respect as history, has Darius arrive in Egypt to quell a revolt against Aryandes at the moment when the Apis bull died and gain great goodwill by offering a huge reward for the finder of its successor. This could be decisive. But in fact we know that a bull died just after Cambyses captured Memphis and was most respectfully treated by him (above, p. 49); so it is not unlikely that in view of his ill reputation the story has been transferred from him to Darius.[11] At this stage Darius' eyes may rather have been fixed on the East; and it is known that about this time he despatched written instructions to his satrap Aryandes about the codification of the laws and sent Ujahorresne on his own from the court to Egypt to carry out policies he wished to have implemented. This seems to suggest that he wasn't going there in person. The revolt in Egypt in 522–21 will in that case have been dealt with by the satrap.

To Jerusalem Darius certainly did not go. But Zerubbabel – despite his Babylonian name a prince of the house of David – was sent in 520 B.C. to take charge there. This will have been no easy task with opposition from the provincial officials when he resumed the building of the temple, and with the messianic rantings of fiery prophets to compromise him. When the governor of Abarnahara (Beyond the Euphrates) intervened, appeal was made to a decree of Cyrus authorizing the work (above, p. 32); and after being sought in vain among the archives in Nebuchadnezzar's palace at Babylon the relevant document was tracked down at Agbatana. The decree in the forms given in Ezra is perplexing; it has even been suggested that what was found was a forgery planted by a Judaean secretary in the imperial chancery, but a twenty-year span is not a long one in official memory. A decree of Cyrus was not to be countermanded, and the rebuilt temple was consecrated in early 515 B.C. This affords the one glimpse of a governor, the Tattenai of Ezra 5–6, functioning in Abarnahara.

The region of Arachosia, which lay south of the Hindukush around Kandahar and probably Quetta, had seen fighting in the winter of 522–21, but Darius' satrap had restored order; and Gandara further east seems to have been at peace. Thatagush, however, had rebelled and not apparently been subdued; so this may have been one of the immediate objects of Darius' eastern expedition. The outcome was that besides Thatagush a new name Hi(n)dush appears in the lists. From the Persian side we learn nothing more, except that on the Persepolis reliefs these two peoples and the Gandarians are all shown in light clothing suitable for a hot climate. The name Thatagush (Herodotus' Sattagydai) has commonly been explained as 'hundred-oxen' land, whether derived directly or as a corruption in Persian of (Median) 'seven-river' land;[12] and it has been identified with the present-day 'five-river' land (Punjab). But Herodotus puts it in a single satrapy (his 7th) together with Gandara and two other peoples, whose total tribute (170 talents) is the smallest in the entire list, while his 20th (Indians) paid more than twice the weight of gold that the 7th did of silver; and he doesn't mention any Sattagydian contingent in Xerxes' army, though cotton-clad Indians were present as both infantry and chariotry. The 20th 'nomos', which is the last in his list (below, p. 79), must correspond to Darius' new conquest of Hindush.

Herodotus' statement on the subject is brief enough to be quoted (IV 44):

Of Asia the greater part was discovered by Darius, who wanted to know where the Indus – one of the two rivers in the world that have crocodiles – discharges into the sea and sent ships manned by people whom he could trust to report the truth, and in particular Skylax of Karyanda (an island off Caria). They started at Kaspatyros city and the region Paktyike and sailed downstream to the east and sunrise, and then across the sea they sailed westward till in the thirtieth month they arrived at the place whence, as previously related, the Egyptian king (i.e. Necho) had sent the Phoenicians to circumnavigate

Libya (i.e. Africa). After they had sailed round, Darius conquered the Indians and made use of this sea.

Presumably, then, it is fair to render the name Hindush by Sind.

Strictly, if we accept this story as correct, we must allow about three years between the building of the ships and the invasion that waited on the news of their arrival at Suez. In fact we cannot believe that the flotilla would not have put in at Hormuz at the mouth of the Persian Gulf[13] to report its progress; and it is difficult to believe that the voyage down the Indus was carried out before Darius had invaded India. But the voyage itself was real enough (above, p. 14), and the results of it were known to Eastern Greeks before the end of the sixth century. Kaspatyros was a city in Gandara (Hecataeus), so the starting point may have been on the lower Kabul river or the Indus above Attock, though the rapids in the long gorge that cuts through the Salt Range could be perilous enough. Before the Warsak dam was built travellers used to float down the lower gorge of the Kabul river on stuffed-skin rafts as being less hazardous than the march over the Khyber Pass to the south; but it is not clear whether the river would have been navigable from Jelalabad. Kabul, formerly suggested for Kaspatyros, can be ruled out because of the cataracts down-river from it. To return to the voyage, we hear of a royal fortress at Opiai down the Indus, then of the desert of which Herodotus knew (the Thar desert – the Indus then flowed in a bed further east than the present one), and lower down of a people called Kallatiai, whom Darius questioned on the subject of their burial customs, twitting them with not burning their fathers when they died, and the Greeks for not eating theirs.[14] Scholars are in general reluctant to make Darius lead the invasion of India in person because they prefer to have him in Egypt. But Herodotus, who commanded such sources of information as were available, certainly understood that Darius went there.

Gandara must be roughly the Kabul river basin, and Thatagush could perhaps be composed of low-lying vales towards the Indus. What Darius presumably did was to conquer the Indus valley south of the Salt Range. There is as yet no evidence that the Achaemenids ever conquered the Punjab; in the last stages of the empire they certainly did not hold it, and Megasthenes, who went on embassies from Seleucus to Chandragupta's court two decades after Alexander, stated categorically that they never ruled in India, while Eratosthenes spoke of the R. Indus as the boundary between Indike on the one hand and the Ariane which the Persians ruled on the other.[15] This of course is by no means decisive; but the commonly held belief that the Achaemenids ruled beyond the Indus gains no more support from the archaeological evidence at Taxila than it has from the literary sources.

It was Europe's turn next. In Ctesias the story is that on instructions from Darius the satrap of Cappadocia, Ariaramnes, crossed the Black Sea with thirty fifty-oared galleys (penteconters) and brought captives back with him; one of them was the Scythian king's brother, and the bitter protests that resulted gave Darius the casus belli he wanted.[16] We have no means of checking this story. A preliminary reconnaissance makes sense. But there does not seem at this time to have been a satrapy of Cappadocia unless the Phrygian one is meant; and as the ships would have had to belong to the Ionic Black Sea colonies, Herodotus would be more likely to know of it than Ctesias. What we can say with some confidence is that the Persians must have crossed the Straits into Europe and set up their bridge-head and supply-bases before Darius got Mandrokles the Samian to construct a boat bridge for his army to cross the Bosporus. Unfortunately we have no pieces of the stelae with royal inscriptions that Darius set up (Herodotus says the people of Byzantium re-used them in an altar of Artemis) and no reflection of the painting Mandrokles dedicated in the Samian Heraeum showing Darius seated and his army crossing on the bridge.[17] Herodotus goes on to quote another stele of Darius at the sources of the Tearos; General Jochmus sought for it in eastern Thrace in 1847 and believed it to have then been recently extant.[18]

The fleet that Darius used was provided by Eastern Greeks, the commanders of the contingents being the men who were bosses of their cities in the Persian interest. While he marched across Thrace and forced his way northward through the Getai, the ships sailed to the Danube mouths and formed a boat bridge for him two days' sail up river. When Darius crossed, the Scythians sent their families away in their wagons with their herds; then keeping only what they needed for food, they withdrew through the wastes in front of him, choking the wells and springs and destroying the forage. Nothing can be made of Darius' march from Herodotus' account of it, which would have taken him more than 2,000 miles; but it seems clear that he never succeeded in forcing a battle. His most effective troops were the donkeys, whose braying kept the horses of enemy raiding parties at a distance. When more than two months had elapsed a Scythian host arrived at the bridge and urged the Greeks to sail away and leave the Persians to their fate. But the commanders knew that their rule at home depended on Darius; so they followed Histiaios of Miletus' advice and merely dismantled the bridge temporarily at its northern end. Darius was thus enabled to return across the Danube. The Scythians blamed the Ionians for behaving like slaves; and Histiaios was afterwards taken into Darius' entourage as an adviser. Darius' Scythian campaign may not have been such a fiasco as the ancient sources make out. But both Herodotus and Ctesias have him abandon part of his army beyond the Danube – in the one case the sick and less serviceable together with the valiant donkeys, in the other the rear divisions;[19] and Herodotus elsewhere speaks of the Scythians following up Darius' retreat as far as the Chersonese (Gallipoli Peninsula). There is no reason to think that they had been constituting a menace to the Persians as they did to Philip II of Macedon in 340 B.C. The enterprise seems rather to have been an imprudent one that showed up Persian limitations.

Darius crossed back into Asia at the Hellespont. He left an army behind to reduce Thrace as far west as the Strymon; its commander, Megabazos, could be the same person as Bagabadush who is named later in a Persepolis tablet as satrap of Arachosia.[20] The sun-hatted Yauna may have entered the royal list of peoples either at this time or twenty years later (above, p. 59). But Skudra seems to have resulted from these campaigns in Europe. To judge by the reliefs it should include the natives behind the Greek coastal fringe in the north Aegean, but the name is a puzzle to which no satisfactory solution has been found.[21] Macedonia at this time first accepted Persian suzerainty, and presumably its people were regarded by them as Greeks. After his Scythian venture Darius had had enough of campaigning and let his generals do the fighting for him in future. The region of the Hellespont was brought under tighter control and two adjacent islands were annexed.

At about this time according to Herodotus Aryandes, the satrap of Egypt, sent an amphibious expedition to Libya on behalf of a refugee queen-mother of Cyrene and destroyed Barka.[22] This accounts for the entry Put in Darius' lists; but nothing is known of any operations in Nubia or beyond since Cambyses' time to account for Kush (the name the Ethiopians of Meroe called themselves by). Aryandes himself seems to have been put to death by Darius some while after. The charge was revolt; but Herodotus insists that he was not in revolt at the time, and that the true cause was that he minted coins as fine as Darius' own gold ones.[23] It could be that Aryandes had offended by mounting an expedition and appointing commanders without reference to Darius. The next satrap known in Egypt was Farnadata, who seems to have continued in office until the Egyptian revolt of autumn 486; the name is no doubt the same as Pherendates and Pharandates in Herodotus (both of whom were commanders in Xerxes' Greek expedition).

After the Scythian expedition Darius seems to have wintered in Sardis. He must by this time have been aware that the free Greeks across the Aegean constituted a problem which, with the intervening sea, was more intractable than any which had confronted his predecessors. At some stage he sent a Persian mission in two modern galleys and a store-ship which was guided by the Greek doctor Demokedes, the purpose being to reconnoitre Greece and the South Italian seaboard (above, p. 17); and he was always ready to annex an island or two. But in the last ten years of the sixth century he occupied himself with organizing his vast empire and building palaces worthy of such a realm. It was only at the turn of the century that his brother Artaphernes, left in Sardis as satrap, referred to him a proposal to gain possession of Naxos and the Cyclades by exploiting Greek civil strife; and as we shall see later, his acceptance of it was the beginning of many troubles for Greeks and Persians.

One other conquest of Darius' may be mentioned here, that of the Sea. The Persians have rarely taken enthusiastically to the water; and their heavy loss of men in the Battle of Salamis was partly due to the fact that they could not swim. There is a certain naiveté at Behistun in Darius' obvious self-satisfaction at his crossings of the Euphrates and in Saka land; at that stage the old Assyrian skills were having to be relearned. He later made use of the Euphrates for transportation, as his Susa inscription (DSf) shows. But what Herodotus specially remarked on was the use that Darius made of the 'Red Sea' and the 'Arabian Gulf' – or, as we should say, the Arabian Sea (or Indian Ocean) and the Red Sea. He had had the coast reconnoitred from the Indus mouth to Suez. He seems to have planted maritime people such as Carians and Ionians in settlements at the head of the Persian Gulf – from the Greek side we know of Milesians deported to Ampe at the Tigris mouth,[24] and from the cuneiform we hear of a puzzling locality called Banneshu which stands in place of Karka in the Akkadian text of Xerxes' daiwa inscription and seems to have been in the same area.[25] The evidence for Phoenicians settled in the Persian Gulf is late and not altogether convincing (two islands in Strabo (XVI 765) called Arados and Tyre); presumably the Phoenicians would not have been forcibly deported so long as they remained loyal subjects, so we may rather think back to the days of Hiram of Tyre and Solomon. Timber from Gandara for Darius' palace at Susa may have been transported by sea. It recently seemed obvious that the Tamukkan of the Persepolis tablets, where supplies were issued to satraps of the southern provinces and Egyptian workers, was the port of Taoke by modern Bushire (below, p. 87), but Hallock has now gone back on the identification. Persis itself lacked suitable wood for ship-building, which was probably not to be found nearer than the Zagros in Elam or Media.[26] In fact, like Sennacherib, Darius may perhaps have used ship-builders up-river in High Mesopotamia. We have no evidence that he had a fleet on the Caspian, as Alexander the Great and Nadir Shah later had.

In the Eastern Mediterranean of course Darius had no lack of ships and seamen to call on. Phoenicia could supply two or three hundred modern warships on demand, and Egypt not much less; Cilicia, Cyprus, and the Greeks of the East Aegean could match them; Darius even had special horse-transports commissioned when he wanted to punish the Athenians in 490 B.C. But these were Mediterranean fleets with a long naval tradition.

With Darius it is difficult to distinguish between strategical and commercial aims. Both furthered his purposes. So with the three most productive and densely populated river lands of the ancient world under his control, the completion of the sea link must have had high priority. We think of the Suez canal as linking the Indian Ocean to the Mediterranean. But to rulers of Egypt the aim was naturally to link it to the Nile; and for a matter of two or three millennia until early Islamic times there seems intermittently to have been a waterway from the Pelousiac arm of the Nile near Bubastis to the Red Sea at Suez. The last Pharaoh before Darius to concern himself with re-opening this canal was Necho, who is said to have left the work unfinished (around 600 B.C.). Herodotus describes the canal at some length, imagining it to have been first completed by Darius (II 158): it was wide enough for two war galleys to pass under oars (so about 80 feet), and its length was four days' voyage.[27] But by the end of Achaemenid times it was already believed that Darius' canal had never been finished; indeed Strabo explains that he was persuaded that the sea at Suez was higher than the Nile in the Delta so that Egypt would have been flooded (XVII 804). Evidently the maritime activity that Darius promoted was not long-lived; Alexander's admiral Nearchus encountered no shipping or facilities for sea travel when he sailed from the Indus to the Persian Gulf. But for the period of Persian rule till 400 B.C. in Egypt a side-light is thrown by discoveries at Tell el-Maskhuta where a shrine of the goddess Hanilat attests the presence of Arab allies in a position to guard the western end of the canal (below, Chap. XVI n.22).

It was once an easy conjecture that Herodotus was romancing about Darius' canal (as also about Xerxes' Athos canal). But fortunately, as often, supporting evidence turned up. There survive parts of four red granite stelae that Darius set up to commemorate the completion of the canal; they were over 10 feet high and inscribed in the usual three cuneiform scripts on the one side and Egyptian hieroglyphs on the other. Darius the King says: 'I am a Persian. From Persis I grabbed Egypt. I commanded to dig this canal from a river by name Pirawa which flows in Egypt (i.e. the Nile) to the sea which goes out from Persis. Afterwards this canal was dug out as I commanded, and ships went from Egypt through this canal as was my desire.' The hieroglyphic texts were more detailed. Chiefs and dignitaries seem to have been invited, perhaps to the opening ceremony; twenty-four or thirty-two ships sailed through bearing tribute, and they are said to have arrived safely at their destination. It is tempting to follow Hinz in believing that this occurred during Darius' state visit to Egypt and that he sailed through the canal on the leading ship. Adulatory speeches were made about the King: 'Never was the like done before'. Scholars generally assume that that final comment was not Darius' own but the customary Egyptian flattery. But Darius was particular about his inscriptions, and after quarter of a century on the throne the past had become fused in his ego. Cambyses by this time was forgotten, and it was Darius who had 'grabbed' Egypt. This verb 'grab-' was a favourite one of Darius', but it was only in his later inscriptions that he declared that all that he ruled had been grabbed by him.

VII The Character of Darius' Rule

Darius' concern that his achievements should not be forgotten is manifest from the outset. When he came with his Persian army in the spring of 521 to relieve Hydarnes and force his way through to Agbatana he passed the foot of the cliff which rises almost sheer for a mile into the sky and was spoken of as Mt Bagistanon by Ctesias. Thanks to the Greek writers the name can be recognized as 'place of the god' (* Bagastana), and the spot was a holy one with springs and a paradise with fruit trees. There was a Median fortress here *Plate 6* (100 yards from Darius' monument), and it could have been in the open valley that Darius fought the decisive battle of Kundurush against Frawartish.

The mountain (Kuh-i Parau) has a prominent forward peak that seems to be what was called 'Sumayrah's tooth' in early Islamic times, and the ancient sources from Ctesias on do in fact ascribe Darius' carved relief on the cliff face to Semiramis.[1] But the monument has nothing to do with the legendary Assyrian queen. In modern times the village at the foot of the cliff has been known as Bisutun (i.e. without columns); the Arab geographers gave some less corrupted forms of the name, from which Sir Henry Rawlinson 140 years ago selected (or perhaps rather coined) the one – Behistun – that has become most familiar to English readers. The smoothed rock-face where the relief is carved is said to be 340 ft above the springs, and the relief panel to measure 18 by 10 ft, with Darius standing 5 ft 8 ins high.[2]

Recent German research has shown a number of stages in the execution of the monument.[3] The relief was carved and an original Elamite text engraved about 520 B.C., followed by an Akkadian version. The relief was completed *Plate 7* with Darius shown lifesize under the protection of the hovering Ahuramazda symbol, to which he raises one hand while with the other he grips his bow; behind him on a smaller scale are his armigers (on the left Gobryas, the other perhaps Intaphernes). Darius treads on the supine figure of Gaumata, behind whom originally eight 'kings of the Lie' were dragged on a rope. It was probably on his Median drive against Frawartish that he noticed the cliff where he could have a victory monument carved; and the conception of such a triumphal relief probably owed its origin to that of King Anubanini (of about 2,000 B.C.) at the Zagros Gates (Sar-i Pol) which he would have passed a few days earlier – despite the difference in composition the theme is strikingly similar.[4] After it was completed two things happened. One, Darius decided that the dignity of the King and imperial people required that his words should be transmitted in his own language and a script devised for it. Secondly, having defeated the Pointed-cap Saka in 519 he could not forbear to add the droll figure of Skunkha at the end of the line, even though that meant effacing the Elamite text there. So at this stage, when copies of his original text of the 'Res Gestae' had already been circulated in the empire in Akkadian and Aramaic, he had his words read back to him and dictated a revised version to be engraved in Old Persian, with the Elamite also to be brought to completion as far as space allowed.

The Old Persian text at Behistun differs from all other Old Persian ones (including those at Pasargadai) in that the word-dividers are angular; and it has also been claimed that in its phraseology it is more tentative than any other. A reputed letter of Themistocles, which is almost certainly a literary forgery of several centuries later but was carefully researched, speaks of 'the letters (i.e. script) which Darius the father of Xerxes recently wrote for the Persians'; and Hellanicus, the contemporary of Herodotus, attributed the Persian writing to Atossa (the name being that of Darius' wife). However, reliefs of Cyrus the Great at Pasargadai are inscribed in Old Persian as well as Akkadian. So some scholars have maintained that the Old Persian script dates back to Cyrus or even the Medes. There is uncertainty what of the sculpture and cuneiform lettering at Pasargadai dates to Cyrus and what to Darius. But recent study has led to one firm conclusion, that the Old Persian there was written under Darius; and at Behistun also further light has been shed on the matter. Fortunately it is only the short fifth column of Darius' text, that dealing with the campaigns of his second and third years, that depends solely on the Old Persian script. The preceding paragraph of the revised version was engraved in Elamite also; and that has recently been read with new accuracy so that any doubts on the meaning of the Old Persian are now removed. What Darius says is 'according to the will of Ahuramazda I have made the writing of a different sort, in Aryan, which did not exist before.' So the problem of the origin of the Old Persian script does seem to be resolved at last.[5] No doubt the Medes and Cyrus used Akkadian and Aramaic for chancery purposes.[6] But there was no Persian script before Darius.

Darius did two excellent things which merit eternal gratitude. One, he had the surrounds of the panel at Behistun dressed smooth so that no later ruler could reach and deface it. The other is that, though cuneiform in its signs, the script he had devised for Persian is influenced by Aramaic to the extent of being almost nearer to an alphabetic notation than a syllabic one. It is wasteful of space compared to the Akkadian at least. But it has only forty-two signs as against 131 in Elamite and far more in Akkadian; and of the forty-two signs six were little-used ideograms.[7] The result of this was that when copies of the trilingual Achaemenid inscriptions came to the attention of European scholars, the script that was Darius' own was seen to be the one that could be deciphered, and from the beginning of the nineteenth century attempts were made to fix phonetic values for signs by substituting the names of kings known from the ancient Greek writers. The Behistun inscription, which H. Rawlinson discovered and studied, provided the material for a more or less effective decipherment of Old Persian in the 1840s; and a key was thus provided for Elamite and Akkadian, which would otherwise have remained unintelligible. Akkadian subsequently gave the clue to the reading of other languages such as Hittite and Urartian. Without Darius and the Greek writers it is doubtful whether any of this could have been achieved.

The Old Persian remained a prestige script, as Darius no doubt intended it to be. He himself, like Shah Abbas, did not read and would probably have thought it beneath the dignity of a noble Persian to do so. Written records and communications were necessary, and for these purposes Elamite and above all Aramaic were used. It is unlikely that Darius had scribes who could take down his words in Old Persian as they did in Aramaic at least. Old Persian was almost confined to royal inscriptions on rock (as at Behistun), on the usual polished stone slabs, on clay bricks, tablets, and tiles (Darius' Susa palace building inscription (DSf) having for long been best preserved on a clay tablet), and on gold and silver plaques. The major inscriptions are commonly trilingual; Aramaic is very rare, but Darius' Egyptian inscriptions have   *Plate 15* hieroglyphs in addition to the three cuneiforms. In the palaces, inscriptions are also found on pillars, door and window frames, and on sculptures. Short inscriptions are found on weights, vessels of stone and the precious metals, and seals. Such objects were sometimes possessed by satraps and potentates; a most handsome crystal seal of Darius I hunting lion in a palm-grove under   *Plate 33* the protection of Ahuramazda may have been given to a high official in Egypt;[8] an alabaster vase with inscriptions of Artaxerxes in hieroglyphs and the three cuneiforms came to light at Orsk, 300 miles north of the Aral Sea in 1971, and a calcite vase naming Xerxes in the same four scripts was found at Halikarnassos. There are a couple of genuine instances of signs of the Old Persian script being used on unilingual seals of private individuals (Kent Sa and Se), and Lewis quotes Boardman for the view that they look provincial (and Sa western);[9] but their rarity is sufficient to show that the script was effectively a royal one.

The script itself is systematically and even artfully contrived[10] It would not need many scribes; so it is unlikely that the mention in Persepolis tablets of rations drawn for twenty-nine Persian lads learning to write and a litre of wine monthly for their instructor refers to the Old Persian script. Of all the kings Darius I was much the most loquacious in his inscriptions, indeed he was even introspective. Xerxes came second to him; but a long text of his found near Persepolis in 1967 repeats in his own name what his father had said in a very personal vein about himself at Naksh-i Rustam (DNb), so it may not be entirely cynical to wonder whether even his celebrated 'daiwa inscription' may not also turn out to be less original than has been supposed. No later Achaemenid wrote anything new, except that Artaxerxes II named Anahita and Mithra along with Ahuramazda and gave some undisclosed information about his rebuilding of the palace at Susa. After Darius' time the language of the script did not develop in line with that of current speech, with the result that artificiality and some inaccuracies appear in the texts; it is this that enables the experts to assign the gold tablets of Ariaramnes and Arsames to a late period (above, p. 8).

Another innovation of Darius' was the minting of a royal coinage. In the sixth century Lydians and Greeks had become quite accustomed to gold and silver coins whose metal value – that is to say, both quality and weight – were guaranteed by the stamp of the ruler or civic authority that issued them; and these coins continued to be struck under the early Achaemenids (the Lydian ones presumably by a King's mint-master in Sardis). In virtually the whole of the rest of the empire silver was used as currency, but generally in the form of bar-ingots or cut-silver which had to be weighed for business transactions; surprisingly, even in Mesopotamia nothing indigenous has come to light that could be spoken of as genuine coinage, though the Lydo-Greek weight-system corresponds to (and even borrows the names from) the Babylonian system for the weighing of the metals. Consequently it will probably have been about 512 B.C., when he got to know Sardis and the Greek cities and was assured of an abundant supply of gold from India, that Darius first recognized the advantage of issuing his own stamped coinage. He concen-

Plate 35   trated on two issues, one of gold and the other of silver, with the menacing obverse type of the mural-crowned King as an archer in the conventional bent-knee running posture. The gold coins were known to the Greeks as Daric staters or simply 'darics'. The Greek word (dareikos) is the adjective formed from the King's name (Dareios) applied to the masculine noun stater. In his *Cyropaedia* Xenophon had Cyrus the Great use darics; consequently some scholars have attempted to dissociate the word from Darius (gold in Old Persian is daraniya-, and other etymologies have been suggested).[11] But Xenophon seems simply to be guilty of one of his anachronisms, and one less notable than that of I Chronicles 29, 7 where our Revised Version has darics current in King David's economy; on the available evidence there is every reason for believing that darics were first minted by Darius. They acquired the nickname 'archers', so that when Persian bribes caused his recall from Phrygia to face a hostile coalition in Greece the Spartan king Agesilaos could remark that he was driven out of Asia by ten (or thirty) thousand archers. The silver coins, which at first seem to have shown the King half-length but later in the bent-knee posture, were called Median 'sigloi' – the Babylonian word which we know as 'shekels'.[12]

Darius is said by Herodotus to have re-organized the empire on a basis of twenty satrapies, each of which was assessed at a fixed annual tribute (below, p. 77). The tribute for all except the 20th (Indian) satrapy was fixed in silver; and it seems likely that Darius intended his coinage to become the normal medium of payment, with gold in a fixed weight ratio to silver of 13⅓ and 13:1 (one daric to 20 sigloi). If so, he underestimated the forces of inertia and cupidity. The greater part of the empire preferred to keep to its old habits, and the Kings could not resist the temptation to hoard the precious metals that came to their treasuries as tribute. Persepolis tablets and Greek writers show workers' wages being paid largely in kind, and the King's courtiers and the troops receiving their daily food (below, p. 139f.). Silver is said by Poly-kritos in the early fourth century to have come in the main as tribute from the western coastlands, and a hoard of that date found at Nimrud in Assyria contained Greek coins mixed with silver rings and vase-handles, while a similar find has been made as far east as the Kabul region. In fact silver was in chronically short supply in Babylonia in later Achaemenid times, and the coins that come to light in the upper satrapies such as Arachosia and Gandara are mostly of Greek origin. Gold came mainly from the east of the empire. The Kings coined only such quantities as were needed for current purposes like military operations, particularly the hiring of mercenaries and the bribing of Greek politicians and parties. The history of the daric is one of avarice and bad faith. The Persian royal issues could almost be regarded as coinage of the Greek world, and so too, on a rather broader front, the silver minted by satraps and commanders in the West for their military needs from the late fifth century on. The King's sigloi had little currency outside Asia Minor; even in the Levant Greek silver coins were preferred.

Darius liked to work through responsible individuals or bodies. At court he had Gobryas and Aspathines as trusty advisers and agents; he also had experts on provincial affairs. Ujahorresne, who had advised Cambyses, was brought to court to advise the new King and receive instructions before being sent back to Egypt. Histiaios of Miletus was brought back not long after the Scythian expedition and kept as an adviser at court for over a dozen years (below, p. 92). Zerubbabel, the grandson of King Jehoiachin, may have been kept at court and briefed before being sent to Jerusalem. Datis the Mede seems to have become Darius' specialist on Greek relations (below, p. 97f.). We get the impression that Darius did not have a regular advisory body such as the Assyrian kings seem to have had, but that he sought advice from those best qualified to give it and then, like Shah Abbas, made his own decisions. He also harboured refugees who might come in useful, such as the exiled Spartan king Demaratos and Skythes of Zankle; and he was beneficent towards Metiochos, the captured son of Miltiades. He took a personal interest in what went on in the provinces. One of the first things he did was to order Aryandes to set up a great commission to collect the Egyptian 'laws' as they had stood at the end of Amasis' reign (i.e. before Cambyses); in the course of sixteen years' work they were codified on papyrus and finally made available in Egyptian demotic and Aramaic.[13] This will probably have been a matter of the patents of endowments, privileges, and immunities granted to the temples by earlier Pharaohs; so it is easy to understand the favour in which Darius was regarded there. But he was equally concerned that his officials should be worthy of the responsibility they carried. Ujahorresne's task on his return was to reconstitute the Houses of Life, or at least that at Sais. These were colleges attached to major temples, where old-inherited priestly learning, cult requirements, and medicine were studied.[14] Ujahorresne could report a few years later that he had set his college in order again, procuring a complement of suitable students (all of good families) and learned men to teach them. The satrap in Egypt was also made responsible on the King's behalf for ensuring that candidates for appointment as temple superintendants were suitable; a missive in demotic from the satrap Farnadata to the priests of Khnum refers to Darius' orders and shows that confirmation of the priests' choice was not a mere formality.[15] One temple superintendant was actually dismissed at El Hibeh in 513 B.C.

The order Darius sent to his 'slave' Gadatas, who may have been his Sardis satrap for a few years after Oroites, contains a rebuke for curtailing the privileges of the priests of Apollo at Magnesia on the Maeander.[16] Carved on stone in Roman times, this could be an ingenious, well-researched forgery; but it is simpler to suppose that it reflected a genuine document in Aramaic. In this case Darius' policy was not so well conceived because in general priests had relatively little influence in Greek city politics.

The Gadatas letter was not just a reprimand. It also commended the governor for introducing fruit trees from Beyond the River (Syria); and Darius would have said the same about the breed of wild mules that was later introduced into the Daskyleion satrapy from Syria.[17] Land improvement was probably one of the things Darius cared about. In the normal way irrigation projects and underground water channels cannot be precisely dated without literary evidence. But in the Great Oasis (Khargeh) west of Egyptian Thebes we have the conjunction of an inscription of Darius I at the Hibis temple that Darius II in fact completed and of underground tunnels of Persian type (qanats or karezes) that brought water through the soft sandstone. Here perhaps is a work that could have been personally ordered by Darius.

With his predilection for responsible government Darius was conscious of the need to ensure that the laws were known to those who would apply them. In Egypt the codification was proceeding, and Darius was later ranked as one of the great law-givers there by Diodorus (I 95). Plato, however, in his querulous seventh letter refers to Darius as the great law-giver of ancient Persia and thereby the conserver of its empire. Olmstead in particular built on this and claimed that he created a penal law-code which is reflected in mentions of the King's law (data) and presumably formed the basis of the Videvdat (Antidemonic Law) which was promulgated some four centuries later.[18] The difficulty is that while Hammurabi's law-code – itself 1200 years old and even then a matter of pious aspiration rather than practical reality – is said to be reflected in phrases in Darius' inscriptions on the re-establishment of the rule of justice, there is no sign of anything that could pass as a body of laws. Olmstead cited in particular the mentions of the King's Law in a Babylonian document of Darius' second year and of his Law in column I at Behistun as evidence for a new law-code. But it is impossible to believe that Darius could have formulated a new code and had it brought into use throughout the empire before he began to dictate his first draft of the Res Gestae in 521 or 520 B.C. What he said there was that at the time of his accession the lands he names 'respected my Law' (DB I line 23), which in the context seems to mean that they recognized his rule or his command. The one other instance of Darius' 'data' cited by Olmstead is a new tax imposed in Babylonia near the end of his reign, which is undoubtedly an instance of a royal command that can not be gainsaid.

There are two directions in which Darius seems to have been active: first, as the Egyptian evidence shows, in having laws or patents made available in writing, and second – though he may not have been the initiator – in having a machinery of permanent boards of judges, which in Babylonia at least included some Persians in their membership, while above them was the satrap to whom appeal could be made (curiously, Stolper adduces an instance under Darius II in which a complaint of Arsames against the Murashu firm was referred from a satrapal tribunal to an assembly of free citizens, presumably at Nippur). It seems most improbable that there was anything corresponding to an imperial law-code; Plato is not an authority to be used in historical matters, and it would be an insult to Darius to father the Videvdat on him.

Darius' new tax (on goods in transit by canal) in Babylonia has been mentioned; it does not seem to be clear whether road tolls were levied. We hear of a naphtha spring at Sadrakai near Arbela and bitumen wells at Arderikka that belonged to the King. In addition to their royal estates the Kings enjoyed the revenues from fish-garths (Lake Moeris in Egypt at least) and water works for irrigation, together with the ownership of huge royal studs in Media and Armenia; very probably they claimed rights to quarries, mines, and salt-workings, and Nehemiah (2, 8) speaks of a keeper of the King's forest in Abarnahara. There is some mention in Pseudo-Aristotle's *Oeconomica* book II of taxes on livestock, on registration of craftsmen, sales, and evidence of a poll-tax. It is reasonable to suppose that the raising of such revenues was part of Darius' organization of a fiscal system.

One of Darius' favourite occupations, it would seem, was building palaces. Greek writers mention one built by him at Sadrakai where the naphtha source was and another on the Middle Euphrates near Semiramis' canal. In 498/97 B.C. materials were being delivered for the construction of the residence of the King's son at Babylon, of which remains of early Achaemenid design came to light in excavation.[19] At Pasargadai Darius continued the work of Cyrus. But the two palaces of his that really counted were Susa and Persepolis (below, p. 158ff.). Work on both must have gone on simultaneously, though the relief sculptures at the latter needed a longer time to complete. By the standards of our generation Darius was fortunate in his architects; for he says everything was built exactly as he wished it (e.g. DPf in Weissbach). The mentions in Persepolis tablets of large parties of workers from Egypt, Lydia, and elsewhere point to conscripted artisans on a scale not unlike Tamerlane's at Samarkand. By 509 B.C. at latest the administrative service in Persis was centred on Persepolis, and it was probably not long after that the treasury of gold and silver was lodged within the fortification there. The King would seem to have spent a lot of his time at Susa, though not in summer when traffic from there came almost to a standstill. It seems as if Darius was in Elam when Ujahorresne was sent back to Egypt; so he may have made Susa his residence very early in his reign. He perhaps came to Persepolis on occasion for the New Year festival (assuming it to have always been at the vernal equinox).[20] The widespread notion that delegates from all the subject peoples came annually there with gifts including okapis, dromedaries, and lion cubs seems to find no support from the Persepolis tablets.. It is of course absurd; the fact that the 7,000 ft pass would be snow-covered is not decisive – Pietro della Valle commented with surprise on the arrival in winter at Shah Abbas' court at Isfahan of a Mogul ambassador who brought an Indian buffalo, elephants, and two baby rhinoceroses; what is decisive is the fact that the peoples of the western empire had no knowledge of Persepolis, for the Greeks would have taken note of it if delegations from Yauna, Sparda, and Put had been

Plates 24–9

travelling there. It does, however, appear that Darius resided in Persepolis in the winter of 495/94 when Datis went to report to him (below, p. 97f.).

The palace at Susa was the principal centre of Achaemenid government except for a period straddling the reign of Darius II when it had been destroyed by fire. In the mid fifth century it was an almost automatic assumption that the King resided there (below, p. 145), and the harem will presumably have been at Susa. Atossa, who must have been a beauty since Cambyses had fallen in love with her,[21] and whom Herodotus spotted as the power behind the throne, presumably ruled the womenfolk there. She does not occur in the Persepolis tablets unless once under the title of the 'banuka' (mistress). Darius' favourite wife, of whom he had an image made in beaten gold, Artystone (Pillar of Justice) the youngest daughter of Cyrus, lived in her residence in Persis; this was at a place whose name seems to be the same as the Kuganaka(n) where a Persian pretender to the Elamite throne in early 521 B.C. had his home. It is a fair guess that this estate was confiscated by Darius and given to Artystone,[22] and that Darius will have called in on her when travelling to Persepolis. From large deliveries of sheep and wine made to her in the tablets it seems likely that Darius visited her in the spring of 503 and again in 498 B.C. (above, p. 14). Artystone had two sons, Arsames and Gobryas. Hinz has credited her with the ownership of a village estate and a carpet factory; and no doubt she would have had a detachment of royal troops assigned to her. One other lady of the highest rank appears in the tablets as having property at Shiraz and elsewhere and being probably visited by Darius. Her name, Artabama, is not one of the five that Herodotus gives for Darius' wives; but he does not give the name of Darius' first wife, the daughter of Gobryas, who was the mother of his eldest sons. Artabama received 2,290 litres of wine in 500 B.C. and seems to have had feasts in places on the Susa road in 499–98; if she was Darius' first wife, perhaps she was travelling to Babylon for her eldest son's installation (he would have graduated from the kardakes by that time). Lewis tells me that he believes he has found mention in the tablets of another wife of Darius whom Herodotus names, Parmys daughter of Smerdis; and Hallock now finds that Abbamush (or-wush), possibly what in Greek is called Apame and resident at Shiraz, is a lady of the highest standing (PFa 14) – we must of course reckon with royal relatives such as the widow of Darius' brother Artanes and perhaps sisters of Darius.

To ensure that no one but his children could claim descent from the founder, Darius married Cyrus' surviving daughters and granddaughter. His oldest sons were by Gobryas' daughter; so there was an expectation that Artobazanes, the eldest of them, would succeed to the throne. Herodotus speaks of the matter as coming to a crisis the year before Darius died (VII 2–4). The decision, to which Demaratos claimed to have contributed his quota, went in favour of Xerxes – probably not so much on the ground alleged, that he was born after his father became King, but because he was of the blood of Cyrus and his mother Atossa was on the spot like Solomon's mother Bathsheba and was formidable.[23] If Herodotus is correct in this, the residence constructed for the King's son in Babylon in the early 490s must have been intended for Artobazanes. There is one argument in favour of this; Darius would probably have been unwilling to remove Artobazanes from the succession so long as his grandfather Gobryas was alive; and Persepolis tablets and his naming as spear-bearer on the front of Darius' tomb seem to show that Gobryas was alive after 498 B.C. In that case the two sculptured Treasury Reliefs, which were designed for the central positions on the *Plate 9* Apadana staircases, may possibly have been intended to portray Darius with his eldest son standing behind him. The argument that they were moved to the Treasury because Xerxes did not wish to be reminded of Darius' first choice is not a strong one; but in itself it is as good as that which makes the King Xerxes with a crown prince behind him who did not become his successor.[24]

Polykritos, who was a doctor at the court when Ctesias left, said that Darius I was the most handsome of men, but that his arms reached down to his knees.[25] This is not specially noticeable on the reliefs; but on the authority of the Avesta long arms were admirable, and the name Makrocheir (Long-arm) which the Greeks had for Artaxerxes I presumably reflects a complimentary Persian name. Attempts to measure Darius' height on the assumption that he is exactly lifesize on the Behistun relief can be dismissed because in that case the other figures would be dwarfs. But the rock-cutting for his sarcophagus at Naksh-i Rustam will not allow him to be more than 5 ft 10 ins tall.[26] On his own profession he was a good bowman and spearman, both on foot and on horseback. When he says that he could control his temper and keep his head in an emergency we have no reason to disbelieve him. He was severe with his subordinates as the Gadatas letter shows, drastic in his treatment of Oroites and Intaphernes, and apparently implacable towards Aryandes. In Herodotus he doesn't appear quick to anger like Cyrus, but he could thereby be the more deadly. He was not sensitive to human suffering, to judge by his wilful deportation of the Paeonians (below, p. 91) and (if it is historical) his impaling of 3,000 leading citizens of Babylon after a revolt.[27] The punishment he inflicted on the 'kings of the Lie' was savage. But it was not unusual; from his point of view it was exemplary retribution; indeed, with his firm conviction that he was Ahuramazda's regent on earth, he need not have doubted that he was acting justly. He didn't like to be crossed, and in his later years he was unremitting in his manoeuvres against the Greeks and especially the Athenians whom he had not been able to punish. But he could behave with clemency if on reflection he found that a man's good deeds outweighed the evil he had done;[28] and he had his soft spots – for Artystone, and for Histiaios whom his brother Artaphernes put to death because he knew that Darius would end up by pardoning him, and for eating pomegranates.[29]

The next chapter will deal with Darius' organization of the provinces. This set the empire on a firm footing. But it did not enhance his reputation. The Story of the Seven indicated that Herodotus' Persian informants had reservations about him. In particular, the comment that strikes home is that while Cyrus was a father and Cambyses a tyrant, Darius was a 'shop-keeper' (III 89). A literal translation might be that 'the Persians call Darius a hawker because he hawked everything'. Apologists of Darius like Junge in his monograph on him[30] have seen in this remark a testimonial to his good management. But the Persian nobles were brought up in a tradition that eschewed buying and selling. The implication is that Darius was not the mirror of Aryan chivalry. Herodotus made the queen of the Massagetai address Cyrus as 'insatiable of blood'. He derides Darius' avarice in the cautionary tale of his opening of Nitokris' tomb over the main gate of Babylon, where instead of the wealth promised he found a message beginning 'If you were not so insatiable of money . . .' (I 187).

Nearly fifty years ago Schaeder argued that the effect of Darius' policies and reforms was to transform an Aryan feudal kingship into an Oriental despotism, and he sought the seeds of decay there rather than in the corruption of the court under his successors.[31] We can now surmise that the transformation was inevitable and even that to some extent Darius was a reactionary in his safeguarding of the privileges of the Persian nobility. Toynbee subsequently divined that the change for the worse came when force of circumstances compelled Darius to abandon Cyrus' policy of rule by consent in favour of repressive partitioning.[32] Darius was of course autocratic, and he certainly increased the distance between himself and his subjects. But here again – granted his need to keep faith with his Persian nobles – Darius seems to have been as progressive as was practicable.

He exerted power. He thought big, and what he did was a matter of urgency. His concept of rule was expressed from the outset in his own phrase (DB I lines 19–20) 'what was said to them by me, night and day it was done'. Herodotus put the matter well when he said that with the accession of Darius everything was filled with 'dynamis' (III 88). The royal inscriptions of his successors show that it was a matter of pride to them to trace their descent from King Darius the Achaemenid.

VIII The Organization of the Provinces

Herodotus tells us (III 89) that after establishing himself on the throne Darius set up twenty 'archai (provinces) which the Perisans call satrapies', appointed archons (rulers), and fixed the annual tribute due from each; to make up these satrapies he selected certain peoples and attached neighbouring peoples to them, and then did the same again further out. Consequently many of the satrapies consisted of several peoples centred on one as a nucleus. When he comes to name the satrapies and their component peoples Herodotus uses a different term, 'nomos', instead of 'arche'. Also in place of archon he frequently uses the term hyparch. We shall normally follow Persian usage and speak of the provinces as satrapies and their governors as satraps.[1] At the same time we must bear in mind that in the Greek writers the word hyparch at least may be used of a governor of a smaller area or a subordinate of a satrap and that the word satrap may also be used of a subordinate in Xenophon and Diodorus – in Babylonia and Judah also the words for governor (pihat and pecha) do not distinguish their rank.

The detail that Herodotus gives can wait for a page or two. At this point one comment ought to be made. To be fair to all, such an apportionment of tribute would need to depend on a survey of resources; so we should not expect it to be completed at one blow. In fact, the Indians (Herodotus' 20th 'nomos') cannot have formed a satrapy until Darius conquered them; the 5th (Syrian) 'nomos' west of the Euphrates had not yet come into being in Darius' sixth year when we know that Ushtani was governor of Babylon and Abarnahara (Beyond the River) with Tattenai as subordinate governor of the latter (and still governor there in Darius' twentieth year); and finally in Ionia the land survey and resulting tax assessment of the cities was carried out by the Sardis satrap, Artaphernes, in 493 B.C., though Herodotus speaks of it as not involving much change in the amount of tribute collected.[2]

At the beginning of his Behistun inscription Darius named the following lands as being in his empire when he assumed the Kingship:

> Parsa (Persis, now Fars)
> Uwja (Elam, Herodotus' Kissioi, now Khuzistan)
> Babirush (Babilu, Babylon)
> Athura (Ashur, Assyria)
> Arabaya (Arabia)
> Mudraya (Misir, Egypt)
> tyaiy drayahya ('those at/in the Sea')
> Sparda (Sardis, Lydia)
> Yauna (Ionia, i.e. Greeks)

Mada (Media)
Armina (Armenia)
Katpatuka (Cappadocia, Herodotus' Syrioi)
Parthawa (Parthia)
Zra(n)ka (Drangiana, Herodotus' Sarangai, later Seistan)
Haraiwa (Areia, now Herat)
Uwarazmiy (Chorasmia, now Khwarizm or Choresm)
Bakhtrish (Baktria)
Sug(u)da (Sogdiana)
Ga(n)dara/Paruparaesana³ (Herodotus' Gandarioi, later
    Paropamisadai)
Saka (land of Sakai, Scythians)
Thatagush (Herodotus' Sattagydai)
Hara(h)uwatish (Arachosia)
Maka (presumably on the coast of the Arabian Sea)

This made twenty-three lands including Persis. Subsequent additions to the list in Darius' later inscriptions are Asagarta (in Persepolis e only, Herodotus' Sagartioi) and Hindush (Sind), Skudra (in Thrace?), Put (Libya), Kush (Ethiopia), Karka (Carians, above, p. 58 and Chap. VI n.3), and the subdivisions of Saka and Yauna (above, p. 58f.). Xerxes added two new names, Daha (Daai, men, perhaps in the sense of 'brigands') and Akaufachiya ('mountain men').⁴ But whether it was he or his father who conquered them, they were not retained in the lists of subsequent Kings, who followed Darius even to the point of naming the Saka beyond the Sea whom he himself had omitted in his late text DSe. The impression given is that at Behistun Darius is naming the principal peoples (or strictly lands) of the empire in 522 B.C., whereas the subsequent additions may be major ones like Hindush or minor ones like Greek islands, Put, and Karka, or even non-conquests like the Saka beyond the Sea.

Herodotus' list of satrapies is as follows (III 90–97) – the numbering is his but will hardly have constituted an official order of precedence:

1. Ionians, Magnesians in Asia, Aeolians, Carians, Lycians, Milyeis, Pamphylians: assessment for tribute 400 talents of silver.

2. Mysians, Lydians, Lasonioi, Kabalioi, Hytenneis: 500 talents of silver.

3. Hellespontioi, Phrygians, Thracians in Asia, Paphlagonians, Mariandynoi, Syrioi (= Cappadocians): 300 talents of silver.

4. Cilicians: 360 horses, 500 talents of silver (140 spent locally on cavalry).

5. Phoenicia, Syria called Palestine, Cyprus: 350 talents of silver.

6. Egypt, with Libya, Cyrene, and Barka: 700 talents of silver, Moeris fishery dues (in silver), corn for garrison troops.

7. Sattagydians, Gandarians, Dadikai, Aparytai: 170 talents of silver.
8. Susa and the territory of the Kissioi: 300 talents of silver.
9. Babylon and the rest of Assyria: 1000 talents of silver, 500 eunuch boys.
10. Agbatana and the rest of Media, Parikanioi, Orthokorybantioi: 450 talents of silver.
11. Caspians, Pausikai, Pantimathoi, Dareitai: 200 talents of silver.
12. Baktrians as far as Aiglai: 360 talents of silver.
13. Paktyike, Armenians and their neighbours as far as the Euxine (= Black) Sea: 400 talents of silver.
14. Sagartians, Sarangai, Thamanaioi, Outioi, Mykoi, islands of the 'Red Sea': 600 talents of silver.
15. Sakai, Caspians: 250 talents of silver.
16. Parthians, Chorasmians, Sogdians, Areioi: 300 talents of silver.
17. Parikanioi, Ethiopians of Asia: 400 talents of silver.
18. Matienoi, Saspeires, Alarodioi: 200 talents of silver.
19. Moschoi, Tibarenoi, Makrones, Mossynoikoi, Mares: 300 talents of silver.
20. Indians: 360 talents of gold dust, valued at 4680 Euboic talents of silver.

Total: 14,560 Euboic talents of silver.[5]

Gifts were brought by the Ethiopians bordering on Egypt (gold, ebony, boys, ivory), the Colchians and their neighbours as far as the Caucasus (boys and girls), the Arabians (incense). Herodotus elsewhere says that the Babylonian satrapy (the 9th) had to bear the cost of feeding the royal court for four months in the year. In his terminology 'Assyrian' includes Babylonian, for which no other convenient name was current (following Sumerian usage they called themselves Black-heads); this accounts for the Greeks making the Assyrian queen Semiramis reign in Babylon, against which Berossos protested. In the above list nos. 2, 3, and 5 are the satrapies of Sparda (Sardis), Daskyleion (Phrygia), and Abarnahara. The Sarangai of no. 14 are presumably Darius' Zra(n)ka. The 17th, 18th, and 19th 'nomoi' are roughly in Baluchistan, around eastern Armenia, and south of the eastern Black Sea respectively.

Herodotus gives a second list (VII 61–95). This is the parade state of the Persian army and fleet as reviewed at Doriskos in early summer 480. The majority of the names in the satrapy list recur here, together with brief descriptions of costume and armour and the allocation to the thirty infantry divisions or other arms. Important as it is, it adds little to the list of peoples in the empire. There are people of the Mysian Olympos, Bithynians, and Ligyes on the north coast of Asia Minor; but the only significant omission that is rectified is the Hyrkanians south-east of the Caspian, who appear frequently in Greek texts. Curiously, Hyrkania is not in the Persian lists of lands either, but it is mentioned (Warkana) at Behistun, where it is subsumed in the satrapy of Parthia (above, p. 56). From other passages in Herodotus we could of course add more names in North Africa and the corner of Europe that the Persians invaded, in Asia we can add the Chalybes on the Black Sea coast, and in India the Kalantiai and Padaioi. We can also add Herodotus' six 'clans' of Medes (above, p. 7) and his ten Persian ones (above, p. 39f.) less the Sagartioi – the Germanioi are known from various sources, including Darius I's Susa palace building inscriptions which name Karmana as a place of origin of a special timber (claimed to be sissoo).[6] One apparent omission from the Behistun list of lands is Cilicia. It was a kingdom ravaged by the kings of Babylon and presumably therefore glad to ally itself with Cyrus, who would consequently have had no occasion to conquer it (below, p. 199); until 400 B.C. it continued to have its own kings, but was used by Darius and his successors as a base for their naval operations as well as providing ships; and according to Herodotus it paid tribute. Herodotus tells us that the Medes were formerly called Arioi (Aryans), and that the Persians had been called Kephenes and were known among themselves and their neighbours as Artaioi (perhaps 'artawan', see Chap. XIV n.33).

Herodotus lists twenty satrapies, and Darius at Behistun named twenty-two subject lands. It was therefore inevitable that modern scholars should seek to identify the two. Not unnaturally Darius was considered the more reliable, and a generation or two ago scholars 'corrected' Herodotus in the light of changes in the Persian lists. A point that is easily overlooked is that Darius' first list of lands subject to him, that at Behistun which forms the basis for all the subsequent lists, is of what was already in being when he became King, so that we are in effect being asked to believe that his main arrangement of the satrapies had occurred under his predecessors. We have only to look at Herodotus' 16th 'nomos', which contains four of Darius' lands, to realize that the two lists are quite incompatible. If we accept Darius' lands as the satrapies, we must reject Herodotus' list out of hand. There are two reasons for not doing this. First, there is considerable internal support for Herodotus' satrapy list from his army list; his army list is not to be brushed aside, for in our generation we have learned that military intelligence can be grossly mistaken about the enemy's strength but is generally more reliable in the identification of units, and it is rarely that an army has exposed itself to the enemy's scrutiny as completely as Xerxes' did on its march to Athens. The other objection is decisive.

If we look at the developed lists of late Darius I and Xerxes we find a total of about thirty peoples. Eight of these at most are shown in other sources to be satrapies or to have satraps after 522/21 B.C., with Media and Sind presumably to be added. Herodotus lists twenty 'nomoi'. Ten of these are identifiable as satrapies, again with Media and Sind to be added. This is a distinctly higher proportion. In Herodotus' list the 1st satrapy (Ionia) seems more or less never to have been separated from the 2nd, and some of the eastern satrapies cause surprise (notably the far-flung 14th and 16th). But his list is not contradicted by what we know from other fifth-century sources. Darius' lists, on the other hand, do not contain lands that can easily correspond to his satrapal seats of

Purush (presumably Poura in Persian Baluchistan) or Daskyleion.[7] What is worse, they contain several non-satrapies: we can cite as examples Yauna in the Sea, Saka beyond the Sea, Karka (Caria only having become a satrapy in 395 B.C.), and probably Arabaya, Put, and Kush. But the crucial one is Athura (Ashur). The name itself implies the Assyrian homeland on the middle Tigris, and it continued to be so named for centuries, surviving in Strabo as Atouria. From Darius' own inscriptions we have two clues for the placing of Athura. The one (in DB) is Mt Izala (the Tur Abdin above Nisibis) on the Armenian edge of High Mesopotamia; it is spoken of there as in Athura. The other is in Susa f; there Athura, whose people brought timber from Lebanon to Babylon, is rendered as Ebirnari (i.e. Abarnahara) in the Akkadian text. Apart from Elam the whole neo-Babylonian empire entered the Persian administrative system as a single satrapy and remained so until Abarnahara was split off. Athura was a land in 522/21, so it cannot in any case mean the satrapy of Abarnahara, which did not exist then; and by partaking of both Babylonia/ Armenia and Abarnahara it cuts across the known satrapy system there.

This is positive proof. In fact, quite apart from the glaring inaccuracies in Darius I's texts (cf. Chap. XVII n.15), the conspectus of peoples in Herodotus is much more complete than that of Darius. Herodotus has failed to include the Arachosians (who are perhaps to be thought of as included in the Parikanioi of the 400-talent 17th 'nomos'); but Darius has not recognized major peoples such as the Phoenicians and Phrygians or the races who lay between Media and the Caucasus and those who were subject to his satrap at Purush. This is a factor that has not been taken into account by the most recent critics of Herodotus.

The only detailed list of Darius' satrapies, then, is that in Herodotus. Many scholars have discussed it in the past, but there is no full modern treatment of it. It has quite recently been suggested that Herodotus made up his satrapies by some means such as reading names off Hecataeus' map, in which case he would have to have invented the sums of tribute.[8] This is a counsel of despair. It is of course possible that he lifted the list from an earlier Greek source; but the information need not be any the less reliable if it did date closer to the time of Darius. One inference, however, does seem fair. Herodotus only knows the 5th and 9th satrapies as separated. By the time they parted company there were almost certainly tribute-paying districts in Europe; but he knows nothing of their tribute. This suggests that his list dates from some time after the Persian withdrawal from Europe (in the early 470s); and it seems to offer the best explanation of his 1st 'nomos', that it is a mistaken attempt to recreate the situation in the West as it had been before the coast of Asia Minor between the Straits and Lycia was lost to the empire. In that case Herodotus' list will have been a more or less contemporary one; and we no longer need to assume that Darius' reorganization was carried out in the early part of his reign. 493 B.C. is the date both of the land measurement in Ionia and of whatever change – if any – in the fiscal system in Persis the switch in the tablets implies (below, p. 86); the creation of the new Abarnahara satrapy must also have occurred within a dozen years of then if Tattenai occupied the same station in Darius' twentieth year as in his sixth.

At a guess, a list in Aramaic in a satrapal chancery might underlie orally transmitted information that Herodotus would have had to pad out as best he could. Apart from the western empire, which was reasonably familiar to the Ionians, there might well be some confusion in his distribution of peoples; and in the upper satrapies, where Skylax was no help, the rendering of names from the Aramaic would be chancy, so that it might be unwise to make any precise contentions depend on detail that Herodotus gives or forms of names like Pausikai and Orthokorybantioi. The absence from his list of Arachosia (one of Darius' lands that was regularly governed by a satrap) cannot but diminish our confidence in his information about Eastern Iran.

The text of Xenophon's *Anabasis* is informative about conditions in the western empire. But at the end it has a list of the governors (archons) of the different territories traversed (VII 8, 25). Modern scholars have been agreed that this is not by Xenophon;[9] but some, including Eduard Meyer and Kahrstedt, have maintained that it nevertheless has good authority. There was admittedly a tendency for satrapies to be divided up in the last century of the empire (below, p. 172f.). But when we are told of governors in Lydia, Phrygia, and Lycaonia-Cappadocia in 401 B.C., we must remember that this was all in the special 'viceroyship' of Cyrus the Younger; so we are not dealing with plenipotentiary satraps. The crux is the Near East, where Phoenicia and Arabia are placed under Dernes, while Syria and Assyria are assigned to Belesys, and Babylonia to Roparas. This would cut across the satrapies of Babylon and Abarnahara. But we are now better informed about the latter. Not only was it a satrapy in the middle of the fourth century but cuneiform tablets record that Bel-shunu (Belesys) was governor of Abarnahara in 407 and 402 B.C.[10] This fortunately shows that 'Beyond the River' was as usual a single satrapy only a year before Xenophon passed that way. A generation ago it was possible to maintain – though rather against the odds – that the three Near Eastern satrapies of *Anabasis* VII 8, 25 were the Arabaya, Athura, and Babirush of the Old Persian lists. But Abarnahara is now unassailable.

There is a mention of one other ancient work 'On the Tributes throughout Asia', which has vanished completely. Its author was none other than Ctesias.

There were satraps before Darius; and to some extent there was fixed tribute, though perhaps largely in kind and possibly ranking as gifts.[11] When Cambyses and his court were near Uruk, food was requisitioned (above, p. 46). And, as has been remarked, Babylonia is said to have been responsible for feeding the King for four months in the year. It is likely that Darius did two things. First, he probably organized the empire in sizeable administrative units, splitting what we call Armenia between a western satrapy and an eastern one (Herodotus' 18th), but in the East forming satrapies by lumping neighbouring peoples together round suitable nuclei. Secondly, the talk of land survey in Ionia in 493 B.C. suggests that he attempted to relate the tribute of satrapies or their component parts to their productive capacity, calculated in terms of silver. The establishment of fixed revenues would not guarantee his subjects against the rapacity of governors and Persian grandees in the provinces; all he could do was to allow for their exactions by fixing the tribute at less than the estimated yield (one of Plutarch's authorities put it at half). But it had one great benefit. It removed the temptation for a governor to extort the highest possible tribute in order to win favour or preferment from the King.

Xenophon can be quite exasperating. In his *Cyropaedia* (VIII 6) he tells us that Cyrus the Great appointed the first satraps to be civil governors but that the garrison commanders in the provinces remained responsible to the King, and he speaks of a King's controller-general who visits the provinces every year with an army and corrects abuses or derelictions of duty. In another of his works (*Oeconomicus* IV 4) he enlarges on this idealistic separation of civil and military control, but he then demolishes it all with his concluding remark 'but where a satrap is appointed the charge of both is combined in him'. This might be thought to imply that by the word 'satrap' Xenophon meant something higher than an ordinary provincial governor and is one of the points that has caused a number of scholars to suppose that Herodotus' twenty 'nomoi' were administrative divisions for fiscal purposes but were not the true satrapies any more than Darius' lands. Before we come on to their views we may note that in practice Xenophon does apply the title satrap in his *Hellenica* to a lady despot who ruled some towns in the Troad under the jurisdiction of Pharnabazos at Daskyleion (III 1, 10–12, below, p. 177f.). So satrap to him was not necessarily an exalted grade.

Until Darius I returned from his Scythian expedition the Achaemenids were fighting almost incessant wars of conquest; no doubt a standing army was kept more or less in being and it could be supported from the spoils of war. But the situation must have changed as the empire ceased to expand; and there had to be a regular system for the calling-up of levies when a large army was needed. Xenophon more than once speaks of marshalling points ('syl-logoi').[12] In his *Anabasis* (I 9, 7) he says that Cyrus the Younger was given command of all those whose marshalling point was Kastollou Pedion (in Lydia east of Sardis) and that he was designated 'karanos' (a word that may be connected with Old Persian 'kara' = host or soldiery). The notion of a few – in fact four – great army commands was put forward by Eduard Meyer. From the oriental side Christensen brought into play the four 'toparchies' into which the Sassanid empire was quartered and sought to project the same arrangement back through Parthian to Achaemenid times.[13] An obvious flaw was that, without Egypt and Asia west of the Euphrates, the Sassanid empire could not have had the same quartering as the Achaemenid. So Ehtécham proposed stepping up the number of Achaemenid toparchies to seven if necessary, but to be reduced to four after Egypt was lost.[14] A difficulty here is the lack of a Parthian link unless by analogy with Armenia. But in any case the theory seems far-fetched.

Junge developed the notion of territorial commands which he called 'Armeebereichen',[15] and he and Toynbee both claimed that these were the true satrapies of Darius. Toynbee in the end felt able to list no less than ten of them.[16] But three more would now have to be added on the evidence of satraps mentioned in the Persepolis tablets (Areia, Makkash, and Purush), so that the emphasis on a few great commands loses much of its point. The trump card that Junge played was Herodotus' statement (I 72) that the R. Halys separated the Median 'arche' from the Lydian, from which he deduced that the whole region from the Aegean to the Zagros was occupied by two great Achaemenid 'Armeebereichen'. But he had not looked at the statement in its context. Herodotus was not speaking of Persian satrapies; what he meant was that before Cyrus' time the Lydian and Median empires met on the Halys. The Junge-Toynbee theory does not seem to have been contested. But it is not clear how far it has won general acceptance. In rejecting it we come back again to the satrapal system as understood by Herodotus.

Great centres like Memphis and Sardis and important frontier posts had strong garrisons (below, p. 110f.). These were imperial troops, and partly Iranian; and in some cases Xenophon might be correct in making their commanders responsible to the King rather than to the satrap. But that is as far as we can go. The marshalling points or 'syllogoi' known are two named by Xenophon, both of which seem to be in Lydia,[17] Uruk in the south of Babylonia where Darius II called a levy (below, p. 102), and possibly the run-down old town of Ur nearby.[18] Situated as they all are on the fringes of the empire, they would be ill-chosen points for the marshalling of army groups. They sound more like mustering points for exercises or local campaigns. Expeditionary forces assembled at nodal points, such as Babylon, Cappadocia where contingents from the highland zone joined up with Xerxes' army that marched from Susa in 481 B.C., Phoenicia for expeditions against Egypt, and Cilicia where army and navy could meet and marines be put on board (as with Mardonios, Datis, and wars in the Levant). As regards command, what evidence we have seems to show that the individual satraps in the satrapies as we know them had armed forces put at their disposal and took the field when necessary. Cyrus the Younger had a more extensive command; but he was sent to the West as 'karanos' and after that he was preparing to fight for the throne. If we find Abrokomas and not the satrap Belesys in command in northern Syria when Cyrus was on the march, it will not be that he held a regular office of 'toparch' of the Near Eastern satrapy group but that he had been appointed by the King as commander-in-chief for a war, whether to resist Cyrus or, as Rehdantz, Judeich, and Olmstead believed, to recover the newly-revolted Egypt. When Thucydides speaks of Tissaphernes as 'general of those below' (VIII 5, 4–5), he may have meant something more than just satrap; the King was ordering a war against Amorges and the Athenians and preparing a fleet, so a commander-in-chief was needed. But even before the era of satraps' armies in the fourth century we can point to satraps in command when fighting was undertaken or contemplated in their territory, not only in the Sardis and Daskyleion satrapies but for instance in Egypt (Achaemenes), and Cilicia and the two Armenias (401 B.C.).

One other restriction on the satrap's powers is generally believed in. That is the royal secretary at satrapal courts. It is often said that the secretary was a King's agent who could report secretly on the satrap's actions. The evidence, however, is negligible. At Sardis in 521 B.C. the secretary opened and read out the messages that Bagaios brought from the King (above, p. 60). But that was surely a normal duty, and it is clear that in the story Bagaios was not at all sure what the reaction would be. The other case which is commonly cited is Hieramenes, who was a co-signatory with the western satraps of the treaty between Darius II and the Spartans in 411 B.C. and may perhaps be mentioned along with the Sardis satrap Tissaphernes on the Lycian Xanthos stele of 412 B.C.[19] He was clearly a person who counted. But Xenophon also speaks of him and his wife protesting (apparently in person) to Darius II in 406 B.C. when Cyrus killed two sons of the King's sister and they seem to have been intimately concerned (if not actually the parents).[20] Probably Hieramenes was not the royal secretary at Sardis but a top-level emissary from the court sent to the West to act on the King's behalf in critical negotiations.

It would seem then that in the normal way the jurisdiction of the satraps embraced the spheres of both civil and military activity. They were responsible for the collecting of tribute, raising of military levies when needed, and for justice and security. Their courts were modelled on the King's and frequented by the Persian grandees in the provinces. Their chanceries were staffed by Aramaic-speaking scribes through whom correspondence was maintained with the royal court and with the local or regional authorities under the satrap's control.[21] Thus Achaemenian seal-impressions are found at Persepolis and at Memphis and Daskyleion, but also at sub-centres as Samaria in Palestine and Lagash in southern Babylonia. The infrastructure of rule in the satrapies will be considered later (p. 173ff.).

Persis was strictly not a satrapy. Being unconquered, it was not subject. So, Herodotus says (III 97), it alone did not pay tribute. This did not apply to all the ten 'clans' that Herodotus named (above, p. 39f.). One of them, the Sagartians, is named by him as paying tribute in the remarkable 14th 'nomos' that seems to sweep round Persis from Seistan to the islands off the south coast of Fars. A district of Persis, apparently in the south-east of Fars, is mentioned in the Behistun inscription as containing the place Tarawa (perhaps modern Tarom) where the pretender to the name Bardiya lived; it is named Yautiya, and is thought to be the Outioi whom Herodotus also places in the 14th 'nomos'. Hinz suggests that these people were made tributary as a punishment by Darius I (Toynbee suggested that the Outioi, Sagartioi, and Makai were all punished in this way); Dandamayev goes further and suggests that only the three principal 'clans' of Persians had exemption.[22] The revolt in Persis at the end of 522 B.C. had been a serious one (above, p. 56). Wahyazdata, the false Bardiya, seems to have won the support of the people there. Dandamayev regards him as a progressive whose aim was to liberate the peasants. If we may judge by Bardiya-Gaumata, whom he was impersonating, we can say that the short section 14 (col. I) at Behistun is concerned with 'misdeeds' as much on the religious as the social plane and we can only read some confiscation of land and chattels into it. The information we have about social and economic conditions in Persis comes from the cuneiform tablets in Elamite found at Persepolis.

Two major caches of tablets have come to light. The larger, comprising the so-called Fortification Tablets, was excavated by Herzfeld in 1933–4 and consisted of many thousands of more or less complete tablets dating between 509 and 494 B.C. A selection of 2087 of them has recently been published by Hallock.[23] The other cache, found by Schmidt in the Treasury of Persepolis in 1936–8, consisted of 753 tablets of which a good selection was published by Cameron.[24] These date from 492 B.C. through Xerxes to early in Artaxerxes I's reign, 458 B.C. At that time, it is assumed, the use of clay tablets was abandoned in favour of Aramaic writing on perishable material such as papyrus or parchment; in fact, since Parnaka, the first controller-general under Darius I, is mentioned as having Babylonian scribes who wrote on parchment, Aramaic was probably in use almost from the outset.[25]

The two series differ in that the Fortification tablets (PF) are mainly records of rations issued and food products transferred and were rendered by the depots in Persis to the central administration in Persepolis, whereas the Treasury tablets (PT) are the records of the disbursements of silver from the Persepolis treasury and have a more limited geographical scope. To a large extent the payments in both cover a similar range of wages, which under Darius were normally paid in kind and in PF were computed so, but in PT were calculated in silver (10 shekels = 1 karsha) and when grain ran short under Xerxes came to be paid partly or even wholly in silver – presumably a commodity market was developing. The standard components of rations were grain, wine (or beer, which seems to have been preferred in the warmer terrain towards Susa, where barley was probably a staple crop), and sheep (especially for people of some standing). The standard exchange rate was approximately 1 sheep = 100 quarts grain = 30 quarts of wine or beer = 3 shekels of silver. Apart from one peculiar mint surcharge document in Akkadian, one tablet each in Greek and Phrygian, and a number in Aramaic, the language throughout is the hybrid one that Cameron has termed 'translation Elamite'.[26]

Elamite being a language with no close kin, the meanings of words are not always certain. The 'shalup' ('gentlemen'), of whom we have already encountered four travelling to Asagarta (?) and can find another party of 460 with 100 boys (PF 1000), may or may not be correctly interpreted as hunters; and the office of 'centurion' (satapatish) also presents anomalies. But a wide range of occupations is certified: for instance, 612 wood-workers of whom Eshkush is the foreman (PT 75); 1149 artisans employed on the 'Gateway of All Races' at Persepolis (PT 79); 32 well-paid copperers (23 of them boys) for whom Hystanes the tax-handler is responsible (PT 54); 42 mixed 'beer-tenders' (PT 46); 72 Carian (?) men, women, and children as stone-workers (PT 37); 55 well-paid mixed wine-makers whose apportionments are set by an Otanes (PT 36); over 1,000 men, women, and children employed in different capacities by the treasury (PT 39 and 66). Tailors and female weavers, craftsmen of various kinds including furniture-makers, herd-masters, irrigation-makers (?), grain-handlers, fruit and wine carriers, a miller, house servants, store keepers, and delivery men are mentioned. There was employment for women in these trades, and generally for children; boys were particularly used for herding animals. Much of what went on seems to have been related to building. In this there was a lull from about 481 B.C. when Xerxes' Greek campaign began; but activity was resumed about 471 B.C. and reached a climax with up to 1,300 workmen at Persepolis around the end of his reign.

The workers are 'kurtash'. This word has been much discussed.[27] It is used to render Old Persian 'maniya' with the meaning a 'domestic'. But it is clearly used in a broad sense for which 'hands' would be our equivalent. Some of the kurtash were free workers, some may have been enslaved as the result of conquest; certainly the majority were of foreign origin. Egyptian stone-masons were used in very large numbers, well over 500 at a time. Indians and Eastern Iranians seem to be found, and also Babylonians, Cappadocians, and Carians. Yauna are mentioned, along with more numerous people who may be Hatti from northern Syria; and we know that Greek masons worked in the quarries near Persepolis.[28] Other possibles are Lycians and Arabs. At the end of the year 495 B.C. a party of 23 men and 12 boys travelled from Sardis to Persepolis with a warrant from Artaphernes, the satrap of Lydia; they drew rations at Hidali on the way up from Susa. Between 503 and 497 B.C. many hundreds of 'Ishkuduru' were employed. These may well have come from Thrace in Europe. But as with the Hatti and Arabs their identity is not certain. The island of Socotra is not out of the question,[29] or they might possibly have come from the oasis of Yazd where Ashkazar seems to be a very old name. We have already come across Irmuziya (presumably workers from Hormuz). The foreigners were not necessarily imported for life. As in Babylonia, they could be brought to perform corvée service for a limited period such as a year and then sent home again. It is ominous that Hallock has reckoned that on an average parties going to Persepolis were two and a half times the size of those leaving it; Lewis has remarked Tamukkan (which has been taken to be the port of Taoke at Bushire) as a place that people leave from but do not come back to. Many of the groups of imported workers show a distribution of men, women, and children that suggests that whole family groups were brought. It has also been remarked by Dandamayev that the rate of remuneration for the workers rose from bare subsistence rations under Darius to a high wage-level that far exceeded any change in the cost of living; but Lewis remarks that the figures are distorted as a result of the famine year 467.

As regards travel the Fortification tablets are the more informative. Parties setting out from Susa commonly had authorization from Darius himself. Traffic dwindled between June and October, when he was presumably on vacation. Rations for travellers were normally issued for a day; so the roadside stations should have been a day's journey apart, as Herodotus implies for the royal road between Susa and Sardis (below, p. 108). The palatial establishment at Jin Jan near Fahlian might be a royal lodge on the route; but the column bases are so exquisitely finished and the situation looking across the river to the snowy mountains of Persis is so attractive that one could wish it to be Kuganakan where Darius' favourite wife Artystone had her château (above, p. 74). Some parties of travellers were quite small, and even when silver was being transported in bulk a guard of ten men was sufficient escort. Evidently internal security was good, as in the days of Shah

Plate 12

Abbas: at the end of Safavid times, 100 years after Shah Abbas, travel was no longer safe, and we may suspect that it was not unlike that 100 years after Darius I also. Most of the people travelling to Persepolis ended their journey there; but there were occasional travellers going on to Areia, Baktria, Gandara, or India.

More than a hundred places in Persis are named in the tablets. Tirazzish and Narezzash or Nariesi were centres and could well correspond to present-day Shiraz and Neyriz. The former seems not to have been on the Susa-Persepolis road at that time but is very frequently mentioned. Hallock has used interconnections of personnel to distribute many place names of the tablets among three areas – around Persepolis, towards Susa, and a perhaps thinly populated area in between.[30] Rakkan, with an exceptionally high number of workers, is presumably the Rakha where Artawardiya gained his first victory over Wahyazdata in 521 B.C.; the name, as Herzfeld saw, resembles the Arabic geographers' Arrajan (Arkhan), an important centre replaced by the modern town of Behbehan, which is about 190 miles by road from Susa; but in that case it would hardly be in the Persepolis area as Hallock placed it. Hidali was on the main road to Susa, and Hallock placed it in the Susa region but now has it in the vicinity of Fahlian; the party of men and boys from Sardis stopped there about the end of 495 B.C. and were followed by Datis a couple of months later (below, p. 97f.). This will surely be the Hidalu where Cyrus I met the Assyrian commander about 640 B.C. when he handed over his son with tribute (above, p. 2). It was one of the three royal cities of Elam in Assyrian times: the Elamite king took refuge at Haidala in the distant mountains in the days of Sennacherib, and Ashurbanipal set up a king in Hidalu. Ghirshman would place it at Shushtar on the R. Karun east of Susa,[31] but that location must now be abandoned. Hallock's new location near Fahlian in fact now suggests that Cyrus I was established in Persis (above, p. 9f.).

The third capital of Elam in the seventh century B.C., rivalling Susa as a royal city though hardly as a metropolis, was called Madaktu. This resembles the Matezzish or Matezza of the tablets, which Hallock regards as the most important place in the Persepolis area after Persepolis itself and a centre for Babylonian, Indian, and Egyptian workers. The first sound in it was w because the Elamite text at Behistun confirms the identity of this name with Old Persian Uwadaichaya, where Wahyazdata was impaled in 521 B.C. Hinz places it in the east of Persis on the ground that Wahyazdata's home was in Yautiya; but this depends on assumptions and in any case is not cogent because Darius brought his 'kings of the Lie' to main centres like Arbela and Agbatana for public display. Hallock placed it north or east of Persepolis because of interconnections with Persepolis, Badrakatash (which he and others recognize as Pasargadai), and the route to India; in fact he now regards it as a dormitory suburb of Persepolis itself.[32] There are however a number of Akkadian tablets recently grouped by Zadok referring to a place Humadeshu; Iranian personal names are preponderant in these particular tablets, and Zadok's identification of the name as Uwadaichaya is at first sight a certainty.[33] The tablets are records of the Babylonian banking house of

Egibi Sons and concerned with loans and the purchase of slaves. Itti-Marduk-balatu, then head of the firm and possessor of a fine old royal name of Isin, seems often to have travelled in person. He had had to borrow one and a half pounds of silver on his first visit to Agbatana when Cyrus was there in September 537; and now, in the last of this little series of tablets, he appears to have been interrupted on one of his visits to Humadeshu and run up a considerable bill. Zadok suggests he was stuck there because of the revolt of Wahyazdata (the dating of the tablet in April of the first year of Bardiya fits better with the pretender's reign in 521, above, p. 56). Before that, in May 524, he was in Humadeshu only fifteen days after being in Babylon. Zadok reckons rather conservatively that at 30 km. a day he could not have got more than 50 km. beyond Susa.[34] Humadeshu cannot have been in the Persepolis area unless the banker was travelling the whole fortnight and averaged over 40 miles a day; so if there is no built-in flaw in Hallock's reconstruction, it seems doubtful whether it is the same as Matezza.

A number of VIPs make their appearance in the Persepolis tablets. At the head of the whole organization in Persis, as a sort of controller-general until about 497 B.C., stood Parnaka (Pharnakes). From his seal it appears that he was son of Arshama, which makes him likely to be a brother to Darius' father Hystaspes, and possibly he was the father of Artabazos (below, p. 167). He was entitled to a daily ration of two sheep, 90 quarts of wine, and 180 quarts of flour; so he must have kept a considerable establishment. Artawardiya, who had defeated Wahyazdata in Persis, drew 50 quarts of wine. The Gobryas who got 100 quarts of beer daily was clearly the paladin and spear-bearer of the King. Aspathines the bow-bearer was ordering payments under Darius and after. Presumably he, like Gobryas, would normally be in attendance on the King, who did on occasion call for his bow (below, p. 93). Leading figures among the authorisers of payments are Artatakhma under Xerxes and Artasyras who continued into Artaxerxes I's reign; Hinz regards them as subsequent holders of Pharnakes' office in Persis – his term for the post is 'Hofmarschall'.

Hinz has in fact attempted a detailed analysis of the whole organization in an important article 'Achämenidische Hofverwaltung'.[35] He believes the 'Hofmarschall' had general charge of the treasury, household and administrative services in Persis (though presumably not of the military establishment). Under him the head treasurer in Persepolis had jurisdiction over a large number of regional treasuries, which were not merely repositories but factories where clothing and tapestries, furniture, fine metalwork, and leather were produced. The employees in each were numbered in scores or even hundreds. Supply departments were responsible for grain, livestock, wine and beer, fruit (no doubt mainly dried, as dates, figs and raisins), and large and small poultry. The chancery had mainly Iranian secretaries who operated through a staff of Elamite and Babylonian scribes; and the higher officials had deputies on whom the day-to-day burden would fall. It is of course not certain that the organization was quite so cut and dried as a study like Hinz' makes it appear. But evidently labour and production in Persis were organized on a huge scale by the central administration in a way that would seem to leave relatively little scope for what we should call modest private enterprise; and sheep-raising was also organized on a large scale.[36] The Persians' criticism of Darius that he made a business of everything is not belied by the evidence from the one province of the empire that in theory was not subject. There is evidently much more to be learned from the systematic study of the great body of Persepolis tablets initiated by Hallock and from comparative analysis of the earlier tablets that were found at Susa.

IX Darius' Feud with the Athenians

It has been pleasantly remarked by Hinz that the Medes loved paradises – the word seems to be Median – or gardens, but the Persians were platform-sitters. The royal Persian reliefs show the platforms. But it is not only a matter of durbars. Darius had his pavilion (tachara) and audience hall (apadana) at Persepolis built on the edge of the terrace, possibly with the plain in full view over a low horn-crowned parapet. When he was at Sardis after his Scythian *Plate 13* expedition he liked to sit outside the city, no doubt enjoying the prospect of the Hermos plain and the ridges of Tmolos chiselled by the westering sun, from which he was shielded by an awning of crimson cloth – for the Persians, in contrast to the Egyptians, disliked the sun on their heads and admired a pale complexion. At Sardis his presence there was predictable enough for an 'impromptu' act to be staged in front of him.[1] A young woman, big and handsome and dressed up in all her finery, crossed his field of view on her way to the spring to water a horse, and presently re-appeared with the stately carriage of one who has a full pitcher on her head, leading the horse and at the same time spinning her distaff. A Greek would have thought nothing of it. But in the Orient it was an unusual sight; for the notion of a lady of rank spinning (or at least weaving) struck horror into an aristocratic Persian.[2] Not so Darius. He recognized that there was good breeding stock here; and the outcome was that a mounted courier set out for Megabazos in Thrace with orders to round up all her race (the Paeonians on the Strymon) and bring them to him. In the event her two brothers, who had arranged the act in the hope of being installed in power at home, were the cause of their nation being deported to Phrygia.

Darius was in no hurry to return home, and he waited at Sardis until Megabazos had finished his Thracian campaign. Presumably he spent two winters away from Susa. It may have been on the return journey that he visited the Rock of Van and had work started on the citadel where Xerxes *Plate 14* later had the inscription (XV) set up in a niche that his father had prepared for it. At a guess Darius was back in Susa at the end of a summer around 511 B.C. and supervising the building of palaces there and at Persepolis. He had been campaigning since about 526 or earlier. He had been to Saka land, the East and probably India, Asia Minor and Europe; and he had been in Egypt with Cambyses at least. Now, with a knowledge of the empire as a whole, he could turn his attention to organization such as was described in the preceding chapter. Artaphernes, his half-brother, had been left behind as the principal satrap in the West, and at some stage before 493 B.C. Megabazos' son Oibares was made satrap of Daskyleion. A Greek island or two were snapped up by his commander (another Otanes, son of Sisamnes), and at some period there was the reconnaissance mission which enabled the doctor Demokedes to jump the boat in South Italy. But for the time being Darius was taking no active steps against Greece.[3]

For all we know Herodotus may be justified in making Darius in 499 B.C. ask who the Athenians were. But his brother had been in touch with them for a number of years. In 507 the Athenians had been threatened with attack by hostile Greek neighbours on three fronts and sent to Sardis asking for a Persian alliance. This involved their envoys in acknowledging Persian suzerainty. The Athenian people promptly disavowed it after the perils had been surmounted, but in Persian eyes this may well have seemed to stamp them as rebellious subjects, in fact as perpetrators of what Darius called 'the Lie'. Presently the exiled Athenian tyrant Hippias, who was now living at Sigeion on the Hellespont, endeavoured to persuade Artaphernes to restore him to Athens. The Athenians sent envoys to Sardis to protest and were warned by Artaphernes that they had better take him back if they wished to be saved. This incensed the self-confident new Athenian democracy.

In the meantime, probably in 500 B.C., Aristagoras, who was in control of Miletus while his uncle and father-in-law Histiaios was detained at Darius' court, saw an opportunity of aggrandisement by restoring some exiled oligarchs to Naxos. He approached Artaphernes with the proposal that they should act jointly, pointing out that the large and rich island of Naxos would provide the Persians with control of the Cyclades and a bridge across the Aegean. Artaphernes referred the matter to Darius, who gave his approval; and an expedition was prepared. Darius' nephew, Megabates, perhaps the 'admiral (?)' of a Persepolis tablet, was in charge with Aristagoras. They had a large force of Persian and allied troops and supplies for four months; the fleet consisted of 200 modern galleys (triremes) which must have been largely Greco-Carian because the commanders Herodotus speaks of seem to have been the men who acted as bosses in the East Aegean cities. Megabates tried to deceive the Naxians by a feint; but they were not taken in, and the expedition proved a failure. According to Herodotus this was due to a quarrel between the two leaders when Megabates punished a Carian captain whose ship he found with no watch set, as a result of which he was said to have secretly sent warning to the Naxians. The quarrel itself is likely enough; Persian discipline will have been less flexible than Ionian and they do seem to have felt vulnerable to attack at night (see Chap. XVIII n.35).

Histiaios had deserved well of Darius at the Danube bridge a dozen years earlier and been given land on the lower Strymon at Myrkinos, where he started to found a city. According to Herodotus the warning that Megabazos gave about the potentialities of the place in timber for ships, silver mining, and the human resources available had caused Darius to change his mind and take Histiaios back to Susa as his adviser; and the story continues that, yearning to get back home, Histiaios sent a message tattooed on a slave's scalp urging Aristagoras to revolt, for he knew that in that case Darius would send him down to the coast to put matters to rights. Aristagoras was aware that the fleet commanders would not revolt because they depended on Darius for their rule in their cities. So he had them arrested while the fleet was lying in a lagoon near Miletus, proclaimed democracy, and then sailed to Greece hoping to gain support. The story of his visit to Sparta and failure to win over King Cleomenes is vintage Herodotus; but at least he left Cleomenes more aware of the Persian menace. At Athens he found the people still smarting under Artaphernes' rebuke and got the promise of twenty ships; Eretria in Euboea also put up five. To make Darius really annoyed Aristagoras sent word to the deported Paeonians to head for the coast, and all of them who wished were shipped over to Thrace. It says little for Persian vigilance that they were landed at Doriskos where the Persian fort and garrison in Europe were situated,[4] and made their way home from there.

When the Athenian and Eretrian ships arrived Aristagoras struck. A commando raid captured Sardis except for the garrisoned citadel, and the city and temple went up in flames. The Persian fief-holders west of the R. Halys rode to the rescue with their household brigades; they caught up with the Greeks before they re-embarked at Ephesus and inflicted heavy losses on them in a set battle.[5] The Athenians then pulled out, leaving the Ionians to continue the war on their own. But Darius had now at last taken cognisance of them. Shooting an arrow up into the sky he prayed to Ahuramazda (Zeus in the Greek) to grant him to avenge himself on them; and he forthwith instructed one of his menials daily before dinner to say to him three times 'Master, remember the Athenians'. This again is typical story-telling. But at a number of places in book V Herodotus' language suggests a Persian source: for instance, Artaphernes speaking of Aristagoras benefiting the King's House (V 31), or the phrase that reminds us of Darius' own (above, p. 76) when Megabazos warns the King that Histiaios has many people who will do what he tells them day and night. Here the mention of the god of heaven is right.[6] Theatrical perhaps; but perhaps Darius was theatrical.

From now on until 480 events take their course. Darius had decided that the Athenians must be punished, and there could be no drawing back. Meanwhile there was the revolt in Ionia. It had not been premeditated. But there was wide enthusiasm for it after the city-bosses had been suppressed; and it was conducted with such determination that in Ionia itself the issue was in the balance until the sixth year (probably 499–494).[7] Mementoes of it survive in the little electrum coins that were struck as a common currency by cities and dynasts between the Straits and Caria.

The Ionic fleet had command of the sea. First it sailed north and brought the Greek cities of the Straits into the war, thus cutting Darius' communications with Europe; then south to Caria, and after that to Cyprus where only the Phoenicians of Amathous stayed out of the revolt. Darius no longer felt inclined to take command himself. But his presence in Egypt about this time (above, p. 66) would suggest that he sensed the danger of the rebellion spreading to the cities of Phoenicia and as far as the Nile valley. For the first time since his accession wars the empire was imperilled. It is no wonder if he did all he could to win the goodwill of the Egyptians. The revolt in Cyprus was in fact quelled in its second year (497 or 496). Though the Ionian fleet on its arrival took up a position to guard the approaches and swept the Phoenicians off the sea, a Persian invasion force succeeded in crossing from Cilicia;

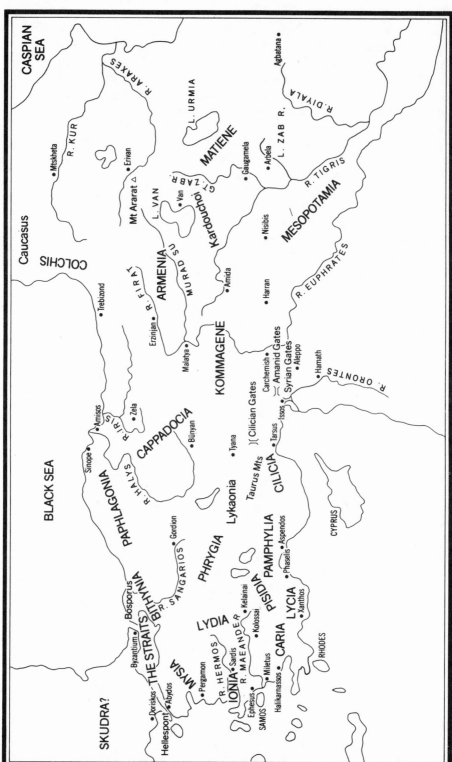

Fig. 6 Asia Minor and Armenia

in the ensuing battle Onesilos, king of Salamis, fought bravely in his chariot, and the Persian commander on his rearing charger was killed; but the Cypriots seem to have been behind the times in warfare, and in the end they broke. The war then petered out in sieges, of which that of Soloi lasted into the fifth month, while the recently excavated Persian siege mound against the wall of Paphos shows how marble dedications from a rustic sanctuary were used for ballast and how the defenders tunnelled under the wall into the mound to fire anything that was combustible in it – interesting also is the apparent evidence that the Persians were using stone projectiles.[8]

Artaphernes had continued to hold Sardis. Persian armies in western Asia Minor under the command of Daurises and two other sons-in-law of Darius meanwhile proceeded to the Straits to secure communications. Daurises was then sent south to Caria, where resistance was fiercer. He won a battle against the Carians, and another against the Carians and Milesians; but then, mis-timing his march to the coast at Halikarnassos, he was annihilated with his army in a night ambush in the rough country of the Pedasians. Hymaies, another of the sons-in-law, did some cleaning up on the Asiatic side of the Straits but fell ill and died. After this, large re-inforcements must have been arriving; and we find Artaphernes and the third son-in-law, yet another Otanes, starting to take the offensive against the cities of Ionia and the Aeolis. At this point Aristagoras seems to have lost heart and sailed away to Thrace.[9] In the meantime Histiaios had been sent down to the coast. But Artaphernes distrusted him, and the Milesians would not have him back. He had big ideas, and might have salvaged some sort of independent duchy in the North Aegean out of the wreckage. But he lacked the resources to implement his schemes; and becoming a raider he was eventually captured on a foraging expedition and decapitated before the King could get to hear of it. His head received honourable interment from Darius as that of a great benefactor of the King and Persians, so that we are left wondering whether it was not really true that but for him the King would never have got back across the Danube.

On its long peninsula Miletus remained unassailable by land. So the issue had to be decided at sea. A great fleet had been requisitioned from the Phoenicians, Egyptians, Cilicians, and Cypriots – 600 ships, the figure that Herodotus gives, is the regular one quoted for a Persian fleet in the Levant or at the Straits. The Ionians, with the Lesbians, mustered 353 ships and waited for the enemy at the mouth of the Milesian Gulf. This was an occasion when the Persians were successful with their political warfare. The Samians, who had distinguished themselves above all others in the battle off Cyprus, now became disaffected. Most of their squadron, which was on the seaward right wing, sheered away as the battle was joined; the Lesbians next to them followed, and in the end the Ionians suffered a crushing defeat (Battle of Lade, probably 494 B.C.). The following spring the Persians' fleet sailed up the coast to the Bosporus, burning the Greek cities, drag-netting the islands, and seizing the good-looking young people for eunuchs and concubines. One of the latter was no doubt the daughter of an aristocrat of Cos who appeared in 479 B.C. at Plataea as the concubine of Pharandates son of Teaspes (probably a nephew of Darius), see below, p. 105). Of the loot from Miletus and its sanctuary at Didyma a huge bronze knucklebone weighing over 200 lb has come to light at Susa.

The Ionian revolt failed. But it had been a tough struggle and long-drawn-out. Herodotus is at his worst here. The only two allied victories he mentions are the first sea battle in which his friends the Samians gained distinction and the ambush in the hills above his home town. There must have been more to a six-year war than that.

Darius now was in a hurry. Already in 493 B.C. Artaphernes was impressing on the Ionic cities the need to settle their disputes amicably and carrying out the land survey which may have distributed the taxation more fairly. Next spring the young Mardonios arrived with a fleet that had been assembled in Cilicia and, to the general astonishment of the Greeks, put down the bosses in the mainland Ionic cities in favour of democratic rule. Evidently Darius was conciliating the Eastern Greeks as he had done the Egyptians five or six years earlier; he wanted their co-operation now that the invasion of Greece was on. It was a political move, no doubt intended also to impress other Greeks with Persian tolerance; and it didn't last long, to judge by the number of bosses we find in 480–79 B.C. The year 492 is the beginning of what is called the Persian Wars. Mardonios was the son of the paladin Gobryas by a sister of Darius, so born about or soon after 520 B.C.; and he was married to Darius' daughter Artozostre.[10] With Megabates, Mardonios, and two years later the younger Artaphernes leading great expeditions, we see three nephews of Darius in high commands, to match the three sons-in-law in the Ionian Revolt. The Achaemenid empire was becoming a family concern like that of Masinissa in Numidia or of the progeny of Ibn Saud in our lifetime (cf. p. 134). Mardonios, who at this point became grand marshal in the West, was an unfortunate choice. He may have been unlucky. But he lacked flair. The punishment of Athens and the pervicacity of Mardonios were to be Xerxes' calamitous inheritance from his father.[11]

Ordering more ships from the Ionians, Mardonios sailed on to the Straits and rejoined his army, which had marched overland from Cilicia. Then he crossed into Thrace to proceed, Herodotus says, against Eretria and Athens. Thrace and Macedonia meekly submitted, so that Persian domination reached to Mt Olympus; some scholars do not believe that the intention was to punish Athens at this stage, but Mardonios could well have expected to enter Central Greece without any serious fighting and he must have been leading a great expeditionary force for some purpose. The army and the fleet moved side by side as far as Akanthos on the neck of the Athos peninsula. In summer the trade wind from the Hellespont can be brisk and benign. But at times it becomes a gale, blowing incessantly for days on end; and then, in our memory, there is not a sail to be seen among the white flecks out at sea. The Athos peninsula takes the full force of this wind. Mardonios can not have lacked advisers with local knowledge. But he let his fleet be caught off a rocky lee-shore in shark-infested waters, and according to Herodotus 300 ships were lost with all hands.[12] Mardonios did not take proper precautions on land either. The Thracian Brygoi attacked the camp by night, killing many and wounding the marshal himself. He stayed on until the recalcitrant tribes were subdued and then returned to Asia.

Having failed with his right hook Darius now tried a straight left. Fighting on land meant cavalry, and the expedition was going by sea this time. So in 491 the fleet was being brought up to strength again and special horse-transports were built. In Greece there was activity. Darius had sent envoys demanding submission (the symbolic earth and water). Many of the Greek states had complied, and among them the Athenians' implacable enemy, the wealthy trading community of Aegina, which lies on the beam as one sails up the gulf towards Athens. It was fortunate for the Greeks that Cleomenes was reigning in Sparta in the 490s. He had not had it in his power to help the Ionians in their revolt. But he struck the old enemy Argos a devastating blow that left her unable to collaborate with the Persians. When Aegina 'medized' he had his obstructive fellow king Demaratos deposed and then with his new colleague crossed to Aegina, where he arrested the offending politicians and turned them over to the Athenians as hostages.

In Athens too things were happening. As the Persian fleet sailed up the coast from Miletus in 493, the Athenian noble Miltiades, who had been ruling a principality of the Outremer on the long tongue of Europe that flanks the Dardanelles (the Thracian Chersonese), was busy packing his belongings. It was he who had unsuccessfully urged the Ionians to leave Darius stranded beyond the Danube; and he now made his getaway in five triremes from his back harbour on the Black Gulf. The Phoenicians were coming up from Tenedos at that moment, and spotting his flotilla as he passed the cape they gave chase and caught the ship his eldest son was in charge of; the remainder escaped. Back in Athens, Miltiades and his partisans were a major force in politics. He was put on trial for 'tyranny'. The chief magistrate after the elections of spring 493 was a 'novus homo', Themistocles, who was also determined to resist the Persians. He may have played a part in securing Miltiades' acquittal; and he was already setting to work to give Athens a secure naval base at Piraeus. The peace party had failed. Themistocles' greatest achievements were to come later. But Miltiades was elected a general, in time to hold command in the field when the Persians came.

Herodotus succinctly remarks of Darius that while all this was happening 'the Persian was doing his thing' (VI 94). The horse-transports were ready and the task-force marched to the Cilician plain to embark on an exciting new amphibious expedition. The figure of 600 triremes for the fleet is probably a conventional one, but obviously it should have been a lot bigger than the 200 used against Naxos. Herodotus speaks of 46 different peoples in this army (IX 27), but that is in fact his figure for Xerxes' army in 480 (below, p. 103). The commander this time was Datis, with whom a nephew of the King, the young Artaphernes, was sent. Datis was a Mede. But there is some ground for thinking that he kept close contacts with Greek statesmen (an ostrakon found in the Agora at Athens calls Aristeides the 'buddy of Datis');[13] and he appears in Greek sources as showing unusual respect for Greek religious sensibilities. He was the one non-Persian that Darius promoted, and his two sons were accepted into the imperial aristocracy. Lewis has perceived that Datis

(Datiya) appears as a recipient of a large beer ration on a tablet newly published by Hallock; he was then returning to Persepolis in January 494 from Sardis.[14] The fleet coasted to Samos, which offers the most sheltered crossing to the Cyclades, put in to Naxos to burn the town and take such captives as could be found, and showed full respect towards the deities of Delos but took children as hostages from the other islands. With the cooling summer breeze and the grapes and figs coming ripe the cruise should have been a pleasant one. Reaching the tip of Euboea Datis spent some time subjugating Karystos and then sailed on to his first main objective, Eretria, which had sent five ships to the Ionians. Eretria held out no more than a week. Its sanctuaries were plundered and burnt, and its inhabitants collected for deportation (Darius settled them at Arderikka twenty-five miles from Susa, where Herodotus (VI 119) possibly visited them). A few days later Datis landed on the open beach at Marathon.

The Athenians sent off a courier to summon the Spartans, and their citizen militia marched out to confront the Persians. They did not bring cavalry and were not taking the risk of exposing themselves in the plain as the Ionians had done at Ephesus and Histiaios on his foraging expedition. The Athenians, 10,000 in number, were joined only by a battalion of Plataean allies. But they were expecting the Spartans to arrive shortly, so it was probably up to Datis to make the first move. Whether he had been re-embarking his cavalry by moonlight for a dash by sea round Sounion to Athens or possibly that the horses were away being watered, Miltiades seems to have received the message and seen his chance. The distance between the two armies had narrowed to less than a mile. Militiades lengthened his front to match the enemy's, keeping the weight on his wings; and in the early morning light the Athenian line surged forward and broke into a double. Madness, the Persians thought; for they had never seen the like before. But the cavalry was away and there was too little time for their arrows to take their toll before the fronts clashed.

The strong Persian centre drove the enemy back. But on the wings they were routed; and the Athenians were able to close the trap and cut down the Persian centre. They then pursued the fugitives to the ships, of which they captured seven. Datis still hoped that by rowing round to Phaleron he could reach Athens before it was properly defended – considering the distance involved it is not unlikely that a striking force had already started before the battle. But the Athenians had reckoned with this. The army hurried back twenty-six miles in the heat of the day, and as the fleet came up they could be seen stationed in front of the city. The oarsmen rested awhile. Then they turned and set course for Asia.

The Spartans arrived at Marathon too late. They were taken to inspect the battlefield and the corpses. At that time they were the professionals in infantry warfare; and it was as well that they should find out about the Persians' equipment and method of fighting before they themselves had to come to grips with them. On the Athenian side the dead were only 192; the Persian losses were reckoned at 6,400 and most of those who fell were the Persian and Saka troops who formed the centre. Herodotus says that until that day 'the name of Medes was a terror to hear'. Now the myth of Persian invincibility on the battlefield was dispelled.

To Darius this meant another expedition, and a much bigger one. Orders went out, Herodotus says, and for the next three years all Asia was convulsed. This would doubtless have been a King's expedition, led by Darius himself as his generals had failed him. But not surprisingly the Persian defeat had caused a change of temper among some of the subject peoples; and at the same time there is one scrap of evidence from Babylonia of precisely this time (the new toll for the King's House on goods in transit by canal) which suggests that Darius was increasing the burden of taxation to cover the costs of his projected expedition.

To the priests in Egypt Darius had been a great benefactor. He had promoted works at Busiris, Edfu, and the Khargeh oasis amongst other places. In 496 B.C. the quarries of the Wadi Hammamat between Koptos and the Red Sea were brought into active use again under the engineer Khnumimbre who had succeeded his father as superintendant there before Cambyses conquered Egypt. In the next four years work there was proceeding apace. Two objects that can probably be dated to this period are the ten-foot-high statues of Darius in grey-green stone which were set up at the temple of Atun in Heliopolis: one, with its base, was found in Susa in 1973 *Plate 15* (see Chap. VI n.3 and p. 163). At the higher levels things no doubt continued to look all right in Egypt. But on 5 October 486 they did not look so well to an official in the imperial service at Syene.[15] His message to the satrap Farnadata has come to light: he must have a guard for the grain barge, otherwise the rebels from Nubia will plunder the stack – they are camping opposite and no longer afraid to show themselves in broad daylight. A more general revolt was evidently not long delayed. It was a later complaint that the palaces of Susa and Persepolis were built from the spoil of Egypt.[16] So it could be that this insurrection of 486 was a popular one caused by the burden of tribute and Persian exploitation.

At the beginning of book VII Herodotus says that Egypt revolted in the fourth year after Marathon, and that in the following year, when he was ready to set out, Darius died, having reigned thirty-six years. Darius in fact died shortly before 1 December 486; but unless (as Kienitz maintains) the insurrection was more or less confined to the Delta, the documents of his thirty-sixth year would suggest that the revolt of Egypt had not got under way as early as Herodotus implies. It fell to Xerxes to subdue it. It didn't take him long because by his second year the quarries were working again and stone vessels were being inscribed for the King; and Herodotus (who admittedly seems to have a year too many in his Persian chronology between Marathon and Salamis) says that after reducing Egypt Xerxes spent four full years preparing his expedition and marched out as the fifth (which was 481 B.C.) was coming to an end (VII 19–20).[17] After the revolt was subdued, Xerxes' full brother Achaemenes was established as satrap. Herodotus tells us that the enslavement of Egypt was now much worse than it had previously been; at least one temple suffered confiscations, and it appears that Xerxes did not assume a titulature as king and divine protector of Egypt but was thenceforward an alien overlord like the Assyrian. Egypt was not a kingdom any longer but a Persian satrapy. One sign of the royal disfavour was the *Plate 15* removal of the two statues of Darius from Heliopolis to adorn Xerxes' new gateway to the palace at Susa.[18]

Babylon began to give trouble next. Greek writers speak of a revolt there with resulting devastation of the city, but not so as to allow us to pin-point it securely in the early years of Xerxes' reign. In fact the dating of tablets from Babylon and its suburbs seems to show evidence of two risings by claimants to the Babylonian throne. The first, that of Bel-shimanni perhaps to be dated in the high summer of 484 B.C., seems to have lasted a week or two. But the second under Shamash-eriba in 482 was evidently more serious and continued into the autumn. Ctesias, who does seem to have dated the revolt of Babylon at the beginning of Xerxes' reign, attributed its capture to Megabyxos, who was one of the grand marshals a year later. Again Xerxes had his titulature changed so that at the New Year of 481 B.C. he was no longer king of Babylon. The wall circuit and sanctuaries were slighted, and the colossal gold statue of Marduk was carried off from the Esagila.[19] No doubt Babylon, like Egypt, not only lost its status as a kingdom but was subjected to harsher oppression. Some scholars date the creation of the Abarnahara satrapy as late as this.

Whether Xerxes had trouble in Judah is not clear. The 'people of the land' there, who must have included deportees from Assyrian times and infiltrated Edomites, were willing to join in worship of Yahweh, but from the time of Cyrus on they resented the new Jewish separatism that centred in Jerusalem. According to Ezra (4, 6) they protested about it in a letter to Xerxes (Ahasuerus) at the beginning of his reign; but nothing more is said, except that this is where the book of Esther fits in its racialistic perversion of Achaemenid history.[20]

The next event in the narrative of Achaemenid history is Xerxes' expedition against Greece. This was epoch-making, and thanks to Herodotus it is well known. Before we turn to it the military state of the empire must command our attention.

15 Statue of Darius I at Susa

16 Persepolis from the air, 1936 (from south-west)

18 Details of capitals at Persepolis

17 Tachara of Darius I at Persepolis

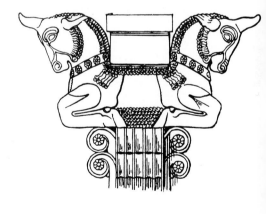

19 Courtiers on Tripylon friezes at Persepolis

20 A detail from the Tripylon friezes

21 A Mede on a Tripylon frieze

22   East front of Apadana and Gateway of Xerxes at Persepolis

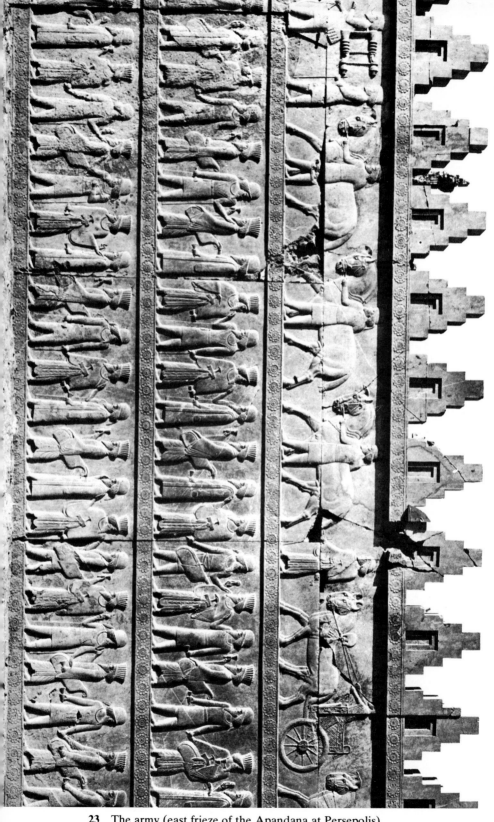

23 The army (east frieze of the Apandana at Persepolis)

24 The Elamites

25 The Babylonians

26 The Lydians?

27 Eastern Iranians

24-9 'Delegations' on the east frieze of the Apadana at Persepolis

28 The Arabs

29 The Ethiopians of Kush

X The Armed Forces and Communications

The 'Immortals', so called by the Greeks at least because their number never varied,[1] were 10,000 strong. All were Persians and infantrymen. The battalion of guards in closest attendance on the King, those who had golden apples for spear butts, numbered 1,000; and in Xerxes' column of march in 480 B.C. two other such footguard battalions are reported (one in front with spears pointing down, the other the select 1,000 within the Immortals), together with corresponding bodies of 1,000 and 10,000 Persian cavalry. Greek writers knew a word like 'azarapates' as denoting a high office at the Persian court, which is clearly a Persian word 'hazarapatish' meaning thousand-commander (below, p. 143). In Persepolis tablets words in Elamite script occur (though of course in non-military contexts there) which are recognized as renderings of Old Persian words for ten-commander and hundred-commander; and Xenophon also speaks of formations of 5, 10, by inference 50, and 100, 1,000 and 10,000 in Cyrus the Great's army. Finally, in his account of Xerxes' army Herodotus has commanders of 10, 100, 1,000 (chiliarchs), and 10,000 (myriarchs, for whom Widengren supplies the title *baiwarpatish), with the commanders of 10 and 100 appointed by the myriarchs, and the chiliarchs and myriarchs appointed by the high-ranking commanders whose names he gives (VII 81). Thus we can take it as certain that the Persian army was built up in powers of ten.

In his *Cyropaedia* Xenophon made Cyrus the Great's original army of Persians consist of 1,000 'peers' and 30,000 commoners who were composed of 10,000 light infantrymen, 10,000 slingers, and 10,000 archers (Cyrus having no cavalry at this stage). This triple division of arms has been accepted by some scholars and brought into relationship both with Parthian and Sassanian institutions and with Indo-European caste and age distinctions.[2] But the fact is that Xenophon does not make Cyrus do battle with such formations; in the *Cyropaedia* his innovation consisted in standardizing his infantry so that the whole force was armed like the 'peers'. In his tomb-inscription Darius I does speak of the spear of the Persian man having gone forth far, but he also declared himself a good bowman and a good spearman in that order (below, p. 134), he had a bow-bearer on equal terms with his spear-bearer, and on his royal coins he had himself shown as an archer. The two weapons therefore were equal in prestige. On reliefs at Susa and Persepolis guardsmen are shown with bow-case and spear, and it seems clear that the infantry man normally carried both. In fact according to Herodotus (VII 61) the Persian soldier wore a soft felt cap, an embroidered sleeved tunic with iron 'fish-scales', trousers, and a wicker shield, and was armed with a short spear, a big bow with slung quiver and cane arrows, and a dagger hanging at the

Plate 35

Plates 11 & 23

right thigh. This costume was of Median origin; and with minor differences the other Iranian troops had the same dress and equipment (Herodotus in fact does not mention shields or body-armour in speaking of them, but it is hardly to be supposed that they lacked all protection).

We may note that the Persian scale-cuirass could be virtually impenetrable, to judge by Herodotus' description of the killing of the cavalry commander Masistios (IX 22). But his account of the battle around Mardonios does make it plain that the Persian infantrymen's body-armour gave less protection than the bronze panoply of the Greek hoplites. Their spears also were shorter, and in hand-to-hand fighting, despite their courage and dexterity, they were at a disadvantage when a Greek hoplite phalanx closed with them. The casualty figures at Marathon (above, p. 98) have shown the disparity, and the battle at Plataea demonstrated the Greeks' confidence in their superiority at close quarters. There were heavier-armed infantry contingents in Xerxes' army such as the Babylonians and Lydians, and there were light-armed levies from the highlanders of Armenia and Anatolia. But there is no mention of these troops being used in battle. Later Greek writers distinguished light infantry (peltasts) from the guards in the Persian military establishment; but this sounds like a subsequent development or interpretation in line with Greek military innovations. Persian military operations in late Achaemenid times will be treated in Chapter XVIII.

The cavalry, Herodotus says (VII 84–88), were armed like the infantry, except that some wore beaten metal head-protection and the nomadic Sagartians, numbering 8,000, used lassoes and daggers. Unfortunately, cavalry have no place in the Persian palace reliefs. But we have an itemized list of the equipment required of the holder of a cavalryman's fief at Uruk in southern Mesopotamia when Darius II called out a levy at the end of 422 B.C.: besides money (a mina of silver) and food, the requirement reads something like horse and harness, saddle-cloth, iron cuirass, helmet with felt neck-guard, shield, 130 arrows, an iron shield attachment, and an iron club and two javelins – there is no mention of additional armour for the horse such as some later Achaemenid heavy cavalry seem to have had.

Plate 23
The King, like his invisible god, went to war in a great chariot pulled by special horses. The chariots appear empty on the Apadana reliefs at Persepolis, and in a plaque from Susa (DSs) Darius I speaks of Ahuramazda having bestowed on him good chariots as well as good horses. But in Xerxes' army the only chariotry mentioned is that of the Libyans and an Indian corps which used wild asses as well as horses; and before that, during the Ionian revolt, we hear of the Persian commander fighting on horseback against the Cypriot chariotry. Scythed chariots are heard of on three occasions in later Achaemenid times. But they were never numerous. Their role seems to have been to charge the opposing line in the hope of disrupting it before the battle was joined; once when used against bunched foragers by Pharnabazos in the winter of 395 B.C., they proved effective. The Babylonian holdings that have been mentioned were of three grades in terms of military obligation: chariot, cavalryman, and bowman.[3] They had already begun to be granted some years before Darius I came to the throne, and the chariot fiefs may have been

something of an anachronism almost from the outset. But until it became usual to make monetary payments in lieu of service, cavalry were certainly to be raised from the fiefs.[4]

Camels were used as pack-animals; in Xerxes' army the Arabs were the only fighting troops mounted on dromedaries. Elephants had been familiar in the Near East. But the Syrian herds were hunted out, no doubt for their ivory, before the end of Assyrian times. Ctesias had heard of their use in war by Indian kings and of their ability to overturn walls; he even speaks of palm trees uprooted by elephants at Babylon. But the Achaemenids do not seem to have used them in their wars of conquest, partly perhaps because of their prodigio..s consumption of fodder and still more of water. Darius III had fifteen elephants at the Battle of Gaugamela in 331 B.C., and a dozen more were on their way to him; but there is no mention in the sources of their being put to any tactical use. Alexander in fact captured them and was thus able to devise counter-measures before having to confront formations of war elephants in India. But it was his Macedonian generals after his death who first developed the use of elephants in battle in Western Asia.

The Persians were adept in the use of cavalry; indeed it was not until the time of Alexander that they were out-classed (below, p. 225ff.). Herodotus' account of the Plataea campaign in 479 B.C. shows them assailing the enemy's positions, operating in his rear, interfering with his lines of communication and denying him food supplies and access to the water on which he depended. It was they who caused the Greeks to withdraw from their forward positions near the river. Where the ground was relatively level the cavalry could ride close up to the enemy line discharging javelins and arrows and wheeling away again; and by this manoeuvre they did seriously harass the opposing Greek line at Plataea. But the Persian cavalry seems to have been baffled when the 1,000 Phocian infantry formed up to resist all-round attack, and in the fight over the body of Masistios they were driven off when Greek infantry reinforcements came up; to judge by this and subsequent encounters, it looks as though they could roll up an exposed flank or cut up disorganized infantry but could not successfully join battle with hoplites in close array. The Persian infantry's normal procedure seems to have been to advance and set up their wicker shields as a hedge from behind which they fired their arrows into the enemy. When these were exhausted they engaged the foe in hand-to-hand fighting. Herodotus tells of two battles which went to the second stage and were long drawn out – that of Cyrus with the Massagetai on the Jaxartes and Cambyses' against the Egyptians at Pelousion. But usually the Persian infantry seems to have expected to make short work of an enemy who had already been harassed and softened up by cavalry and missiles. Marathon has shown that the Greeks' aim must be to avoid moving in the plain where they would be exposed to cavalry action and to come to grips on more or less even ground before the Persians' missiles could take effect (above, p. 98).

Herodotus (VII 61–88) lists no less than forty-five different peoples (and one name missing) from whom contingents were levied for Xerxes' Greek expedition, not counting a dozen or so whose contribution was to the fleet. The infantry were brigaded in twenty-nine divisions under commanders whom he names. There were considerable differences in their arms, which are described in detail, and in their armour, on which Herodotus is sometimes more sketchy. It has often been claimed that Xerxes would not really have taken such a motley assortment of peoples with him and that what Herodotus presents is the paper strength of the entire land forces of the empire. This would involve some sort of document to which he or an informant had had access. But some of the information he gives is not of the sort that could be extracted from a record, as for instance the horse-scalp headgear with erect ears and mane worn by the eastern Ethiopians, the long palm bows, stone arrowheads, and red and white body colouring of those from Nubia, or the Arabs with long bent-back bows to their right. These must depend on ocular evidence and are just the sort of thing that would have been noted and remembered by people who saw the army move past. In any case this was not a task force but a King's expedition in which the entire empire was expected to participate. If the King went, all must go (the whole household, wife and all, Herodotus makes Xerxes say), and to ask for exemption for even one of several sons incurred a sentence of death.[5] In theory no one should not go.

Herodotus describes the column of march when Xerxes left Sardis in the spring of 480 (VII 40–1). Likewise the dawn march-out of Darius III from Babylon in 333 to do battle with Alexander is described by Curtius Rufus (III 3, 9–25), though with an eye rather for the spectacle of pomp and luxury than for military organization. Collating the two descriptions we can see in what state the King set forth for war. He was attended by Magi with their altars and sacred fire; they made libations, incantations and sacrifices as needed. The empty chariot of Ahuramazda was drawn by eight white horses with the charioteer following on foot; and in Xerxes' equipage ten sacred Nesaean horses preceded it. The white horses of Ahuramazda may be an old convention, for Herodotus has Cyrus punish the R. Gyndes because one of the sacred white horses drowned in it on his campaign of 539 – this reminds us of the sacrificing of white horses by the Magi at the Strymon and of the horses as sacrifice to the sun in Cyrus' procession in the *Cyropaedia* (VIII 3, 12 and 24). Xerxes himself rode in a chariot, but he had a covered carriage to change into when he wished to relax. A golden stool was carried in readiness for him to mount. Darius III brought his mother and his wife with him and each had her own carriage, while the ladies-in-waiting seem to have been mounted; fifteen carriages contained the King's children with governesses and eunuchs, and 360 concubines rode – it is not said what on, but as they were wearing royal habiliments they will hardly have suffered the indignity of being packed into camel panniers like Shah Abbas' much more numerous womenfolk. We do not know how large a family Xerxes took with him, but he did bring children because Herodotus tells us that his illegitimate ones were entrusted to Artemisia to take back from Athens to Asia by ship (VIII 107).

A well-known Persian habit has been that of beginning an expedition or long caravan journey with a short evening's march. This practice, which allows people to return home for things they have forgotten, is one that dies hard. Xenophon in fact made Cyrus the Great institute it (*Cyrop.* VI 3, 1).

We hear of mess tents and luxurious furnishings , and of gilded and silver

Plate 23
(top left)

tables and chairs. The safari canteens of the King and his nobles included gold and silver vessels with gem-encrusted cups (three or four tons of them were captured after the Battle of Issos). Darius III had valets to see to his wardrobe, and 365 pages are mentioned. We also hear of his portable ointment chest; and 40 perfume makers as well as 46 chaplet-weavers were listed in the inventory of captured stock drawn up by Parmenion in Damascus.[6] Cooks, bakers and orderlies rode; Parmenion's inventory recorded 277 confectioners, 29 pot-boilers, 13 makers of milk dishes, 17 drink-mixers, and 70 wine-strainers. The banquet that Mardonios' kitchen staff prepared at Plataea after the battle astounded the Greeks by the extravagance of both the food and the décor. Victuals were of course requisitioned from the subject peoples, but the King himself had viands and sheep brought with him from home. The King could not drink ordinary local water, so a train of four-wheeled mule carts carried boiled 'golden water' in silver urns (below, p. 140). As regards stabling, we hear of the bronze manger that stood by Xerxes' tent which Mardonios had at Plataea. The King travelled with a war chest. Herodotus gives an instance of Xerxes' generosity when he gave his host at Kelainai 7,000 gold staters, and Mardonios was left in Greece with a plentiful supply of gold, both coin and bullion, and of silver. Curtius Rufus speaks of 600 mules and 300 camels carrying Darius III's supply of ready money.

Xerxes' Immortals commanded great respect and indeed were pampered; they had concubines and numerous attendants who travelled in carriages, and special food was transported for them on camels and other baggage animals. It is hardly likely that the select Persian cavalry fared any less well; and the great nobles must have taken households and retinues to the war, though we only happen to hear of the wife of Xerxes' brother Masistes and of a Coan girl, concubine of one of the twenty-nine infantry commanders, who issued from her closed carriage with her ladies-in-waiting in all their finery after the battle was over at Plataea. She was fortunate that her father was a friend of the Spartan commander-in-chief; the rest of the concubines captured were divided up among the spoils.

In siege warfare the Persians used the traditional methods of blockade and stratagem, siege mounds and mines under the walls. Xenophon in the *Cyropaedia* makes Cyrus use moveable siege towers, which is no doubt an anachronism. Herodotus tantalizingly remarks that the Persians brought engines of all sorts against Miletus at the end of the Ionian revolt (VI 18); these would include rams and what A.W. Lawrence speaks of as ram-mantlets, possibly also some form of catapult (see Chap. IX n.8).

To turn to the navy, the standard ship of the line was the trireme. This is known to us almost entirely from Greek sources.[7] It was 110–120 ft long and designed for 170 oarsmen who were arranged in three rows or banks on either side; but it was extremely narrow, and the overall oarspan is reckoned at less than 40 ft. Triremes were superseding penteconters in the fleets of Greek maritime cities in the second half of the sixth century. The Phoenicians were not behindhand in this development; at the Battle of Lade in 494 B.C. (above, p. 95) they, together with the Egyptians, Cypriots, and Cilicians,

provided a Persian fleet, reputedly 600 strong, to engage the 353 triremes of
the Eastern Greeks. The total complement of a trireme was reckoned at 200,
which allowed for deck-hands and a detachment of armed marines. According to Herodotus the Persians put an additional 30 marines on board each
ship in 480 B.C.; from this we may infer that there was a continuous deck
across the ship which served as a fighting platform. In this respect the Persian
triremes seem to have differed from the allied Greek ones; for it was only in
the next decade that, perhaps as a result of their experience in 480, the Greeks
seem to have experimented in fitting their triremes with continuous decks. In
480 the triremes on the Greek side presumably carried their fighting men on
bow and poop platforms.

So far as we know, the triremes on both sides in 480 B.C. were in other
respects fairly well matched. Those of the allied Greeks, of which Athens
produced more than half, are said by Herodotus to have been the heavier,
while those on the Persian side, especially the Phoenician, were the better
sailers. Morrison believes that the reason for this difference is that Xerxes had
his triremes drawn up on the beach and dried out at Doriskos in the early
summer of 480 in preparation for the battles ahead; but the outcome of the
Battle of Salamis three or four months later does seem to suggest that it was
not just a matter of the bilges but that the allies' ships were the sturdier. Also
with the increased weight on top the Persian ships may have been more easily
affected by a swell. In conditions of their own choosing, with calm water and
plenty of sea room, the Persians might expect to have the advantage. At the
same time, triremes normally depended on putting in to shore for the night.
When they came within range of hostile coasts the Persian ships could not
operate very effectively in advance of the army, with the result that their
freedom of action was circumscribed and they could not choose where they
would fight the allies.

As regards the marines, the Athenian triremes are said in the recently
discovered 'copy' of Themistocles' decree to have carried only ten men-at-
arms and four archers each. But this is a dubious source.[8] Some at least of the
ships in the Persian fleet appear in Herodotus as having their own fighting
men on board, the Egyptians being specially mentioned for their prowess. In
addition he speaks of them all as carrying thirty Persian, Median, and Saka
marines. It could be that this was an ad hoc measure to increase their fire
power and boarding strength in narrow waters where their superior ma-
noeuvrability would not avail. From Herodotus we gather that there were
quite a number of cases in 480 in which the fighting men on one side or the
other succeeded in gaining possession of an enemy ship; but it would appear
that at Salamis the Greeks achieved their victory mainly by the use of the ram
to cripple and wreck the enemy, and that the Phoenician ships at least were
more fragile than the Greek.

Political warfare was a weapon that the Kings understood, and they had
the advantage of undivided rule and ample funds for dividing their adver-
saries. Lydia seems to be the only one of their major conquests which was
achieved without the help of treachery from within. Hand in hand with this
went the use of espionage for military intelligence. Cambyses had sent spies

into Ethiopia before he marched south from Egypt. Xerxes, like his father, was concerned to divide the Greeks who remained outside the empire. In the autumn of 481 agents were sent to the Greek mainland to demand submission from all except the Athenians and Spartans and to prepare for the reception of his army; when they rejoined him on his march through Macedonia the following summer the cooperation of nearly all the peoples of Thessaly and central Greece had been obtained,[9] while in particular the oracle at Delphi, to which the Greek states were turning for advice and encouragement, was preaching defeatism. The Greeks of the West could not be attacked by the Persians at this stage. But it can hardly be coincidence that while the Phoenicians were playing a vital part in launching the great expedition from the East, their daughter-city of Carthage undertook an assault on the Western Greeks, landing an armada under Hamilcar in Sicily at the same moment as Xerxes was entering Greece, and so preventing the despatch of reinforcements to the homeland.

The year 480 was of course the turning point in Achaemenid expansion. Any successes that were achieved in the last hundred years of Achaemenid rule came largely through intrigue and bribery, and by tampering with the loyalty of mercenary leaders on the opposite side (for the fourth century see below, Chapter XVIII); in the fifth century only Megabyxos, who reconquered Egypt, seems to have been capable of pressing an offensive with vigour (below, p. 168f.).

An expanding empire needs good communications, just as a decaying empire needs bad ones that will hamper an invader's progress. In this the early Achaemenids acted as worthy successors of the Assyrians. In preparation for his expedition to Greece Xerxes had a road made in Thrace which the natives regarded with wonderment a generation later; it is also possible that the rock-cutting for a path over the shoulder of the Trojan Mt Ida was his doing,[10] and we may assume that the whole of his route as far as Macedonia had been surveyed and put in good condition in advance of his march. We have little information about the road network generally in the Achaemenid empire. Of the utmost importance was the highway which led from Babylon over the Zagros Gates and by Behistun to Agbatana, whence it continued across the plateau to Rhages, the 'Caspian Gates', and Eastern Iran (what Curtius Rufus called the 'via militaris'); and on the ground there are road traces in Persis, including a stretch of rock cutting which may be Achaemenid on the route linking Persepolis to Pasargadai.[11] But the only specific information we have is about the roads from Susa to Persepolis and Sardis to Susa. The former is known to us through the Persepolis tablets (above, p. 87f.). It seems to have had staging posts a day's journey apart at which rations were issued, and current study of the tablets is placing them in their order. In Darius I's time the road did not touch Shiraz and so probably went by the Tang-i Khas pass up from Fahlian to the vicinity of Anshan (at Malian) as it was to do in Arab times;[12] but in later Achaemenid times, when travel was less secure, it may have taken a longer southerly route as in modern times when Shiraz is its goal.

Herodotus gives a description of what he calls the King's Road running from Sardis to Susa (V 52–3). It had royal staging posts and caravanserais everywhere, and the whole length of it ran through secure inhabited country. At the crossing of the R. Halys on the borders of Phrygia and Cappadocia there were gates and a big guard house, and again double gates and guard houses where the road entered the north-east corner of Cilicia (in Melitene near modern Malatya). After the crossing of the Euphrates the route was through Armenia to Matiene with ferries across the Tigris, two rivers of the same name (the Upper and Lower Zapates or Zab), and the Gyndes (Diyala), and so to the Kissian country (Elam) and Susa itself.[13] The total number of staging posts was 111; the distance was reckoned as 450 parasangs, which Herodotus makes 13,500 Greek stades (short furlongs). Reckoned from reported staging figures and modern road maps it should be all of 1,600 miles. Herodotus goes on to call it 90 days' march at 150 stades a day. But presumably the staging posts were a normal day's journey apart for ordinary travellers. Of the track itself there is possibly some evidence. The line of an ancient road leading eastward from Gordion in Phrygia must be that of the King's highway, and the course it takes between the burial mounds shows that it does not go back earlier than the sixth century B.C. The cuts made across it by the excavating team revealed a packed gravel surface 20 to 21 ft wide with a border of kerb-stones, but of course there is no telling whether it was like that in Achaemenid times.[14]

On roads such as this the Achaemenid royal mail could travel fast. The term 'angaros' that the Greeks knew for a King's messenger goes back to Akkadian, and the Assyrian king Tiglath-Pileser III had introduced a fast relay service; so the system was not a Persian invention. But the Achaemenids perfected it. Herodotus tells us (VIII 98) that nothing human travels faster than these messengers. At each day's journey a horse and man are stationed; and when a message comes, neither snow nor rainstorm nor heat nor night prevents the man from completing his course with the utmost speed, each messenger handing over to the next as in a torch race. This is quite different from the couriers whose speeds have been recorded in modern times, as the Tatars of the imperial Ottoman postal service who could keep up 100 to 120 miles a day. Assuming that there was a fresh courier at each staging post (i.e. at about fifteen-mile intervals), the King's mail could proceed day and night practically at a gallop. So in favourable conditions the 112 stages might well be traversed inside a week.[15] There were probably only a limited number of trunk roads in the empire where the angaros-system was used. We should expect Memphis and Baktra to be linked to the capitals in this way. But whether there was an express dromedary service across the Syrian desert is unknown.

We are not told of tolls on the trunk roads. But the Persepolis tablets show that travellers required authorization and were normally escorted; and two stories, that of the slave whom Histiaios sent from Susa to Miletus with a secret message tattooed on his scalp and that of Demaratos' tablet with the wax blank, both depend on the assumption that a traveller would be searched – the roads being guarded, Herodotus says (V 35). Fire signals are said to have been used by the Persians. Warning beacons had of course been used from time immemorial (e.g. in Babylonia); but the relaying of messages by beacons was a novelty if Herodotus is correct in having Mardonios signal his arrival in Athens in this way. Messages were passed in Persis by men shouting across valleys, but this could only be a localized phenomenon; Darius I in Scythia had an Egyptian whose voice could carry across the Danube.

The Achaemenids maintained some bridges on their main routes. What we hear of is boat bridges, which seem to have been in normal use on the Tigris in Babylonia, the R. Physkos at Opis (by Baghdad), and probably on the Pasitigris (Karun) by Ahwaz, over canals in Mesopotamia, on the Euphrates at Thapsakos (below Carchemish), and on the Halys; Tamerlane at least had one on the Oxus by Termez. We also hear of ferries. These are not mutually exlusive because the big rivers may flow too strongly for boat bridges in flood time, in high flood sometimes too strongly even for ferries. No doubt stuffed (or inflated) skins were in general use locally. Some of the bridges we read of were specially constructed for particular campaigns: those of Darius I and Xerxes over the Bosporus, Danube, Hellespont, and Strymon, Cyrus the Great's on the Jaxartes, and perhaps that of Cyrus the Younger over the Maeander; Alexander had to build a bridge on the Persepolis road. In some parts of the empire there was a lack of bridges, as on the Iris and Thermodon rivers on the south coast of the Black Sea. There, as also along the south coast of the Caspian, no road was kept up because in these regions a regular Persian presence does not seem to have been maintained.

The one bridging feat of which we have a description is that of Xerxes at the Hellespont.[16] Two boat bridges were constructed to span the Dardanelles. Herodotus speaks as though they were both built at the same place where the stream was seven stades across. The downstream one, of 314 boats, was probably there (the so-called Heptastadion, in fact 1,400 yards across); the boats were aligned with the current and it was anchored against the land wind. But the upper bridge, of 360 boats set at an angle to the current and anchored against the wind from upstream, may rather have started from the tip of Abydos (Naǧara Point) three miles or so to the north. Egyptians and Phoenicians built these bridges, the latter weaving cables of white flax, and the former of papyrus which were of the same thickness but lighter in weight. The completed bridges were damaged by a storm and repaired with two flaxen cables and four papyrus ones to each bridge. The cables were winched tight with wooden 'donkeys'. Planks laid crosswise formed the roadway, with brushwood and trampled earth on top. Hedges ran along the sides so that the animals would not panic. One bridge (the upstream one) was used by the infantry and cavalry while the baggage train and attendants crossed on the other. Somehow it was contrived that ships could pass through gaps in midstream.

The preparations for Xerxes' march entailed a good deal more than this. A short day's walk down from the bridges on the European bank the Athenian colony of Elaious afforded calm anchorage just inside the narrows. The Phoenicians and others of the Persian fleet used it as a base for three years before Xerxes' crossing. From there they organized working parties for the digging of a ship canal at the neck of the Athos peninsula which was intended to obviate the danger of another storm disaster like that suffered in 492 B.C. (above, p. 96); the sides of the cut were stepped down to allow the spoil to be passed upwards. Like Darius I's canal to Suez, the Athos one took two ships abreast. Breakwaters at the ends prevented silting. A market was set up in a meadow there and flour was sent to it from Asia; presumably the workers were on a par with the 'kurtash' of the Persepolis tablets (above, p. 87), so the appearance of a market is relevant to them. The same work-force was responsible for the Strymon bridge. Supply dumps for the invading forces were built up at four places that Herodotus names between the Dardanelles and the Strymon, and also in Macedonia.[17] Herodotus speaks of foodstuffs for men and animals, while Theopompus' description of the contributions sent for the campaign against Egypt in the early fourth century included salted meat piled up into what looked like mountains and bales of 'books' – presumably stationery for bureaucratic needs.[18] From Herodotus we learn that royal scribes were in attendance on the King to note down details of the different contingents and the names of those who distinguished themselves in the fighting. We happen to hear of medical kit (myrrh and cotton bandages) being carried to treat wounds, and of the fleet setting up a white stone marker on a dangerous reef.

The agents Xerxes sent into Greece in 481 B.C. put the requisitioning of supplies in train. From Herodotus we hear that it was disaster to have to provide the 'King's dinner'; the estimate, no doubt exaggerated, of the cost to the Thasians was 400 talents of silver (VII 118–20). Notice having been given long in advance, the corn stocks were apportioned and flour was being ground months beforehand, the best cattle were found and fattened up, poultry and waterfowl were kept in hen-houses and ponds – apart from fruit, we have the same essentials as were provided for by the supply departments of the Persepolis tablets (above, p. 89). Gold and silver wine-cups and vessels and other things necessary for the royal table were manufactured. A marquee was set up for the King (it may have been his own one with gilded posts and a dome like the sky – Herodotus also speaks of tapestries in his suite which he left behind with Mardonios). As the King departed in the morning his retinue pulled the tent down and took away all the furnishings and valuables that had been provided. Herodotus says the people were practically driven out of house and home and the only thing they had to be thankful for was that the King did not dine twice a day.

Before passing on to the events of 480–79 we may briefly consider the static forces allocated to imperial security and defence. Our knowledge of the garrisons is patchy, depending mainly on Greek writers and dossiers in Aramaic from Egypt, though something may be learned from excavations (not least from cemeteries of what may have been military colonies in North Syria and the south of Palestine).[19] Important satrapal centres had imperial garrisons. Memphis had a state arsenal with workshops and a mixed force in the White Fort that included Semitic and other troops from the western provinces, Babylonians, Sakai, Caspians, and Chorasmians, and seems to have numbered 16,000 mouths to judge by the grain quota.[20] Sardis always had a garrison. On the other hand, the satraps in Daskyleion, which was well placed to command the Straits, and in Armenia about 400 B.C. seem to have had household troops, but we do not hear of imperial garrisons there. The client king in Cilicia paid for the upkeep of a considerable force of cavalry in his country. Persepolis seems to have had a small garrison; and guards were stationed at frontier and river crossings. In Egypt, besides Memphis there were contingents of troops (apparently mainly Semitic with Persian or Babylonian bimbashis) at various centres.[21] Syene with Elephantine (Yeb, which had a Jewish military colony) formed the seat of the southern command at the First Cataract; for transporting supplies they had boats, whose repair was a charge on satrapal funds. The garrison at Yeb is certainly older than the Persian conquest and probably of before 587 B.C. Thebes, Abydos, and Hermoupolis had military detachments. The different nationalities may have been segregated by battalions. The establishment also included native Egyptians, of whom Herodotus tells us there were two great territorial regiments in Lower Egypt (II 164–68). There may still have been detachments on the eastern (Pelousiac) arm of the Nile, though not on the scale of the foreign military settlements of Saite times at Migdol and Tahpanhes; at Tell el-Maskhuta in the eastern Delta there was a sanctuary of the Arabs' goddess Ilat which almost certainly yielded the silver bowl dedicated to Qainu son of Geshem, king of Kedar (below, p. 175). Remains interpreted as store-houses could indicate an important supply base at Tel Jemmeh on the other side of the desert south of Gaza, but they cannot be proved to date as early as Achaemenid times. In Babylonia there were fief-collectives that had been granted to foreigners such as Indians, peoples of Anatolia, Armenia, and Syria, and perhaps Sakai (Gimirrai) (see below, p. 203); but though no doubt military in origin they will hardly have constituted a force in being.

In the North-east of the empire Cyrus the Great's string of forts near the Jaxartes has been mentioned (above, p. 37). Darius I had defeated the Pointed-cap Saka, and he or Xerxes later added Daha to the list of subject peoples. So Persian rule may have been carried down into the steppe east of the Caspian. But in late Achaemenid times the great oasis of Khiva or Khwarizm (Chorasmia) seems to have had its own ruler; and when we find Sakai in the Persian armed forces we should perhaps think of them as borderers who were induced to join up for pay and opportunity for loot. This would be a small price for the Persians to pay for tranquillity on a long open frontier. We do not hear of further trouble there in Turkestan. Similarly the camel-leading bedouin of the Arab lands seem to have brought their gifts regularly, and down to the late fifth century B.C. at least Persian authority was respected as far as Dedan with the kings of Kedar apparently recognized in the Hejaz and Negev, and at Darius' Suez canal. The impression we have is that on both these frontiers peace was maintained with relatively little exertion of force. We may credit the Persians with good organization and firm discipline, and probably also with tolerance in handling the frontier peoples.

On the evidence above all of Xerxes' expedition Persian preparation at this time was first class from the point of view both of political warfare and of the movement of large forces by land and sea. The weakness, if we must look for one, was in the higher command. The King had little experience of war. The lesson of Marathon had not been learned. Too great faith was placed in the valour of the King's forces when fighting under his eye, and too little account taken of the free Greeks' will to resist. The Persian command did not have the strategical grasp to impose its own pattern on the fighting, and Persian professionalism in mounting the expedition and delivering men and ships to the battle fronts was not enough to ensure victory.

XI Xerxes' Great Expedition

To make a single war the subject of a whole chapter in this book may seem ill proportioned. But as the preceding chapter has indicated, it is the one major operation of the Achaemenids in their prime that is recorded in sufficient detail for us to see the Persians close up and evaluate their strength and weaknesses.

The story of the Persian expedition into Greece in 480–79 is well known.[1] No comparable event has been more momentous in the history of European civilization than its repulse. And it is easy to persuade ourselves that it was little short of a miracle that the allied Greeks emerged victorious. But we know the story only from the Greek side. The familiar picture that we in Europe have inherited, that of the King with half the East at heel repelled by a handful of resolute Greek patriots whom he expected to trample underfoot, is a heartening one for lovers of freedom. It is not entirely realistic. As regards sheer numbers, the fact that the population of the Persian empire was many times that of Greece is balanced by the fact that there were far more Greeks in the world than Persians. What is more to the point is that a campaign at so great a distance from home in an ill-explored and difficult terrain was a very audacious enterprise. It involved risks that Xerxes did his best to insure against by such preparations as could be made in advance; and to that extent he deserved his moment of triumph when he sacked the city of those Athenians whom his father had long been at such pains to punish. The Delphic priests expected him to win. But on the allied side there were leaders who calculated that a Persian conquest of Greece might be averted if the Athenians and the Spartan alliance united in resistance. The event proved them correct. It was bound to be a struggle in which chance could make or mar and generalship prove decisive. On the second count, if not also the first, the allies were fortunate.

The momentousness of the Persians' defeat does to some extent depend on the magnitude of the forces they brought to bear; though in any circumstances the repulse of a King's expedition must have ranked as a very serious setback. In their elation the victorious Greeks could hardly fail to exaggerate the enemy numbers. So when we learn that the epitaph of the Peloponnesians at Thermopylae, which was presumably set up only a year later, speaks of four thousand men doing battle with three hundred myriads, we can accept three million as the 'common knowledge' figure for the Persian land forces which no loyal Greek patriot would have cared to question at the time, but we are not obliged to believe it ourselves. Herodotus a generation later did not believe it. Instead, he has a curious story (VII 60) of Xerxes' infantry being counted by a penning process at Doriskos in Thrace and found to number

1,700,000 (thus, with his figure of 100,000 for the mounted troops added, making a total of 1,800,000 fighting men brought from Asia), to which he adds 300,000 Greek and other foot soldiers picked up en route between the Straits and Thermopylae (his grand totals for the whole expedition VII 184–87). We cannot seriously believe his figures either.

Herodotus' break-down of the Persian army offers a different line of approach to the problem (VII 61–88). Under Xerxes there were six marshals; and beneath them came twenty-nine noble Persians in command of infantry corps, each of whom had an unspecified number of myriarchs (divisional commanders of 10,000 men) subordinate to him (above, p. 101). If it were to be assumed that as usual the multiplier was ten, each of the twenty-nine divisions would have been 100,000 strong; and with Herodotus' figure of 100,000 mounted troops a total of 3,000,000 fighting men would be reached. Herodotus has not himself used this method of computation. But it is tempting to believe that we have here the basis of the 'common knowledge' figure of three millions. Many modern scholars have therefore accepted the twenty-nine infantry corps, but with the difference that their commanders were themselves the myriarchs or divisional commanders; with the Ten Thousand (Immortals) under Hydarnes to add to them, we should thus have thirty divisions of 10,000 foot. It has been further suggested that, with five divisions of foot and one of cavalry, each of the six marshals would have commanded an army corps of 60,000 men; this is of course mere conjecture, but task forces of 60,000 men do appear twice in Herodotus' account of the operations (Artabazos escorting the King back to the Straits in VIII 126, and the Achaemenid Tigranes defending Ionia in IX 96). So a figure of up to 360,000 fighting men is not unconvincing. By Napoleonic standards it would not be specially large.

Some of the modern scholars who use Herodotus' figures in this way have maintained nevertheless that what we thus deduce from him is not the actual size of Xerxes' field army but the paper strength of the entire Persian military establishment: either, many of the more outlandish contingents mentioned were not taken on the Greek expedition, or only three of the six army corps were used (the others being left in reserve). These contentions do not carry conviction. It is the more outlandish contingents, for instance those from Ethiopia and eastern Baluchistan, that depend most on visual rather than documentary presentation in Herodotus' list (above, p. 104); and there does not seem to have been any regular peace-time military establishment – apart from guards divisions, household brigades, and static garrison, levies would be produced from the satrapies to the number required for an expedition. On the contrary, when the King went all must go (above, p. 104). Even the cautious uncle Artabanos, who contributed four sons as commanders and was himself to stay behind as caretaker of the Royal House, escorted Xerxes as far as the Hellespont. So if we have arrived at a reasoned figure for the strength of Xerxes' army we have no valid excuse for proceeding to cut it down drastically. At most we can question whether some of the divisions like that from the Persian Gulf islands could easily have numbered 10,000; on the other hand nations such as the Medes, 'Assyrians', Baktrians, Indians, Cappadocians with their neighbours, and the combined Phrygians and Armenians could have greatly exceeded that figure – even the Lycians, a small nation whose ancient population has been reckoned at no more than 200,000, provided 10,000 men for the fleet.

Some scholars have preferred to ignore the transmitted figures and judge by what they regard as logistically or demographically plausible. Figures of 100,000 and less have been proposed; it has even been claimed that it was not the twenty-nine divisional commanders but the six marshals who were the myriarchs. But such numbers are less than the Assyrian kings normally put into the field from only a small fraction of the same territory, and very much less than Shah Abbas could muster, according to Herbert and de Laet. The emphasis on supply dumps and swarms of grain ships and other commissariat vessels, on rivers drunk dry in regions not then denuded as they are now,[2] and the construction of two bridges over the Hellespont with the time reported to have been spent in crossing them[3] all point to a much bigger army. So too Herodotus' statement that Mardonios, who remained in Greece with an army that was judged sufficient to finish the war, made a selection of eastern contingents which amounted to barely a quarter of Xerxes' forty infantry and mounted divisions. This is not to say that all the needs of the great Persian army were satisfied; in particular, it was known to have suffered severe hardships on the return march to the Straits.

The figure here accepted for Xerxes' army, of more than 300,000 fighting men, is probably higher than most scholars now allow. But it rests on inference from the sources rather than on guesswork. The point that needs to be stressed is that the army depended on a complicated supply system in which the accompanying fleet played a large part. When that organization was disrupted after the naval defeat at Salamis, the bulk of the land forces had to be withdrawn to Asia in haste.

Fortunately there is less room for manoeuvre with the numbers at sea. On the allied side we can accept as approximately correct the figures of 310 (or 300) triremes at Salamis (Aeschylus) and 380 as what would seem to be the campaign total (Herodotus). Through the Ionians Xerxes should have been kept accurately informed about Greek naval strengths until 480 B.C. His informants might have underestimated the number of new ships that the Athenians were currently launching; on the other hand there were sixty Corcyraean ships which failed to arrive on time. If we assume that Xerxes was relying on the Carthaginians to pin down the western Greek fleets in Sicily he might have reckoned on not being confronted by much more than 400 triremes in battle; otherwise 500 and more. By their opposite results (above, pp. 93 and 95) the two battles in the past between Persian and (Eastern) Greek fleets would have suggested that ship for ship they were probably fairly evenly matched. But Xerxes had to make allowance for unforeseeable losses by storm and misadventure, the greater distance from his fleet bases and repair yards, inferior fleet stations, and inadequate knowledge of Greek waters and sailing conditions. In addition to this, his fleet would have a role to play in supporting his land forces in their advance, and it did on occasion need to be divided; and finally he was likely to have to fight where the enemy chose to offer battle. Great numerical superiority was therefore necessary. At Lade the Eastern Greeks had manned 353 triremes; and though the figure of 600 for the Persian fleet there might be an exaggeration, the total number of ships involved will hardly have been less than 800, all of which came from ports that were in Xerxes' empire in 481–80.

The Greek 'common knowledge' figure for the Persian fleet in 480 is not certain. Aeschylus in his *Persae* of 472 B.C.[4] gave Xerxes a strength of a thousand ships with 207 specially fast ones. Strictly this applies to the fleet at Salamis, but it would be hypercritical to suggest that the tragedian was distinguishing the strength of the battle fleet there from a total campaign strength. Herodotus has the same figures, which would be in people's memory, and he makes the total that which Xerxes brought from Asia. But he adds the 207 to the thousand, which our text of Aeschylus does not seem to do. Herodotus did not, however, really believe that Xerxes had 1,207 triremes at Salamis; and though half-heartedly speaking of Persian losses being made good by fresh requisitioning, he not only has 600 triremes destroyed by the storms but remarks that thereby the great disparity in numbers between the two fleets was providentially lessened. The figures he gives for ships manned by the Eastern Greeks are very moderate compared with what they raised at Lade, and this applies particularly to the islanders who could see a prospect of freedom in a Persian defeat. The four peoples of the Levant who had provided 600 ships at Lade now contribute a total of 750. This could be an exaggeration; for instance, the Phoenician fleet, which Herodotus makes 300 ships,[5] could be the same as the 207 fast ones of Aeschylus. But even with some scaling down of the Levantine figures the total of triremes in the Persian fleet cannot have been much less than 1,000. In addition, Herodotus speaks of 3,000 smaller craft with a total of seamen that he estimates as about equal to that in the battle fleet (where the standard complement was 200 a ship).

On land the drivers and supply teams, tailors, smiths, saddlers, adjutant and quartermaster staff, sewers and seneschals, servants, and harems must have run into six figures. It would be difficult to say which of the two arms of the service had the greater numbers. The balance between land and sea forces emerges as different from that in Herodotus because scholars for the most part are not prepared to scale down the number of oarsmen in a trireme in the way that they scale down everything else (except the Immortals). But something around 750,000 people must have been on the move with the King. On the allied side something over 80,000 combatants fought in 480 (nearly all at sea). In 479 almost 40,000 hoplites and 70,000 light-armed took part at Plataea (some of them, Athenians especially, fought both at sea in 480 and on land in 479), and in addition the 110 ships at the Isthmus in 479 will have involved another 25,000 men. The relatively small number of heavy infantry on the Greek side is explained by the fact that in their armies only men of some socio-economic standing served as hoplites, whereas the property-less and immigrant could take an oar. Among the Persians a higher proportion of the adult males must have served in the line regiments.

The allies owed a great debt of gratitude to the Egyptians. It should not have taken the Persians nine years after Marathon to prepare the invasion of

Greece. Clearly it was not only Darius' death but much more the Egyptian revolt that caused it to be delayed. For the Greeks each of the last years, and even months, of the decade was crucial. About the winter of 483–82 a rich vein had been struck in the silver mines of Laurion in southern Attica. It was originally proposed that the bonanza should be shared out among the citizens of Athens. But once again (to judge by banishments) the Athenian politicians favourable to Persia seem to have been losing ground. Themistocles succeeded in persuading the responsible democratic assembly to start a crash ship-building programme instead. With a goal of 200 triremes Athens was trebling her naval strength. Many of these ships were first entering the water as Xerxes approached, and without them a Greek victory at sea would have been unlikely.

To turn at last to the narrative, for which we depend almost entirely on Herodotus, Xerxes must have set out in the spring of 481 B.C. The marshalling point for the contingents (other than those from western Asia Minor) was Kritalla. Its position is not known; but since it was in Cappadocia it must have been east of the Halys bend. Xerxes was evidently following the line of the 'royal road' this far, and not the 'southern highway' by Syria and Cilicia that was used by Mardonios' land forces in 492, Cyrus the Younger in 401, and Alexander in 333; obviously the passage of the Cilician Gates would have *Plate 41* taken more time than he could afford. As it was, his two bottle-necks will have been the Euphrates and Halys crossings, but presumably he had the bridges widened or doubled. On the central Anatolian plateau he evidently forked left from the line of the 'royal road'. At Kelainai the King and his army were entertained by the second richest man in the empire, Pythios. Plutarch speaks of him having a gold mine; but mines in the satrapies would probably have been at the King's disposal, and it is simpler to assume with Herodotus that he was a great land- and sheep-owner. After a 1,600-mile march the Persians arrived at Sardis and wintered there. Meanwhile across the Aegean Athens and Sparta had convened a Hellenic congress and decided on resistance.

In the spring of 480 Xerxes set out for the Hellespont. He is said to have paid a courtesy visit to Troy, like Alexander the Great and Mehmet II (the conqueror of Constantinople) after him. At Abydos a marble grandstand had been built so that he could survey his army and fleet. Herodotus tells us that after congratulating himself on his good fortune Xerxes wept at the transitoriness of human life, for of all that great concourse not one would be alive in a hundred years' time. The bridges at the Dardanelles had already been repaired. The crossing is said to have occupied seven days and nights, Xerxes himself traversing the upstream bridge on the second day; and by the end of the week the advance guard should have been arriving at Doriskos by the Hebros mouth where Darius had established the Persian headquarters in Europe. The warships were hauled up and dried out on the beaches there; the army was marshalled in readiness for an advance in three columns along the Thracian coast, and Xerxes marched out probably about the beginning of June. On the way he himself made a detour to see the Athos canal with his

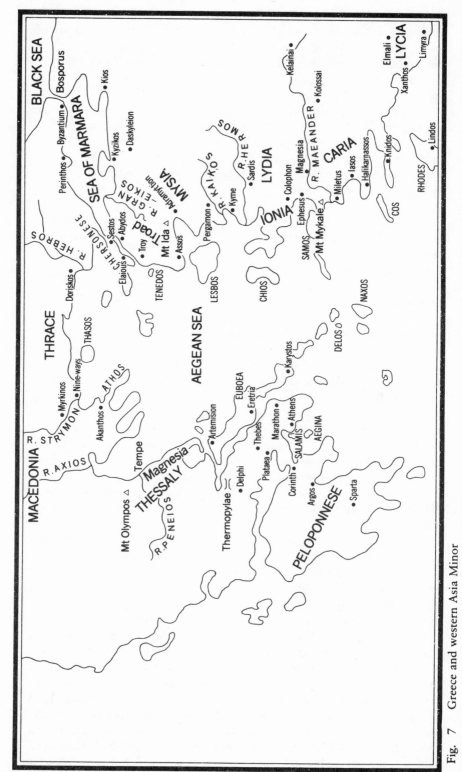

Fig. 7 Greece and western Asia Minor

ships passing through; and while the army was forming up in the plain of the Axios (Vardar) river and his advance troops will have been widening the forest tracks leading over to Thessaly, he made an excursion in his Sidonian royal yacht to view the gorge of Tempe where the Peneios flows through between Olympus and Ossa. If we trust Herodotus, he would appear not only to have been an admirer of the picturesque but to have been interested in the possible effects of building a barrage there.

The powerful Thessalian family of the Aleuadai at Larisa had already espoused the Persian cause. The rest of the Thessalians had in the main opted to resist the invader; and the first allied defence plan was to include Thessaly, which involved a force of Athenians and Spartans being sent north. But reconnaissance showed that while the pass of Tempe could be blocked, the mountain barrier to the west was more easily traversable, and the Thessalian plains could not have been closed to the Persian cavalry. So Thessaly had to be abandoned and the Mt Oeta line, which offered good co-ordination with the fleet, was eventually selected instead. This position was in fact an excellent one. The narrow pass of Thermopylae between the steep mountainside and the sea could be held indefinitely by a few thousand hoplites, while immediately to the east the narrow, dog-legged sea-lane between the Central Greek coasts and the long island of Euboea was ideal for a fleet lying in wait for the enemy. The two positions were interdependent; and since the allied action on land had to be defensive, a decisive result could only be achieved at sea. But the Spartans, on whom the leadership of the Greek allies devolved, were in a cleft stick. If the fleet were defeated, an army sent into Central Greece would be endangered. They would therefore have preferred to defend the Peloponnese with a barrier across the narrow isthmus of Corinth. But the Athenian fleet was essential to the whole defensive plan, and Athens lay outside the Isthmus. They therefore allowed one of their two kings, Leonidas, to proceed to Thermopylae, but with no more than 300 select Spartan hoplites. He had some 6,000 other Greek hoplites to assist in holding the pass at Thermopylae; but to the defence of the high marching track by which it is outflanked (the Anopaia) he allotted no more than 1,000 Phocians who knew the terrain.

The war opened at sea. And the first blow was struck by the legendary kinsman to whom the Athenians prayed, Boreas. The allied fleet lay secure at Artemision near the north tip of Euboea. To reach the strait the Persian fleet had to sail along the inhospitable lee-shore of Magnesia, and a three-day storm caught them on the beaches there with many of their ships riding at anchor. Herodotus has a minimum of 400 Persian triremes wrecked there, and also another 200 which were sent round Euboea on the seaward side only two or three days later. These losses must be greatly exaggerated. At all events the Persian fleet was able to enter the narrows and take station across the strait from the allies. In the first two rather tentative evening exchanges the allies seem to have had the advantage; but a more general engagement provoked by the Persians was harder fought, with the heavy-armed Egyptian marines excelling themselves and half of the Athenian ships suffering damage. It was followed by the withdrawal of the allied fleet because the position on land had not held.

The Persian advance had been so timed that the fleet would not lack the support of the army on shore. On his arrival in front of Thermopylae Xerxes reconnoitred Leonidas' position, after which he seems to have waited four days while his army closed up and the fleet regrouped. Then he had his throne set up where he could watch the fighting and sent crack infantry regiments into the pass. But Leonidas countered with a flexible defence, in which the Greeks seem to have showed themselves the better trained in manoeuvring; and at the end of two days Medes, Elamites, and even the Immortals had taken a knock without achieving a break-through. Xerxes then sent out Hydarnes and the Immortals at lighting-up time with a local guide to round the Greek position by way of the Anopaia path. In the first light of dawn they brushed aside the Phocian battalion on the col and were soon set on the downward track. On learning that his position was turned Leonidas sent off most of his force, and himself stayed with his Spartans and the Boeotians to cover their escape. Before evening the last stand was over and a Spartan king lay dead. The Persians had their losses also; Herodotus' figure of 20,000 sounds excessive, but Xerxes had two of his brothers to mourn.

There was now no line north of the Isthmus that the allied land forces could hold against an army the size of Xerxes', and work on the wall there proceeded night and day. The fleet had withdrawn from Artemision. But it must take up a position on the flank of the Persian advance, and it must also have an island base since the Persian army would overrun the mainland; so Salamis was the most suitable station. There the allied fleet concentrated.

Thermopylae was an important Persian victory. It cost the allies Central Greece and would have ended the war if the Athenians had not been prepared to abandon their land and shrines and homes to the enemy. As regards future strategy the allies had taken the measure of their opponents and knew how defeat might be avoided; Xerxes had no doubt acquired a healthy respect for Greek hoplites, but he could not have seen any of the fighting at sea and had probably been given too rosy an account of it. Food supply must inevitably have been an important consideration; it is impossible to tell whether the Persian army or the allied fleet and Athenian refugees on Salamis would have felt the pinch the more seriously. But the season was slipping by and Xerxes may have been unwilling to defer the issue for long when he was so far away from the nerve-centres of his empire. About early September he was in Athens, where a few die-hards on the Acropolis were overcome; and the good news of his success was promptly relayed to his uncle Artabanos in Susa. Darius' words on his tomb-front, which were on record in the palace archives, may have sounded in his son's ears: 'Then shalt thou know, then shall it become known to thee, the spear of a Persian man has gone forth far; then shall it become known to thee, a Persian man has delivered battle far indeed from Parsa.' In fact 3,000 miles.

The Persian fleet was now at Phaleron, whence the twenty Athenian ships had sailed to join the Ionian Revolt and incur the wrath of Darius. A few miles up the coast were the narrows where less than a mile of placid water separated the island of Salamis from the shore which the Persians now held. Xerxes may have contemplated the possibility of effecting a crossing by a combination of mole and boat bridge; but if so, the work should have been started before, and not as Herodotus says after, the battle. Certainly nothing could come of it. The accepted Athenian account of the events leading up to the battle was that in his guile Themistocles, who is generally agreed to have been the principal architect of victory, sent a personal message to Xerxes that the allies were no longer minded to fight and would slip away during the night. Themistocles was a person to whom stories of one-upmanship and repartee attached themselves. In general they are not believed. But Aeschylus can hardly be inventing when he has the Persian fleet spend the night at sea patrolling the exits from the Salamis channels. When day came the Greek seamen were rested and fed, and manning their ships for battle. Xerxes' instructions to intercept the fugitives must have included the order to bring the enemy to battle, because in the morning he was himself ensconced under a golden canopy on the slope overlooking the strait and the Phoenician ships had penetrated the narrows.

In the ancient accounts of Salamis we find a wealth of incident but no clear picture of the formations of the fleets or their situation in relation to the coasts. When they clashed the Phoenicians held their own for a time. But the Athenians had contrived to work round them, pinning them against the shore where they had too little sea-room and fouled one another. A morning swell up the channel may have added to their disorder. As more squadrons of the Persian fleet pressed forward to show their prowess under the King's eye, the Phoenicians could find no escape. Some of their commanders ran their ships ashore under Xerxes' throne and went up to protest. Meanwhile the Eastern Greeks who had come up the channel were engaged by the Spartan admiral and so were unable to take the pressure off the Phoenicians; they manoeuvred more successfully, but the Phoenicians had been trapped and the Aeginetans were positioned to fall on the flank of those who tried to pull out from the mêlée. Some of the Persian contingents may not have entered the battle at all; in particular, there is no mention of the Egyptians in Herodotus' account, and later Greek writers surmised that they had been detached to guard the western exit towards Megara. But all in all it was a diminished and dispirited host that returned to Phaleron roadstead. Aeschylus perhaps makes the Persian herald exaggerate when he announces that never before in one day did so numerous a multitude perish. But the dead included the chief admiral Ariabignes who was one of Xerxes' brothers, Syennesis the client-king of Cilicia, and perhaps two sons of Darius' daughter Mandane,[6] not to mention a select force of Persian infantry who had been landed on the islet in the mouth of the channel. The allies had fought hard and resourcefully. They prepared to resume the battle when the enemy returned to the attack. But morale on the other side had snapped. The army remained in position. But a day later the roadstead was empty; the Persian fleet was on its way back to the Hellespont.

The whole situation was now changed, and Xerxes was in serious difficulties. Without a fleet the Peloponnese could not be conquered. Winter was only a month or two away; and with the prospects of unrest after such a reverse he must return to Sardis to keep the empire under surveillance. But to abandon his new Greek conquests would be an admission of defeat and a failure to equal his predecessors in glory; and Mardonios' reputation could only be retrieved by a victory over the recalcitrant Greeks. So it was decided that Mardonios should stay behind in Northern Greece with selected divisions of the army while the remainder went back to Asia with Xerxes. The Greek sources speak of Xerxes' return march as almost headlong flight and fraught with disaster; certainly there would be hardship as autumn gave way to winter. But Artabazos escorted the King to the Straits and still had his corps in fighting trim as he made his way back to Mardonios.

Xerxes was to live for another fifteen years. But at this stage he is passing out of the narrative. Thanks to Herodotus, he is of all Persians the one we feel most for as a person. But there are two different Xerxeses. The Athenian and Spartan tradition that dominates the descriptions of the fighting gives us the familiar portrait of the vainglorious despot whose troops are driven forward under the lash, cruel to the point of beheading the engineers and sea captains who were not successful, and panicky in defeat. He is even said to have had Leonidas' corpse beheaded and impaled after Thermopylae (true to his habit, Herodotus abstains from moral judgement when he relates this, but 100 pages later he gives vent to his feelings in the withering scorn with which he makes Pausanias reply to the suggestion that Mardonios should be treated in the same way). As against all this, Herodotus' information about Xerxes from Persian sources and Asiatic or exiled Greeks offers a quite different picture. He had presence; in the whole great host no one appeared 'more victory-worthy than Xerxes to hold the command'. He was capable of large designs and generous impulses, and true to his word; and though emotional and perhaps vacillating, he normally had a chivalry or magnanimity that his father seems to have lacked. The admirable discipline of the Persian troops suggests that he inspired their reverence. On other grounds we may suspect that he was self-righteous, less probably (as some scholars believe) a religious bigot (below, p. 148). But if we follow Herodotus, he more than once showed good sense when overruling his subordinates – in releasing the Greek spies caught in his camp at Sardis so that they could report home on Persian strength and efficiency, and in preventing a corn ship from being seized on its way to Greece because it was taking food where they were going. When he first brought Xerxes on the stage Herodotus made clear that Mardonios was Xerxes' evil genius, and that it was the god's will that it should be so.

But at the end Herodotus is adverse. He has Xerxes disappear from view entangled in a disastrous amour which results in the killing of his brother Masistes, and then almost immediately he concludes his History with the cautionary tale of Cyrus explaining to his followers that hardy country breeds hardy men and if they move down to settle in richer lands they may expect not to rule others but to have others rule them. He doesn't accuse the Persians of lack of courage. But he does leave us with the thought that luxury and lack of self-discipline were having their effect on Xerxes and those around him.

Mardonios selected the Persian, Median, Saka, Baktrian, and Indian contingents from Xerxes' army. If we work on the myriad theory he may have had some 60,000 foot and perhaps 30,000 cavalry in addition to his Theban and northern allies. But he was blocked by the Isthmus wall, and with no fleet he could not attempt a diversion. He did his utmost to entice the Athenians into making a separate peace on favourable terms; and when that failed he invaded Attica again and finished off the work of destruction there. At last after midsummer 479 the Spartans with their allies succumbed to Athenian pressure and marched out across the Isthmus under the command of the Spartan regent Pausanias. Mardonios withdrew from Attica and took up a position beyond Mt Kithairon on the edge of the Theban plain, where he felled the trees and made a stockaded camp more than a mile square. The allies crossed the mountain and confronted him on the Asopos stream near Plataea. Neither side would launch an attack on ground of the other's choice and the two armies faced each other for a fortnight. The Persians were experimenting with the use of cavalry and found a weak stretch of the allied line where the ground was level. The Greeks in the line there were hard pressed for some time by the repeated assaults of squadron after squadron. But as his brigade wheeled round after an attack the cavalry general Masistios' Nesaean charger was hit by an arrow and threw its rider, and in the ensuing mêlée the cavalry were beaten off. After this, however, they did cut up a supply train on the pass behind the Greek lines; and when finally they succeeded in choking the fountain that the Greeks depended on, Pausanias gave the order to withdraw a mile or two up the slope.

The Greek retreat during the night seems to have been badly executed. The different groups became widely separated; and in the morning the reconnoitring Persian cavalry found the Spartan division isolated on the slope. Mardonios, who had stationed himself on the left opposite the Spartans, thought his opportunity had come and ordered his infantry forward to the attack. The Persians advanced within bowshot and from their hedge of wicker shields started to fire their arrows into the enemy. This was where generalship counted. Pausanias held his men back under the hail of arrows until Mardonios' hinder ranks had closed up and flexible manoeuvring was no longer possible. Then he gave the command and the Spartan phalanx advanced down the slope. As the ranks of the Persians were crushed in Mardonios and his thousand guards were engulfed in the battle; they fought fiercely, but when he fell the rest fled to their stockade. The Thebans, who were committed beyond redemption to the Persian cause, reacted strongly. Their hoplites held up the Athenian advance, their cavalry helped the Persians to escape to their stockade, and they inflicted the only serious casualties on the allies when they cut up 600 men who were incautiously hurrying across level ground to be in at the kill. There was great carnage in the stockade because with such large numbers Pausanias dared not risk having prisoners at large. Apart from the 600, the allied casualties were astonishingly light: of the Spartans, 91 killed, of the Athenians, 52. On the Persian side we do not know what kinsmen of Xerxes perished; there had been a reshuffle of commanders and Herodotus does not give names. It is sometimes said that Mardonios' error was that he let himself be killed in the battle; but more probably his fatal error lay in his selection of troops the previous autumn.

Artabazos has also been blamed for not attacking the victors. But his lack of confidence in Mardonios did not lower him in Xerxes' esteem. He was presumably coming up with other Iranian divisions. But when he saw the rout he turned about and led his men northward at top speed. By outpacing the news of the battle and proclaiming that Mardonios was following on his heels he got through Thessaly unmolested. The Thracians harassed him, but with the remnant of the army he reached Byzantium by the inland route, choosing the Bosporus crossing out to fear that the allied fleet might have control of the Dardanelles. His future and that of his descendants was to lie in that pleasant corner of Asia.

After Salamis the Ionians had become restive. Those who were islanders saw freedom dawning, and refugees came to Greece urging the allies to send their fleet to liberate them. When he had returned safely across the Straits into Asia Xerxes proceeded to Sardis. This was only three days' march from the Ionic coast, and he therefore brought the residue of his fleet south to guard his flank. The Phoenicians were sent home; and as the Egyptian marines had been retained by Mardonios, it will have been mainly East Greeks who remained. Leotychidas, the Spartan king, who was now in command of the allied fleet, was persuaded to cross to Samos. The Persian fleet withdrew and hauled their ships ashore on the south coast of Mt Mykale, where there was a Persian army to protect them; cutting down trees, the Persians made a fortified encampment there. The allies landed nearby and closed in to the assault. The Persians lined up behind their hedge of shields. But their Ionic subjects were not to be trusted; and according to Herodotus resistance collapsed before the Spartans could work round the mountainside to the camp. The commander of the Persian army, Tigranes, and the admiral Mardontes both fell in the battle. In popular belief the battle of Plataea was fought in the morning and that of Mykale in the afternoon of the same day. If that were true the allies must have had many thousands more men mobilized than were estimated above. But on balance it seems more likely that Plataea released man-power for Mykale.

This last battle comes almost as an anticlimax. But it had far-reaching results. A Spartan king had led the allied Greeks across the Aegean and raised the Ionians in revolt, and the Athenians under the command of Pericles' father had made the major effort and then gone on to capture the Persian fortress at Sestos on the Hellespont. The allies were thus committed to protecting the Greeks in the King's territory.

The myth of Persian invincibility was now shattered, and the Phoenician navy was discredited. Europe, Eastern Greece, and for the time being Cyprus opposite the Phoenician coast, were lost to the empire. But the most serious loss was that of the Persian man whose spear had gone forth far. Whether or not he might have had a chance if he had kept the heavy-armed non-Iranian infantry together with light-armed mountain-bred skirmishers to harry the Spartan phalanx, Mardonios had in fact retained the Iranian line divisions as being the best fighting material; and the only Persian infantry who were not with him were a guards battalion or two with Xerxes and whatever household troops Artabazos had. Many of the Persian cavalry should have escaped with Artabazos. But the Immortals and the Persian line infantry division (that under Otanes in 480) must have perished in the war, together with some thousands of Persian marines. Adding in the Persians with Tigranes at Mykale we might reckon at least 25,000 Persians dead. The numbers might be made good in a generation. But the former military ascendancy could never be regained.

The trouble with the Persians from the time of Cyrus had been that they took war too much to heart. Conquest was a matter of royal and national honour; and it was axiomatic that Persian arms must prevail. In his own way Herodotus illustrates this with a charming anecdote about Darius' Scythian campaign (IV 134). The Scythians had at last judged the time ripe and drawn up their line for battle. But suddenly, before it could commence, they began milling around in great confusion and soon there was no army there for the Persians to fight. When he enquired where they had gone Darius learned that a hare had started up and the enemy was off in pursuit of it. These Scythians are not taking us seriously, Darius said; and Gobryas wrily agreed that they were impossible people who were making fun of them, and the sooner the Persians got out of their country the better.

XII Narrative of Middle Achaemenid History

The chapters that follow will be as much concerned with Achaemenid rule after 479 B.C. as before it. So at this point the historical narrative may be carried down in summary form through the next two or three generations. After their defeats in 480–79 the Persians had no fleet in being, and in 478 Pausanias, the victor of Plataea, sailed to Cyprus and liberated the island (or at least the Greek cities there). After this he cleared the passage of the Straits by capturing Byzantium; but his harsh treatment of the allies, coupled with what sounds like the beginning of treasonable negotiations with Artabazos, caused his recall; and in 477 the Athenians took over the leadership of the allied forces which were continuing the struggle against the Persians. They were fortunate in having an inspiring commander, Miltiades' son Kimon, who made the most of the new reputation for invincibility that the Greeks had won for themselves. The next year saw the Persian grandees and garrison commanders driven out of Thrace except Maskames, son of Megadostes, whom Xerxes had made governor of Doriskos; this was not Greek territory, and all attempts to unseat him failed. Maskames and his descendants are said to have received annual gifts for their prowess from both Xerxes and his son Artaxerxes. One other Persian would not submit tamely; this was Boges at Eion by the Strymon mouth, who was besieged through the winter (probably of 476–75) and finally threw himself into the flames rather than surrender.

For several years after this we know of no allied operations outside the Aegean. But in 469, or soon after, Kimon sailed to Caria and with a confederate fleet set about cutting out Persian strong-points as far as Phaselis on the border of Pamphylia. Meanwhile Xerxes had had ten years for counter-preparations. An army was sent under Pherendates to the R. Eurymedon in Pamphylia; and it was joined by a fleet raised from Phoenicia and Cilicia, which was commanded by a bastard son of Xerxes, Tithraustes.[1] Kimon went boldly in to the attack and was victorious on both land and sea on the same day. Accounts of the fighting vary; but in the main naval action, which Kimon seems to have fought in the river, Thucydides speaks of 200 Phoenician ships destroyed and captured and the contemporary Athenian epigram of 100 captured with their complements. On land the defeat of the Persians was total; it is clear that morale was at a very low ebb. To the Athenians and their allies the profit from loot, ransom money, and sales, with slaves selling at about one-thirtieth of a talent each, must have made the Levant seem an Eldorado.

One satisfaction it would be ungracious to deny Xerxes before his death. Themistocles was banished from Athens and eventually went into hiding on

Persian soil. Sent up concealed in a closed carriage in the guise of a lady for the harem – so we are told – he mastered Persian and then appeared at court to receive the reward offered for his capture. He was honourably treated by the King and given the grant of a fief in the West, where he settled down in affluence at Magnesia by the Maeander. The ancient writers disagree on the point whether the King was Xerxes or his son; and none of them inspires confidence.[2] But if it were correct that Artabanos (or Artapanos) was the chiliarch who received Themistocles, Xerxes would have to be right;[3] and in any case it is not entirely easy having Themistocles on the run as late as 464 B.C. In August 465 Xerxes died, murdered in his chamber by Artabanos in collusion with the eunuch of the bedside. The story goes that there were three legitimate sons, of whom one was satrap in Baktria while Darius (the eldest) and Artaxerxes were at court – according to Ctesias (Phot. 20 = 38B) Hystaspes was the second son and Artaxerxes the youngest. After the deed was done Artabanos contrived to pin the murder on Darius and have him killed by Artaxerxes, who thus came to the throne. He thereupon attempted to kill Artaxerxes; but in the event it was he who died, while the King escaped with a flesh wound. Artaxerxes then found himself involved in a war with the satrap of Baktria (his brother Hystaspes or, according to Ctesias, Artapanos), from which he is said to have emerged victorious after a battle in a sandstorm.

Artaxerxes I was nicknamed 'Long-arm' (Makrocheir in Greek). He was dead before Ctesias arrived at the court, and Herodotus' narrative did not reach down to his reign. So of all the Kings of substance he is the one of whom we hear least.[4] After his opening struggles he settled down to a reign of forty years, in which according to Plutarch he maintained a reputation for mildness and magnanimity. He is said to have been physically ample and (like his father and grandfather) handsome. But when Cornelius Nepos, our informant here, adds to this his 'incredible military valour' it is questionable whether he is drawing on details of Artaxerxes' early struggles which are not known to us (as King he was dissuaded from going in person on the Egyptian expedition). Nepos may have in mind Herodotus' etymology of the name.[5] The main events recorded are the revolt of Egypt under Inaros, which the Athenians fomented and the veteran marshal Megabyxos eventually suppressed, and the rebellions of the indomitable marshal himself (below, p. 168f.). The Egyptian revolt ended in a major disaster for Athens and her allies, though a rebel named Amyrtaios remained active in the Delta possibly for a dozen years more; it looks as though the scare was such that in 454 B.C. the treasury of the confederacy was moved from Delos to Athens. But in 450 Megabyxos' Athenian counterpart, the veteran Kimon, who had been ostracized and was back again from exile, patched up the bad relations that had developed between Athens and Sparta and led a fresh expedition of the confederacy with 200 ships to Cyprus. The Persians had been helping the Phoenicians to regain their position there and were assembled in strength with a large fleet under an Artabazos and an army in Cilicia reputedly under Megabyxos. Kimon himself died in the course of the campaign and the key Phoenician city of Kition did not succumb to the siege, but the rebel was re-inforced in the Delta marshes and the confederates were victorious on both land and sea at Cyprian Salamis, with the result that the Athenians were in a position to negotiate with the King from strength.

With Kimon died the last of the Athenian statesmen who still wanted to keep the war against the Persians going; so in 449 B.C. the Athenian democracy was more than ready for peace. Artaxerxes had tried to set the Spartans against them ten years earlier, sending Megabazos with a large stock of gold for bribes. But he had had no benefit from it. Now with the Athenians again aggressive in Cyprus it was worth surrendering his claim to the East Greek cities and their coastal neighbours if he could obtain a guarantee that there would be no more interference in the Levant. He had nothing to thank the Spartans for; but he had good reason to hate the Athenians, and it is to his credit that royal honour submitted to discussing concessions with them.

This was the thirtieth anniversary of the battle of Plataea, and Pericles rescinded the oath taken by the allies there not to rebuild the temples destroyed by the 'Mede' – work on the Parthenon started a year later. But peace with Persia could not be publicly announced without Athens either reducing the annual war contributions that the allies paid in the confederacy or admitting that they had become tribute-paying subjects. A published text of the agreement would have been embarrassing to both Persia and Athens. But it seems fairly certain that a prominent Athenian, Kallias son of Hipponikos, went up to Susa and negotiated it with the King (and, no doubt to his dismay in so delicate a matter, encountered there an embassy from Argos which was sent to make sure that in the changing circumstances its old bond of friendship with the King was renewed).[6] Fourth-century Athenian pamphleteers and orators could cite this 'Peace of Kallias' according to their brief. The gist of the assumed agreement seems to have been that the King would not send warships beyond Pamphylia or invade the belt of Greek and associated cities along the coast of Asia Minor round to the Bosporus, while the Athenians for their part would not interfere in the King's territory. It is not clear whether the King was to receive tribute from any territory in the possession of Greek cities on the Asiatic mainland; but Herodotus certainly understood that what the Persians claimed as theirs was Asia and the barbarian (i.e. non-Greek) peoples who inhabited it (I 4).

After this the Persian empire seems to have been quiescent. Egypt was pacified under the new satrap Arsames (see Chap. XII n.11). Megabyxos, who had risen in revolt, was reconciled to the King; and in Judah there could be no open opposition to the vigorous new governor, Nehemiah, since he had the King's support. We know of no troubles in the East after the revolt in Baktria. Relations with the Greeks could now be left to the western satraps to deal with. The lull in the second half of Artaxerxes I's reign does not necessarily imply firm rule – a gradual weakening of Persian control of the more distant parts of the empire would have been unlikely to filter through the headline-hitting memorabilia of Ctesias himself and the news-flashes of Photios' scriptorium. But for at least a quarter of a century the King didn't need to bother his head about the Greeks, the more so because they were becoming increasingly involved in their own hostilities and (from 431 B.C.)

outright war between the Athenian and Spartan alliances. Olmstead goes beyond the evidence when he makes the King (or, as he says, the Persian government) use Thargelia and other Greek courtesans as secret weapons to keep him abreast of Athenian state secrets, though Plutarch does say Thargelia lived with many eminent Greeks and made them well disposed towards the King.[7] But Artaxerxes had to take notice in the end. In the winter of 425–24 the Athenian commander at Eion on the Strymon intercepted a Persian named Artaphernes on his way to Sparta with a message from the King in 'Assyrian script' (which here should mean Aramaic):[8] in it the King acidly remarked that many ambassadors had come to him from the Spartans but none of them said the same thing; would they please send men with Artaphernes to clarify what it was they wanted. The Athenians tried to make capital out of the interception and sent Artaphernes back with ambassadors of their own; but when they reached Ephesus they learned that the King was dead. Artaxerxes in fact died in 424 B.C. His wife Damaspia is said to have died on the same day. Their only son Xerxes was the successor.[9]

We are now in the hands of Ctesias for the next few years. As regards the succession Babylonian tablets are evasive – best to continue dating by a dead King if you don't know who will be the new one. Of the illegitimate sons of Artaxerxes three were of consequence. One, Sekyndianos (Phot.) or Sogdianos (Diodorus) – perhaps Sugdyana – seized the throne by murdering Xerxes in his bed after a drinking bout when he had reigned only forty-five days.[10] Another, Okhos, was satrap in Hyrkania and married to his half-sister Parysatis. The couple rejected the blandishments of Sogdianos. Parysatis at least had considerable estates in Babylonia and may have been able to call up followers there. The usurper had meanwhile alienated the palace troops, not least by killing their commander in a personal quarrel. Okhos raised an army and was joined by the commander of the household cavalry and the satrap of Egypt.[11] Sogdianos had to surrender and was put to death after occupying the throne for six and a half months; Okhos then became King with the title of Darius (II). A few years later he had to contend with a revolt of his full brother Arsites. The driving force here was Megabyxos' son Artyphios, who may have succeeded his father in Syria. Artasyras, who appears again later as King's Eye at Kounaxa, was Darius' commander; he suffered two reverses against Artyphios but finally got the better of him by seducing his Greek mercenaries, and the two rebels were put to death. All this happened after 417 B.C. if this Arsites is the royal kinsman Arishittu who owned property in Babylonia.[12]

We must make allowance for Ctesias' love of the sensational. But it does look as though the 'Year of the Four Emperors' marks a change in the rules that the Persian nobility could not fail to apprehend: there could be a half-black Mikado. The three sons of Artaxerxes who contested the throne and Parysatis, who seems to have been the most strong-willed of them all, were not only illegitimate but, according to Ctesias, all born of Babylonian concubines; and those who did the plotting for them were mainly eunuchs, of whom one, the Paphlagonian Artoxares, eventually attempted to supplant Darius II (below, p. 136). Something of the prestige of Kingship must have vanished. As we have seen, the surviving son of Megabyxos revolted against Darius. Ctesias reports that at some time in his reign Teritoukhmes, son of a Hydarnes, who had succeeded his father as a satrap[13] and been compelled to take a daughter of Darius II in marriage, repudiated his allegiance and had to be killed.[14] In Egypt there are signs that trouble may have been brewing up before the revolt started there at the end of his reign (see Chap. XVIII n.4). Darius' last five years were occupied with rebellions nearer home. According to Xenophon one in Media (409 or 408 B.C.) was quickly settled; but in the humid jungle land (modern Gilan) where the western Elburz drops to the Caspian the people the Greeks called Kadousioi also revolted and could not be brought to heel. And before this there was a potentially serious revolt in the West by Pissouthnes, who as son of a Hystaspes is likely to have been either a grandson or nephew of Xerxes.

Sardis fades out of the picture after 479 B.C. when Xerxes left the West. Being barely two days' march from the territory of the confederate Greek cities of Colophon and Ephesus, it may have seemed too vulnerable a situation for a Persian satrap when Kimon was on the warpath; and it is tempting to suggest that for a while the satrapal seat was further inland (perhaps at Kelainai, where we know of a royal palace later in the century that was in fact said to have been built by Xerxes on his return from Greece).[15] But after the 'Peace of Kallias' (449 B.C.) Sardis was once again safe, and Pissouthnes had become satrap there at some date before 440 B.C. He was not above meddling in Greek affairs, though not to the extent of involving Persia in war with Greeks;[16] and he engaged Greek mercenaries for his service[17] – perhaps a sign that he had an inkling of what might happen after Artaxerxes died. Here we know too little. If it were the case that the younger Xerxes was known to be too incompetent or debauched to rule, Pissouthnes could have foreseen the danger of being put in a position where as a legitimate heir to the throne he must either reign or be consigned to the cinders. Under Darius II he rose in revolt. We have no indication that this was synchronized with the revolt of Megabyxos' son, but a date about 416 B.C. would fit both. Tissaphernes, son of a Hydarnes, was sent with two other nobles to overcome Pissouthnes; and after this was achieved by seducing his Greek mercenary commander, Tissaphernes stayed on as satrap in Sardis. But Pissouthnes' son Amorges maintained the revolt on the coast with Athenian support from 414 or earlier to 412 B.C. This drew Darius II into intervening against the Athenians in their war with Sparta; and from then on the King never ceased to be a potent force in Greek internal and inter-state politics.

The history of the Achaemenids in their last eighty years will be taken up later (Chapter XVIII). For the present purpose it may suffice to say that about 408 B.C. Darius II sent his second son Cyrus to assume command in the West; after giving the Spartans the aid they needed to defeat the Athenians, Cyrus built up an army with a strong Greek mercenary corps, and in 401 B.C. he marched against his brother Artaxerxes II who had succeeded to the throne in 405–4. He fell in battle at Kounaxa near Babylon. Artaxerxes II's forty-six year reign was one of almost uninterrupted decline of the central authority. He did succeed in clearing the Spartans out of Asia Minor and in

387 B.C. putting an end to war on the Greek front. But all his attempts to reconquer Egypt failed; and as the central power lost credibility satraps and vassals ceased to respond to control. It was only in the 340s that his more ruthless successor Artaxerxes III succeeded in re-establishing a semblance of the old imperial unity.

XIII King and Court

Cyrus the Great had the reputation of being kind and father-like; evidently he was approachable. Brought up in the purple, his son Cambyses proved to be a tyrant. Darius was strong-minded but he was a capable administrator and man of affairs who knew how to make use of advisers; and not having had a royal up-bringing he came to power by his own exertions and understood the need for unremitting effort. While maintaining the domination of the Persian nobility, he increased the distance between himself and his subjects; this appears not only in his own written words but in the reliefs where as King (or, some would say, in the guise of 'royal hero') he is elevated to almost superhuman stature and strength, towering above other men or nonchalantly throttling lions and stabbing monsters. Xerxes would seem to have been brought up in the shadow of his father, thus as King following in Darius' footsteps and perhaps too rigidly observing established protocol. The King was beginning to be imprisoned in a binding code of regal honour and Persian national pride, receptive of the flattery of courtiers and officials who would say only what they thought the King would wish to hear; from this it could be no great step to a court in which subservience became a cloak for venality, corruption, and in due course treachery – in fact the royal circle and harem whose scandals Ctesias enjoyed retailing. Darius' exaltation of his own status had the effect of making his successors too remote from what we should now call the grass-roots.

Plate 17

The pinnacle of power was a lonely perch. The King lived largely in seclusion; he is said by Xenophon to have prided himself on being inaccessible;[1] when he met his subjects or counsellors there seems to have been no frank discussion but monologues addressed with due reverence to the King. His physical powers must be unrivalled, with the result that it might be lèse-majesté to anticipate him at the kill.[2] He must do everything on a grander scale than others, and he was not supposed to revoke an order, still less go back on a promise that he had given. All men under the King's rule were his slaves,[3] so he had power of life and death. All property was at his disposal; and since he was the fountainhead of justice it was axiomatic that he could do no wrong. This appears in Herodotus' story (III 31) of Cambyses receiving the reply from his royal judges that they knew no law against his marrying his sister but there was one that the King of the Persians could do what he pleased.

To make a tragedy of Xerxes' 'hubris' in his *Persae* Aeschylus had to bring in a steadying voice of reason and moderation in the middle of the play. He therefore conjured up the ghost of Darius, who with supreme poetic licence is made to reprobate his son's presumptuousness in bridging the Straits and making war on the Athenians. In these circumstances Darius is presented as a semi-divine being; and though the ghost speaks of Xerxes as mortal the chorus is permitted to address Atossa as wife of a god and mother of a god, on which a scholiast made the obvious comment that the Persians call their kings gods.[4] Alexander the Great was induced to believe, or at least to wish others to concede, that he was a son of Zeus; and Curtius Rufus makes a flatterer encourage him to accept divinity by saying that the Persians worshipped their kings among the gods (VIII 5, 10). Isocrates also made a rhetorical remark about the King receiving homage due to a god. Some scholars therefore claim that the Persian Kings were worshipped as gods. But there is in fact no evidence that they were even deified after death (the statement of an Alexander historian that the Magi who guarded his tomb sacrificed a horse monthly to Cyrus the Great in no way proves it); and Darius' inscriptions show that deification did not enter his thoughts. In Egypt a Pharaoh was divine. But in the Near East, as in Greece, the notion was – and for 1,500 years had been – universally rejected as long as divinity was regarded as supernal. In general, legitimate kingship involved two factors: royal descent and selection by the appropriate deity. These are the two points that Darius stresses at the outset in his Behistun text, and we have seen Cyrus's propaganda claiming one or the other to justify his successive conquests.

Though not divine the Persian King was the elect of Ahuramazda, whose regent he was on earth. It was therefore, as we have seen, a sovereign imperium that he received. In early Achaemenid times the King seems to have designated his successor by delegating the kingship of Babylon to him; but after Xerxes repudiated that throne in 482/81 B.C. the practice was discontinued. In selecting Xerxes, who was son of Atossa and Cyrus' eldest grandson, Darius set a precedent of preferring the first son born in the purple which is said to have helped to whet Cyrus the Younger's ambition to win the throne in place of his elder brother.[5] It would seem that after Xerxes there was a normal expectation that a King's eldest son would succeed him,[6] and Artaxerxes II did actually designate his eldest son as his successor. Intrigue and in-fighting as often as not produced a different result; but no one except Artaxerxes III was bloodthirsty enough to put all possible rivals to death in the way that Parthians and Ottomans did or even blind them as the Safavids commonly did. The empire was fortunate in the longevity of the survivors of the accession struggles. Between 522 and 337 B.C. six Kings averaged over 30 years' reign each. To lend legitimacy to their rule the successors of Artaxerxes I assumed the time-honoured throne names by which we know them: according to our Greek sources both Darius II and Artaxerxes III had been named Okhos (Wahauka), Artaxerxes II Arsakas, and Darius III Kodomannos, while Arses may also have taken the name Artaxerxes (IV) – as did Bessos in 330 B.C.

Fairly clearly Darius I, like Shah Abbas, did not read or write ('it was inscribed and was read off before me', he says at Behistun). From the Greek writers we get some idea of Persian education; but it applies only to the nobility, and there was no place for what we should call intellectual pursuits. From what we can gather, the sons of Persians of note were weaned from the harem at the age of five (when for the first time they were allowed in the presence of their fathers), and until they were twenty or more they were brought up at the royal court (or in the provinces at the satraps' courts). Emphasis was laid on speaking the truth and learning the examples that the legends provided; older children might listen to the judgements of the royal justices. Herodotus says that among the Persians the thing most prized after valour in battle was to be the father of many children (I 136); we can understand that the aim was to contribute the maximum to Persian military strength, and the result must have been a population explosion at the higher social level. The young underwent a hard training in the physical skills that were needed and the accompanying virtues – the observation of Chardin in the seventeenth century and later travellers that it was only in adult life after the age of twenty that they learned to deceive is echoed in the ancient sources such as Xenophon's *Anabasis* (I 9, 3–4). They were practised in riding, shooting the bow and throwing the spear, in hunting and tracking. Darius himself declared in his tomb inscription: 'trained am I both with hands and with feet; as a horseman I am a good horseman; as a bowman I am a good bowman, both afoot and on horseback; as a spearman I am a good spearman, both afoot and on horseback' (Kent). As in Greece, music seems to have played its part. Royal princes no doubt did not lack for companions of their own age and learned leadership in field exercises. But there is no hint of their receiving training in the exercise of royal power. When Cyrus first turned over the kingship of Babylon to his elder son Cambyses, he may have had in mind that he should gain experience in government; but in effect a satrap was in charge there; and the kingship of Babylon, which Xerxes also held before his father's death, may seem to have been as titular an office as the Viceroyship of Tabriz in late Kajar times or the Princedom of Wales at the present day.

Cyrus the Great left two sons and three daughters behind him, all by the one wife, Kassandane. As a usurper Darius I was concerning himself with creating a dynasty. He made use of his closest relatives. His father commanded in Parthia in 521 B.C., and Parnaka who was made controller in Persis (above, p. 89) was probably his father's brother. Of his own three younger brothers known to us one, Artanes, died, but Artaphernes (who was a half-brother according to Herodotus) served for many years as satrap in Sardis, and it is probably the other brother Artabanos who appears in a Persepolis tablet of 500 B.C. as satrap of Baktria – two key posts in West and East. By his six known wives Darius had a considerable progeny. The husbands of four daughters of his were army commanders in the West in the 490s (and another in 480); seven or eight of Darius' nephews held commands at different times in the West, while one, Sataspes, was put to death by Xerxes after failing to expiate a crime of passion by completing a circumnavigation of Africa. Of Darius' twelve known sons eleven went on the expedition to Greece in 480 B.C. (see Chap. XI n.6). Key satrapies were by then going to princes of the blood royal. Darius had made up for his lack of royal fathers by 'having children whom he might make princes in all lands'. In an expanding and belligerent empire such numbers could be accommodated and still leave room for other noble Persian (or at least Achaemenid) families who tended to form their own little dynasties in some of the satrapies (below, p. 171).

The Persian King recognized no equal in the world. There could be no concert of powers, or even balance of kingdoms such as the ancient world saw in Hittite times or in the generations before Cyrus and after Alexander. The King could not marry a foreign princess or give his sisters and daughters in marriage abroad. His daughters could be bestowed on high Persian nobles as a reward for good service or possibly to limit their ambition – an honour that does not seem always to have been acceptable.[7] By the compact of 522 B.C. the King might take wives only from among the families of the Seven.[8] This did not prevent him from having concubines; but from the reign of Xerxes on it created a distinction between legitimate sons and bastards, of which latter only Darius II was able to establish himself successfully on the throne (it was said that Artaxerxes II would have preferred a bastard to be his successor rather than Okhos, below, p. 222). It was partly as a matter of policy that Darius I had half a dozen wives; three of them were the princesses in whose veins flowed the last of the blood of Cyrus, two were daughters of the paladins Gobryas (Darius' first wife) and Otanes (already said to have been in Cambyses' harem), and the sixth was his brother Artanes' only child. Xerxes seems to have had only one wife, the pitiless and long-lived Amestris, daughter of Otanes;[9] we also hear of a couple of amours of his. From then on the Kings appear as virtually monogamous – at least from Ctesias we gain the impression that Damaspia and Parysatis were the sole accredited partners of Artaxerxes I and Darius II, Dinon spoke as though there was only a single queen, and we have plenty of evidence of sincere affection, or at least confidence, between husband and wife. Indeed it is Darius I whose marital relations seem to be the exception. The children of all his wives ranked as legitimate. But Atossa, eldest of Cyrus' daughters, may have had a special position. Junge perhaps went too far when he dubbed her 'Königin des Reichs', a phrase which recalls the 'Queen of the Nation' of Sassanid times and 'Glory of the Empire' (as the Kajar heir apparent's mother was called). But it has been suggested that she is the 'banuka' (Mistress) of a Persepolis tablet. Presumably she enjoyed the authority in the harem that was commanded by queen-mothers such as Parysatis and, at the end of the empire, Sisigambis. This was nothing new in the Near East. Sammuramat, the supposed historical prototype of Semiramis, is thought to have ruled Assyria for several years in the ninth century until her son took over, and the mothers of Esarhaddon and Nabunaid appear alongside their sons in the realm (the latter died in 547 B.C., having remained physically and mentally sound and 'with meat and drink agreeing with her' to the age of 104, while the former obtained the throne not only for Esarhaddon but on his death for Ashurbanipal).

Ouseley long ago remarked that women have no place in Achaemenid court art. But if we may judge by what we hear of the queens, Persian women could be masterful, and Amestris and Parysatis were more bloodthirsty than any of the Kings except perhaps Artaxerxes III. They could own considerable properties. A sizeable city called Anthylla on the Canopic branch of the Nile was reserved to the Persian Queen for the provision of shoes, and some villages in North Syria were named 'Parysatis' girdle'. Plato speaks of the queen's 'girdle' as rich country nearly a day's journey in length and adds her 'veil' and other unspecified items of adornment; we are reminded of Athens which was assigned to the revenues of the Sultan's harem in the mid eighteenth century and administered through a voivode by the Chief Eunuch. Parysatis also owned villages east of the Tigris and land in Babylonia (perhaps her own inheritance);[10] we have already mentioned Artystone's properties in Persis (above, p. 74). Herodotus speaks of a personal 'army' as a typical Persian gift from the King to a royal lady (IX 109).

The fourth-century Greek writers spoke of 360 concubines in the King's harem – one for each day of the year; and Darius III was reported to have lost 329 when he fled from Alexander in Syria. Compared with the Parthians, Sassanids, and Safavids this seems a niggardly quota: the Suren had 200 carriage loads, Chosroes II 3,000 or 12,000 women, and Shah Abbas 4,000 according to Herbert; Jahangir the Mogul contented himself with 1,000 (Coryate). According to Herakleides of Kyme 300 concubines slept by day so that at night they could watch over the King with music and song by lamplight. Herodotus speaks of the women in Smerdis' harem taking their turn, but at that early time they may have been fewer and perhaps all wives. When the King went on safari they were transported in closed carriages so that they should not be seen by ordinary human eyes. Candidates for the harem, likewise closeted, were sent up from the provinces, though not so far as we know selected in accordance with specifications of ideal beauty such as the Sassanid Chosroes II circulated to his governors. In Ctesias we hear of the Babylonian concubines whose children aimed at the throne (above, p. 129).

Eunuchs were needed to serve in the harem but came to assume an increasingly important role in the life of the court generally. They of course had a long history in the Near East; we even hear of Greeks engaged in this form of slave trade from the early sixth century B.C. Xenophon seeks to justify the usage, which he dates back to Cyrus the Great in Persia – Hellanicus said that the Persians learned castration from the Babylonians. In Herodotus we meet one, Hermotimos of Pedasa in Caria, who, he says (VIII 104–05), rose to be the most highly esteemed of all Xerxes' eunuchs, was sent on a commission in Mysia, and was put in charge of the royal children when they were shipped back from Greece in Artemisia's trireme. We have no reason to suppose that at that stage eunuchs aspired to be more than trusty servants, though one belonging to Xerxes' cousin Sataspes was able to escape with a fortune when his master was put to death. Under Artaxerxes I eunuchs gained more influence at court. Nehemiah rose not only to be King's cup-bearer – a position that under Cambyses was filled by a high noble's son – but to procure for himself the governorship of Judah. If we trust Ctesias, Artoxares the Paphlagonian was sent on important missions by Artaxerxes I and became a king-maker after his death; eventually he learned to his cost that the one thing a eunuch could not do was to become King himself. Artoxares acquired great wealth if he is the Artahsaru whom Babylonian tablets show as owning villages and having a staff of officials in the 420s.[11]

Artaxerxes I according to Ctesias had one legitimate son and seventeen by his concubines, and Artaxerxes II is said to have had three legitimate out of 115. The progeny of the harem must have built up into a social problem. Curzon spoke of the 'plague of royal drones' – the 'shahzades' who kept courts and harems and lived on pensions, occupying lucrative positions in the provinces of Iran under Nasreddin Shah in the nineteenth century. We hear of next to nothing comparable to this in Achaemenid times.[12] On the other hand we read in Curtius Rufus of a company of 200 who were the noblest of Darius III's 'propinqui' and flanked him on the march, and a body of 15,000 effeminate-looking 'cognati' of the King whose place in the column was in front of the royal wardrobe (III 3, 21 and 14). The propinqui were presumably relatives of the King, and the cognati perhaps represent a wider circle of kinsmen who frequented the court as pensioners, clocking in for their breakfast and escorting the King when he went travelling or hunting. The number 15,000 was regularly given as that of the King's guests at his table; so we may suppose that the ever-accumulating swarm of 'royal drones' was mainly retained in the King's entourage (perhaps serving in the guards regiments) and not let loose on the provinces of the empire. It is perhaps not fanciful to think of these kinsmen when we look at the carved stone balustrades with their files of courtiers and gentlemen-at-arms trooping into the reception rooms at Persepolis.

Plate 19

At his coronation ceremony at Pasargadai the King was expected to consume a peasant meal of fig-cake, turpentine wood, and sour milk, probably as a reminder not so much of the humble origin of the Achaemenids (Achaemenes being evidently regarded as a foundling) but of Cyrus' meagre fare there before the decisive battle with Astyages (above, p. 27). This together with Herodotus' story of Cyrus speaking of hardy countries producing hardy warriors, is at the root of a moralizing Greek tradition of Persian native frugality which in due course yielded to luxury as the spoils of empire were opened to them. There will of course be a certain element of truth in this. But as with the Romans, that pristine simplicity that we are taught to admire always recedes into a more distant past as we try to trace it back. The Pasargadai site shows us that Cyrus the Great had no scruples about opulence. He does not seem to have hesitated to take over the elaborate Median court style and dress; and his satraps were expected to imitate his prodigality. Luxurious living was easily come by because it was at the expense of the conquered peoples. But the besetting fault of the Achaemenids was rather their covetousness. There are exceptions, and probably, avaricious as he was, Darius I was the most notable. But in general they tended to regard wealth as something to be hoarded and not used to create prosperity. They had treasuries in their different royal seats; at Persepolis we hear of a treasurer (ganzabara), deputy treasurer (upaganzabara), and a large staff. According to Polykritos in the fourth century the gold and silver were kept in the form of valuables or bullion, and coin was only struck as needed. Paradoxical as it may sound, their hoarding of wealth was probably a worse fault of the Kings than their profligacy.

In the last hundred years of the empire diplomatic missions were constantly going up to the Persian court from the Greek cities; and a lively curiosity was thus aroused among people unaccustomed to such a display of pomp and extravagance. In Persian eyes the Greeks lived in penury, unable to lay a bed fit to sleep on and finishing their meal before any serious eating had begun (while still hungry, Herodotus says). The Greeks on their side found much that as moralists they could impugn, but envy was not far away. The literature on the subject of the Persian court was mostly ephemeral; but we have a wealth of citations in later writers (especially from Athenaeus), and at points we can supplement the written word with the visual evidence of Persian reliefs.

The King was an impressive sight; Herodotus leaves us in no doubt of that. He presented so colourful a spectacle that later writers likened him to a peacock. Despite the many representations of the Kings on reliefs scholars are not yet agreed whether his robe was in two pieces or (as it would rather appear) one; the folds on reliefs reflect a Greek style of carving, but the costume itself was reputedly Median.[13] Xenophon, whose *Cyropaedia* is particularly informative here, describes what sounds like winter wear: a long purple overmantle, full in the sleeves and embroidered with designs in gold, on top of a striped robe or tunic and crimson trousers. A high flat-topped cap (the 'kidaris') distinguished the King; it was probably of felt, and we are told it had a scented blue and white ribbon. On the evidence of the monuments a

Plate 8   crown was worn in public, as at Behistun where Darius I's crenellated mural crown makes its first appearance; it was not unique to him, and in particular it graces the lapis lazuli head of a beardless prince from Persepolis in Teheran.[14] The King had a golden sceptre, and out of doors a parasol was held over his head to preserve his complexion; like other noble Persians he was at pains to protect himself from heat and cold. His throne was high; it had a footstool and a purple canopy that rested on columns. Jewelry hung from the King's ears, neck, and wrists. Plutarch transmits to us an estimate of 12,000 talents (say, £3 million gold) as the value of what Artaxerxes II stood up in.[15]

Plate 9   Pages with wands were the ushers. The master of audiences whom we see on the Treasury reliefs was probably the 'hazarapatish' or chiliarch (below, p. 143f.). He inclines his body forward by way of reverence; his raised hand may be keeping his breath from approaching the King. Scholars seem now inclined to believe that this is the posture of obeisance which the Greeks called 'proskynesis' and regarded as due only to the gods; and the gesture is interpreted as blowing a kiss.[16] But Herodotus speaks of the Persian obeisance as 'falling down' before a superior and even 'on one's head' before the King (I 134, VII 136), and in Curtius Rufus it is described as lying or prostrating the body on the ground, and with the chin touching the earth; a dissenting Theban ambassador was said to have got away with dropping his ring on the floor and stooping to pick it up. It is difficult to believe that Macedonians would have found the posture on the reliefs so excessively degrading that they refused to comply. Hands must be kept in the sleeves by those who approached the King. Servants in close attendance were muffled lest their breath touch him. Napkin and scent bottle were held in reserve, a fly whisk

Plate 9   was at the ready, and censers stood in front of the King. Reliefs show us

servants of various kinds and ferrashes carrying rugs or robes, whips, and the   *Plate 23*
King's stool for mounting. Within the palace the King walked on purple   *(top left)*
carpets which no feet but his might touch. They are spoken of as of Sardis. But
since Macedonians and Greeks set great store by tapestries and carpets,
generally with animal designs, that were produced in the Near Eastern lands,
the reference may be to colour rather than provenance.[17] The King was not
expected to go on foot outside the palace; it was probably as true in
Achaemenid times as in recent memory that out of doors all Persians of
dignity would ride however short the distance they had to cover. Artaxerxes
II was the freak in this respect – marching on foot all day up the mountain
paths of Gilan at the head of his troops, in all his royal robes with his shield
and bow-case and finding the humblest food palatable.[18]

According to Ctesias and Dinon the King dined 15,000 guests, and the
meal cost 400 talents. Herakleides of Kyme is quoted at some length by
Athenaeus (IV 145–46):

> the attendants at the Persian King's table bathe and dress in
> white, and they spend nearly half the day seeing to the dinner.
> Of the King's guests some dine outside in full view of the
> public, others indoors with the King. But even the latter do not
> dine with the King; there are two apartments opposite one
> another, and the King breakfasts[19] in one while his fellow-
> diners are in the other. The King can see them through the
> curtain in the doorway, but they cannot see him. Occasionally
> however on a feast-day they all dine in one room with the King
> in the great hall. If, as often happens, the King has a drinking
> party, up to a dozen guests may be called into his presence by a
> eunuch after the meal is finished. They drink with him, but not
> the same wine, and they sit on the floor while he reclines on a
> couch with gold feet; they go away when they have drunk to
> excess. The King generally breakfasts and dines alone, though
> on occasions his wife and some of his sons dine with him.[20]
> During dinner the concubines sing and play on the strings for
> him; one acts as soloist while the rest sing in chorus.

It sounds extravagant, Herakleides remarks. But, the quotation from him
continues,

> in fact the cost of the dinner will be found on examination to
> have been calculated economically; and the same applies with
> other Persians of the ruling class. A thousand animals are
> slaughtered daily for the King; they comprise horses, camels,
> oxen, donkeys, deer, and above all sheep. Much poultry also is
> consumed – ostriches, geese, and cocks. Modest helpings are
> set before the diners, and each carries away what is left over at
> the breakfast. The greater part of the roasts and breadstuffs,
> however, are carried out into the courtyard for the guards and
> light infantry that the King maintains, and they divide it up into

equal portions of meat and bread. So they are paid in rations by
the King whereas in Greece mercenaries get their pay in money.
In the same way other Persians of the ruling class have all the
foodstuffs put on the table at once. When the guests have
dined, what is left, which is mainly meat and bread, is given by
the table superintendant to the servants, so that in this way
each gets his daily food. The most honourable of the King's
guests get leave to attend at breakfast only, thus avoiding a
second journey and being free to entertain their own guests.

Athenaeus seeks to justify Ctesias' and Dinon's estimate of 400 talents by
comparing the cost of Alexander the Great's much smaller dinner parties. But
it does seem excessive; and he has just cited Theopompus as saying that when
the King visits any of his subjects 20 or even 30 talents are spent on the dinner
– this could include gold vessels and furnishings that were carried away by the
retinue.[21] The figure of 400 talents could well have no better foundation than
the estimate in Herodotus for feeding Xerxes with his army (above, p. 110).
What did almost scandalize the Greeks was the amount of meat the Persians
ate, quite apart from all the sweetmeats. Herodotus also speaks of an annual
dinner which the King provided on his birthday, when he anointed his head
and gave presents (IX 110) – in fact, he says, all Persian men give a birthday
feast, sacrificing an animal according to their means (I 133). Also annually on
the festival of Mithra the King danced the shield-dance in a state of
intoxication.

As regards payment in kind we have seen such a system at work in the
Persepolis tablets. In a mainly non-monetary economy it evidently continued
in theory at least as the notional remuneration of office-holders such as the
satrap of Babylonia (Hdt I 192) and the basis on which Themistocles was
given three towns to provide him with bread, wine, and fish.[22] Lewis has
charmingly remarked that the story that Cyrus the Younger revolted because
his dinner allowance did not satisfy him may not be so silly as Plutarch
thought.[23] Subordinate governors fed local notables at their court (150 in the
case of Nehemiah at Jerusalem and of Iranian nobles in later times). A mean
figure of 1,500 at satraps' tables might seem reasonable.

The King drank choice wines, especially (Posidonius said exclusively) the
Chalybonian which was the drink of great kings of old; it was made from
vines above Damascus. With true oriental fastidiousness the King could not
stomach the local water when travelling and had cart-loads of his easily
digestible boiled 'golden water' brought from the Choaspes at Susa; but back
in Susa he demanded water from distant rivers such as the Nile and even, it
was said, the Danube.[24] Incense came in the biennial gifts from Arabs who,
Herodotus says, were not subjects of the King. Scents were in demand; among
various oils mentioned that of the Karmanian thorn may have been made
from acacia. The royal unguents achieved fame because of the capture of
Darius III's travelling ointment chest by Alexander; the most exotic was a
skin-cream of gum-ladanum boiled in lion's fat, to which saffron and palm
wine were added. Many people were employed in devising new refinements

for the King's whims. Other specialities of the court that are mentioned were wheat from Assos in the Troad (perhaps fetched there from Eresos in Lesbos) and salt from the oasis of Ammon. Ctesias seems to have been the principal authority on the royal cuisine but he was criticized for failing to mention pepper and vinegar.[25] A remarkably comprehensive list of foodstuffs and flavourings consumed daily at the King's breakfast and dinner is given by Polyaenus (IV 32); precise quantities of each are stated, and the menu in 'Media' differs from that in Susa and Babylon (where for instance half the wine is from grapes and half is palm-wine). The whole is said to have been inscribed in the palace on a bronze pillar which Alexander the Great was able to make his men read – thus allowing a stratagem. There is no word of this in Plutarch or Athenaeus, and the invention of the bronze column seems too ridiculous to stem from Ctesias or Dinon; but Polyaenus, who was hard-pressed to fill eight books with stratagems and stronger in resource than research, may have found such a list in some little-known book.

As regards doctors, Darius I maintained Egyptian specialists;[26] but when he dislocated his ankle it was a Greek, Demokedes, who put it right; Demokedes also cured Atossa when she suffered from a breast swelling.[27] He subsequently made his escape; and according to Hinz' spirited interpretation of a Persepolis tablet a court apothecary named Ziwakka had the task of treating the King for a couple of months there – at least Aspathines did authorize two months extra rations in arrears for a person of that name at the end of September 494 B.C.[28] A generation later we hear of another Greek doctor at the court, Apollonides the Asklepiad of Cos, who restored Megabyxos to health after he had nearly died of his wounds. He is said to have come to a bad end after he prescribed intercourse as a cure for Megabyxos' sexy widow Amytis but aggravated her malady by his treatment; our knowledge of him, however, comes from Ctesias, who was an Asklepiad of the rival school of Knidos. Then Ctesias himself seems to have been a doctor at court for seventeen years (above, p. 21); and another Greek, Polykritos of Mende, was there when he left. Babylon does not seem to have produced leading doctors. We may smile at Herodotus when he tells us with approval that the sick were brought to their doors to obtain advice from passers-by (I 197); but it is probably symptomatic of a failure to rise much above a combination of magic and the old pharmacopoeia. The Houses of Life were the repositories of medical lore in Egypt (above, p. 71); it could be that even before Hippocrates the Greek medical schools were producing the best general practitioners, but the Egyptian doctors at the court have not had a fair press.

We have mentioned that the King danced the shield-dance which the Greeks called the Persikon at the Mithra festival – this was the occasion in the year when he was required to get drunk; the Persians danced for exercise, taking to it as naturally as to riding.[29] They drank heavily but did not become disorderly; Cyrus the Younger is said to have prided himself on his ability to drink more than his brother and carry it better. Herodotus implies that the Persians normally deliberated when drunk and reviewed their decisions next day when sober (or vice-versa). They had a passion for gold cups; Ctesias says

that when in disgrace they were punished by being served off terracotta. Song had its place. We hear of a minstrel at Astyages' court; and deeds of gods and men (not least of Cyrus the Great) entered into the repertory for children, though we also hear of an ode on the 360 different uses of the palm.[30] Stringed instruments were used, and there was a Persian mode of flute playing. Wood-working obtains mention as a royal hobby, though in this the Achaemenids are not likely to have compared with Seljuks like Aladdin Keykobad. The pastime which the Kings most favoured was the traditional
Plate 36   oriental one of hunting. Hundreds of beasts of burden will have been loaded with netting and a great tract of country fenced in. The beaters then drove the game to the King. Though not perhaps on a par with the Shahs of 500 years ago, or even the Duke of Shiraz (in Shah Abbas' time) who is said to have had 20,000 beaters and a train of 600 camels for the netting, the Achaemenids certainly made a great carnage; and the 'royal drones' could have earned their keep here. Wives, or at least concubines, were not left behind. With their liking for beautiful surroundings and shade the Persians of course made a virtue of planting trees. In addition to the numerous paradises of which we
Plates 28–9   read, the Apadana reliefs of Persepolis show young pines flanking the roadway;[31] trees were planted around the Tomb of Cyrus; Xerxes adorned a great plane tree in Lydia with gold and set an immortal custodian in charge of it (in the event it is the tree that has been immortalized as the 'ombra vegetabile' of Handel's *Largo*); Parysatis evidently had palm trees planted at the grave mound of her son Cyrus' mercenary leader Klearchos; and Xenophon has Cyrus the Younger tell Lysander that he himself planted trees in his park at Sardis and would never dine without having sweated from some exercise of military training, gardening, or the like.

Novelties were always much sought after, and the King gave lavish rewards to their inventors. Prizes were also given for military turn-out and achievements, athletics, having the most children, for interpreting the King's dreams, and even for removing the most scorpions on the King's route. In gentle mockery the Greeks later said that Gaugamela (Camel Pasture), where Alexander won his decisive victory in 331 B.C., was so called because it had been given as a prize by Darius to the camel that put up the best performance on his Scythian expedition. The Achaemenid is the one period of Iranian history in which we do not seem to hear of robes of honour being presented by the rulers; but it must be an accident of our sources, because they had already appeared as presents to Persian emissaries in pre-Achaemenid texts at Susa. The Achaemenids were not alone in being past-masters in the art of torture. From Ctesias and those who drew on him we know more than a dozen ways in which Darius II and Parysatis inflicted the death penalty, some almost exquisitely horrible. Half of them were among those used by the Sassanids (who added trampling underfoot by elephants) and down even into Kajar times when a less lingering method of despatch was devised by blowing the victim out of a gun.

We have seen that eunuch chamberlains and cupbearers were becoming more influential under Artaxerxes I; and in the last years of the empire Bagoas had almost attained the supreme power when Darius III compelled him to drink first (below, p. 225). But this should not blind us to the fact that there were leading positions at court which were held by Persian nobles. We know of Darius I's spear-bearer and perhaps two successive bow-bearers (Gobryas, Intaphernes and certainly Aspathines); we hear nothing of these offices under his successors, but the places are filled on their carved tomb fronts. Xerxes' charioteer, Patiramphes, was son of Otanes. The Greeks found a source of amusement in the official they called the King's Eye. Xenophon in his *Cyropaedia* expressly stated that this was not a unique office, and he claimed that the King had many 'eyes' and 'ears' who kept him informed. As regards the 'ears' he has the support of a fifth-century papyrus from Elephantine which speaks of 'listeners' (a word corresponding to Old Persian 'gaushaka') in Achaemenid Egypt. So we can accept that the raj had such informers; indeed Herodotus traces secret informers back to the beginning of the Median kingdom under Deiokes. But according to Plutarch (probably following Ctesias) there was an official with the title of King's Eye who brought Artaxerxes II the news that his brother Cyrus was dead on the battlefield; and the three fifth-century Greek writers, Aeschylus, Herodotus, and Aristophanes, all speak as though the King had a trusty servant who was called his Eye. Schaeder examined the question from a philological angle and found reason in his study of later Iranian institutions to project back into Achaemenid times a court title such as 'spathaka' ('he who spies').[32] This is of course not proved; but it seems better founded than recent ingenious theories which impute to the Greeks or Aramaic scribes a misunderstanding of the word and seek other connections in later Iranian titles or alternatively relate the title to the divine eye of the sun. It does not seem possible to project back into Achaemenid times a regular office of Secundus ad Regem – Xerxes says his father made him 'after himself greatest' (XPf), but that was a matter of Darius nominating his successor. There was one position in the Achaemenid hierarchy which could outweigh all others in power and influence; but that was the chiliarchy, to which we now turn.

Chiliarch is a Greek term meaning 'commander of a Thousand'. In Ctesias, confirmed by late writers, we hear of an important court official called the 'azarapates',[33] who would seem to be the master of the royal audiences. That this represents an Old Persian word 'hazarapatish' (commander of a thousand) is confirmed by two facts: first that Alexander appointed a chiliarch in imitation of the Persian court set-up, and second that what we should call the Grand Vizier at the Sassanid court was called the 'hazarbadh'. From the Greek writers we can piece together that this officer in Achaemenid times not only controlled the King's audiences but brought in messages and commanded the wand-bearing pages or ushers. One passage in Plutarch, which gives us the name Artabanos (Ctesias' Artapanos) for the chiliarch who received Themistocles in preparation for his audience, refers to a second chiliarch present at the court (Roxanes);[34] but everything else points to its being a unique office, and Plutarch may have uncritically combined two versions of the story which named the chiliarchs of Xerxes and Artaxerxes I. When we add to this the command of the King's bodyguard of a thousand,[35]

Plate 9

the chiliarch would be a powerful figure; the duties seem to fit admirably with the figure in military costume whom we see saluting the King on the Treasury reliefs.

We have clear evidence of the chiliarch's importance in the fourth century when Tithraustes dealt with Konon,[36] took charge in the West when Tissaphernes had to be removed, and continued in the post at court for most of the reign of Artaxerxes II, and when the audience-master Aristazanes was said to be Artaxerxes III's most trusted friend after the eunuch Bagoas.[37] The office thus seems to have been one of considerable trust from at least the end of Xerxes' reign. Before this we know of Hydarnes, son presumably of the paladin Hydarnes. He was commander of the Immortals in 481–80 B.C. but insisted on returning from Greece with the King while the main body of the Immortals stayed behind; he would therefore seem to have had the King's special bodyguard of a thousand under his command and so have been the chiliarch. It was he who received the two Spartans who were on their way to Xerxes to expiate blood guilt; curiously Herodotus places him in the West at the time (VII 135), but it might make better sense to suppose that in this case Herodotus has misunderstood and that Hydarnes received them at court as chiliarch. We do hear of a chiliarch with Darius I on his Scythian expedition.[38] But our authority, Clement of Alexandria, is an unreliable one, and his attribution to the venerable early mythologist Pherekydes is improbable; what we can reasonably conclude from this is that some writer thought he could improve on Herodotus, but we cannot say whether he was justified in doing so. If a unique office of chiliarch-hazarapatish could in fact be traced back to early in Darius I's reign, then we need have no hesitation in regarding Prexaspes as the hazarapatish under Cambyses; he was the King's right-hand man and dealt with callers, and Herodotus names him as the official who brought in the messages (III 34). Junge, to whom we owe the fundamental study of this office,[39] was led into assigning to its holder the control of the chancery, the King's council, and the treasury, of which the last at least was based on arguments that are now no longer tenable; but he was probably right in seeing the hazarapatish as potentially (and often in practice) the most important person at court after the King from an early stage in the history of the empire. In that case we could suspect that with his high-ranking spear and bow bearers Darius I was spreading the duties so that no one official should have too great a share of the power.

Herodotus tells us of three occasions when a King summoned the most eminent Persians in his train or at his court to sit in council with him – Cambyses to give his last instructions in Syria (III 65), Darius to plan the death of the rebellious satrap Oroites (III 127), and Xerxes to decide whether or not to make an expedition against Athens (VIII 8). Apart from these specially convened meetings and the councils of war that Xerxes held at the Hellespont and in Greece, we have no word of any council of state. The Book of Esther, which does not lack patches of local colour, speaks of 'Seven princes of Persia and Media which saw the King's face and sat the first in the kingdom' (1, 14); and this was at one time regarded as evidence of a Council of Seven consisting of the seven families of the Magus-killers. In fact, with

Darius as one of the Seven and Intaphernes' family wiped out, there could only have been five of them to form a King's council. But the number seven still stands. First, Ezra seems to have claimed that he received his firman to establish the law in Jerusalem from 'the King and his seven counsellors' (7, 14); and secondly, on his march to contest the throne and already acting as King, Cyrus the Younger summoned the seven noblest Persians in his train into council to court-martial his relative Orontes who was caught negotiating with the King.[40] We know of King's judges, who were appointed for life and evidently were available at court when the King had cases to submit to them. So since both known instances of councils of seven were concerned with law, it is tempting to assume that the King had a panel of seven judges whom he could call into council; indeed though the Book of Esther has no historical value, the seven Persians there were consulted by Ahasuerus (Xerxes) as wise men who knew law and judgement. There is no evidence of anything that we could call a council of ministers; only in Sassanid times did the sort of specialization of functions appear that would justify the use of the term 'minister'.

In general we find in all the Greek writers that the King regularly made decisions on his own responsibility; and the same appears in Darius I's instructions to his officials in Egypt and Artaxerxes I's appointment of Nehemiah to the governorship of Judah. State records, however, must have been kept, as Greek and Old Testament writers indicate. That this could create a problem is shown by the story of the search for Cyrus' decree referring to the Jerusalem temple (above, p. 61). Cyrus and Cambyses may not have had a single central repository for their archives, and Agbatana seems to have continued as a functioning centre.[41] But under Darius I a centralized record system must have been needed. Greek writers speak of the King moving seasonally from one capital to another, like our mediaeval sovereigns who moved around with their courts consuming their revenues on the spot; and there is ground for believing that they took vacations at their high-altitude palaces in high summer. But their archives could hardly have been transported with them; and the distances are such that each of these royal progresses would have involved weeks of travelling if the whole court was on the move.[42] The Fortification tablets show that Darius on occasions visited Persepolis, and Lewis has worked out that he spent winter 495–94 at least there. But except in high summer his normal residence seems to have been Susa; and Aeschylus, Herodotus (two dozen times), and the Old Testament writers regularly speak as though Susa was the recognized capital and seat of the King. In a couple of instances we can even correct them (Aeschylus making Darius' ghost rise from the tomb at Susa, and Herodotus placing Cambyses' palace and the killing of Smerdis there). For a time after the Susa palace had been burned down under Artaxerxes I Babylon seems to have been favoured by the King's presence. But apart from this, Achaemenid rule from early in Darius I's reign seems to have been centred on Susa.

In early Achaemenid times the empire was becoming less feudal and more bureaucratic. Thanks to Darius I its financial structure was securely organized, though with an increasingly high proportion of the revenues going into the well-stocked treasury. Provincial government was equally firmly organ-ized, and the military establishment was well maintained. Darius had evi-dently given personal attention to communications in his huge empire, to the control of officials in the satrapies, and the enforcement of law. Reasonably firm centralized rule probably continued for a couple of generations after him; and Achaemenid government at that time may have compared not unfavourably with that of Tudor England. There was of course no parlia-ment, still less the federal diet of representatives of the subject peoples that some scholars have sought to find, though the Persian habit of subjects with a grievance flocking to the King's or governor's gate and making loud protests is as old as the Achaemenids.[43] But the real weakness that one can perhaps detect after the reign of Darius lay in the absence of a consultative body to which the King could regularly turn – in fact the absence of a council of chief officers of state on whose collective wisdom and individual experience he could draw in reaching decisions. This might have helped to obviate the dilatoriness, the lack of stability in major matters of policy, and the clashes of personality that resulted from arbitrary rule.

XIV Old Persian Religion

Darius I regarded himself as being under the special protection of Ahuramazda. If we add together what he says in his various royal inscriptions, Ahuramazda is a great god, the greatest of the gods, he made this earth and yonder sky (a phrase that Darius found apposite on cliff faces, as Naksh-i Rustam and Mt Elvend, where the sky was far away in the zenith), he created *Plate 5* man and well-being for man, he created Darius and bestowed the Kingship on him, he gave him the good land possessed of good horses and good men, he gave him the great kingdom with mountains and flat land, this side of the sea and the other side of the sea, this side of the desert and the other side of the desert, in fact this great earth far and wide; divine blessing in life and in death, many children and long life will be upon those who worship him; by the favour of Ahuramazda may their farmsteads, their livestock, and their labourers be assured to them, may Ahuramazda protect the land from invaders, famine, and the Lie.

There is nothing that Darius did or was but he attributes it to Ahuramazda's favour; and the scope of the god's omnipotence seems to increase as we follow his royal inscriptions down. It is implicit in Darius' thought that in the world-wide struggle between good and evil Ahuramazda is the upholder of Justice, and so with his aid Darius is triumphant over the Lie – Ahuramazda delivered the rebels into his hand. Darius casually mentions the 'other gods that are' as also assisting because he was not hostile.[1] But he allows them no role. He does not name them, nor do any of his successors in their inscriptions until Artaxerxes II recognizes Anahita and Mithra along with Ahuramazda. On a baked brick stamp at Susa (DSk) Darius says 'of me is Ahuramazda, of Ahuramazda am I'; so we should be justified in speaking of the god of Darius in the way that we speak of the god of Abraham.

The inscriptions clearly indicate the polarization of Justice (or Truth) and the Lie. Apart from this, the Persians of Achaemenid times were notable, to judge by contemporary evidence, in worshipping the triad of deities Ahuramazda, Anahita, and Mithra, who were to be the principal divinities in the Avesta, in worshipping fire as divine, and in having the Magi as their priests. This religion had a wide currency among the Iranians, and there is no sign of any feeling that it was the exclusive property of a chosen people to be jealously guarded from outsiders; otherwise the cult of the Persian deities would probably not have been so dominant in parts of Anatolia as it was in post-Achaemenid times. Equally there was no attempt to force Persian religious beliefs and practices on subject peoples who had deities of their own. The Kings did destroy some sanctuaries of alien gods, but this was by way of retaliation or punishment and not with intent to suppress other religions. The one possible exception occurs in Xerxes' daiwa inscription (XPh),[2] where the King speaks of a place (unnamed) in which he destroyed a 'daiwadana' or sanctuary of daiwa (false gods) and worshipped Ahuramazda in their place. It follows, and is distinct from, the mention of a land that was in revolt when he came to the throne; so it doesn't refer to Egypt. Sanctuaries were demolished at Babylon in 482 B.C. (above, p. 100), and some scholars believe that it is these that are referred to; but it is difficult to see how Ahuramazda could effectively have replaced the existing deities there. An attack on Anahita and Mithra seems very unlikely. The talk is of one sanctuary with a plurality of deities, whereas Anahita and Mithra never seem to have been worshipped together; and people with Mithra-names were frequent in Xerxes' entourage – we know at least five from literary sources, let alone those at Persepolis and in Egypt. Possibly some other daiwa of old Iranian religion were involved. The fact that the place is in the singular needs stressing, because failure to recognize this has given rise to the belief that Xerxes banned daiwa at large.

The Kings generally lent their support to the established religions of their subjects; we know of examples of this policy in Babylonia, Elam, Egypt, Jerusalem, Sardis, and the Greek fringe; and the great Asianic temple estates with their hierodules seem to have come through into Hellenistic times in good shape. More remarkable perhaps was the Persians' readiness to adapt themselves to the syncretistic trend that was in the air. When for instance they claimed that their destruction of Greek sanctuaries was revenge for the burning of that of the Lydian Kybebe at Sardis,[3] when (as we are told) they learned from Assyrians (i.e. Babylonians) and Arabs to sacrifice to the heavenly goddess (Mylitta and Alilat),[4] or when Tissaphernes sacrificed to Artemis at Ephesus[5] and later rallied the neighbouring Greeks to defend her,[6] we may suppose that they were prepared to see in those deities the equivalent of their own Anahita, whom the Greeks on their side were willing to equate with Aphrodite or more frequently Artemis (less commonly with Athena).[7] Ahuramazda could be equated with Zeus (particularly distinguished as Zeus Theos or Megistos) and with Bel, and the Achaemenids may have seen a reflection of him in Yahweh. The respect with which the Persians normally treated the Greek Apollo may have been due not only to his ownership of important oracles but to a resemblance to Mithra (not least in relation to the sun, with which Apollo was beginning at this time to be associated); the Aramaic text of the recently found trilingual of Achaemenid date at Xanthos in Lycia names Artemis as such but gives an equation of Apollo with an Iranian by-name of Mithra that was current in Syria.[8] Dedications to Egyptian deities by Persian officials in Egypt from the reign of Xerxes on are probably as much a matter of the inclination to conform as of syncretism. In fact the mixing of Iranian and native names in families settled in Babylonia and Egypt, and also in Lycia, could imply increasing assimilation to the native cultures. Many foreigners in Egypt worshipped the gods of the land, though others had names compounded with Near Eastern deities.[9] The same of course applies in Babylonia, where a prince of the house of David was named Zerubbabel and Mordecai (from Marduk) could be thought of as the name of

Esther's Benjamite cousin and guardian. Persian officials no doubt preferred not to be implicated in the religious dissensions of the subject peoples – hence the reluctance to authorize the restoration of the temple of Yahweh in the Jewish military colony of Yeb (Elephantine) in face of opposition from the temple authorities in Jerusalem.

Unlike Mithra, who belonged to the old Indo-Aryan pantheon in pre-Iranian times, and who is attested in Mitanni (in High Mesopotamia) 800 years before Darius, Ahuramazda has the appearance of being a late-comer – not in the fact of being a sky-god but in his composite name and his involvement in the struggle of Justice against the Lie. The word Mazda goes back before 700 B.C. as a Median name-component; but Ahuramazda's first appearance seems to be in a list of deities found in Ashurbanipal's library (Assara Mazas).[10] The geographical limits of his worship before Darius cannot be fixed. By the time he came to dictate column V of his Behistun inscription Darius had become conscious of his own position as a worshipper of Ahuramazda as against rebels or enemies who were not, and he there declared that the Elamites and the Saka of Skunkha were not; but unfortunately he did not go back to the campaigns of his 'annus mirabilis' and say which of the 'kings of the Lie' were or were not worshippers of his god. At least it would seem, to judge by the Saka, that not all Iranians were. On the other hand, the Elamite text at Behistun calls Ahuramazda 'the god of the Aryans', while the father's name of the Syennesis of Cilicia who lost his life at Salamis in 480 B.C. is given by Herodotus as Ōromedon, which might imply some recognition of Ahuramazda west of the Euphrates before the time of Darius I.

Herodotus tells us that the Persians made no statues of their gods because they considered it folly to visualize them in human form. At the time he seems to have been correct in this, and the same could be said of the Medes since the Assyrian kings had found no images of gods to carry off among the spoils from Median campaigns. But the royal reliefs from Behistun onward show what looks like a bust of the King riding the air on the tail and wing-span of a bird of prey and hovering overhead when the King performs his royal functions or even when he goes hunting lion in a palm grove. This was at one time taken to be the 'fravahr' (a sort of soul-angel) of the King; but more generally it has come to be recognized as the god of the Achaemenids, the very similar Ashur symbol on Assyrian monuments lending mutual support to the interpretation as the deity. Shahbazi is currently arguing that it is not the god but the 'khwrenah' (Fortune) of the King; and Moorey has claimed that this emblem served as the war standard of the Kings which the Greeks took to be a golden eagle – a difficult contention because the Parthian king is also said to have had an eagle standard carried before him and the Greek mentions of the Achaemenid standard are fairly explicit;[11] it seems simpler to allow that the royal standard was an eagle and perhaps connect it with the legend that Achaemenes was nurtured by one. Certainly the identity of the winged bust is open to argument.[12] In favour of the view that it represents Ahuramazda are the fact that it seems to appear on independent satrapal coins (as of Datames) and above all the postures: the King is raising his hand as though in adoration

Plate 10

Plate 33

Plate 5

to a superior being, and the bust has its two hands held out as though in blessing and bestowing a ring on the King. The physical likeness of god to King would not be out of keeping with the reciprocal ownership expressed on the brick stamp DSk (above, p. 147).

To judge by later sources the worship of the Persian deities was well established in Asia Minor, especially in Lydia where it must have been introduced by Iranian officials and fief-holders in Achaemenid times,[13] and in Cappadocia and Armenia.[14] Artaxerxes II, who set a precedent by naming Anahita and Mithra in his royal inscriptions, is said to have imposed the cult of the former with images of her at places in his empire as far removed as Damascus and Sardis and at Baktra. In later times her cults seem to have been dominant not only in Asia Minor but in Elymais (behind Susa) and Media; she was of course worshipped at Agbatana, Persepolis, and Susa, and according to Zoroastrian texts Zranka (Seistan) was a stronghold of her worship. Some scholars assign her a Baktrian origin as the goddess of the R. Oxus (or of the Jaxartes and even the Volga!), but there does not seem to be evidence to show that she was an old 'Aryan' deity. As Anaitis she won a place in the Hellenistic republic of deities. It may be an accident of our sources that makes her appear the most venerated member of the triad; but it does seem that fire worship was mainly her domain. Mithra also was widely worshipped to judge by the frequent appearance of the word in compound names throughout Achaemenid times and after. Aramaic inscriptions on vessels found at Persepolis have given rise to a belief that Mithra's sacred haoma drink was officially used in ritual there. But now it is not clear that there is any indisputable evidence that it was or any certain mention of the god Mithra in the Persepolis tablets.[15] We are however told that the King celebrated the Mithra festival by getting drunk, and horses were said to be sent from Armenia to the King at the Mithra festival.[16] A theophoric personal name Haomadata belonged to a military commander at Elephantine about 460 B.C., and the odd haoma – name is perhaps to be recognized in the Persepolis tablets. Cults of Mithra have not often come to light in the Hellenistic world prior to his rise to fame in the wake of the Roman armies; but he is nevertheless attested in Lydia, Phrygia, Pontus, Cilicia and the Taurus, Commagene in the Euphrates bend, the Crimea, and on Baktrian coins.

Herodotus noted the essentials of the Persians' religion.[17] He says that they had no statues, temples, or altars; to Zeus (i.e. Ahuramazda) they sacrificed on mountain tops; they also sacrificed to sun and moon, and to earth, fire, water, and winds. Strabo says almost the same in his account of Persian religion, following Herodotus closely despite the interval of over 400 years.[18] The primitive-seeming animism occurs in Zoroastrian scriptures and is exemplified in Herodotus' narrative of Xerxes' march when he speaks of the Magi burying human victims at the Nine Ways road junction and sacrificing at water crossings and to placate a gale – offerings to rivers and mountains have also been read into the Persepolis tablets.[19] But as regards the alleged lack of temples and altars we may note that in fact Strabo goes on to speak at first hand of walled sanctuaries or shrines and of ash-altars; and – to pass over the cults we know were established by Artaxerxes II – the places of worship ('ayadana') of which Darius spoke at Behistun must have had some substance if he could claim to have restored them after their destruction by Gaumata.[20]

On the archaeological side fire altars seem to be adequately attested in Achaemenid times. At Naksh-i Rustam the tomb reliefs of Darius I and his successors show the King in adoration before an altar, and just round the corner from the tombs there is a pair of solid rock altars with deep sockets in the top which until recently scholars believed to be no less ancient.[21] At the Pasargadai site a mile north of the palatial campus there is a pair of stone plinths which seems to have stood in an enclosure; one had steps, presumably for ascending to the sacred fire. The matter can be taken further. In Seistan west of the Helmand, at Dahan-i Gulaman where an Italian mission recently discovered some large buildings and traces of a short-lived major settlement (apparently of early Achaemenid date) on the edge of the drifting sandhills, a row of three hollow stone altars on stepped bases was found; they were enclosed in a porticoed building almost 180 feet square. Altars are therefore attested, and in fact Soviet scholars have claimed that fire altars can be traced back to the fourth millennium B.C. down the R. Tejend in Turkestan.

Plate 5

Fig. 8

As regards monumental cult buildings, that at Dahan-i Gulaman had not only the three altars in the open court but a multiplicity of ovens and tables backing the pillars in the porticoes; it must be as old as Herodotus, but its form is unique and its function inexplicable. This is the one fairly certain fire cult building of Achaemenid date. There is, however, a clear record of a building explored by Dieulafoy three miles from Susa which had a four-columned room with a porch at the back of a court 60 ft square, and with porticoes and corridors surrounding the complex. In both cases there were stairways leading to a higher level from the corridors. In Dieulafoy's building no altar was noted, and his attribution of the construction to Artaxerxes II by comparison of the column bases can only be regarded as an approximation, though the theory that it was a temple built by him for Anahita is attractive. A not dissimilar complex has been noted at Kuh-i Khwaja in Seistan; but Gullini's dating of it in Achaemenid times has no support from finds there. Stronach has excavated a pre-Achaemenid fire temple with altar at Nush-i Jan (south of the Great Khorasan road) which Ghirshman seeks to identify with the 'daiwadana' destroyed by Xerxes, and Ghirshman believes that fire temples with an interior court open to the sky can be followed back into the second millennium B.C. (as at Choga Zembil).

It seems clear that Herodotus went too far when he said that the Persians in his day had no altars, and he can hardly have been right if he meant that they had no cult buildings at all. It is, however, not easy to define a standard form for sanctuaries in which the sacred fire was guarded because in almost every case there is doubt about either the dating or the purpose served. This applies especially to two types of installation which readily catch the eye. One consists of the tower-like buildings at Pasargadai (the Zendan of Solomon) and Naksh-i Rustam (the Kaaba of Zardusht, above, p. 36), which are 24 ft square and 41–47 ft high. It is agreed that they are both of Achaemenid date, the Zendan being presumably of Cyrus' era. They are so

Fig. 9

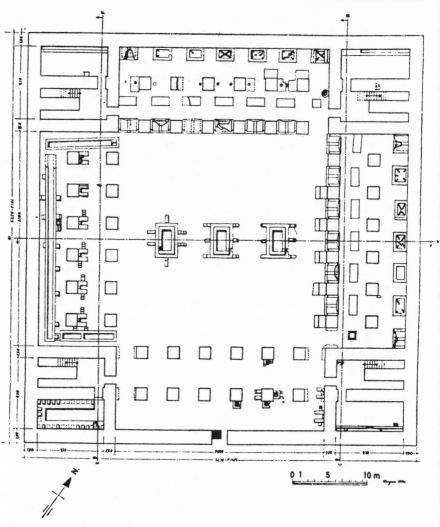

Fig. 8   Plan of cult building at Dahan-i Gulaman. (By courtesy of Professor U. Scerrato, from *East and West*, Vol. 16, Nos. 1–2, March–June, 1960.)

similar that it is unlikely that they were built to serve different purposes. It is not likely that they were tombs because no monarch other than Cyrus would have been buried at Pasargadai. It is also unlikely that they were archive strong-rooms because there would hardly have been one at Naksh-i Rustam. Ritual repositories of some sort are a possibility, and there is a stronger case for treasuries if Naksh-i Rustam is the Nupishtash of the Fortification tablets (above, p. 34). But on the whole the most favoured explanation is fire temples, though it is far from clear where the fire would be tended. A simpler tower at Nurabad in the valley to the west of Shiraz has been cited as a parallel, but its date is uncertain and it could simply have been a guard post. The other type of installation is the raised terraces which carried buildings

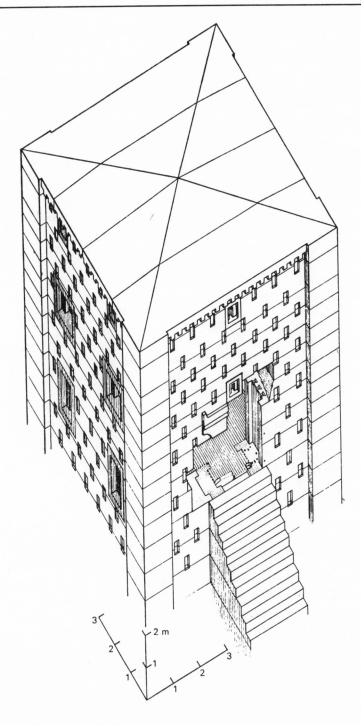

Fig. 9   The Zendan at Pasargadai. (From David Stronach, *Pasargadae*. Courtesy of Oxford University Press.)

that seem to have been sacred, such as that at Masjit-i Solaiman and other places in the Elymaean territory (Bakhtiari country) in the hinterland of Susa.[22] These must surely have served the fire cult; and they have been brought into connection with the 'high places' to which Herodotus says the Persians went up to sacrifice to 'Zeus'. But Herodotus in fact speaks of 'the highest points of the mountains', which does not fit with these terraces; and apart from Masjit-i Solaiman, where there may be some faint trace of use as early as the fifth century, they seem to date to the post-Achaemenid era.[23]

In their religious habits as described by Herodotus the Persians were especially concerned with purity. Fire and water must not be defiled. It was forbidden to wash in a river, and nicety and privacy were observed in the performance of bodily functions. Concessions must have been made to troops on the march because otherwise no military movement would have been practicable. Fire being divine, burning of the dead would be pollution. Bodies were waxed before interment; and the Magi at least exposed their dead for laceration by dogs and birds. Ctesias is said to have taken Herodotus to task for saying that the Persians didn't burn their dead, but we are not told what he himself had to say about it. In Herodotus' account sacrifices were made without fire, libations, flute-playing, and other accompaniments that the Greeks were accustomed to; a Persian making a sacrifice would take the animal to a clear spot, and wreathed usually with myrtle he would pray for blessings not only on himself but on all the Persians and the King; then having killed and (he says) boiled the animal he set out portions of the meat on herbage (preferably clover). But a Magus was needed to chant a 'theogony' – probably a hymn about the gods like the later Yashts. The need for a Magus should perhaps be stressed because it implies that for the 'layman' a pre-scribed devotional routine did not suffice to maintain the requisite communion between him and the divine.

Plate 31   The Magi are a puzzle. Herodotus speaks of them as a 'clan' of the Medes (above, p. 7), Strabo as a Persian tribe (XV 727). Scholars have sought a home for them at Rhagai or in Atropatene (Azerbaijan) or around Behistun; but though they may be recognizable on Luristan bronzework of centuries earlier there is no clear evidence for a particular location. Certainly they are depicted officiating on tomb fronts in Media that may be of Achaemenid date (Dukkan-i Daud near the Zagros Gates and that at Eshakvand south of Behistun which Herzfeld took to be the sepulchre of Gaumata);[24] and – for what it is worth – Ammianus Marcellinus in late Roman times spoke of them as occupying their own lands in Media.[25] It may well be true that the Magi were of West Iranian and indeed Median origin; Frye believes that in Eastern Iran minstrels were more prominent than Magi.[26] But by the end of the Persian empire, when the upper satrapies became known to the Western world, the whole Aryan (Iranian) race could be spoken of as being at one with the Magi in their doctrine of cosmic dualism, which implies that they all had them as their priests.[27] We thus find that the development of the catholic Zoroastrianism of the Avesta seems from its geographical horizon to have been working itself out in North-eastern Iran but that the religion that evolved was that of the Magi.

Our sources do not present the Magi as theologians. They functioned as officiating clergy and were essential above all to the fire cult. In Cappadocia, where they were numerous in Strabo's day, they tended the unquenchable fires with their fur caps peaked forward, their mouths muffled, and holding bundles of tamarisk or other stems in their hands; this fits well with the figures on the tomb front at Dukkan-i Daud and a sacrificial relief from the satrapal centre of Daskyleion. It is not clear whether in Achaemenid times it was possible to become a Magus without having been born into the 'clan' – the only evidence that seems to point to this is of the beginning of the Christian era.[28]

The Magi are said to have worn white robes and lived a life of privation, and they had a curious habit of killing with their own hands birds, snakes, ants, and other undomesticated creatures save dogs and their kin. They may perhaps have had something of the dervish in them. What we hear of their activity in the sources is mainly in the royal employment. The King had Magi in attendance. They led march-outs and processions. They sacrificed, poured libations, chanted their theogonies and lisped incantations. They might be called upon to interpret dreams or portents. At Persepolis, where there is evidence not only of a fair number of Magi but of offerings to Ahuramazda and other deities such as the Elamite god Humban, they were recipients of rations and wine. Presumably Persian grandees kept Magi at their courts. The Tomb of Cyrus had its guardian Magi who sacrificed a horse monthly and received a generous meat allowance.

It would seem that as clergy the Magi were subject to their temporal masters in the period that concerns us and not to high priests; so we cannot think of them as forming a church with its own hierarchy, doctrinal instruction, or endowments. In Achaemenid times there does not seem to be evidence of a caste system like that which gave priests and judges a place next to the nobles in the Sassanian social hierarchy. They may possibly have been a tribe like the Levites, but not a caste like the Brahmins. If we reject the Seven's claim that the occupant of the throne whom they killed was a Magus, we have no evidence that Magi were politically active; Ctesias and Dinon would have told us if they had been, and the royal reliefs do not seem to give them a place in court circles. But we do hear of one Magus being Cyrus the Younger's tutor in a version of Cyrus' attempt on his brother which has the tutor reveal the plot;[29] and in the Smerdis story as Herodotus received it it was evidently considered believable that a Magus should be left as caretaker of the royal household. Probably, then, some Magi were put in positions of trust; but there is no reason to suppose that they were able to assert themselves as a corporate body, and we do not hear of them inflaming the passions of the public like Hebrew prophets or Islamic mollahs.

The god of Darius was of course the god of Zoroaster (Zarathushtra). Darius invariably calls his god Ahuramazda. This is in origin two words (Ahura = Lord, Mazda = Wise); but they are fused into one word in all his texts (as also in the later tablets purporting to be prayers of his royal ancestors, p. 8). The Assyrian list of gods, which should date to the mid seventh century or earlier, gives the two words in the same order (above, p. 149). In theory therefore we might suppose that the Gathas of Zoroaster, in which the god is addressed by either name singly or by the two in either order, carry us back in oral tradition to an earlier stage when the god's name was not yet stereotyped.

Zoroaster appears in the Gathas as having thought out his conception of ethical dualism and his divine mission in solitary communing, and being unsuccessful in his preaching at home (wherever that was) as having then moved supposedly to Baktria (or at any rate somewhere in Eastern Iran), where he found a protector in the kavi (kinglet) Gushtasp of whom he made a convert in due course. By the fourth century after Christ Gushtasp seems to have come to be identified with Darius' father Hystaspes;[30] and at some subsequent stage a legendary chronology was produced which would place Zoroaster in the late seventh and the sixth century B.C. Many scholars accept this identification, which opens the way to a range of exciting speculations about the political and religious relationships of Zoroaster, Cyrus, and Darius. There are two obvious difficulties in the identification: first, since he was an Achaemenid with his roots in Persis, Darius' father could not have been a hereditary ruler in Baktria; and second, the names given to members of Gushtasp's family in the Gathas do not fit at any point with those that we know from Herodotus and Darius' own inscriptions. But a further difficulty occurs when we turn to other Greek sources. Though Herodotus doesn't mention him, knowledge of Zoroaster's name seems to have reached the Greeks in his time. Xanthos of Lydia spoke of Zoroaster as having lived 6,000 years before Xerxes' invasion,[31] and fourth-century Greek writers give similar computations; also – assuming he is Justin's authority here – Ctesias at the end of the fifth century had it that Zoroaster was a king of the Baktrians who was attacked and killed by Ninos, which would put him back into a very distant mythical past. We need not take the dating in these writers very seriously – Pliny pertinently remarked it as astonishing that the memory and lore of Zoroaster should have survived so long without writing. But what it does indicate is that their Persian or Median informants cannot have thought of Zoroaster as a figure of at all recent history; and the memory of a religious leader as individual as Zoroaster should have remained vivid among them if he had been living in the time of Cyrus. This rules out any possibility that the Gushtasp of Zoroaster was the son Hystaspes whom Xerxes made governor of Baktria, and the notion that Darius preceded Zoroaster can be dismissed. It seems reasonable to assume that Zoroaster lived well before the time when Achaemenid rule was established in Iran and probably before the time of Ashurbanipal's list of deities, but – little though it helps us – later than the domestication of the camel.[32]

Darius shows the same intense concentration on the one creator of all and omnipotent deity as Zoroaster did. He does not himself speak of Justice (arta) or of false gods (daiwa); but his son Xerxes introduced both in his daiwa inscription (XPh).[33] In common with Zoroaster, Darius recognized the enemy as 'the Lie'. We can probably attribute to both a special concern for sedentary cultivation; both expected justice to have its reward through Ahuramazda in this world and the hereafter, and both stood in a like exclusive personal relationship to the god. It would be strange if Darius was not acquainted with Zoroaster's doctrine.[34] But that does not mean that the hard-headed King let himself be implicated in the religious movement that surfaces in the Avesta. In fact Benveniste has drawn attention to the absence of names of Zoroastrian inspiration in the Persepolis tablets and likewise the absence in Zoroastrian texts of the forms that are found in theophoric names at Persepolis.[35] The special virtue of Ahuramazda in Darius' eyes was that with his persecution of the Lie he formed the perfect heavenly counterpart for a Great King who looked for justification in enforcing universal rule on earth.

It is of course possible that Darius brought Zoroaster's creed to the Persian court from north-eastern Iran, where he may have served on Cyrus' last expedition or possibly lived as a youth with his father in the Parthian satrapy. But this is speculation. Since with him Justice invariably prevailed, Darius' dualism was less pronounced than Zoroaster's, and he may have come near to being a monotheist like the Second Isaiah. Xerxes was his father's son; a further reflection of the terminology of the Gathas of Zoroaster has been remarked in his use of the word 'artawan'. Some scholars maintain that the Zoroastrian reformed calendar was adopted by the Achaemenid court in 441 (or 481) B.C.; but this seems speculative and objections have been raised.[36] What is certain is that the liberal-minded Artaxerxes II named the triad of great deities in his inscriptions. Presumably the court will have embraced the Zoroastrianism that developed from the fusion of the prophet's personal religious doctrine with the larger body of theolatric beliefs and practices that made up Persian religion. Of this the Magi were the ministers. For the Western world the greatest contribution of the Achaemenids in the religious sphere may have lain in the encouragement given – possibly by the example of their own supreme deity but more clearly through the royal favour – to the development of Yahwism. But in general their religion was one that seems to have been salutary in its effects. Canon George Rawlinson gave a judicious appraisal of it over a century ago when he wrote that the religion of the ancient Medes and Persians was of a more elevated character than is usual with races not enlightened by special revelation.

XV Palaces and Art

Thanks to their conquests the Persian Kings commanded vast resources and could afford to build on a lavish scale. The open campus that Cyrus the Great laid out (above, p. 36) perhaps reflects a not too distant nomadic background and (despite the citadel on the north) no great pre-occupation with security. Darius was more fortress-minded. The two great palace complexes which he constructed as capitals were Persepolis and Susa (above, p. 73f.).[1]

At Susa a low hill was levelled up with a filling of gravel to provide a surface of about ten acres standing at a height of 60 feet above the stream bed. The main palace, known to the Greeks as the Memnonion, was enclosed in a bastion of the thick mud circuit wall, with a gate pylon against which Xerxes *Plate 15* was to erect the two Egyptian statues of his father. Owing to restriction of space the palace seems to have formed a close complex of courts, corridors, *Fig. 10* royal apartments, and service rooms, with the Apadana standing on its own platform as the most impressive building. Stone was in short supply and the *Plate 11* relief decoration was mainly in enamelled bricks. Apart from fragments of reliefs and some components of the Apadana columns very little remains of the main palace. A second palace, or at least Apadana, came to light in 1969 on a very low brow across the Shaour stream a third of a mile away. It consisted of a great columned hall with flanking porticoes and is assigned to Artaxerxes (II) by inscriptions; though large by any other standards, it cannot compare with Darius I's huge Apadanas and may have been run up to serve as a reception hall while the main palace was under reconstruction after a fire in the reign of Artaxerxes I. Strictly, Susa was in the satrapy of Elam (Uwja), not in Persis; but to Herodotus (as III 30) it could rank as 'to Persians'.

Darius' fortress at Susa was presumably habitable before 509 B.C., after which time he is shown to have been normally resident there. The Apadana and gate pylon may not have been completed for another decade or two. But the existence of royal apartments there, as at Agbatana, may be presupposed; and, in fact, when he makes Darius the founder of the palace there Pliny is in disagreement with Strabo (who assigns it to Cyrus) and by implication with Herodotus also (above, pp. 33 and 52). At Persepolis, however, Darius expressly claims that there had been no fortress before he built his; and though there may have been residences in the vicinity the first major project, probably occupying several years before about 513 B.C., was the construc- *Plate 16* tion of the vast terrace. With an extent of thirty acres, which would allow a much greater range of buildings, and local supplies of a hard, dark limestone that could be laboriously carved by skilled stone masons, the Persepolis palace-complex was inevitably a longer-term project than Susa; and scholars

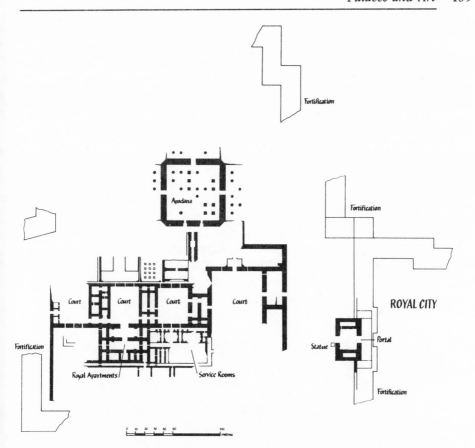

Fig. 10   Plan of Palace of Darius I at Susa. (From J. Perrot in *Proceedings of IInd Annual Symposium on Archaeological Research*.)

now tend to assume that Darius directed his main work-force to Susa first. The terrace at Persepolis measures about 1,400 by nearly 1,000 ft. At points the levelled rock of the hill skirt obtrudes; but in the main there is a deep filling behind the platform wall, which rises to some 50 ft. The terrace or platform was reached from the flat ground below by twin returning staircases of 111 steps which were 23 ft broad and shallow enough for troops of riders to ascend; there seems also to have been a smaller stair on the south leading up to the Treasury.

The complex of buildings on the platform took generations to finish; indeed the overall plan was never quite brought to completion. What can be attributed to Darius I is the earlier parts of the Treasury, the Tachara (Palace of Darius), which was virtually finished during his lifetime, and the Tripylon, the main structure of the Apadana, and the mud fortification wall with quarters for the guard. At the same time, not only was a single axis adhered to by later Kings when they built there, but it is claimed that the original lay-out of underground conduits dictated all subsequent construction. In particular, the Tripylon is not itself a palace, but it is so monumental a porch as to imply

Plate 17

Fig. 11

that to the south a palace altogether more grand than the Tachara was
envisaged by Darius. Godard has thought of the platform surface as being
deliberately divided into three functional areas – reception halls, treasury,
and barracks.

Darius may be credited with some originality. The lay-out on the platform
at Persepolis offers variety, especially in the exciting changes of level between

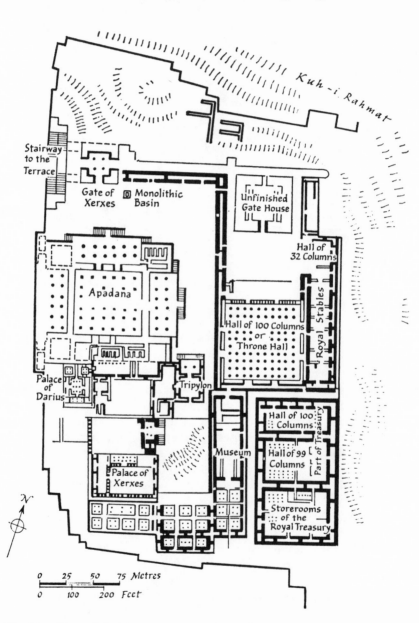

Fig. 11   Plan of the Terrace at Persepolis. (After Hauser, Courtesy of Chicago
Press.)

the different building podiums which allow for communication by the ornamental returning and Palladian staircases that seem to have been an Achaemenid speciality. At Pasargadai, as Nylander demonstrated, Cyrus employed teams of Lydian and Greek masons after the conquest of Sardis; the technique and tools used were those current in Eastern Greece; and not only do the tooling and dressing and the setting and jointing of the blocks with clamps and dowels follow Greek practice, but the architectural syntax of columns and mouldings was basically Greek.[2] Darius in the interval had served in Egypt and seen a different range of masonry and architectural effects. The distinguishing feature of his Tachara is the Egyptian cavetto mouldings; and his spectacular cruciform tomb at Naksh-i Rustam, which measures about 75 ft high and 60 ft across the arms in the 200-ft high cliff and served as a model in every detail for his successors, probably owes more to Egyptian high-rise carved frontages than to any Anatolian rock tombs he may have seen. In general, however, Darius continued the Lydo-Greek tradition of Cyrus, constructing great columnar halls (now square rather than oblong) flanked by colonnaded porticoes. His liking for the grandiose appears in the enormous size of many blocks in the Persepolis terrace wall and the sculptured footings, in the height of the columns (65 ft in the Apadana) with Ionic shafts whose slenderness resembles that of California redwoods, and in the extreme elaboration of the capitals; the feet of his columns were also made more ornate with delicate carving and a new kind of tapering bell base. The synthesis is not always harmonious, but the general effect is impressive. The jointing and finishing, with the claw-chisel now in use, was of fine workmanship under Darius and Xerxes.

Plate 3

Plate 5

Plate 18
Plate 12

Darius' Tachara rose high and overlooked the plain. The polished darkstone frames of doors, windows, and alcoves now stand in isolation, the intervening walls of mud brick having perished – hence the modern name 'Hall of Mirrors'. The jambs had relief sculptures with the King (or his heroic counterpart, see Chap. V n.26) dominant, but in the rear (northern) quarters servants were carved instead. Since food is also carried some scholars have thought that the Tachara served as a dining hall. In the south-east of the platform was the Treasury, built by 509 B.C. and enlarged about 493 by Darius, then added to by Xerxes. It seems probable that the building to the west of this and its long extension westward served for the growing needs of storage rather than (as Schmidt believed) the harem. The Apadana, with thirty-six interior columns and another thirty-six in its three porticoes, was grand, no doubt hung with tapestries inside and awesomely dark. The carving of the sculptured friezes of podium and staircases was completed under Xerxes, but the plan of the building had been laid out before Darius started to mint his royal coinage to judge by the foundation deposit.[3] Recent investigations have led to the belief that the Palladian stairway on the east was an addition to a more modest original design. The Tripylon is preceded by a charmingly unpretentious double staircase whose balustrades bear reliefs of courtiers, and could have been what the ancient writers would call the King's Gate. It is of the time of Darius I, as also presumably were the mud quarters of the military on the east side of the platform. More precise information about

Plate 17

Plate 22

Plate 19

the sequence of construction may come from Nylander's and Roaf's studies of mason's marks on the principal buildings.

The 'Gateway of All Lands' (Gate of Xerxes) with its colossal Cherubim (pairs of human- and bovine-headed bison) faces the head of the great stairway of the terrace; with its Assyrian-type monsters it might well have been envisaged by Darius himself, but inscriptions show that it was built by Xerxes. South-west of the Tripylon Xerxes built a palace ('Hadish') on a high podium; and he and his son Artaxerxes I constructed more in this area, including a triple-stairwayed reception-complex (Palace H) in the space on the west which was later rebuilt by Artaxerxes III. The main building that Artaxerxes I completed after his father's death was the so-called Hall of 100 Columns (Throne Hall). On a square of 225 ft it occupied more ground space than the hall of the Apadana, though it was little more than half the height. Here again the sculptured decoration is on the door jambs, with the King despatching monsters or enthroned in state with guards and subject peoples lending him support. On Godard's theory this hall will have been the assembly room of the military, who would thus have occupied the whole eastern half of the platform to the north of the Treasury. Ctesias makes Xerxes remove from Babylon to 'Persians' (i.e. Persepolis); this follows his account of the Greek expedition (with no indication of the length of time that intervened). In fact the Treasury tablets show that after a lull from early in his reign there was an upsurge of building activity at Persepolis about 470 B.C. It does not seem to have outlasted the completion of his unfinished buildings by his son, and after that no King would appear from inscriptions to have been active there till Artaxerxes III. In this period the prestige of Parsa may have rested on the growing sequence of royal tombs which occupied the cliff face at Naksh-i Rustam and then spread to the slopes at Persepolis itself. Frye considers that Persepolis was by this time a venerable relic and has characterized it a 'provincial Versailles'.[4]

As a residential complex Persepolis presents problems. The Treasury, which (like the Hall of 100 Columns) shows traces of the fire of 330 B.C., has yielded relics of vessels and other trophies and valuable objects which were stored there. But in general the palace complex seems to show little sign of the running water, sanitation, or kitchens that might be expected. Over the last thirty years the remains of an increasing number of palatial buildings have been discovered in the plain in front of the terrace. No doubt grandees will have had residences there; but in one case at least a residence which seems to have had a large garden with an ornamental lake is identified by an inscribed column base as the Tachara of King Xerxes. It is possible that the palaces on the fortress platform served for formal receptions and ceremonial purposes but that the King may have preferred more spacious accommodation in the plain for himself and his harem. There is reason to suspect that a loosely built-up town may have extended for miles here.

Darius was at pains to record that many different peoples of empire contributed labour and materials to the construction and decoration of his Apadana at Susa. If we add the new tablet DSaa to the texts that make up DSf some twenty-six or twenty-seven peoples are mentioned (see

Chap. XVII n.15). This redounds to the glory of Darius. But it also implies that the imperial archictecture and ornamentation of the Achaemenids was a composite which had no firm base in any native or national tradition.

The main vehicle of Achaemenid art was relief sculpture.[5] Sculpture in the round is known. The foreparts of Assyrian-type monsters (some with human heads) are found in carved portal-Cherubim and the crowns of capitals. But the colossal granite figure of Darius I – one of a pair made in Egypt – which was found at Susa in 1973 is the only substantial piece of large-scale statuary to have come to light yet,[6] other surviving figures in silver and lapis lazuli being statuettes which would not have been more than a foot high. The relief sculpture begins with Cyrus. In the absence of evidence for a major art-style attributable to the Medes, the most obvious models to follow would have been Assyrian. Cyrus, however, was eclectic (above, p. 43); and Sardis and Yauna, as well perhaps as Syria, offered a new range. The sculptures of Palace P at Pasargadai show drapery folds whose inspiration was clearly Greek; but scholars now tend to date them to the time of Darius, though the presence of such folds at Behistun shows that the mode is older than Persepolis. The Behistun relief must have been a nightmare for the carvers. Details such as Darius' beard and crown have been lovingly sculptured. But the relief-planes are not consistent, and while the motifs are in general Assyrian the style seems indeterminate. Apart from the drapery folds nothing looks Greek.[7] It was in the reliefs of the Tripylon staircase that the characteristic court style of Darius began to be evolved. As with the Parthenon frieze, artisans from different backgrounds must have worked side by side fashioning in stone a repertory of standard designs and poses; and so a team will have been formed. Like the west frieze of the Parthenon the Tripylon does not lack scrabbly work done by apprentices or unskilled carvers; but standards were imposing themselves, and habituation to a common style will not have prevented the introduction of new subtleties within the general framework. After this, in the long, superimposed friezes of the Apadana staircases Achaemenid art went on to realize its full potential as an archaic art in the decade or so around the beginning of Xerxes' reign.

Plate 15

Plates 7 & 8

Plate 19

Plate 20

Plates 23–9

Compared with Behistun the friezes of the Tripylon are informal. They show a variation of pose and an interest in incident – the swinging bow-case incommoding the man behind, the head turned round to expostulate, the snatched conversations – which would suggest that Greeks had a hand in the design; and the rounding of contours and modulations of the surface in what is relatively low relief are best matched in Greek sculpture of the late archaic period. At the present time quite contradictory opinions can be held on the part played by Greeks. At one extreme scholars point to the rarity of mentions of Yauna on the Persepolis pay-roll (which is partly belied by scratchings done by Greeks on blocks and in the quarries there). At the other extreme we may adduce the Ionian Telephanes of Phocaea, who (the elder Pliny says) was on a par with the greatest of Greek sculptors but was little known because, some said, he spent his time in the workshops of Xerxes and Darius, and we may even proceed to recognize in him the grand master of these friezes. It is still largely a matter of subjective judgement.[8]

The special qualities that made this imperial Achaemenid art impressive seem to be the clarity, composure, and timelessness of the King's world: on the negative side an effortlessness – Nylander speaks of 'pictograms of slow movement' – that makes for grand art rather than great art. There is no attempt to imitate the vigour of Assyrian scenes. Battles and hunting do not figure on the Persian reliefs, and banqueting is only hinted at by food-carrying attendants. In principle, as buried foundation tablets and monuments skied on cliff faces show, it was to the god that the King addressed his record. But a main aim of the palace sculptures was to exalt the King (see Chap. V n.26). The range of the court themes was in fact exhibited (or intended to be exhibited) very nearly complete on the Apadana staircases, where the King *Plate 9* was to be shown enthroned with the crown prince behind him and his court *Plates 23–9* officials in position, his men-at-arms and the military establishment at his back, and the subject peoples approaching him with gifts.

Faults and weaknesses can be observed. The spacing is not always satisfactory. Human figures tend to be stocky and flat-footed, lacking suppleness at the joints, especially in the springing of the arm at the shoulder. On the whole the figures of the Apadana tend to be better proportioned than those of the Tripylon, and the more glaring anomalies of scale have been avoided; but even when allowance is made for the paint and applied gilt ornament which will have enhanced the decorative effect, the long files can be monotonous, the more so for the lack of feminine. On the other hand, with the studied differentiation of the appearance, dress, and equipment of a couple of dozen peoples of empire – many of them lacking any precedent in Near Eastern art – Achaemenid sculpture displays a fair degree of originality within the limits that Darius set for it. The different types of horses, chariots, and camels, the zebus, and the antelope and giraffid from Africa have been depicted with perceptiveness, as also the dress, equipment and hair styles of different peoples; and several more or less distinct ethnic physiognomies are rendered. The offerings brought were no doubt typical – some, like the ivory tusks from Kush and the pots (presumably of gold dust) from Sind, being distinctive, whereas metalwork, caskets, and cloth were brought from different regions of empire.[9]

Much of the detail is realistic. But there is a good deal that is symbolic. At Behistun all the 'kings of the Lie' are shown bound on one rope; but in fact some were dead before others rose in revolt. Elsewhere his subjects are shown supporting (and indeed lifting) the King; but their positioning in tiers is impossible, and sometimes it is nothing less than the canopied dais for the royal party that they are carrying. So it is very improbable that the reliefs at Persepolis were intended, as many scholars believe, to portray particular ceremonies that took place there (above, p. 73).

This court art was imposing and attractive. It served the purposes for which it was invented; and while there may have been a tendency towards greater refinement under Xerxes there was no incentive to radical change. When he was in Athens in 480 Xerxes could have seen statues in which the tensions of the archaic style were being relaxed. But Achaemenid art in fact

30 Persian dignitary in tomb painting at Karaburun near Elmali (Lycia)

31 A Magus on a gold plaque (Oxus Treasure)

32 Chased gold armlet with griffin terminals (Oxus Treasure)

33   Crystal cylinder seal of Darius I (impression)

34   Chalcedony cylinder seal and impression
with Iranians in battle (Oxus Treasure)

35   A daric (enlarged)

36 Cylinder seal of the King hunting (impression)

37 High valley in Media by Jowkar

38   The citadel mound at Bampur

39   The Tigris with Roman bridge below Diyarbakir (Amida)

40 A mountain village above Salang in the Hindukush (Paropamisadai)

41 The Cilician Gates above Tarsus

42 Coin portrait of Tissaphernes

43 Coin portrait of Pharnabazos

shows no awareness of the new impulses that were then making themselves felt in Greece, and of course the Eastern Greeks were no longer subject to the Persians after 479 B.C.[10]

The palaces of Babylon and Susa have yielded remains of friezes in enamelled brick. This medium was one current in both centres but little used *Plate 11* at Persepolis. In his Susa building inscription Darius spoke of Babylonians as the makers of the baked bricks; but his texts alternatively speak of Yauna resident in Babylonia. In all probability the remains of such friezes found at Susa belonged to the buildings of Darius I and Artaxerxes II. But the repertory of subjects is restricted to guardsmen and files of monsters; and though the colours lend vivacity the medium is not one that permits great subtlety.

According to Chares of Mitylene, who was Alexander the Great's chamberlain, a romantic Iranian story of Odatis (perhaps Hutautha, Atossa) and Zariadres, brother of Hystaspes, held such an appeal for 'the barbarians (i.e. Persians and the like) inhabiting Asia' that it was constantly depicted in their sanctuaries, palaces, and houses.[11] Unfortunately there is no archaeological evidence to support this;[12] indeed painting (which strictly speaking is referred to) has left virtually no trace in the Achaemenid centres. But the medium was used in the Persian West. The best evidence so far comes from two chambered tumuli recently conserved by Machteld Mellink near Elmali in northern Lycia (see Chap. XVI n.32). The first, dated about 525 B.C., shows painted scenes of daily activity; but the iconography is not Persian, and the medium is that of Greek mythological painting. The second tomb, at Karaburun, is of the early fifth century. It depicts a grandee whose physical appearance, costume, and surroundings seem wholly Persian. In different scenes he is shown trousered and mounted in battle and enthroned in what appears to be a funeral procession. But in the principal one he reclines on a couch with moulded feet. His mantle is green, flesh is pale as befits people who seek the shade, mattress and cushions were brightly painted; the man's head dress would have been of chequered cloth with jewels. A low table is shown as bearing fruit, branches, and green leaves for chaplets. The grandee wears *Plate 30* typical bracelets with lion's-head endings, and the vessels (done in white to indicate silver) that he and his attendants hold are of normal Achaemenid forms. The attendants are also dressed in the Persian manner, and one holds a coloured straw fan. In this painting Persian life-style is presented with elegance and with the sureness of touch which comes from an established Western artistic tradition.

The Karaburun tomb illustrates more clearly than the dynastic reliefs (above, p. 180) the directness and freedom with which Greek techniques and artistic forms could be used in the service of grandees in western Asia Minor. In this art the rejection of the female, which is almost a total ban at Persepolis, is not observed and the range of themes includes battles, hunting, banqueting, the funeral cortège, files of horsemen, and Magi at sacrifice. At the same time the numerous Achaemenian seals that seem to have been made in the West show a command of royal Achaemenid motifs as well as current Greek forms.[13] It would not be surprising if Sardis, the metropolis of the Persian West, had become a more creative focus of 'Persian' art in the fifth century than the royal capitals, and Persian grandees in the West may have acquired keener appreciation and been better served artistically than those at court. In the fourth century, as the peoples west of the Euphrates came to absorb the new cultural impulses, one no longer has the feeling of Persian and Greek meeting over the heads of those who lay in between. Something of a common art-style was spreading from Western Asia Minor and Greece to Cilicia, Phoenicia, where works like the Satrap Sarcophagus from Sidon show Greek artists already active in the fifth century, and even Judah.[14]

Plates 26, 31–4, 36

Plate 33

Minor arts flourished in the Persian empire as they had long done in western Asia. Among the works of fine craftsmanship that were most prized were vessels in the precious metals such as animal-tipped drinking horns, jars with animal handles, cups, bowls, and fluted jugs, dagger hilts and chased or inlaid sheaths, gold disks and plaques, gold torques and penannular armlets with animal endings, gems and seals of different kinds, and jewelry with bright-coloured inlay of lapis lazuli, garnet, and turquoise. These were prestige objects such as might be given to high officials (as for instance the cylinder seal of Darius found in Egypt (see above, p. 69) and vessels with royal inscriptions) or exchanged among grandees and foreign princes as far away as the Balkans or Central Asia.

Some of the sources of production are known or can be surmised. Finely decorated weapons will have been made in many regions. But polished stone vessels made principally for Xerxes bear inscriptions that fix their origin in Egypt, and others of chert at Persepolis were manufactured in Arachosia. A number of Achaemenian stamp seals are proved to be products of Sardis by owner's names in Lydian characters. At Susa Darius spoke of Medes and Egyptians as the gold-workers. Metalwork seems to have been a speciality of the people of Media and the northern Zagros, who had assimilated stylized Mesopotamian motifs long before they came under Persian rule; Medes and other peoples of the confines of Anatolia are shown as carriers of metal vessels and ornament on Persepolis friezes, and find-places might perhaps suggest that such craftsmanship was most at home in the Anatolian and North Iranian lands. Egyptians were active in the production of such prestige objects. Their forms and motifs are often distinctive, and Greek craftsmanship can be unmistakable (as in the Lycian tomb paintings, many fine satrapal coins, and of course seals). The treasure discovered in 1877 near the Oxus shows a mixture of artistic traditions; what contribution the Eastern Iranians had to make in Achaemenid times is not clear, but it may not have been negligible (below, p. 193).[15] The different elements are not easy to distinguish; this is illustrated by Scythian (Saka) craftsmanship, in which the old animal style was overlaid with Mesopotamian motifs, and from the sixth century with Greek naturalistic forms also.

At Susa and Persepolis, then, a court art-style was created which can fairly be termed Achaemenid; and its special idioms, with the prestige that they carried, were widely diffused and taken into the repertory of craftsmen in many regions of the empire. But the Achaemenid style was a composite with no growth from within. The Persians themselves seem to have been promoters and patrons rather than practitioners in the arts.

XVI Satraps, Hyparchs, and Fief-holders

Under Darius son of Hystaspes Achaemenid rule was becoming a family affair, with Sardis and probably Baktria governed by brothers of his, and with his sons-in-law and nephews commanding expeditions in the West. If we add the information from other sources to that of Herodotus, all of two dozen brothers, first cousins and brothers-in-law appear to have gone with Xerxes in 481–480, and the key satrapies of Baktria and Egypt were held by full brothers of his (Masistes and Achaemenes). Unfortunately, Herodotus' narrative ends with 479 B.C. and we lose track of the collateral branches of Hystaspes' family unless possibly a son of Artabanos was satrap of Babylonia some time in the middle of the fifth century.[1] Similarly we lose track of the line of Darius' bow-bearer Aspathines, whose son, named Prexaspes, was an admiral in 480. One family which we can follow more or less continuously in the West until the time of Alexander is that of Artabazos who was a trusted commander under Xerxes in Greece and stayed on at the Straits in what was to become a hereditary satrapy at Daskyleion – Pharnabazos was a great-grandson of his. Artabazos was son of Pharnakes; and the Pharnakes (Parnaka) who was Darius I's controller-general in Persis was son of Arsames (above, p. 89). So Artabazos could have been the son of a brother of Hystaspes.[2]

The Seven agreed on special privileges (including that of inter-marriage) for themselves after the coup of 522. Intaphernes was presently put to death with all his kinsmen except one unnamed son, and we hear nothing more of Ardumanish (or whatever his name was), though his father's name Wahauka was later current in the royal line if it is what the Greeks called Ōkhos. One thing we must remember is that our information relates almost entirely to the western half of the empire so that Persian nobles settled or employed in the East disappear from view. Also, in trying to follow up the descendants of the Seven we do not often find fathers' names given outside the pages of Herodotus. So when we meet an Otanes or a Hydarnes or Gobryas we cannot be sure to what family he belongs. In fact we do know that the Gobryas who was a commander in 480 was the son not of the paladin Gobryas or of his daughter but of Artystone and Darius, and that an Otanes active in the West was the son of a Sisamnes, while a Sisamnes was son of a Hydarnes. Otanes and Hydarnes are fairly common names in the Persepolis tablets and other sources. In the second half of the fifth century men with what is presumably the name Hydarnes occur as a sirdar in Egypt (Widrang), as a satrap who was succeeded by his son Teritoukhmes (Idernes),[3] and as the father of Tissaphernes (Widrna); but we cannot say whether any of them were of the paladin's family. So too with a Gobryas who was satrap of Babylon about

420 B.C. and – probably the same person – one of Artaxerxes II's generals in 401 B.C.

Old Persian Gaubaruwa, spelt Kambarma in Elamite transcription, is Akkadian Gubaru and Greek Gobryas. It is not always accepted that the Gobryas who is Darius I's spear-bearer on the tomb front at Naksh-i Rustam was the same person as the Gobryas who was acting as Cyrus' governor in Babylon in autumn 539. But the Gobryas of 539 ought to be the Gobryas who became satrap of Babylonia four years later and continued so under Cambyses; and it looks a straight run-through from Gobryas' attendance at the King's court near Uruk in 528 (above, p. 46) and Darius' marriage with Gobryas' daughter to Darius' admission to the plot of which Gobryas was one of the prime initiators. From that point on Herodotus and Darius' monuments fairly well prove the identity of Darius' father-in-law, general against the Elamites, spear-bearer, and right-hand man on the Scythian campaign. Of his governorship of Babylonia a little is known.[4] From 521 B.C. he was presumably in attendance on the King, whose daughter he is found escorting in 498 B.C. (see Chap. IX n.10). At Nakshi-i Rustam he is called the Patishuwarish. It would make sense if this could mean 'deceased'. But in fact it can hardly not be the same word as Strabo's Persian tribe of Pateischoreis, and it calls to mind the region Patusharra in Assyrian royal annals which is located on the Median plateau towards Mt Bikni and the salt desert. Presumably Gobryas was not an Achaemenid, but at Behistun Darius does call him a Persian. His father's name was Mardonios, and he gave that name to his son by Darius' sister who met his end at Plataea in 479. We know nothing more of the family than the Mardonios had a son Artontes who was concerned to recover his father's body.

Bagabukhsha (Megabyxos) the paladin is called son of Datuwahya at Behistun. According to Herodotus his son Zopyros recaptured Babylon for Darius by mutilating himself and so gaining the confidence of the Babylonians who believed it was Darius' doing, for which service he received Babylon as a fief (III 150–end). This is, however, difficult to believe because the revolts there occurred after Darius' death (above, p. 100); and here for once Ctesias is to be preferred when he has Zopyros killed in the revolt after Darius' death and his son Megabyxos reconquer Babylon. After this, Megabyxos the son was a marshal in the Greek expedition of 480. If we believe Ctesias, he had cause to complain of the promiscuousness of his wife Amytis, who was Xerxes' daughter; but his sense of grievance did not prevent him from betraying the plot to murder Artaxerxes I after his accession; he was severely wounded in the resulting fight, but recovered thanks to skilful treatment by the Greek doctor Apollonides. After Lower Egypt had revolted under Inaros in the late 460s and the satrap Achaemenes at the head of an expeditionary force was killed in battle at Papremis (about 459 B.C.) Artaxerxes tried to divert Athenian aid from Egypt by wholesale bribery in Greece (above, p. 128). But when that failed Megabyxos was put in charge of an amphibious expedition, and after recapturing Memphis and so relieving the garrison in the White Fort he succeeded in penning the Athenian fleet at Prosopitis Island nearby. After a one-and-a-half-year siege he drained the channel and captured the ships; a supporting Athenian fleet of fifty ships sailed in without knowing of the event and was destroyed (455 B.C.). Megabyxos was then able to return with Inaros and a body of Athenians as prisoners, leaving a royal prince Arsames as satrap (see Chap. XII, n.11) and the whole country pacified except for the rebel Amyrtaios in the marshes.

We know from Herodotus and Thucydides of Megabyxos' success in Egypt and of his son Zopyros' defection, but for the rest we depend on Ctesias. Megabyxos is said to have negotiated an armistice on conditions, and when in due course Inaros and fifty Athenian prisoners were done to death by Amestris, the queen-mother, he felt his honour compromised; so he returned to Syria, where he was probably satrap, and proceeded to revolt. It was only after he had routed two expeditions sent by the King, personally wounding both commanders as he had previously done Inaros, and himself sustaining a wound, that honour was satisfied and he consented to be reconciled to his sovereign. If he was commanding the army in Cilicia in 450 B.C., his revolt probably belongs to the early 440s; it must have been over before Nehemiah went to Jerusalem in 445 B.C.; G. Rawlinson saw in his condonement a weakness in Artaxerxes I's character and a dangerous precedent for future revolts. Restored to court, Megabyxos was imprudent enough to anticipate the King in a lion-hunt; and after his wife and her mother Amestris had begged for his life he was sentenced to permanent exile in the 'Gulag Archipelago' of the Persian Gulf. Five years later he made his way back disguised as a leper, received a free pardon, and was the King's table-companion until his death at the age of 76.

Of his two sons who had fought valiantly with him during his revolt one, Zopyros, later went into exile at Athens and lost his life in a raid on Kaunos in East Caria; the other, Artyphios, who had perhaps succeeded to the Abarnahara satrapy, revolted against Darius II and twice defeated the King's forces under Artasyras, but eventually his Greek mercenaries were seduced from him and he ended up in the ash-pit (above, p. 129). That seems to be the end of the family. But in Megabyxos the battle-scarred marshal we have a rare sketch of a noble Persian in the fifth century. His life story has no doubt been sensationalized by Ctesias; but even so we may surmise that if there had been a few others with his heroic temper and high code of honour Persian arms would not have sunk so low. In an article (in *AJP* 101 (1980) 79–96) which contains much of interest on the Persian armed forces Rahe has contended that Megabyxos revolutionized warfare by the combination of oriental cavalry and Greek mercenary hoplites, thus setting the example for Cyrus the Younger; but this does not fit well with the Egyptian terrain or his addiction to single combat.

With Otanes (Utana) and Hydarnes (Widarna) we quickly lose direct contact, but fortunately not for good. Otanes was a most noble Achaemenid and in Herodotus he appears as the senior member of the Seven. At Behistun he is called son of Thukhra, but Herodotus calls him son of Pharnaspes (and so brother of Cyrus' wife Kassandane). This could be a case where two names were current, as with Bardiya – Thukhra might be a nickname 'Rufus'. Otanes has the distinction that his is the only name apart from the King's that appears on brick-stamps of Darius' palace at Susa. He went on a special mission to restore Syloson to Samos (above, p. 60), but after that he does not appear on the active list under Darius. We can probably assign a son or two to him among those that Herodotus names as sons of Otanes in the army of 480 B.C.: Smerdomenes the marshal (whose mother was a sister of Darius), and perhaps Patiramphes who was Xerxes' charioteer and Anaphes who commanded the Elamite division. It would be surprising if the paladin himself lived to take the field then; so the Otanes who commanded the Persian foot division and was the father of Xerxes' wife Amestris is a problem. But Ctesias makes Amestris the daughter of Onophas and in fact names Onophas in place of Otanes in his list of the Seven, while Anaphas appears elsewhere an an alternative form of the paladin's name.[5] So there is a connection of some sort, if a faulty one. Hydarnes was last definitely heard of in Media in 521 B.C.; it has recently been suggested that Persepolis Fortification tablets show him in authority there down to 499 B.C.[6] He had a son Hydarnes who commanded the Immortals in 480.[7] Herodotus speaks of the son as being at one time 'general of the coastal men in Asia' (VII 135), which has given rise to a belief that he was made satrap of Daskyleion; but his regular office may rather have been that of hazarapatish (above, p. 144). A Hydarnes is also mentioned by Herodotus (VI 133) as the recipient of an accusation against Miltiades; the context is Western, but the date could be at any time between the Scythian expedition and 493 B.C. Sisamnes, son of Hydarnes, who commanded the Areian division in 480, may have been another son of the paladin.

In later times great prestige attached to being descended from one of the Seven – in the Latin writers 'a septem Persis oriundus'. A number of grandees in fourth-century Asia Minor were so descended (for instance, the satrapal family of Mithradates of Cappadocia and of Kios, and that of Roisakes and Spithridates of Lydia). Some of them were probably of Otanes' line, which is assumed to have been established in a tribute-free despotate in the north of Cappadocia with a palace perhaps at Gazioura by the R. Iris.[8] Two or three of these noble Persians were able to retain or regain their rule after the Macedonian conquest; but it is not easy to distinguish the posterity of Otanes, though the royal line of the Hellenistic kingdom of Pontus could more easily be in descent from him than, as was claimed, from Cyrus the Great.[9] In Armenia a Persian ruling line ended near the close of the third century B.C. in Orontes who was said to be a descendant of the paladin Hydarnes;[10] an ancestor of his named Orontes was commanding Armenians under Darius III and is found holding the satrapy of Armenia after Alexander (317 B.C.), while an earlier Orontes, who was rewarded with the King's daughter as his bride after the battle at Kounaxa (401 B.C.), was satrap in eastern Armenia or Matiene.[11] It is therefore a prevalent assumption, though not without difficulties, that the Hydarnids held a hereditary satrapy in Armenia under the later Achaemenids as well as continuing to rule there after Alexander. The kings of Commagene in the Euphrates bend claimed descent from the same Orontes who married Artaxerxes II's daughter Rodogoune, but used it to trace themselves back to Darius, with no mention of Hydarnes.[12]

After his accession Artaxerxes I is said to have replaced existing satraps with his own friends.[13] This is the lowest ebb in our knowledge of Achaemenid rule. In Baktria the satrap rebelled as claimant to the throne; Megabyxos may perhaps at this time have been given Abarnahara, and we know names, though not dates, of several satraps in Babylon, of whom one named by Ctesias as satrap about 450 B.C. was Artaxerxes' brother. But Achaemenes remained in Egypt until he fell in battle, and there was no change at Daskyleion. What in fact is striking is the long tenure of office even at the top satrapal level. Achaemenes had governed Egypt for quarter of a century before his death, and – assuming Ctesias' Sarsamas (see Chap. XII, n.11) to be the same person – Arsames had half a century in office, though he spent three years back home when he went on vacation in 410 B.C.. Pissouthnes was satrap of Sardis for quarter of a century at the least before he revolted.

The impression we get is that the major satrapies were allotted to princes of the royal house and not normally passed on from father to son; the emoluments of office were perhaps too valuable. This applies to Babylon, Baktria, Memphis, and Sardis; unfortunately we know virtually nothing of holders of the satrapies of Media and Susa. Minor satrapies could more readily be left in the hands of Persian nobles with experience of local conditions as long as they saw to it that the tribute was paid. Daskyleion, which became less important after the Persians had pulled out of Europe, affords the best-known example. Artabazos' family held the satrapy for ninety years until Pharnabazos was recalled to marry the King's daughter Apame. Pharnabazos' handsome teenage son, who was left behind, was driven out by 'the brother' (presumably of Pharnabazos), and he was befriended by the Spartan king Agesilaos;[14] but after the seat had been occupied by one of Pharnabazos' former aides (Ariobarzanes), Artabazos, generally believed to be the son of the royal marriage, recovered his father's heritage; after a chequered career he ended up in Eastern Iran, while one of his eleven sons, Pharnabazos, stayed to command the Persian fleet in the Aegean in 334–332 and took a part in the struggles after Alexander's death. Abarnahara also shows a tendency to be hereditary: a son of Megabyxos may have succeeded his father there, and we find satraps of the name Bel-Shunu (Belesys) in the last decade of the fifth century and again sixty years later. Ctesias speaks of a satrap Teritoukhmes under Darius II who had succeeded his father Idernes and of a city being held for his son to take over if he had not been poisoned by Parysatis, while Oudiastes, who replaced him, was succeeded by his own son; the name of the city, Zaris, seems to point to Zranka (Seistan). The evidence for a hereditary satrapy of the Hydarnids in eastern Armenia has been presented. In the fourth century there were new satrapies with rulers who succeeded from father to son, as in Cappadocia, where Datames expanded the governorship that he had inherited from his father, Kamisares, and his son Sysinas held what he could after him, and Caria which was ruled by a native dynasty continuously through the last sixty years of the empire. The established families will have owned great possessions in their satrapies and had their own court circles. We find Pharnabazos and Datames more than once using their relatives and dependants to carry out missions or military operations for them; this was especially helpful when there was underhand work to be done.

Under Cyrus the Great the satrapal system would seem to have been universal with one notable exception; this was Cilicia, whose ruler (Syennesis) evidently continued in office in virtue of his spontaneous adhesion to the Persian cause. He seems to have been tributary but responsible for his own military security. Cambyses and Darius I probably allowed some exceptions on the fringes of the empire. Cyprus had submitted voluntarily to the Persians in the time of Cambyses, and its city-kings may have been more or less autonomous until the Ionian Revolt. In Egypt the defeated Pharaoh failed to behave as a vassal and was replaced by a satrap of Cambyses; but the families of princelings of the Delta and Libyan marches were retained as minor rulers, and in those of Inaros and Amyrtaios sons were even put in power after their fathers had revolted and been conquered;[15] this was of course no easy territory to control, so the fact that the policy led to recurring revolts does not necessarily mean that it was a bad one. When he defeated Skunkha and his Sakai Darius did not install a satrap but set up a native chieftain of his own choice. In Arabia and Ethiopia rulers like Geshem of Kedar, whom Nehemiah had to confront, were probably not expected to do more than acknowledge Persian suzerainty and send the statutory gifts; the despatch of an imperial official to Dedan in the time of Geshem's son Qainu was probably caused by the outbreak of hostilities with Tema, near which the graffito recording it was found (for some sort of trouble with an Arab king in 411 B.C. see Chap. XVII n.4). In the generation before 479 B.C. Macedonia ranked as a vassal kingdom. For the rest the empire was nominally under satrapal control, though of course there were forested mountain regions which may never have recognized Persian authority.

The reign of Darius II was marked by revolts in different parts of the empire (above, p. 129f.) and no doubt by a weakening of the central authority. Mountain tribesmen were becoming increasingly impatient of control, and by the early years of the fourth century a trend towards more compact and manageable satrapies is recognizable. Darius II is himself said (by Ctesias) to have been appointed satrap of Hyrkania by his father; since Hyrkania seems normally to have been contained in a larger satrapy (that of Parthia ostensibly in 521 B.C. and again under Darius III)[16] it is possible that this was a temporary expedient to give him a benefice or keep him away from court. Surprisingly – for they were in revolt at the time – we read in Plutarch of an archon (satrap) of the Kadousioi named Artagerses who was killed defending the King in the battle of Kounaxa. The situation in Asia Minor is masked by the overriding command entrusted to Cyrus the Younger from 408 B.C. and to some extent also to Tissaphernes between 401 and his execution in 395 B.C. But after Kounaxa Syennesis may have been punished for hedging his bets; and Caria became a satrapy under native dynasts after the death of Tissaphernes. Cappadocia emerges as a satrapy which included the north-east corner of Cilicia (Melitene).[17] It is doubtful whether Ionia ever ranked as a separate satrapy. Phrygia in the middle of Anatolia is a puzzle. In the Greek writers the term 'Phrygian' in a satrapal context normally refers to

Daskyleion (Hellespontine Phrygia); and though there are some mentions of people in charge in inland Phrygia we do not receive the impression that it had a separate satrap empowered to act on his own authority, so it could be a matter of subordinates or King's emissaries for a special purpose. In the East, where Herodotus' grouping of peoples in satrapies is obscure, we can at least infer that there had been some re-arrangement by the time of Darius III, with new satrapies of Karmania, of Areia as distinct from Parthia, and reputedly even of the Tapouroi in the east of Khorasan; Zranka by then went with Arachosia.

From the time of Darius I governors of satrapies were Persians. Apart from the curious appointment of a man of Halikarnassos named Xeinagores as successor to the Syennesis of Cilicia who perished at Salamis in 480 B.C.,[18] the earliest known exception is the Belesys (Bel-Shunu, so probably a Babylonian) who was satrap of Abarnahara before the end of the fifth century. Lewis has remarked that being himself half a Babylonian Darius II may have been more partial to them than his precedessors.[19] After this Kamisares, whose son Datames enlarged his original province in south Cappadocia and was the most warlike satrap of his time in Anatolia, is said to have been a Carian who had a Scythian wife with Paphlagonian connections; and it was an old native family – that into which Syennesis' daughter had married – that held the satrapy of Caria from 395 B.C. It is interesting how notables from Caria were rising in the world through their combination of native shrewdness and a Greek cultural facade. Cyrus the Younger in 401 B.C. committed the charge of Aeolis and Ionia and of his fleet to an Egyptian (or possibly Carian) of Memphis, Tamos, who had been one of Tissaphernes' lieutenants, and Tamos' son Glos held similar charges under his father-in-law Tiribazos (below, p. 216). Eastern Iranians do not appear in our sources as satraps. The restless Orontes, who betrayed his satrapal colleagues in 362 B.C., is called a Baktrain. But if he is the Orontes, who was son of the King's Eye Artasyras, married to Rodogoune, and supposedly a Hydarnid, his family must have been Persian (see Chap. XVIII n.27).

There was no uniform infrastructure of Achaemenid rule in the satrapies, and no general system for the collection of tribute can be discerned. Babylon and Egypt had been kingdoms with a developed administrative system of their own which the Persians were content to maintain in being. Under its satrap Egypt continued to be divided into nomes, each with a governor (fratarak) and treasury; administrative and judicial responsibility was vested in these governors. Widrang (presumably Hydarnes, and so a Persian) was promoted from military commander of Upper Egypt to the governorship of the southern nome in the late fifth century. In Koptos Atiyawahy, son of Artames, was governor under Darius I and Xerxes; his brother, who may have succeeded him about the beginning of Artaxerxes I's reign, had a fine Iranian name Ariyawrata (Ariarathes) but adopted an Egyptian name Dedhor or Takhos. Their mother was named Qandu and may have been an Egyptian.[20] Functionaries with Persian names appear in documents. On the other hand, district governors appear with Egyptian and Babylonian names; and surprisingly high offices were held by Egyptians, such as Ujahorresne (above, p. 48), and Ptahhotep the head of the Treasury in Memphis and Ahmose the commander of the military under Darius I. Khnumimbre was director of works and commanded soldiers, and Osorwer had a mansion and district in the South. It is notable how many such dignitaries date to the time of Darius I before the revolt of 486 B.C. In both Egypt and Babylonia the habit of officials and fief-holders with Iranian names giving their sons native names (and less frequently the reverse) increases the difficulty of assessing the ethnic mix in the upper classes. In Babylonia there were presumably Persians commanding garrison troops as in Egypt, and perhaps acting as city governors (a Persian is also mentioned at the end of the empire as governor of an island in the Gulf in Strabo XVI 767). The great sanctuaries were important social and economic centres and owned land and slaves, but some financial control seems to have been exercised by royal superintendants. Panels of judges appear in the tablets; they contained a small but significant proportion of Persian names (below, p. 203).

To a considerable extent Persian dominance in both Babylonia and Egypt must have been maintained through landowners. The satrap Arsames had great possessions in Egypt, with native bailiffs administering them and Cilician and other slaves taken into his employ and even branded; he also gave orders as though he were the owner of far-flung estates in Abarnahara and Mesopotamia. Other members of the royal house, Warohi and Widdaps, appear as absentee landowners in Egypt. The King of course had vast possessions; and members of the royal house who owned estates in Babylonia in the later fifth century were the queen Parysatis, Arishittu (presumably Darius II's brother who revolted), and Menostanes (a son of Artaxerxes I's brother, Artarios, who backed Sogdianos, above, p. 129). Many Persians of standing and veteran soldiers of the imperial army had received fiefs with the obligation of providing military service, though as time went on this was commuted into money payments. Temples and the larger landowners must have played an important part in the provincial administration and the maintenance of law and order.

In Abarnahara we do not know of a permanent satrapal seat. Sidon, the premier Phoenician city, which (as recorded on Eshmunazar's sarcophagus) received the coastal stretch of Sharon south of Mt Carmel from a Persian King (Artaxerxes I?) in return for services rendered, had a royal park for the Persian King's use, and there was a palace with columns in Persian style; but it had its own city-king. It must have been an important centre because Diodorus speaks of Persians who were there when it revolted after Artaxerxes III's abortive campaign against Egypt (below, p. 223). Tripolis and Damascus have also been claimed as the satrap's residence, and Askalon is also said to have had a palace in the fourth century. But the one satrapal palace that we hear of, that of Belesys in 401 B.C., was in the north near Aleppo. So far as we can judge, there was a variety of local governors, whose chanceries would maintain contact with both the satrapal court and such lesser centres as there were within their jurisdiction. These local governors were city princes in Phoenicia and Cyprus, elsewhere perhaps priestly rulers, native despots, and tribal shiekhs.[21] When Nehemiah was sent, in 445 B.C. as is generally accepted, to take up office as the King's special governor in the run-down city of Jerusalem, his action in rebuilding the wall circuit was seen by the neighbours who hemmed Judah in as portending revolt, and protests were promptly made by their governors; for Jerusalem had the reputation of being a rebellious city and had been the seat of mighty kings (after David captured it from the Jebusites). In this context we meet three dynasts whose families continued to wield power after them – Sanballat in Samaria, which had been the capital of the kingdom of Israel and whose territory was largely peopled by Assyrian deportees from Babylonia and Syria, the Jew Tobias of Amman across the Jordan, and the Arab Geshem of Kedar[22] who may have been occupying Edom as far north as the palace of Lachish, together with representatives of the Philistine administrative centre of Ashdod.[23] Recent excavations have yielded wine-jar stamps and sealings in Judah and Benjamin, with several names of governors which are in general Jewish or at least Semitic. As against this, two or three men with Persian names appear as officials or people of influence in the Biblical books (as Mithradates and Sathrabouzanes in Ezra/Esdras), and Bagohi may perhaps have been a Persian governor in Palestine.[24] Parysatis and Arsames had their estates (a bailiff or two at places like Damascus having Persian-sounding names), and the royal estate in Esdraelon might go back to Achaemenid times, though no Persian architectural elements have come to light in the palace at Megiddo. But though tombs at Shechem and elsewhere yield culture-objects of Achaemenid types, there seems to be no evidence of a Persian presence in Abarnahara on a scale comparable to that in Babylonia. Abarnahara had submitted with a good grace after Cyrus' capture of Babylon and fitted easily in a multi-national empire. Much of the province had suffered such upheaval and deportation in Assyrian times that ethnic consciousness was lacking, and there was no inclination to revolt and so give grounds for conquest and confiscations. Important peoples like the Hittites and Aramaeans, the Philistines, and the Edomites had more or less lost their identity, as the Midianites, Amorites, and Amalekites had done earlier. Only the Phoenician cities, which housed the last, now highly civilized remnant of the old Canaanite stock, and the hard core of Jews of the Covenant of Sinai, who saw in Jerusalem the sole seat of a supreme, jealous god, proved capable of national aspirations when the Persian empire seemed to be collapsing.

It is commonly assumed that Achaemenid rule in the empire had a pyramidal structure with a territorial basis. Leuze set up Abarnahara as the model of the devolution of authority: King-Babylon satrap-governor in Abarnahara-district governors. But Abarnahara cannot be regarded as one of a plurality of divisions of the Babylon satrapy; and after it became an independent satrapy, the satrap was the only intermediary between the King and a diversity of dynasts, high priests, and sheikhs. On the evidence of Nehemiah it is claimed that Judah was subdivided into twelve administrative districts and there is some correspondence between them and the find-spots of the jar-stamps; but they present anomalies and it is questionable whether they can have had any official standing. It is more likely that each district governor or ruler had his own internal arrangements. There were, however, treasurers in the province since the King could give Ezra a warrant to draw on them for his needs.

Western Asia Minor ought to be more informative because we hear a good deal about the military and diplomatic encounters of Persians and Greeks there (especially in the years around 400 B.C.). But unfortunately the Greek writers do not explain in what way satrapal authority was delegated; and as they use the terms 'satrap' and 'hyparch' loosely, the information they give is ambiguous. To take an example from Herodotus that at first sight seems clear, we are told that the Persian Sandokes, who was in command of a fleet squadron captured off Artemision in 480, was hyparch of Kyme in Aeolis. If Kyme had a Persian governor we should expect other Greek coastal cities of equal importance to have had them – which does not fit with the general picture of native tyrants or oligarchies running the cities in the Persian interest. But as we read on we discover that it was at Kyme that the Persian fleet spent the following winter; so probably Sandokes' appointment depended on Kyme with its sheltered bay being a fleet base for Xerxes' expedition; and the same applies to Artayktes, the hyparch of Sestos on the Straits in 480–79. We again hear occasionally of Persian 'hyparchs' in the coastal areas or cities under Tissaphernes and Cyrus the Younger. But inevitably they appear at places where negotiations or military operations were taking place; and we cannot tell whether they had a particular territorial jurisdiction or may not rather have been lieutenants whom the satraps despatched to sensitive points as needed. In general the impression given is that the Persian satraps in Western Asia Minor were frequently on the move and normally conducted negotiations themselves, and not that they were in the habit of acting through subordinate district governors.

In the coastal plains we find a mixed Persian and medizing Greek military presence in the King's land. Evidently Persians did not care to be settled in too close proximity to the sea after 480 B.C.; Kimon's operations in the years following had presumably cut out any Persians within easy reach of his fleet, and the treaty of Kallias secured the territory of the Greek cities from encroachment. But where a plain was shielded from the sea or stretched deep inland the Persian presence was stronger. The situation in the Kaikos valley in 400 B.C. is particularly well known thanks to Xenophon's privateering there.[25] The high citadel of Pergamon and two smaller ones lower down the valley were occupied by Greek families in exile – the descendants of the Spartan king Demaratos and of Gongylos who had no doubt gained his fief as a reward for acting as secret agent between Xerxes and Pausanias.[26] Both families had men-at-arms at their disposal. There is also talk elsewhere of a Greek fief at Gryneion on the coast; and during the Ionian Revolt a Persian called Harpagos had had a sufficient body of troops in the north-west of the valley to be able to intercept Histiaios' raiding party at Atarneus. In the plain was a Persian, Asidates, who lived with an armed retinue in a tower-compound, while a certain Itamenes had troops of his own in the neighbourhood. Besides this, Xenophon speaks of Assyrian heavy infantry and royal mercenary Hyrkanian cavalry up to eighty in number arriving from Komania with 800 light-armed infantry, and forces including cavalry from other places in the neighbourhood, of which two are named. The pattern seems to be one of fief-holders and possibly also military settlers who between them were responsible for keeping the peace, though of course the larger contingents of troops may have been specially despatched to the area to counter the threat from Xenophon's corps (which was the rump of the Ten Thousand who went up with Cyrus). It looks as though these fiefs left no room for native land-owners in the fertile country there.

There is possibly some evidence from place names like Hyrkanian Plain and Darius' Village (and, Strabo XIII 629 adds, Cyrus' Plain) for Iranian military settlement in western Asia Minor; there may also have been Bak-trians in the west. In the inland plain of Colophon we more than once hear of men with Iranian names who brought non-Greek troops into play (Itamanes and Stages). In the Maeander valley Themistocles was given the region of Magnesia as a fief (above, p. 127). According to Herodotus the land in the plain there had been taken over by the Persians after the fall of Miletus (while the rough hill-country was turned over to the pastoral Pedasians from behind Halikarnassos). An interesting side-light on this has appeared on an inscrip-tion of the hellenized city of Amyzon in the hills to the south;[27] it records the grant of citizenship in 320 B.C. to two men with fine Persian names, Baga-dates and his son Ariaramnes, no doubt to the benefit both of the city, which thus gained territory in the fertile land, and of the landowners, whose title to it would have been secured by the attachment.

In Lycia there is contemporary evidence from funerary inscriptions in which local dynasts vaunted their prowess. That Persians left their mark on the upper stratum of Lycian society is suggested by the themes of their tomb-reliefs and more clearly by the frequency with which Persian names occur in the inscriptions of the cities in post-Achaemenid times[28] – even allowing for some specious adoption of noble Iranian names for prestige purposes in Roman Asia Minor (as with two freedmen calling themselves Mazaios and Mithridates who erected a market gate at Ephesus in honour of Agrippa). But the contemporary inscriptions, including those on coins, show that men with Persian names were prominent in Lycia in the late fifth and early fourth centuries: besides two satraps of Lydia, names such as Harpagos, Otanes, Mithrapates, Artembares the Mede, who may have been a satrap's lieutenant, and Arsames seem to be recognizable. Unfortunately it is difficult to determine the position of these men in the power-structure. On the whole the ones named seem to have inserted themselves as despots in western Lycia among the contending native dynasts; so we may be dealing in part with mixed families engaged in local power-struggles rather than with a regular Persian governing and fief-holding establishment (see below, p. 200f.).[29]

One other region on which the spotlight is turned is the corner of Asia adjoining the Dardanelles (the Troad). Here the inland cities of the Scaman-der basin had been enrolled in the Athenian confederacy; but in the second half of the fifth century they worked loose. The three principal ones came into the hands of a Greek (or hellenized Dardanian) who built up a despotate under the jurisdiction of the Daskyleion satrap, to whom he regularly paid over the tribute. When he died , sometime after 414 B.C., Pharnabazos the satrap looked round for someone to replace him with; but the widow, Mania, convinced him that she was her husband's equal, added the little coastal towns to the principality, paid over the tribute regularly, and joined the satrap in his campaigns against the recalcitrant hill tribes of Mysia and Pisidia.[30] Her armed forces, which provided garrisons for the cities, seem in general to have consisted of Greek mercenaries; but it was clearly understood that she was a vassal ('hyparch' is Xenophon's term) of Pharnabazos with obligations of providing military contingents as well as tribute. Her principality seems in effect to have been an extended fief. Other 'hyparchs' in the Daskyleion satrapy can be named: in addition to the satrap's relatives we hear of Pytharchos of Kyzikos, who was given seven towns by Cyrus, perhaps Timagoras of Kyzikos who received gifts and was an agent of Pharnabazos, the noble Spithridates who had a force of 200 cavalry and connections with the Paphlagonians, a noble family (of Pharnabazos' close associate Ariobarzanes) at Kios, and further east the Persian Rathanes who held Gordion against Agesilaos, Epixyes on the route inland in the 460s, and a 'dynast' at Tyana who was put to death by Cyrus the Younger along with a royal official there; among others the military commander Memnon at the end of the empire. In the Lydian satrapy we hear of Amyntas to whom the town of Alabanda was given, a 'house' of the satrap Tissaphernes in Caria (which had perhaps been confiscated when he overthrew the rebel Pissouthnes' son Amorges), the noble Ariaios who was at home at Kolossai, and the palace that Cyrus the Younger frequented at Kelainai. On the borders of the two satrapies was Arsakes in the rich land by Adramyttion. We also know of people like Miltiades' son Metiochos and Phylakos of Samos (and in Ctesias of Lykon who betrayed Pissouthnes) who were given fiefs by the King, presumably in the West. There were also a number of Greeks and a Carian whom the satraps used as agents and advisers, including Tissaphernes' military expert, Phalinos of Zakynthos; such people also might expect to be rewarded with fiefs.

The household troops of these 'hyparchs' were brought into action locally against raiders such as Histiaios, Thrasyllos (409 B.C.), and Xenophon. But they could also unite to form a field force. In fact Herodotus relates that after the Ionian raid in 499 B.C. the Persians who held 'nomoi' (apportionments) west of the R. Halys rallied to Sardis and pursued the Greeks to Ephesus. There were of course also the static garrisons (above, p. 110f.), and satraps had their own sepoy brigades: Pharnabazos had 400 cavalry (and two scythed chariots), Tissaphernes took 500 cavalry when he went up to Babylon to warn the King, and Cyrus the Younger had an escort of 600 cavalry when he went up. Tissaphernes had a very much larger force of cavalry, as well as infantry, in 395 B.C., but he had by then received strong reinforcements for an offensive against Agesilaos (below, p. 214). The overall impression we receive is that both militarily and politically the normal Persian presence within these satrapies depended on what Xenophon would call 'hyparchs' but we can probably regard as large fief-holders.

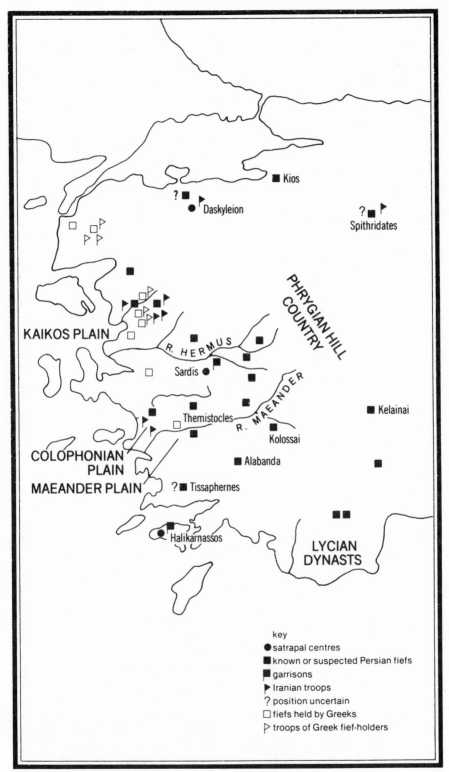

Fig. 12   The Persian presence in western Asia Minor

The literary testimonies have now been reviewed. Except in Lycia there is hardly anything to be derived from contemporary inscriptions. But inscriptions of Hellenistic times, when Greek came to be widely used by the Asianic peoples, give evidence of the survival of Persian proper names in various places; the combination of such names with the continuing worship of Anahita which is attested by coins and inscriptions (above, p. 150) helps to locate Persian families which were still flourishing in Asia Minor.[31] Achaemenian and Greco-Persian seals would provide particularly valuable information if their find-spots were recorded; and to some extent the same is true of ornaments and silver vessels of Iranian types, though as prestige objects they could easily find their way outside the limits of Persian rule and it is not easy to distinguish what is Persian. The occasional tomb seems to betray a Persian presence, as the so-called 'pyramid tomb' at Sardis, reliefs perhaps from a tomb at Daskyleion, and a tumulus with two chambers equipped with couches, which was recently excavated at Ikiztepe in eastern Lydia and contained silver vessels and an incense-burner similar to those on

Plate 9   the Persepolis Treasury reliefs. Classical reliefs from such monuments found in Lycia, Lydia, and elsewhere show dynastic themes such as riding, hunting, banqueting, and audience scenes. In some cases, as on the reliefs from

Plate 30   Daskyleion and, in a different medium, the paintings in the tomb at Karaburun near Elmali in northern Lycia, figures and décor appear that have been classed as Iranian (above, p. 165) and the first impression is that Persian influence was increasing in the fifth century. But the general character of many of the scenes is dynastic without necessarily being more Persian than Anatolian.[32] Adding together the literary and other evidences it is possible to

Fig. 12   produce a tentative sketch-map marking places where a Persian presence can reasonably be surmised.

The pleasant, fruitful valleys that lead down from the Lydian hill-country seem to have been a favoured area for Persian fiefs. In southern Cappadocia, where the route over the Antitaurus from the Euphrates crossing descends towards the upper Halys plain, water streams in abundance over a cliff in the valley at the village of Bünyan among groves and orchards and forms an ideal setting for a paradise; a Persian (or at least Iranian) domain here is proved by the discovery of a fire altar with a relief showing a Magus. Persian grandees will have lived in places like Bünyan and Kelainai which could be beautified with lodges, woods, animal parks, gardens and orchards, with fountains of running water, and fish-stocked streams or lakes – we get a good idea of what they liked from Xenophon's descriptions of Kelainai and Daskyleion.[33]

The distribution of these fiefs in the West may have depended partly on the opportunity to confiscate – Lydia, Lycia, and the Greek fringe had been conquered by force of arms. But it depended also on fertility of the soil and congenial surroundings for the Persian way of life. Consequently a Persian presence seems to have been lacking in the unproductive mountain regions. This appears in the literary sources. Some communities of the Trojan Mt Ida seem to have been annexed for the first time during Darius I's reign; Themistocles went into hiding in a Greek hill town of the southern Aeolis where the King's writ did not run; a Persian noble Orontes went to Mysia in revolt

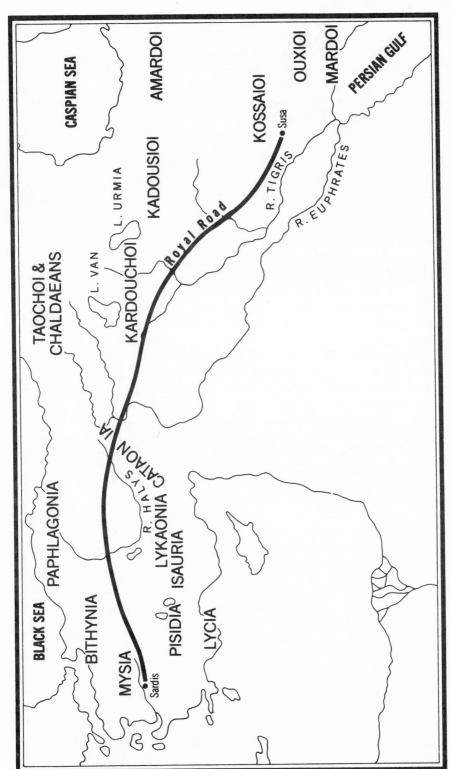

Fig. 13   Trouble-spots in the Empire

against Cyrus the Younger (below, p. 222), and the Oxyrrhynchus historian says the majority of the Mysians were not subject to the Persians in 395 B.C. Even in the tranquil period after the treaty of Kallias Pericles could take an Athenian fleet along the shores of the Black Sea, making contacts and installing settlers on its southern coast. Paphlagonia appears as independent in fact, if not in name, until the satrap Datames broke through to capture the gluttonous ruler Thus (supposedly his cousin) after 380 B.C. and in due course seize Greek cities of the coast. It seems clear that the Persian presence had stopped short of the coastal ranges of Paphlagonia.

Around the late fifth century, when we have the benefit of Xenophon as an informant, we hear of punitive expeditions against the refractory mountain peoples of Mysia and Bithynia in north-western Asia Minor, and apparently also in Pisidia to the south, in Lykaonia, Isauria, and Kataonia on the south and east edges of the Anatolian plateau; and in most of the region between Armenia and the far end of the Black Sea the tribesmen were not under Persian control; the same is true of the Kardouchoi in Kurdistan where Turkey now borders on Iraq, the Kadousioi and Amardoi south of the Caspian, and tribes of the Zagros like the Ouxioi and Kossaioi who in later Achaemenid times are said to have demanded passage money from the King when he travelled up to his summer capitals. In the mid fifth century, Herodotus says, the royal road from Sardis to Susa ran through secure, inhabited country all the way. This is no doubt true. Persian garrisons, guard-posts, and the household troops of 'hyparchs' will have kept the lifeline secure, just as the 'militaris via' to eastern Iran was kept secure in Seleucid times. But even in Herodotus' day it is doubtful whether the mountain country was held under effective control by a Persian military presence; at best it would probably be a matter of occasional punitive drives to teach the tribesmen a lesson and round up the equivalent of tribute. Security on the roads was certainly a problem, because we hear of Cyrus the Younger having highwaymen blinded, and even with his special firman from the King Ezra had qualms about taking a large caravan from Babylonia to Jerusalem without an armed guard (since the journey was made with sheep and cattle and took no less than four months, a crossing of the Syrian desert can be ruled out).

The 'trouble-spots' known from the sources are shown on Fig. 13.

XVII The Extent of the Empire

Persis and to a large extent Media were mountain country. Stretching from Kurdistan to Fars, the Zagros consists of a broad band of parallel ranges which generally increase in height as one ascends from the side of Mesopotamia and reach altitudes approaching 12,000 ft in Mt Elvend above Hamadan (Agbatana) and 15,000 ft in the highest part further south-east. Only sparse and often stunted oaks now grow along the valley sides, but from the Greek writers we learn that there was a continuous broad forest belt in ancient times. Parallel chains of valleys, between which the rivers from time to time switch trellis-wise through tide-worn breaches in the ridges, offer good land between the 2,000 and 6,000 ft levels, and the precipitation is generally sufficient for pluvial agriculture. In the main these valleys are not only fertile but often very long. But in the south of Persis they are more discontinuous, and with the greater heat and less abundant water the cultivable patches are more restricted. Nevertheless from the Greek writers we learn that between the torrid coast-lands, which had no trees save palms, and the wintry snow-bound mountains inland the intermediate zone of Persis was temperate, with grass, damp meadows, vines and other fruits, with gardens, clear streams, and lakes, and in places woods containing game.[1] Within these lands altitude makes a great difference; low down the corn may be harvested as early as February, while higher up the autumn sowing may not yield a crop till the following August.

Of the Achaemenid capitals Susa, like Babylon, is situated down in the flat land. But it is separated from Mesopotamia by the marshes of the Chaldaeans, and its contacts were as much with the Iranian lands as with Babylon. In fact its language, which survived as Khuzi for a millennium and a half after Darius I made his capital there, is thought to be related to Dravidian such as the Brahui of Baluchistan. Because of the lack of wind the plain of Elam can be exceptionally sultry. But in one respect it differs greatly from Babylon. The rivers that drain the main stretch of 400 miles of the Zagros converge fan-wise on the plain of Susa, which consequently has been well situated to dominate the exits of their valleys and control the winter quarters of the mountain tribes. In contrast to this, Persepolis and Agbatana lay beyond the watershed of the Zagros, with altitudes straddling 6,000 ft, which are normal levels on the plateau. Thanks to Mt Elvend Hamadan is supplied with water, but it is snow-bound in winter.[2] Around Persepolis the hills were presumably clothed with a vegetation that is now lacking; and with the help of irrigation, which seems to have been in use there ages before the Achaemenids, the basin of the R. Kur will have constituted a fertile enough terrain to judge by the clusters of minor sites that have been noted up the valley and to west and

Plates 4 & 16

south of Persepolis; the cultivated area will have been much greater than now if the Lake of Neyriz was dry land (the Greek writers knew of no lake, but Strabo speaks of a great fertile vale in eastern Persis which the rivers traverse). The settlement pattern here, as on the plateau land of Media in 317 B.C., is likely to have been one of numerous villages.

The Zagros provides abundant high summer pasture. The Achaemenid Kings were said to have had breeding grounds for as many as 150,000 Nesaean horses in Media. But the abundance of pasture creates a problem. Sedentary cultivators farming the mountain valleys will not have fodder for large herds of stock in winter, and it needs nomads to take advantage of the high grazing. Thus the picture for many centuries has been one of nomadic tribes who spend the winter in low-altitude camping grounds, which they

Plate 37 leave in April to reach the high valleys during May and the upper mountain slopes in June, and begin to descend to warmer levels about October; in this way they find fresh grass for their stock for most of the year. Inevitably a satisfactory symbiosis of cultivators and nomads is difficult to achieve; if government does not intervene, the nomad tribesmen tend to become dominant to the detriment of cultivation. As far as the archaeological evidence goes, it did recently seem to be a fair conclusion from the surveys which have been carried out in the central Zagros in and around Luristan that, in contrast to Early Iron Age and Median times, settlements of Achaemenid date were almost non-existent; and Achaemenid forts seem to be lacking also. But Stronach's down-dating of pottery from the sites alters the picture,[3] and Ghirshman has discovered a cluster of citadels with sacred terraces and habitations in the Bakhtiari mountains up-country from Susa which he would like to date from the beginning of Persian occupation perhaps about 700 B.C. (above, p. 152ff.). So it is not certain that Achaemenid rule resulted in an increase of nomadism at the expense of the cultivatorrs. What we can infer from the density of the oak cover reported by the Greek writers is that cultivation was not far advanced; it is the sedentary cultivators, and not the nomads with their modest fuel needs, who destroy the forest.

In the collapse of the empire we hear in the Greek sources of predatory peoples (acorn-eating as their successors in recent times) who had been accustomed to exact tribute or passage-money from the Kings and tried to resist any armies in transit through their territory.[4] These were the Mardoi (a Persian 'clan'), the non-Persian Ouxioi, from whom may have come the name Uwja (modern Khuzistan) by which the Persians knew Elam, and the Kossaioi in the central Zagros, with the Elymaioi in the hinterland of Susa. Some of these are said to have possessed both high mountain and cultivated lowland, and there is mention of villages of the Kossaioi and of nomads in Persis; possibly some of them might pass as transhumants rather than nomads. But we are told that when he unexpectedly attacked these peoples in winter and conquered them, Alexander the Great founded 'cities' and tried to turn them into cultivators instead of nomads – an attempt that has been made by other rulers, usually without any lasting success.

We have seen (above, p. 39f.) that Herodotus spoke of four out of the ten Persian 'clans' as 'nomads' (i.e. pastoral people). One was the Mardoi. But the most interesting case is the Sagartians. Their territory, called Asagarta, is mentioned both in Darius I's early inscriptions and, it would seem, in Persepolis tablets; and it was evidently in Media. Since the claimant to the throne who rose in revolt there was publicly impaled by Darius' command at Arbela, it is commonly supposed that Asagarta lay to the north in what is now Iraqi Kurdistan. But Darius chose important centres for executing the rebels; and the Sagartian, like the Mede Frawartish who was executed at Agbatana, had previously been brought to the King's Gate. So the place of execution could be giving us the whereabouts of Darius and not of the Sagartians. It is curious that Herodotus speaks of them as being Persians and speaking Persian, and at the same time places them in a satrapy – his 14th – which seems to stretch from Seistan round the south to the Persian Gulf islands. It may be legitimate to conjecture that as nomads they spent the summer in the high Zagros in Media, where Darius' Median general defeated them in 521 B.C., but descended to winter camping grounds in the south where the tax could more easily be collected from them. This would be the same pattern as that of the great Kashgai nomad confederation in the last half-millennium.

The Sagartians are said to have provided 8,000 cavalry in Xerxes' army, and we hear of Mardoi, and later of Ouxioi and Kossaioi, in Achaemenid armies. Nomads make good soldiers if agreements entered into with them are honoured. So it could be that the Achaemenids deliberately allowed them a free hand. What does appear certain is that control by the central authority weakened over the years: communication between Susa and Persepolis was maintained without interference in Darius I's time (above, p. 87f.), and the number of apparently inhabited settlements in the Persepolis archive already runs to well over a hundred; but in the later years of the empire passage through the tribal areas had to be paid for. A similar pattern appears in the northern Armenian region where in 401 B.C. Xenophon noted that the Taochoi and Chaldaioi were independent but providing troops in the satraps' armies.

The survey of the provinces of the empire that follows is of necessity a sketchy one (this is the case especially with Egypt and those western lands of which more is said in other chapters). There is a considerable quantity of ancient literature, much of which stems from the Alexander historians and later writers who used them like Strabo, and there is a wealth of modern specialized books and articles on which this survey has drawn. References will not normally be given because to do so would be interminable.[5]

The plateau of what is now called Iran is not all flat behind the Zagros; in particular there is tolerable upland village country in the north and east of Media, and an irregular mountain chain, rising in places to granite massifs over 13,000 and 14,000 ft in height, dispenses water for the important centres of Yazd and Kerman on its inner edge. But for the most part the aridity is such that there can only be desultory, if not precarious settlement in the interior away from the encompassing mountain skirts. Certainly bedouinization in Mongol times and the long-distance raids of the Baluchis over the centuries have caused the abandonment of many little settlements that once existed. But at best there can only have been small oases, usually at some distance from one another, and hardly providing cross-routes unless (as in Arab times) domed cisterns were maintained on waterless stretches. The large number of ruins of mud-built compounds that catch the eye on semi-arid land give an impression of a larger population that is probably false; in the main they are not contemporary but successive habitation units.

The interior of Iran could always be crossed by well supplied travellers on a line where the underlying transverse ridges still break the desert surface, from Yazd or Nain to Tabas and the 'eastern highlands' – when he took this route in 1902 Sykes on the way rescued two travellers who were inarticulate from thirst. On either side of this crossing is salt or sand desert. That to the north (Dasht-i Kavir) was apparently traversed in 316 B.C. by the indefatigable warlord Antigonus in an attempt to take his rival Eumenes by surprise; but there does not seem to have been any regular established route across it, and the normal road eastward from Media has always been along the foot of the Elburz through the so-called Caspian Gates and Parthia (which we are told the Kings had to hurry across for lack of sustenance) or by a crossing of the eastern Elburz into Hyrkania (Gorgan). The desert to the south-east (the Lut or Karmanian desert) sinks to altitudes as low as 850 ft on its west side according to Gabriel and is near to being impassable. In 1810 Pottinger noted that couriers could go from Kerman to Herat in eighteen days, but he says the risk of perishing was very great. A route eastward from Kerman crosses the south of the Lut. Both Alexander's general Krateros and Antiochus III traversed it successfully; but the Afghan invaders lost a third of their force and all their baggage there in 1719, and the Seljuk Sultan Alp Arslan in the eleventh century is reported to have been in dire straits on the west side of the Lut. We have remarked that Cyrus the Great gave the name Benefactors to the people who succoured him on the R. Helmand (above, p. 29f.); his successors must have taken care to ensure adequate supplies on journeys or campaigns to Eastern Iran. Even so the danger from scorching sand-laden winds was not negligible in these southern deserts; whole armies are rather vaguely reputed to have been overwhelmed by them, and the names given to the deserts, such as Lot, Death, and Despair, are sufficiently evocative.

East of Persis lay Karmania. In Darius I's Susa building inscriptions Karmania is named as a source of timber. But Karmanians do not figure in the Old Persian lists of peoples; so Herodotus may have been right in speaking of them (his Germanioi) as one of the 'clans' of Persians. Nearchus said that they lived and fought like the Persians except that they used donkeys instead of horses even in war. Ctesias, on the other hand, named them among eastern Iranian peoples. In late Achaemenid times there seems to have been a satrap there; and difficult as it is to envisage in any case, Herodotus' 14th 'nomos' would be beyond belief if it did not encroach on Karmania. With its high mountains Karmania should not have lacked fertile valleys, as Marco Polo recognized when he saw the country newly ruined; it was also said to have mineral wealth. The modern site of Kerman (Bardasir) in the north is at the earliest a foundation of Sassanid times. The principal port was Hormuz (Harmoza) near the mouth of the Minab (Anamis) river. The centre where

Alexander the Great camped on reaching Karmania was at five days' hard travelling from Hormuz, whence Nearchus came up to report to him. This rules out Sirjan with its important Islamic site on the west side of the mountain massif (above, p. 40). The recently investigated site of Tepe Yahya on the edge of a cultivable plain towards the south of Karmania was important in prehistoric times, and it has an Achaemenid level with traces of substantial mud brick buildings. But for supplying an army Jiruft on the Halil (Div) Rud seems much the most suitable region. Nothing definitely earlier than late Hellenistic seals has been reported from there. But the enormous, river-devastated site of Shahr-i Dakyanus that Abbott and Sykes both noted near Sabzevaran, certainly to be identified with Marco Polo's Camadi, could well cover a settlement of Achaemenid date and rank as Ammianus' elusive 'Carmana omnium mater'. Sykes and Stein overestimated its distance from Hormuz; road maps now show that Nearchus could have reached it in five days if he had kept up a speed of about thirty miles a day.

East of the central desert rise the 'eastern highlands' of the modern state of Iran, which allow many pocket communities to exist in a relatively temperate, though windy environment. Beyond their south end, approached only across arid wastes from the west, is the sunken, low-lying alluvial basin of Seistan. The extremes of temperature there are exceptional. Winter blizzards are matched by the 'Wind of 120 Days' which blows with ferocity through the summer; it drives the loose sand in dunes which can overwhelm cultivated land and settlements or equally denude the ground so that Stone Age artifacts lie exposed on the surface (as Yate and McMahon first noted at Shahr-i Sokhta). Deaths from freezing as well as heat stroke and dehydration were sustained by the McMahon mission in 1903–5, together with huge losses among the camels. Rainfall is minimal and there are scarcely any trees except for a few palms and the occasional string of tamarisks. But the basin serves as the sump for the drainage of the south-western Hindukush. Of the rivers whose spring flow replenishes the swampy lagoons of Seistan the greatest is the Helmand (or Hidmand, in the Avesta Haetuma(n)t = 'with dams', Etumandos or the like in the Greek writers). Split into channels it irrigates the soil so that a delta-land with abundant crops and cattle is created in the midst of desert; the fertility of Seistan was fabulous before Tamerlane and his successor destroyed the irrigation system. The river from time to time changes its course, and human settlement has had to move accordingly – not to mention the international boundary whose fixing gave rise to the McMahon mission. Seistan (Sakastene, named after the Sakai who were planted there by the Parthian Mithridates II in the second century B.C.) is the land which the Greeks knew as Drangiana (the Sarangai of Herodotus, Zranka in Old Persian, Zaranj in the Arab geographers). Its inhabitants were said to live like the Persians except that they had little wine to drink. Among the ruined sites of principal cities two have yielded remains of Achaemenid date: Dahan-i Gulaman to the west of the Helmand dam, where remains of a large settlement are reported and several substantial structures of Achaemenid type, including a most remarkable cult building, have been excavated (above, p. 151) – the place was apparently abandoned before late Achaemenid times;

and secondly Nad-i Ali east of the dam (and so in Afghanistan), where a fortified palace on a brick terrace was found. Zarin or Zaris seems to have been the principal ancient name here; known from Ctesias, who gives no location, the name is restored from Parin in Isidorus and Aris in the Tabula Peutingeriana, both in this region.

From Seistan the valleys of the lesser, northerly rivers provided communications with Areia; but the easy route to the east was by the great bend of the Helmand to the junction with the Argandab river at Bist or Bost (Bust). The Helmand was capable of providing a fertile ribbon of land between the sand deserts until marauding Baluchis made settlement there impossible; it was densely inhabited in the time of the Arab geographers, who spoke of walking all the way on the roofs of houses. In this sector lived the Benefactors (Euergetai) of Cyrus the Great. Bist was an outpost of early Islam. Having a suitable climate for their war-elephants, it became the winter capital of the Ghaznavids almost a thousand years ago, and imposing ruins of their era line the banks of the Helmand for several miles. But the great citadel must conceal earlier levels; its name seems to occur in more or less corrupt forms in late classical writers, and coins of the Greco-Bactrian rulers and an Achaemenid stone weight have come from it. The Arabs found the people of Bist unexpectedly civilized, as Alexander did the Euergetai.[6]

Camel-borne marauders familiar with the few water-points could cross the sand deserts of what is now south-western Afghanistan. But for travellers and armies the only route to the East from the Helmand at Bist has been up the green valley of the R. Argandab which leads to the big oasis-complex dominated by the city of Kandahar; thence an imperceptibly rising trough dotted with homesteads provides easy going to Ghazni, and so on to the Kabul region, with no hardship other than the deep winter snows on the stretches at the 8,000 ft level. The Argandab valley at Kandahar acts as a pass between the treeless slopes of the Hindukush and the desert of sand. It cannot be other than the R. Arachotos of the Greek writers (Avestan Harahwaiti), and the oasis-complex should have been the heart of the ancient province of Arachosia. This was one of the lands listed in the Old Persian inscriptions (Harauwatish); and it had a satrap in 522–21 B.C. and later. The name is not to be found in Herodotus; in the Arab geographers the region of Kandahar was known as Rukhkhaj.

The extent of Arachosia is also a problem. It is questionable whether the Old Persian lists name any land or people between Arachosia and the sea on the south. The Behistun inscription seems to imply that, as far as Darius I knew, Kapishakanish, which we should expect to be Kapisa in the Koh Daman plain north of Kabul, was then included in Arachosia; Darius also names Arachosia as one of the regions from which ivory was brought for his palace at Susa, and Darius III is said to have had elephants from there, while Strabo later spoke of Arachosia as reaching to the Indus. It can hardly have extended to the region of the Khyber Pass because Gandara (Paropamisadai) must be fitted in there; but possibly it took in the ragged, stream-rent edge of the plateau further south, together with the torrid plain of Kucchi which stretches from the Bolan Pass to the lower Indus. The seat of the satrap in 522–21 was named Arshada.

We could expect this to be in the oasis-complex of Kandahar. The name Kandahar itself is of uncertain origin; for scholars assign it with equal confidence to Alexander, to the Suren Gondophares in Parthian times, and to later refugees from Gandara. But at Zor Shar on the west of the modern city recent soundings have proved the existence of a fortified settlement going back to the Achaemenid era, so there was a town there for Alexander to give the name Alexandropolis to.

Between the extensive deserts on the south of these regions and the open sea lies the tract known as Makran (already known as Makarene in Roman times). Except at its west end, where the donkey-breeding Bashakird country adjoins the Strait of Hormuz, Makran is contained in the Persian and Pakistani provinces of Baluchistan, reaching almost to the confines of the lower Indus. For the most part it has a broad coastal strip, which is too torrid to support vegetation and has been sparsely inhabited by primitive communities whose sustenance and necessities of life came from fishing. From the time of Nearchus' voyage in 325 B.C. they have been known as the Ichthyophagoi ('Fish-eaters'). The barren hills that bound the coastal plain are scored by dry watercourses with tamarisks; they support some goats and golden-skinned deer. The general physiography of the interior is one of strings of spiky hills which run nearly parallel to the coast and long valleys which separate them. Movement in a west-east direction is relatively unobstructed except where sand dunes pile up. But though there are places where water suffices for palm-groves and settlements, the valleys are mostly arid with only scanty xerophytic vegetation; and the heat and long waterless stretches have made travel hazardous, while flash floods that result from rainstorms on the hills not only further the denudation of the terrain but add to the dangers of travel (Alexander the Great's army experienced one to its cost). In the belief that Semiramis and Cyrus had traversed this country and lost almost all their men, Alexander was moved to emulation and came through with great hardship and heavy losses in 325 B.C.[7] Jalaluddin of Khiva also returned from India through Makran in A.D. 1223 and is said to have lost the greater part of his army.[8]

The exploratory journeys of Aurel Stein, Sylvia Matheson, and others over the years have revealed the existence of numerous sites in Makran dating before and around the third millennium B.C., and it is clear that some areas that are now uninhabitable had settlements then. It seems at the present time to be the prevailing view that there has been no appreciable climatic change since chalcolithic days in Iran; and if that is so, the desiccation – for such it is – was presumably due to human exploitation and over-grazing of the land which reduced its capacity to retain moisture. To this may perhaps be added the inhabitants' disinclination to spend much effort for little return by conserving what rain-water does fall; Sykes quoted a Baluchi saying which expresses an attitude of mind, that when the Almighty created the world Baluchistan was formed from the refuse material. Life has indeed remained primitive in Makran. The Greeks reckoned that its inhabitants were autochthonous and incapable of articulate speech, the Arabs found that though Moslem in name they were savage and spoke a jargon, and Sykes remarked a resemblance between their utterance and that of their camels. From their absence in Alexander's train it is assumed that camels were not bred in Makran, which is unpromising country for them; but they have been maintained by the Baluchis for transportation on their long-distance forays and can now be seen pulling carts and ploughs. As the people of the coast satisfy almost all their needs from fish and whales, so in the interior the palm serves for most purposes.[9] The Baluchis, though dominant there, took possession of Makran only in the last thousand years or so. The native substrate is Dravidian (Brahui), and it is presumably they who represent the straight-haired Ethiopians of Asia in Herodotus' 17th 'nomos'. The Parikanioi listed with them were no doubt 'pairika' (= heathen, kafirs). The same name appears in the 10th (Median) 'nomos', where even recently it has evoked fanciful identifications (not only Hyrkania but even Fergana); in fact Sargon II knew a Barikanu in the Median Zagros.

No conqueror could take more out of Makran than he is prepared to put in; and in view of the inhospitable nature of the country we can hardly expect the Persians to have maintained much of a presence there. In 325 B.C. Alexander came from the Indus delta and forced his way through a couple of peoples (Arabitai and Ōreitai) of whom it was remarked that they had from long ago been independent, after which he spent sixty days traversing Gedrosia until he came to its 'palace' (i.e. satrapal centre) at Poura. In all this stretch there was no vestige of imperial authority, and we have to assume that there was no satrap in Makran east of Poura. Poura was fairly certainly on the

Plate 38 Bampur river, and it was probably at Bampur itself rather than Fahraj (Pahra, now Iranshahr);[10] it will thus have been not more than ten days' march east of the centre where Alexander camped in Karmania inland from Hormuz. That Poura had been a satrapal seat from early Achaemenid times is highly probable because a Persepolis tablet of 500 B.C. records the issue of grain to the satrap of Purush (PF 681). In the Alexander historians the name Gedrosia evidently covered most of Makran. It is curious that there is no name in the Old Persian lists that can be applied here. Maka, with the ethnic Machiya that most scholars relate to it, is found in the lists from Behistun onwards, and has often been taken to be Makran. But two tablets also of about the middle of Darius I's reign (PF 679 and 680) record provisions for satraps of Makkash, which therefore cannot cover the same ground as Purush. The positioning of Maka in the lists is ambiguous, and the prevalent identification with the Mykoi of Herodotus' 14th 'nomos' is conjectural. From the time of Alexander the Great onward Makai was a name the Greeks gave to a people in the eastern end of Arabia (roughly Oman). It is of course not impossible that Mykoi and Makai are one and that they straddled the Strait of Hormuz (Oman itself has often been subject to Islamic rulers of Fars or Kerman).

The ranges of the western Hindukush are divided by rivers of which that of Herat, the Hari Rud, preserves the name of the ancient Areia (Haraiwa). There is an arduous route from its valley to the passes above Kabul which may possibly be referred to in Strabo. But security would have presented a problem, and these passes are blocked during the winter; so the normal route to the East has been the circuitous one by Kandahar, while that to Baktria ran along the northern skirts of the Hindukush. Apart from the Buddhist wonders of the Bamiyan valley, the interior of this mountain mass has little to offer save summer grazing for nomadic groups.

East of Areia must lie the land which is called Gandara in the Old Persian lists but appears as Paruparaesana[11] in the parallel texts at Behistun. The known associations of Gandara are with the Indus. But under Alexander the name Paropamisadai stood for a mountainous region and an existing satrapy; we are told that it stretched down to the Indus, but the city that Alexander founded in the Paropamisadai was at or near Kapisa in the wind-swept Koh Daman plain at an altitude of near 6,000 ft. Presumably, as Tarn surmised, it and Gandara were geographically distinct but were united administratively. East of the Kapisa region is Nuristan ('Land of Light'), which was known as Kafiristan until its inhabitants were made to embrace Islam just over eighty years ago. It is a country of high mountains and steep inaccessible valleys, each with its own dialect of a language said to derive from an Indo-Aryan more archaic than Sanscrit; presumably until the end of the past century the people there had remained undisturbed for several thousand years, though Tamerlane is said to have crossed their country and suffered the indignity of having to be lowered down a cliff in a basket. Of the companions of the Gandarians in Herodotus' 7th 'nomos' the Sattagydians are unplaced (above, p. 61); Aparytai might possibly be the Afridis of the Khyber, but the recent equation of Dadikai with Tadjiks is untenable because the latter name originated on the western borders of Iran a thousand years later in reference to the bedouin, while Marquart's identification with Dardic peoples is speculative.

Plate 40

Darius I's Indian conquests have been mentioned (above, p. 61f.). The wealth of gold that Herodotus tells us came from there has perplexed some scholars; indeed Arrian spoke of Alexander finding none there. Darius says that gold for his palace at Susa came from Sardis and Baktria. But the Baktrian rivers have not produced gold, except for a little that Le Strange cites high up the Oxus (Pyanj) in Wakhan. Tarn suggested it was brought to Baktria from Siberia, and that the fabulous gold of India was a fable; but if so it was one that died hard, for the gold, silver, and copper in Shin-tu (by then calling itself In-tu) was being remarked by the Chinese traveller Hiuen Tsiang a thousand years later. North of the Indus bend the Hindukush runs up to the mountain-knot of the Pamirs. It has often been asserted that the most easterly Saka whom the Achaemenids claimed as subjects inhabited the Pamirs or even Chinese Tartary (Sinkiang); and the Kaspioi who (with Sakai) formed Herodotus' 15th 'nomos' are placed in Kashmir. But the Pamirs are not, as was supposed before Curzon's journey of 1894, a plateau forming the 'roof of the world', but a terrain of high rugged mountains with deep valleys whose floors are at 12–14,000 ft altitude; and passes are only open for five months of the year. It is difficult to believe that the Persians would have wished to rule these isolated lands. In any case Darius speaks of the limit of his empire as being the Saka beyond Sogdiana and not beyond Baktria, which implies that we should look towards Tashkent and the region of the Hunger Steppe rather than south of the Alai range. This was the frontier on the Jaxartes that Cyrus the Great was concerned to secure by his string of forts.

The Paropamisos or Hindukush constituted a barrier which made the upper satrapies or north-eastern provinces of the empire another world. From its northern slopes rivers run northward towards the Amu Darya (Oxus) but, except in the east, they die without penetrating the broad belt of steppe and sand dunes that flanks its southern bank. Where they reach the mountain foot great fertile oases are formed, notably those of Balkh (Baktra), Khulm, and Kunduz. On the north side a row of rivers descends from the Alai mountain range and provides oases in strips and patches reaching to the Oxus. North of the western Alai range again is the valley of the R.Zarafshan (Polytimetos) with great oases such as Varakhsha, Bokhara, Karshi (Nautaka?), and Samarkand, which formed the heart of Sogdiana. It is disappointing that though their general location is fixed, the known cities of Achaemenid date in these satrapies – Zariaspa (Baktra), Marakanda (Samarkand), Aornos (if at Khulm), and Margush (Merv) – have barely revealed any trace of themselves. But in the last generation a good number of lesser sites have been discovered by Soviet teams, especially on the north bank of the Oxus; and it is clear that in the valleys there – the Shirabad, Surkhab, and Kafirnigan, and the Wak-shab (i.e. Oxus)[12] – there were in Achaemenid times agricultural communities which depended on irrigation networks. According to the Greek writers the Oxus divided Sogdiana from Baktria. Where it leaves the mountain zone north of Baktra this will have been true; but Soviet scholars familiar with the terrain are no doubt right in assuming that these valleys which descend to the Oxus from the high mountain chains on the north belonged to Baktria. Tarn in fact remarked, with a touch of exaggeration, that the Oxus was to Baktria what the Nile was to Egypt.

Sogdiana had its rich valley lands; it stretched to the Fergana Gate and the Jaxartes (Syr Darya) with Cyrus' line of forts there; and it had hill strongholds of local 'barons' which Alexander had trouble in reducing. But its glories belong to later epochs. Remains of the Achaemenid era have not come to light yet. It is on the Oxus, and especially its northern side-valleys, that a pattern has begun to appear: this is one of open settlements for the rural population in groups which centre on a mud-walled stronghold of a local 'baron'. In Alexander's time Baktria passed as a land of open villages. By 128 B.C. (Chang-kien) the villages or towns were walled; and it would appear that there was a steady advance in urban settlement under Seleucids, Greco-Baktrians, and Kushans. Whether the first urbanism at the great centres like Baktra came with the Achaemenids or preceded them is not yet clear; but it is likely that, as at Charsadda (Peukela) in Gandara and perhaps at Kandahar, settled Achaemenid rule may have promoted the process.

The Iranians of the upper satrapies were remarked on as physically big; they were warlike, and the nobles with their retinues provided first-class cavalry. They seem to have had something of a heroic temper which could express itself in minstrelsy and oral epic. Compared with the Medes and Persians, who were in contact with the civilizations of the Near East, they were rough and little addicted to luxuries. Their technology, in the use of iron for instance, seems to have been less advanced. But it is now being asserted that in both pottery and monumental building they had their own distinctive forms; and while absorbing both Achaemenid and western motifs, much of the artisanship and style that marks the famous Oxus treasure (above, p. 166) is now claimed as having an individual character that can be considered Eastern Iranian. In fact there seems to be a growing tendency among scholars to divide what the Greeks called Ariané (the whole of Iran) between East and West, not so much on the lines that the Greeks did when they said that east of the Caspian Gates people were less civilized, but in the sense that beyond Seistan and the Atok (the skirt of Khorasan against the Kara Kum desert) there was a distinct Eastern Iranian civilization which was in process of forming itself when the Achaemenids arrived there, and which absorbed Persian influences without losing its own cultural entity.

This is a matter in which it is at present prudent to suspend judgement. On the evidence it would still seem perverse to deny that Eastern Iran was backward by comparison with the West. But its culture may not have been simply derivative; and it must have been mainly through the upper satrapies that Iranian artistic influences reached the steppe folk of Central Asia. To some extent the odd community of Greeks deported to the upper satrapies by the Achaemenids may have contributed to the cultural synthesis; but the strong Greek presence there that Narain postulated in his disagreement with Tarn finds no support in either the literary or the archaeological record.[13]

The words 'baron' and 'seigneur' which are customarily applied to the local grandees of the upper satrapies pre-empt inportant social issues; but what had been inferred from the literary sources seems to have gained confirmation from recent field survey. The question that therefore arises is who were the 'barons'. We could be dealing in the main either with Persians who had been granted fiefs there or with a native nobility which retained its dominant position. The satraps of Baktria tended to be Achaemenid princes – we can name four or five of them – and they will have had their retainers and their estates. But it is not known whether Baktria was conquered or consented freely to Persian rule; and when the satrap rose up and contested the throne with Artaxerxes I, we don't know whether the nobles gave him their support in such a way as to involve confiscations and land-grants to Persians. In isolated cases it is fair to assume that for instance Artasyras, general and King's Eye around the late fifth century and father of the supposedly Hydarnid satrap Orontes, was a 'Baktrian' in the sense of a Persian settled there (above, p. 173); but in general the names that occur in the sources cannot help. Junge and Frye have assumed a Persian 'colonization' of the upper satrapies, as in Anatolia; Bickerman, Altheim, and in general the Soviet scholars take a native nobility for granted, as indeed Tarn seems to have done. The probability is that there were both, with the distinctions becoming smudged by intermarriage.

In these north-eastern lands all but the greatest rivers die out as they advance into the plains, their energy spent in supplying water for irrigation; even the Zarafshan river which nourishes Sogdiana fails to reach the Oxus. In its lower course to the long delta-oasis of Khwarizm the Oxus runs through desert: on its left bank the gray 'howling wilderness' of Kara Kum whose surface varies between hardened clay, salt flats, and sand dunes, with occasional brackish wells and a sparse population of antelopes and wild asses; on its right the Kizil Kum with its sea of soft reddish brown sand forming great billows. In this region the heat and cold are extreme, the temperature of the sand surface being said to have a diurnal range of up to 140°F. As in Seistan it is likely that a good deal of land that was once cultivated is now covered over by the wind-blown sands.

On the south side of the Kara Kum desert, at Merv and from the terminal basin of the Hari Rud-Tejend north-westward along the Atok the supply of water for cultivation has given rise to flourishing settlements at different times. But the archaeologists do not appear to have found any substantial remains of Achaemenid date to match those of prehistoric and Parthian times; it would seem as if the steppe horsemen who succeeded the settled cultures of the Bronze Age in the current view were still dominant. Towards the Aral Sea, however, the great programme of field research undertaken by Tolstov has brought to light a new civilization of the first millennium. At that time a branch of the Jaxartes (Zhany Darya) ran south of west to reach the Aral not far from the eastern arm of the Oxus and with natural channels and a network of canals a huge crescent-shaped area was made available for settlement; Tolstov spoke of it as the 'Venice of Central Asia', but it is a Venice some 400 miles long formed of the delta-lands of the two rivers. Many of the walled sites are said to be of the fourth-second century B.C.; but what goes back to Achaemenid times includes an important fortified centre (Chirik Kala) where the tombs of kings or chieftains seem to have been. Fortified compounds are reported with a huge inner yard, presumably for animals, and apparently with long corridors or rows of rooms to house whole communities as the Viking long houses did. Evidently there was dense habitation with what is spoken of as mass-employment of slave man-power and specialized craftsmanship; Soviet scholars even speak of an 'industrial revolution'. Tolstov regarded the civilization as a Saka one which commenced in the seventh-sixth century B.C.

Geographically this corresponds excellently to what the Greeks remarked: the 'Araxes' (i.e. Jaxartes)[14] with many large islands and mouths, split up into many channels, one arm going to the Hyrkanian Sea (presumably by joining up with the Oxus), while the remainder flowed into 'the other sea on the north' (the Aral). In the royal inscriptions of Darius I in Egypt the Saka that he claimed as subject to him are referred to as being of the marshes and of the plains. Strabo tells us that a large grouping or confederation of the nomadic folk was the Massagetai with whom Cyrus fought beyond the Jaxartes, and that some of them lived in mountains, some on plains, and some in marshes and on islands. From the Greek sources we gather that they kept stock and caught fish, with the implication that they were not cultivators of the soil. One of the nomadic peoples that made up the Massagetai was called Apasiakai – a name that Tomaschek a century ago interpreted as Apa-saka ('Water Sakai'); so the name Apasiak was given by Tolstov to his marsh folk.

The Zhany Darya and its channels are said to have dried up before the beginning of the Christian era; and after that the fertile basin was confined to the Oxus and its delta-lands. This is Khwarizm or Chorasmia (the name given as Uwarazmish in the Old Persian texts), and it is here that the Chorasmians seem to have been living when Alexander the Great came to the Oxus. A curious problem now presents itself. Hecataeus at the end of the sixth century spoke of the Chorasmians as living east of the Parthians and having plains and mountains; but there are no mountains near Khwarizm. Darius in his Susa building inscriptions mentions a dark shining stone as brought from Uwarazmish. This is generally taken to be turquoise, whose sources are in the hill country of eastern Khorasan, and Khwarizm is in any case a most unlikely source for any such stones. It has been said with some justice that Darius is singularly unreliable in his naming of the places from which materials came for his palace, so his testimony might be disregarded.[15] But Herodotus also has a contribution to make. He tells the often-quoted story (III 117) of a mountain-ringed plain into which a great river called Akes flowed and from which it discharged through five outlets until the Persian King (unnamed) blocked the exits to form a 'sea' and then acquired a considerable revenue when the water was dispensed through sluice-gates. The plain, he says, was on the borders of the Chorasmians, Hyrkanians, Parthians, Sarangai, and Thamanaioi. The name Akes is not otherwise known. Scholars mostly place the plain in Seistan, in Khwarizm, or on the southern borders of Turkestan on the Hari Rud-Tejend or the Murgab, though the R. Akesines (Chenab) has not escaped mention; but with the clues given it fits no more easily on a map than the Garden of Eden. The Chorasmians, however, are there counted as neighbours of peoples of the Iranian uplands who are separated from Khwarizm by 400 miles of gray desert. And Herodotus is not making a casual reference to the Chorasmians; in fact he says that it was to them that the plain had belonged until the Persians took it over. This strange story is at the root of the recent speculations about a Great Chorasmian state before Cyrus' conquest (above, p. 29). But it affords a firmer basis for the widely-held view that the Chorasmians only entered Khwarizm during the course of Achaemenid times and had previously been occupying the east of Khorasan roughly in the space between Parthia and Areia. At the end of the empire at least the Chorasmians seem to have been independent; but their relationship with Tolstov's Apasiaks is inscrutable.

The Sakai or Scythians were in general nomadic people of the steppes. Some of them had caused havoc in the Near East in the seventh century; but later, according to Strabo (XI 512), the generals of the Persians attacked them at a nocturnal celebration in eastern Asia Minor and wiped them out – Herodotus had most of them wiped out by Kyaxares at a banquet (I 106). Generally speaking, they appear in our sources as a fringe people who curtained off the North from the Danube right across the Eurasian steppes. Herodotus was not sure that the Massagetai were a Scythian nation, but usually they have been accepted as such. Darius I speaks of three lots of Saka. The third – those beyond the Sea – were the ones he invaded on his expedition across the Danube. The others were known as 'tigrakhauda' and 'haumawarga'. The epithet 'tigrakhauda' means 'pointed-capped'; and though all Saka were shown on Achaemenid reliefs as wearing pointed caps, the Saka under Skunkha are spoken of in column V at Behistun as wearing pointed caps, while Skunkha himself at the end of the line of rebels is so grotesquely hatted that the identification imposes itself.[16] Darius attacked these Saka by crossing a sheet of water; so it now seems not unlikely that their habitat was Tolstov's marshland. The word 'haumawarga' has tended to be taken as meaning 'preparing (or consuming) haoma', which was the sacred inebriant that was specially associated with Mithra. To an external viewer distinctions between such Sakai would not be obvious; so Herodotus remarks on the pointed caps of the Sakai in Xerxes' army and at the same time calls them 'Amyrgian'.[17] But Darius distinguishes them. If the Pointed-cap Saka were those of the marshes, the Haumawarga must be those of the plains; and it must be the latter whom Darius spoke of as being beyond Sogdiana when he defined the limit of his empire opposite Kush (the other opposed pair being Hindush and Sparda).

Plate 7

These northern nomads were interconnecting, and some racial mixture is only to be expected. The graphic representations of Saka cavalrymen who were stationed at Memphis in Egypt show some with Mongol features; skulls from supposedly Saka burials of the mid first millennium B.C. by the Ili river south of Lake Balkhash are reported to be of basically European type but with Mongoloid features, and it is more remarkable that the description of Scythians in the Hippocratic Corpus reveals definite Mongol traits. There are a number of known Saka names that can be claimed as Iranian, but – unfashionable as the suggestion is – there could also be Turcic ones (see above, p. 37).

Herodotus' 16th 'nomos' is very far-ranging. But Parthia and Areia would go together, the Chorasmians may have been close neighbours of both, and Sogdiana would naturally be attached to them if the satrapy included Margush (Merv) at the time. Caspians appear twice in the list – in the 11th 'nomos' with Pausikai, Pantimathoi, and Dareitai, and in the 15th with Sakai. Dareitai suggests Dara and the Atok east of Nisa, and Pausikai could conceivably be the Apasiakai, while later Greek writers knew of an extinct people called Kaspioi with a territory called Kaspiane in the eastern Caucasus[18] along with an adjoining region Sakasene on the northern border of Armenia (whence also, it would seem, the Sakesinai in Darius III's army of 331 B.C. came). So it is perhaps preferable to place the 15th 'nomos' west of the Caspian Sea and the 11th on the other side. In the gloom of their humid jungle and forest at the eastern end of the Black Sea the Colchians, who were not subjects but brought gifts, would then have been western neighbours of the 15th 'nomos', whose satrapal centre may have been at Mtskheta by Tiflis.

Patrokles, who was sent to investigate the Caspian region a generation after Alexander, reported that there was a regular trade-route from India by the Oxus to the Caspian and thence by the Kur valley to the Black Sea. This has not commended itself to all ancient historians. But intrinsically it is not unlikely, because trade will follow routes where heavy tolls can be avoided; and if in the decline of the empire Achaemenid control lapsed there, the Kur route would have been attractive, as it was in the early nineteenth century for trade between Persia and the West, which avoided Ottoman tolls until it was stifled by the extension of the Russian protectionist tariff to Georgia.

As Herodotus says, the Caucasus was the barrier that set the limit to the advance of the Persians. The Arab geographers called it the 'mountain of languages'. Like Kafiristan it was a refuge of forgotten peoples, and Strabo talked of seventy different tongues being spoken there (Pliny, citing Timosthenes, spoke of 300!); at least fifty are reported even at the present day. At the south-east corner of the Caspian Sea was the low-lying piedmont of Hyrkania (Warkana in the Behistun inscription), with its capital at Zadrakarta (possibly at Tureng Tappeh, where a circular fortification of Achaemenid date is now reported). Now called Gorgan, it is a land of forested mountainsides leading down to yellow fields and thick copses; with numerous muddy streams, thatched houses, and well nourished animals, the countryside now has a rustic charm. But possibly during antiquity, as in recent times until Russian rule was established in Turkestan, it was underdeveloped because of the destructiveness of the steppe nomads. The name Hyrkania does not figure in the Old Persian lists of peoples or Herodotus' 'nomoi' – at different times we hear of it being incorporated administratively in Parthia; but Hyrkanian troops were in regular use under the Achaemenids. The southern shore of the Caspian is also prosperous now at the foot of the steep, deciduous-forested slopes of the Elburz. But in ancient times, as again until quite recently, its protection may have lain in its impenetrability. Trees and dense brambles (which Curzon 100 years ago said were known to the inhabitants as their champions or wrestlers) denied access to marauders as they did to Alexander the Great. In what is now called Gilan, where swords rust and bowstrings rot, the Kadousioi (or Gelai) more than once successfully defended themselves against Achaemenid armies; like the Byzantines of Trebizond they were protected as much by the humidity and luxuriant vegetation as by their own martial prowess – it is not fortuitous that Lazistan and Gilan are now the two regions with flourishing tea plantations in Turkey and Iran.

Armenia appears as a land in the Old Persian lists. But Herodotus has two 'nomoi' there, and Xenophon confirms this when he speaks of two satraps whose forces the Ten Thousand encountered in 401 B.C. The eastern one (the 18th) comprised the Matienoi, who overlapped with Media in Kurdistan, the Saspeires roughly in Azerbaijan, and the Alarodioi who seem to have preserved the name Urartu or Ararat. Azerbaijan became a satrapy after Alexander's death and promptly became independent under Atropates, from whom it received its name Atropatene.[19] The other 'nomos' (the 13th) embraced Paktyike (which is untraceable) and Armenians as far as the Black Sea. From the early ninth century B.C. there had been a flourishing kingdom in central Armenia around the eastern arm of the Euphrates (Murad Su) and Lake Van, which in time extended its rule in all directions and especially to the Araxes (Aras) valley behind Mt Ararat. The people were Haldian (in Xenophon Chaldaioi) and apparently Hurrite; they are known both from the Assyrian annals and from their own (undated) royal inscriptions. This realm came to an end about the beginning of the sixth century, not long after the collapse of its one-time rival Assyria; and since the Medes were campaigning west of Armenia by 590 B.C. (above, p. 26), there is little doubt who swallowed up the Vannic kingdom. But in the Araxes valley around Erivan the destruction of the capital of Teishebaini (Karmir Blur) about the same time has been attributed to Scythians on the evidence of arrowheads of the triangular type used by them (though not peculiar to them). Urartian influence has been postulated in the development of Median and Achaemenid architecture, though without any very cogent argument. But certainly the Urartians were advanced in their construction of canals to bring water to their fortresses and garden cities as early as 800 B.C.[20]

The old name Urartu continued to be used anachronistically in Akkadian, but in the Old Persian inscriptions the land is called Armina; and the dominant ethnic element became one which called itself Haik and, unlike the Urartian kings, spoke an Indo-European language. According to the Greeks the Armenians were emigrants from Phrygia; but they may have been settled in Western Armenia perhaps even in Hittite times. There is no sign of settled life in Armenia after the collapse of Urartu. The same, however, is true of Armenia before the emergence of the Urartian kingdom; and yet in the thirteenth and twelfth centuries B.C. Assyrian kings found numerous tribes and petty chieftains there. In the same way Xenophon found no lack of villages; so it is a matter of their remains being too slight to catch the traveller's eye.

In general, Armenia is high-lying and provides abundant pasture after the snows recede in clouds of steam. Somewhere north of the Euphrates Xenophon found seventeen foals being reared for the King as tribute. As in his time, the houses are – or until recently were – dug like burrows into the earth in many regions; and in the four or five months of snow people and animals have gone to ground. But Xenophon found the villages organized under their headmen and well stocked with meat, wheat, raisins, beans, and old scented wine. Palaeobotanical research seems to indicate that the present bare, treeless landscape has resulted from over-exploitation of the land in post-Achaemenid times. Remains of Achaemenid date are reported at Altin Tepe near Erzinjan in Western Armenia and in the east at Haftavan Tepe near Lake Urmia and at Arinberd and Armavir in the Araxes basin. The Rock of Van will also have been a citadel since Xerxes set a trilingual inscription in the cliff

Plate 14   where his father had had a niche prepared for it.

South-east of Armenia, in what presumably was Matiene, is a region of narrow fierce gorges extending to the drainage systems of the Zab rivers; the Armenian king Tigranes I in the early first century B.C. was able to give seventy valleys to the Parthian and later recapture them. There is no word of cities here; but presumably there were semi-independent groups of villages in the valleys, with abundant grazing on the plateau of Iranian Kurdistan to the east. In the hilly country from which the Tigris breaks out to enter the High Mesopotamian plain the Ten Thousand forced their way through an independent people called Kardouchoi against whom, as they were told, a Persian army of 120,000 had been sent and not a man returned because of the bad terrain. In this land, called Gordyene in the Roman era, other Iranian elements seem to have taken refuge in historical times, so forming the now more widespread race known as Kurds. They have never acquired a national identity; it has been their lot to be divided between major powers, Iranian on the one hand and Armenian or Anatolian on the other (and since the collapse of the Ottoman empire among a plurality of ethnically disparate states).

West of the Euphrates is Asia Minor, whose name Anatolia (=Orient) corresponds to the Asiatic part of the Middle Byzantine empire. Like what is now Iran, Anatolia has an extensive plateau revetted on all sides by mountain ranges. It has a central salt lake (Tatta) and an expanse of arid steppe further west (the Axylos in which thorn bushes would not grow), together with a series of inland lakes in the south-west (Pisidia). But with an average altitude of 3,000 ft it is not so elevated as the Iranian plateau, and the principal rivers have forced their way through the mountain chains, thus greatly reducing the barren areas. Heavy storms occur in late spring (the 'Forty Afternoons' Rains'), and in ancient times the plateau was better wooded and (from evidence of olives) milder in winter. So conditions generally were more favourable to settlement than on the Iranian plateau.

A major power centred on Phrygia had possessed itself of the interior of Anatolia in post-Hittite times. But when it collapsed under Midas (Mita) in the early seventh century, a new dynasty in Lydia (the Mermnads) built up a kingdom which stretched from the Greek fringe on the west coast as far as the Halys and came to blows with the Medes east of that river in 590 B.C. (above, p. 4). To the south of this, despite the incursions of Nebuchadnezzar's successors, the ruler (Syennesis) of Cilicia seems to have joined in mopping up the lesser principalities of eastern Anatolia, so that his realm included Mt Amanos and seems to have reached to the Euphrates crossing at Isoli (Tomisa, 'ad Aras') in Melitene (Malatya). The evolution of this kingdom is difficult to explain. In Aramaic the satrapy was called H(i)l(i)k, and the Greeks believed that coastal Cilicia was occupied by a people (Kilikes) who had moved there from the Aegean; but in Assyrian and Babylonian texts the Cilician plain seems to have been called Que or Huwe, while the name Hilakku was applied to adjacent hill country. North of Cilicia the broken country between the Halys and the Euphrates was known as Cappadocia (Katpatuka in the Old Persian lists); reaching as it did to the Black Sea, it never seems to have had any political coherence. To Herodotus these people were Syrians.

It is difficult to gauge the degree of Iranian penetration west of the Euphrates before the time of Cyrus the Great. In the bend of the river south of Malatya the Assyrian kings had encountered men of Kummuh (Commagene) bearing names that would pass as Median; but it is suggested that they could be Indo-Aryan (Mitannian) rather than Iranian. The name of a Syennesis of Cilicia, Ōromedon, has been mentioned (above, p. 149); but the royal deity was the Baal of Tarsus, and the known proper names in Cilicia and of Cilician (hlk) slaves acquired for the satrap Arsames in Egypt seem generally to be Asianic (Luwian). Similarly, Magi and the cults of the Persian deities were widespread in Cappadocia, and when coins of Syennesis were struck in the second half of the fifth century the legends were in the imperial Aramaic and not Greek; but the great sanctuaries with their villages of hierodules were Asianic (Ma and Kybebe). So it would look as though the strong Iranian presence was superimposed on a basically Anatolian rural population. Cappadocia had fertile valleys in its mountainous north towards the Black Sea, especially on the lower Halys and among the affluents of the R.Iris. But mainly it was pastoral, with horses, mules, and sheep reared for despatch to the Persian King. Fourth-century coin hoards have been claimed as indicating great economic development there in later Achaemenid times; as merchandise, of course, horses and mules have the great advantage of not requiring overland transportation, but it could be more a matter of the profits of mercenary service.

Phrygia was sheep-raising plateau country except in the west, where the highlands form a watershed and give rise to the rivers Maeander and Hermus which flow to the Aegean. Its biggest city in 395 B.C. was said to be Kelainai by the sources of the Maeander, where Greek influence was felt early; in the east Xenophon speaks of Tyana as being in Cappadocia, though Phrygian inscriptions come to light there. According to Herodotus the Daskyleion satrapy included Cappadocia as well as Phrygia. The inner edge of the Taurus between Ikonion (Konya) in Phrygia and Tyana carried the trunk route

Plate 41 ('southern highway') from the West to the Cilician Gates, where the stream was constricted to a pass a few feet wide between cliffs. The Taurus above this stretch was occupied by predatory mountain peoples (Lycaonians and Isaurians).

The south coast of Asia Minor has two fertile plains – that of Cilicia, where the Taurus sheers away inland, and the piedmont of Pamphylia. Otherwise the mountains descend abruptly to the sea. There was a sprinkling of Greek colonies along this shore, with other large centres like Tarsus of which some may have been superficially hellenized. West of Pamphylia is the bump of Lycia. With deep valleys between forested mountains that rise to 10,000 ft, Lycia had the benefit both of good harbours and of seclusion. The Lycians called themselves Trm̃mili (perhaps the Turmiriya of Persepolis tablets as well as Tarmilaa of Babylonian). Though conquered by Harpagos about 540 B.C., they continued to have native dynasts such as Kybernis(kos), who commanded the Lycian contingent in Xerxes' fleet in 480 B.C.: many of them struck their own silver coins. Isocrates said that no Persian ever got control of Lycia. But dynastic inscriptions of Xanthos name two satraps of Lydia (Tissaphernes and Autophradates); and Mausolus, the satrap of Caria, was competing with a native despot, Perikles of Limyra, for possession of the cities, while his youngest brother Pixodaros was named in 337 B.C. as satrap of Lycia as well as Caria in an inscription of Xanthos with texts in Lycian and Greek, and in Aramaic as the official language of the Persian raj.

The Lycian grandees were pleased to employ Greek architects and artists for their tomb monuments, and like the Etruscans they readily embraced the Greek mythology. But their reliefs equally depict scenes of hunt, war, audiences, and banqueting which display the despotic life style (not infrequently with figures in what is claimed as Persian dress). The Lycians continued to preserve their language and script; and in the prevailing syncretism they retained more of their native divine and theophoric names than other neighbours of the Greeks (above, pp. 148 and 177). The Carians on their west had made common cause with the Ionians as mercenaries in Egypt and probably on colonial enterprises, and they had joined with them in the revolt of 499–494 B.C. With their many small dynasts and their religious confederations they absorbed Greek culture as it filtered down the social scale until Mausolus made them adopt Greek forms and institutions in the fourth century. The name Karka, recently proved to be Caria, appears in the Old Persian lists before the end of Darius I's reign (above, Chap. VI n.3). But Caria did not in fact become a satrapy until 395 B.C. when Tissaphernes was executed. The first satrap was a Carian of a leading family; if this was Hyssaldomos, he was almost immediately succeeded by his son Hekatomnos, whose five children ruled in succession for almost fifty years. Mausolus, who was satrap about 377–353 B.C., extended his rule in Lycia and Eastern Greece. He was commemorated by a grand temple-tomb on a high podium, whose sculptural adornment was the work of leading Greek masters; the style and mythology were Greek; but native traits can be recognized, and figures in Persian costumes appeared in hunting and banquet scenes and among the standing dignitaries.

The Greeks had long been known to the Near Eastern peoples as Ionians (Yawani, in Old Persian Yauna). Those of the west coast of Asia Minor had been subjected after Cyrus conquered Lydia. Herodotus makes a 'nomos' (his 1st) of them and their neighbours as far as Pamphylia. But Darius I named Sparda (Lydia) as the limit of his empire opposite Hindush, which suggests that he didn't recognize another province beyond Sardis; and the jurisdiction of the Sardis satraps under Cyrus and Cambyses, Darius I, and Artaxerxes I is known to have reached to the coast.

The great Lydian plain was the heart of the Sardis satrapy. Sardis with its high citadel was the one city there. It yielded gold from the river Paktolos. With its lively Greek contacts it must have impressed Darius as the centre of a monetary economy and advanced trading community; he stayed a long time there, and it was probably not only strategical considerations that induced him to leave his brother in charge. Because our sources are Greek we could very easily overestimate Darius' interest in Greeks and things Greek. But he was forward-looking; and in his contacts with individuals and his choice of appointments in the West he would seem to have recognized the potential of the Yauna, who were overtaking the old civilizations of the Near East and Egypt in the cultural and intellectual spheres.

Plate 13

From Daskyleion the other western satrap could control the lowlands of Mysia, Bithynia around the R. Sangarios, and the plateau as far as Cappadocia. Paphlagonia, however, was less tractable with its ranks of mountain ranges running parallel to the coast for 200 miles and no easy route across them. Herodotus named the Paphlagonians also in the Daskyleion satrapy, and they were serving with Xerxes in 480 B.C. But what we hear of them later suggests that Persian control was normally lacking there. From time to time a native chieftain might succeed in uniting the country, but there was no organized kingdom either then or later; Alexander the Great was content to accept nominal submission from them without tribute being exacted, and this had probably been the position 100 years earlier. Towards the east end of the Black Sea the coast becomes more humid and the mountains higher; it is difficult to believe that the Persians continued to exact a 300-talent tribute from Herodotus' 19th 'nomos'. It has been remarked that the Persians maintained no road all along this coast (above, p. 109).

The great plain of the two rivers Tigris and Euphrates stretches 700 miles from the foot of the Armenian mountains to the Persian Gulf. The shelf at the north end, at about 1,500 ft above sea-level, affords fertile patches where streams emerge; but the expanses of flat ground below it are too dry to be inhabited in comfort through the summer months, and so have tended to lie open to the nomadic peoples of the Syrian waste. On the east the Tigris, with the shelves and mountain valleys of the Assyrian homeland, yields winter cereals and temperate fruits. But the Euphrates below Thapsakos flows through an aromatic steppe on which ostriches, bustards, and wild asses ranged in Xenophon's time, and away from the river the only population will have been a moving one of what were later known as Skenite Arabs whom Xenophon did not encounter because Cyrus' army was no easy prey for them. This steppe land of Upper Mesopotamia, however, gives way above Babylon to the alluvial deposit of the two rivers, and with good soil and an altitude of not much more than 150 ft dates will ripen easily. So Lower Mesopotamia should be a land of plenty. In antiquity, with a network of canals taking water from the Euphrates (which has a higher bed than the Tigris), it produced fabulous crops of grain (principally barley, which stands up better to saliniza-tion than wheat) and food, slats, and fuel from the date-palms, which are likewise tolerant of salinity. While stock-raising and production of flax and sesame oil were important, it was the palm-groves that proved to be the most valuable land and dates were the common medium of exchange, debts being made payable in them. Indeed in later Achaemenid times the date may have been to Babylonia what 150 years ago the potato was to Ireland. The cuneiform tablets that have come to light are informative about land tenure and the economy. But they have hardly anything to say about long-distance trade. Metals and good timber must have been imported, and there is mention of cloth and barley exported to Elam.[21]

The information obtained from the tablets is slanted and therefore could be misleading. The firm of Egibi had been commercially active before Cyrus was born; and it continued in Babylon for half a century after his death. But in the fifth century a new type of banking house evolved. The unique archive which has been recovered consists of 730 tablets unearthed in 1893 at Nippur south-east of Babylon and concerns the House of Murashu. This firm was based in Nippur; and though its dealings extended to Babylon, Susa, and other centres, it is not likely that it was the only one of its kind. It went in for usury; but its main functions were those of an agricultural credit bank and estate management agency. It came to own land, canals, and means of production. It could provide animals, seed, implements, and machinery for

raising water. It managed estates for absentee landlords, leasing plots, emp-
loying labour, paying the taxes, and delivering the rent to the landlord. Small
holdings were commonly grouped in a collective (hatru) – an arrangement of
long standing in Babylonia where the supply of water and upkeep of canals
necessitated co-operation. The work of the Murashu firm may at least have
been beneficial in ensuring efficient organization. The period covered by this
archive is half a century beginning in 455/54, and three sons and three
grandsons of the founder were involved in the work. For the last seventy years
of the empire Babylon is mute so far as published tablets go, but no doubt it
was suffering.

Herodotus speaks of a satrap of Babylon (Tritantaikhmes) receiving a
bushel of silver daily and having both a huge stud and villages charged with
the maintenance of his Indian hounds. The King received tribute and various
taxes. Members of the royal family had estates; Menostanes, Arsites,
Arsames, and Parysatis are mentioned in the Murashu archive (see above,
p. 174). The Persian presence is also indicated by names such as Bagamiri,
Tiridatu, Ibradatu, Aspadasta, and Ishtabuzana. To maintain the law and
settle disputes there were benches of judges for different canals and the
Sea-land, and tribunals of the satrap and Parysatis are heard of; in the
Murashu archive about one in four of these judges has a Persian-sounding
name. There is no comparable archive concerning the temples, but without
doubt they also were great landowners and employers of labour. They
received their tithe; but as in pre-Achaemenid times, royal overseers were
appointed to exact the King's dues.

Lower down the scale came the lesser fief-holders.[22] Bowman's fiefs seem
commonly to have been combined in the collectives, as also the holdings of
minor officials and tradesmen. In many cases troops from the provinces were
grouped in collectives in Babylonia; the list of them includes Saka, Indians,
Areians, Armenians, Melitenians, Moschoi (Phrygians?), Syrians, Lydians,
Arabs. Various other nationalities appear in the Murashu archive. Altogether
about a third of the proper names that appear are reckoned to be non-
Babylonian; but such a statistic can be misleading when, for example, a man
with a Jewish name gave his son a Babylonian name and the grandson was
given an Iranian one. The resident Egyptians are said to have had their own
quarter in Babylon, as also the Elamites; and Tyrians, who were presumably
descendants of those deported by Nebuchadnezzar, had a separate organisa-
tion of their own in Nippur.

The great estates of Persian nobles and of the temples had large numbers
of workers who were presumably on a similar footing to the 'kurtash' of the
Persepolis tablets (above, p. 87). Some may in effect have been serfs or slaves,
others labouring for hire. Men came seasonally from Elam to work at the
harvest, and conversely Babylonians were sent to do a year's corvée service at
Susa. At least the craftsmen of the Eanna temple at Uruk were free workers
since they could negotiate terms with the King (above, p. 31); it would seem
likely that many village communities were dependent on great landlords or
on the cities with their temples and rentiers.

There can be little doubt that Persian domination caused hardship to the natives. At first commodity prices rose sharply. But taxes were due to the treasury in silver; and as it accumulated there, silver became scarce, so it was interest rates that took flight (up to forty and fifty per cent in the later fifth century). A bowman's fief would not suffice his children if divided among them. The water rate demanded could amount to a quarter or a third of the gross yield. Borrowing to pay taxes led to mortgaging, and many small-holders must have sunk to the status of hired labourers. In the mid fifth century Herodotus remarks on the poverty that compelled the Babylonians to prostitute their daughters; and it is unlikely that conditions did not deteriorate after that. Ur in the south is thought to have been particularly hard hit because its prosperity had depended on the Persian Gulf trade.

On the credit side the temples may not have fared badly; certainly Babylonian astronomy was at its height in the two centuries of Persian rule. But the one remarkable achievement was the mixing of races that set the example for the cosmopolitan civilization of the near East after the conquest by Alexander. What resulted from the 'Pax Persica' was syncretism and cultural assimilation on a scale that had not previously been thinkable.

What lay 'Beyond the River (Euphrates)' was known by that name (Abarnahara). Its shape is roughly triangular. But the habitable lands are confined to a belt stretching on an average 100 miles inland from the Levant coast, the rest of the triangle being the Syrian desert. Except for a kink where the Litani river breaks through westward to the coast, the whole of this belt is divided longitudinally by the Asiatic end of the great rift valley, which runs from Cilicia east of the Amanos up the Orontes to the Beqaa between Lebanon and Antilebanon, then down the R. Jordan to the Dead Sea. West of this divide the rainfall is sufficient to allow pluvial cultivation. To the east conditions are variable; in the north the prosperity which is attested by remains of Roman date was lost for ever with the Arab invasion. It seems to be proved that deforestation and soil-erosion have greatly diminished the cultivated areas in what was Abarnahara; but even in the east such favoured spots as the oasis of Damascus are still fertile enough. As regards routes, Abarnahara could be reached from Babylon up the Euphrates valley to Thapsakos (below Carchemish) or more circuitously round the borders of Mesopotamia by Nisibis and Harran; and it could be traversed lengthwise from Aleppo in the north to Hamath in the Orontes valley, and either by the Beqaa or by Emesa (Homs) and Damascus to Megiddo in the plain of Esdraelon, thence down the coast to Gaza. For a desert crossing from Babylon the route by Palmyra has the advantage of water points at intervals; a more direct route by Rutba was taken by the Ottoman posts which travelled due west from Baghdad.

The Abarnahara that Cyrus the Great took over from the Babylonian kings was an extaordinary mixture of peoples. In the north there had been Hittite principalities which once reached up the Orontes valley as far as Hamath; south of them the prevailing population had been the Semitic Canaanites, and the southern stretch of the coast had come to be occupied by the five cities of immigrant Philistines who gave their name to Palestine. These three peoples were culturally advanced. But two numerous quasi-Arab peoples had moved in: in the north the Aramaeans who took their toll of the Hittite cities and gained possession of Syria as far south as Damascus, and in the south the 'children of Israel' who occupied the hinterland of Palestine with parts of Transjordan. The Canaanites were in due time destroyed or absorbed, and it was only in Phoenicia that a remnant of them could stand its ground. The Philistines, despite their higher technology, were unable to withstand the superior numbers of the Israelite tribes once they were united under David, and the Aramaeans of Damascus and as far north as Hamath were also subjected. So from their new capital of Jerusalem David and Solomon in the tenth century were able to rule most of Abarnahara. After Solomon's death, however, the kingdom broke in two. It was not long before the Assyrians became aggressive again, deporting peoples that they conquered; and when the northern and more powerful Israelite kingdom collapsed with the fall of Samaria in 722 B.C., its territory was settled with deportees from Babylonia and Hamath. The southern kingdom, however, survived under Hezekiah; and being the seat of Yahweh, the god of all Israel, Jerusalem was acknowledged as the religious centre of a much larger area than the small kingdom of Judah. The combination of religious and nationalistic fervour that was in due course engendered enabled the Jews to retain their identity after Jerusalem fell to Nebuchadnezzar in 587/86 B.C. and a large part of its people was deported to Babylonia.

In Phoenicia the Canaanites (called Phoinikes by the Greeks) occupied a coastline of headlands and bays that lent itself to the planting of cities, of which Sidon and Tyre were the greatest. As in Cyprus the cities were ruled by kings. The Phoenicians may have had some infusion of sea-raider blood; at any rate they were unusual among Semites in their readiness to take to the sea; Hiram of Tyre had built a merchant fleet to trade in the Red Sea in a joint venture with Solomon, and the Phoenicians were becoming active in the Western Mediterranean not very long after that. The Lebanon, which rises to 10,000 ft in the north, provided them with a hinterland rich in timber and iron ores. Syria provided wool, and the sea provided murex for dyeing cloth purple; and glass manufacture was another speciality of theirs. They had an art-style that drew largely on Egyptian motifs and were skilled ivory carvers. And their Canaanite literature provided the models for Hebrew tracts and belles lettres. Being a talented people they took advantage of cultural as well as commercial contacts with Athens in the fifth and fourth centuries and their cities were among the leading centres of the Hellenistic world after Alexander. In Achaemenid times Sidon was the principal Phoenician city and had a palace in the Persian style of architecture. The Phoenicians were loyal subjects until the failure of successive Persian expeditions against Egypt finally provoked them to revolt in the mid fourth century; unfortunately this led to the destruction of Sidon. The Abarnahara satrapy included Cyprus, where Phoenician colonies co-existed with the Greek cities; with wooded mountain, good cornland, and copper ore, the island was generally prosperous.

The southern end of the Levant coast had been occupied by the Philistines after the repulse of the Sea Peoples who attacked Egypt in the early twelfth century. The shore there consists of dunes and swamps; and they did not exploit the sea as the Phoenicians did. Behind the broad coastal plain south of the Carmel lies a fruitful foothill country (the Shephelah). In the north, Galilee is fertile, as also the plain of Esdraelon. Further south the hill country is less so, but the Canaanites had learned to make watertight cisterns, thereby extending the limits of habitation; and to the Israelites from the desert it appeared a land flowing with milk and honey. Dipping far below sea-level, the Jordan valley is near-tropical and very fertile; on the Dead Sea there were balsam plantations, and a perfume industry at Engedi which is dated to Achaemenid times. In the south Palestine shades off into desert.

The administrative divisions of this part of Abarnahara have been mentioned (above, p. 174ff.). We hear something about conditions in Judah when Nehemiah went there in 445 B.C.[23] Such larger landowners as there were do not appear to have been Persians. Silver for paying taxes was hard to come by, and usury, mortgaging, and enslavement were endemic. Nehemiah was able to win over the Jerusalem populace to his religious reforms by building a city wall, abolishing interest and cancelling debts, and giving the numerous Levites jobs in the temple service. Having the support of the King he was able to feed 150 notables, and at the same time to forgo the 'governor's bread', which sounds as though it would have been no light imposition on the people. His activity seemed at the time to be of purely local interest; Herodotus knew of circumcision as practised hereabouts, but he did not know of the chosen people and their god in Jerusalem.

Shalmaneser III in the ninth century knew Aribi as a geographical term; Tiglath-Pileser III received tribute from a couple of Arab queens, and the record of Ashurbanipal's ninth campaign contains mentions of Kidrai, and once of Nabatai. The Kedarites (Kidrai) were brought to heel by Nebuchadnezzar and Nabunaid. But in the fifth century, while evidently acknowledging Persian suzerainty, Geshem and his son Qainu seem to have been dominant from Tema and Dedan (Al Ula) across Edom and Sinai to the 'land of Goshen' and the edge of the Delta (above, p. 175). The Edomites appear to have been dissipated in the course of the sixth century; so it may have been Kedarites who aided Cambyses in his invasion of Egypt. The Nabataeans seem to have become predominant there in the fourth century. Darius spoke of Arabaya as a land, and Herodotus of annual gifts of incense from the Arabs. The incense country is Dhofar on the south coast of Arabia east of Hadramaut, and myrrh comes from the west of Hadramaut. We know of two occasions when fleets of his sailed along this coast, so Darius should have known the sources and dealt with the producers direct or through the Makai. But the rulers of Hadramaut, like those of Saba (Sheba) and Ma'in (Mina) in Yemen, should not have been known to the outside world as Arabs – that was the term that they themselves applied to the bedouin on their borders.

These were literate people with an active commerce. Sabaean kings are mentioned in Assyrian annals, and Minaean merchants planted an emporium in Dedan in the fourth century when Kedar seems to have been in a decline. They knew of the 'Medes' (i.e. Persians), but there does not seem to have been any confrontation between them. Arabaya to Darius was presumably 'Arabah', the desert of indefinite extent in which bedouin (Arabs) lived. The

Achaemenids were concerned to keep the peace in Dedan; but there is no evidence of their attempting to settle the bedouin on the fringes of the cultivated lands as the Romans did. By 333 B.C., however, the Arabs were ceasing to be contained, to judge by those who had moved into the Lebanon and gave trouble to Alexander the Great.

Egypt was the Nile (Ha'p, in Old Persian Pirawa), and as far as the Achaemenids were concerned it was a single political unit. It was more turned in on itself than Babylonia. By the end of the fifth century it had succeeded in ridding itself of Persian rule. Artaxerxes II had expeditionary forces collected three times at least with the intention of reconquering it; and there were other unsuccessful attempts by his successor which led to the kings of Egypt fostering revolt in Abarnahara. In 343 B.C. Artaxerxes III did finally recover Egypt.[24] Half a dozen years later it was in revolt again. Most scholars now place the seizure of the throne by Khabbash at this point rather than in Xerxes' time; and Khabbash, whose reign lasted more than one year, may have fled southward with his forces and be the Nubian Kmbswdn of Nastasen's inscription (above, p. 48). It was the misfortune of the Egyptians that their land was recaptured under Darius III just in time for Alexander the Great to invade it and take possession by right of conquest when he accepted the surrender of the Persians there.

XVIII Narrative of Later Achaemenid History

When Artaxerxes I died in 424 B.C. the empire had lasted a century and a quarter. So far as is known there had been no fighting for over twenty years, and in the West the non-interference pact with Athens had worked satisfactorily. The seizure of power by Darius II provoked widespread revolts; but this was mainly a matter of fellow-Iranians disputing his title to rule, and it was only in 414 B.C., when the Athenians' support for Pissouthnes' bastard son Amorges upset the long peace, that the Persian King again became involved with the Greeks (above, p. 130). The result of this new involvement is a flood of information about Persian activities in the west of the empire, and an increasing interest in Persian affairs on the part of Greek writers that continued unabated until the end of Achaemenid rule. The trouble is that since they were Greeks the writers' prime concern was with the history of contending Greek states, so they give no consecutive narrative of Persian history as such. But Persian grandees make frequent appearances on the stage, and a few of them are seen close enough up to come to life. Bearing in mind Canon Rawlinson's dictum that the history of an Oriental monarchy must always be composed mainly of a series of biographies,[1] we need no justification for using the known personalities as pegs on which to hang a narrative of Achaemenid history in its last eighty years.

Tissaphernes was son of a Hydarnes. It is not practicable to make Xenophon say that he was the brother of Artaxerxes II's wife Stateira (and so, if we believe Ctesias, of Teritoukhmes son of a Hydarnes, whose family – no doubt of the Seven Families – was wiped out by Darius II).[2] Diodorus (XIV 26) has him given a daughter of Artaxerxes II in marriage after the death of Cyrus in 401 B.C. But no other writer mentions it, so it is questionable whether he was a son-in-law of the King. Tissaphernes later appears as owning a residence in Caria, and some scholars have suggested his ancestral home was there; but he may have confiscated it on the death of Amorges who was holding out at Iasos in Caria in 414–12 B.C. His dominant position among the high nobles of the court and Xenophon's knowledge of a brother of his who never appears in the West[3] tell against a provincial origin; so perhaps also does the fact that Ctesias speaks of him and two other nobles being 'sent forth' by the King to deal with Pissouthnes. Tissaphernes has had such a bad press that it is only fair to him to say at the outset that in an epoch when disloyalty was becoming the norm he remained the most loyal subject of the two Kings whom he served.

Some scholars who view matters from the Oriental angle have been unwilling to think of Athens as a power comparable to the Achaemenid. But the example of Carthage and Venice suffices to show what a single maritime city can achieve; and Athenian policy was as audacious as any. This time, however, the Athenians overreached themselves. Only a year or so after they committed themselves to supporting Amorges, the armada they had sent to conquer Syracuse was completely destroyed in the late summer of 413 B.C. This was a devastating blow. It meant the end of Athenian sea-power for a short time and the arrival of a Spartan fleet in the East Aegean. It was obviously in the interest of Persia as well as Sparta that the Greek cities there should be wrested from Athens' grip and cease paying tribute to her. Tissaphernes also had a more immediate aim in which the Spartans could assist. While he led his own troops to fight at Miletus, he persuaded them to put in to Iasos, where by taking the place by surprise they were able to capture Amorges and hand him over to Tissaphernes. The profits from loot and the sale of captives were considerable, and for a short time harmony prevailed. But like that between Queen Elizabeth I of England and the Grand Turk, the alliance that was struck in 412 B.C. was an unholy one that boded no genuine co-operation. Despite the fact that he had bought captives from them for a tenth of the going rate for slaves, Tissaphernes lacked funds to pay for the continued maintenance of the Spartans' crews; and the Spartans could not in decency liberate Greek cities from Athens on the understanding that they would become tribute-paying subjects of Persia. Darius II will have understood the logic of this. A Phoenician fleet of 147 ships had therefore been mobilized and was brought as far as Aspendos in 411 (like that of 440 B.C. it is a ghost fleet, but Tissaphernes' assurances that it really existed were believed and Thucydides is emphatic about it). Its maintenance must have been a heavy expense to the King, who obviously intended it to be used to sweep the hated Athenians off the sea. But Athens was recovering rapidly, and Tissaphernes may not have cared to risk losing it.[4] In any case he was finding it a useful bargaining counter with the Spartans, who were not matching up to his expectations any more than he to theirs.

These Persian grandees were men of dignity and noblesse. They were only too easily affronted by bluff egalitarian Spartans. So when the grand Athenian aristocrat Alcibiades presented himself as an adviser, Tissaphernes was quick to recognize a more congenial spirit and perceive the advantage of a two-faced policy: by encouraging the contending Greek powers to wear one another out he might hope to regain the revenues of the Eastern Greek cities without much effort or risk. But the trouble was that he did not have Darius' sanction for such a policy. So when the Spartans in disgust sailed north to the Straits in response to an invitation from Pharnabazos, the satrap at Daskyleion, Tissaphernes suffered a serious loss of face. He chased up to the Straits in an effort to win them back, but without success.

Pharnabazos seems to have been the great-grandson of Artabazos who received the satrapy soon after 479 B.C. (above, p. 167); and he had only very recently succeeded his father Pharnakes in office. He threw himself into the struggle with enthusiasm, providing pay for the Spartans as well as himself maintaining troops on land. At the Dardanelles he led his cavalry into the sea to rescue the grounded Spartan ships. When their fleet was destroyed at Kyzikos in 410 he succoured the seamen with clothing and provisions and gave them the forest under Mt Ida for ship-building. He cannot be blamed for their lack of success or for the punitive Athenian raids on his and Tissaphernes' territory. In later life he was to be the King's son-in-law and a procrastinating field marshal with faded laurels to rest on; but in his prime he seems to have been a tolerably adept cavalry brigadier. To his cost he formed enmities, one with the artful but unceremonious Spartan commissar Derkylidas whom he reported to the admiral for punishment, and another by offending the retiring Spartan admiral of 400 B.C. Anaxibios. He was also not on good terms with Lysander, and he seems to have wronged one of his principal nobles, Spithridates (see Chap. XVI n.14). He may also be suspected of intriguing against Datames later (below, p. 217). So the appearance of geniality that distinguishes him from Tissaphernes in Xenophon and their

Plates 42–3   coin-portraits could be deceptive.

By 409–8 Pharnabazos had spent a lot of money; and having been reduced to the necessity of buying off the Athenians as well as paying the Spartans, he had begun to take the same view of the Greek war as Tissaphernes had done. But Darius II refused to contemplate negotiating with the Athenians and sent his second son, Cyrus, to take over as commander instead.[5] Ctesias has Cyrus born after his father became King, but he did not realize that in that case he could not have been more than fifteen years old when his father appointed him;[6] and the passage in Photios where the information is said to have come from Parysatis herself (49 = 42B) commands no more respect than the other statements about her (above, p. 22). Of Cyrus we receive a favourable impression because he came too late to have his conduct examined by Thucydides and he aroused Xenophon's unstinted admiration. He certainly possessed drive, the gift of cultivating friends, and – it would seem – personal magnetism. But Xenophon's claim that he only began to think of revolt when he had been treated with ignominy by his elder brother after their father's death is unconvincing. It may or may not be true that (as Plutarch relates) he actually tried to murder Artaxerxes during the preparations for his coronation at Pasargadai; but from our text of Xenophon's *Hellenica* we learn that the year before he was summoned to his father's bedside he had murdered two of his cousins for not paying him the homage due to the King,[7] and of those in Darius II's confidence Hieramenes (above, p. 85) as well as Tissaphernes distrusted his intentions, while his mother's determination to see him on the throne must have been an open secret.

Cyrus wanted Spartan support for his bid for the throne, and he needed the Greek war ended so that mercenaries would be seeking employment. He was also fortunate in having a very capable and accommodating Spartan admiral, Lysander, to deal with. Mutual confidence was at once established in 407 B.C. and Cyrus contributed lavishly to the conduct of the war. The next year saw a set-back. The admiral of 406 was a forthright Spartan who presumably neglected the douceurs to the palace officials; he took offence at being kept waiting at Cyrus' 'gate' when he came for money and began to have second thoughts about Greeks being allied with Persia. But after some initial successes he lost his life and the greater part of his fleet in the hard-fought battle of Arginousai (406 B.C.); and after that the rules were bent at

Sparta and Lysander was sent out again. Cyrus then gave him the support which enabled him to defeat the Athenians in the Dardanelles before the end of the next summer and so bring the long war to an end.

Cyrus had in the meantime been recalled by his father. The reason Xenophon gives in his *Anabasis* is simply Darius' mortal illness; but the passage in his *Hellenica* makes the murder of the two princes the cause. Darius fell ill in the north of Media, where he had gone for the campaign against the revolting Kadousioi; and he died in 405 or early 404 (in Babylon according to Ctesias).[8] Artaxerxes II was his successor; and Parysatis moved heaven and earth to have Cyrus exonerated and sent back to his command in the West. Cyrus' concern after that was with winning over Persian notables to his cause and raising an army with which to march against his brother. The cover story for his overt activity was local hostilities. At the same time he had large bodies of Greek mercenaries collected for him as shock troops and stashed away across the water, and so he was almost ready to start by the time that Tissaphernes had hard information and posted off with his 500 horsemen to warn the King. Cyrus was running short of money to pay his mercenaries; but he could rely on extorting it en route, so did not need to strip the silver from his bed (as Tissaphernes had once magniloquently declared himself ready to do for the Spartans), or even chop up his own chair.

On his march in 401 B.C. Cyrus had problems to face. For a small mobile army the best route to Babylon was that by the Cilician Gates;[9] but this required the collaboration of the Syennesis at Tarsus and so had to be worked for. Syennesis was cunning enough not to risk negotiating in person with a suspected rebel – in the event he had a son planted in either camp, but at this stage he had to be dummy while his wife Epyaxa played the hand. She went to Cyrus at his camp in Phrygia with money to pay his troops. The fiction of a local campaign in Anatolia could still be kept up, and with her guards she accompanied him for a fortnight; there was speculation how far their intimacy went. Epyaxa may not have been greatly impressed by the size of the army. But after she had been put at the receiving end of a mock charge by the Greek hoplites and bolted along with the market-stall men, she was clear which side was the one to back. As Cyrus proceeded along the 'southern highway' she slipped off, followed by 1,500 Greeks under Menon who entered Cilicia on the west. On reaching the Gates Cyrus found the heights occupied against him. But a day later the pass was clear because Syennesis had received news of Menon's 'invasion' and returned to Tarsus to defend his stronghold in the mountains behind the city; eventually, after a token sacking of the capital he was prevailed upon to come to terms with the conqueror and supply money to pay the troops, receiving in return a gold-bridled horse and just such costume and ornament as nobles wear on the Persepolis reliefs. Another serious problem of Cyrus' was that of keeping his force of some 13,000 Greek mercenaries moving forward as his true objective became increasingly apparent. The rank and file had been engaged for service in Anatolia; and it needed loyal support from the leaders in his confidence and promises of pay increases and a lavish donative before the point of no return was reached on the east bank of the Euphrates.

Plate 41

Cyrus did not cross the Amanid Gates pass by which Darius III was to descend in Alexander's rear in 333 B.C. He had more mercenaries arriving at Issos in the innermost nook of the Levant, together with sixty Spartan and Ionic ships; and this put him in a position to outflank the fortified coastal pass that Xenophon called the 'Syrian Gates'.[10] In the event there was no opposition to him either there or at the Euphrates. Abrokomas, who had an army in Phoenicia conventionally estimated at 300,000 men and was responsible for safeguarding it, had burned the boats on the Euphrates at Thapsakos and was on his way back to the King, whom he rejoined eight weeks later – five days too late for the battle.[11] Cyrus was fortunate in finding the river so low in mid July as to be for once fordable; and his march down the left bank was not difficult, though some attempt was made to scorch the earth as he was approaching Babylonia.

Artaxerxes II waited until the end of August for contingents to reach him from the eastern provinces. He lacked his brother's élan; indeed we are told that he was not even a good horseman. His victory over Cyrus at Kounaxa north of Babylon owed nothing to his generalship. Of three Greeks present who wrote accounts of the battle none saw it as a whole; but two things are clear. On Cyrus' right wing beside the river the Greek mercenary corps (the 'Ten Thousand') carried all before them but did not break off from their pursuit to take the King's centre on the flank. And second, sighting his brother in the middle, Cyrus plunged in frontally against him and was struck down before he could deal him a mortal blow. When it comes to apportioning the blame, both ancient and modern critics are divided between Cyrus' impetuosity and his Spartan mercenary commander's cautiousness. Since Cyrus' death decided the issue the greater part of the two armies probably had no taste of action. According to Xenophon, Tissaphernes led a cavalry charge that carried him through the lines of the Greek light-armed to Cyrus' camp; and Diodorus, whose battles have to be slogging-matches, makes him the hero on the Persian side. The King had been struck on the chest by Cyrus and lifted on to a horse by his indispensable aide Tiribazos. He may – to follow Plutarch's source – have assumed in the hush of battle that all was lost; but a sound of wailing came to the attention of the King's Eye Artasyras, who was presently able to report to his master that Cyrus was dead. Of the Greeks not one had been killed; and though they had not had time for breakfast before the battle and found their camp stripped when they returned, they spent the night happy in the belief that they had won. Artaxerxes' army had been withdrawn from the field.

Of Artaxerxes' four marshals whom Xenophon names – each allegedly commanding 300,000 men – Abrokomas had not arrived in time; and of two others (Gobryas and Arbakes) nothing can be said. The Persian leaders who were around after the battle were Tissaphernes, who was the other marshal, together with his brother and the queen's brother, Ariaios from Kolossai in western Phrygia, and Orontes, the King's Eye's son. Ariaios had commanded Cyrus' non-Greek troops and was in charge of his left wing in the battle; this does not seem to have been held against him, but he could no longer afford to befriend the Greek mercenaries. Orontes must have rendered some service;

for he was given a daughter of the King as bride and was heading with her for the satrapy of Eastern Armenia (see above, p. 170). Left to clear things up, Tissaphernes did his best to eliminate the Ten Thousand, especially by murdering their officers at a parley. But he was in a hurry to return to Sardis and possess himself of the Greek cities; and when the Ten Thousand set off northward with newly elected leaders and devised means to reply to his long-range sniping, he left them to make their way up into Armenia with the winter blizzards ahead. While he went back to the West they forced a passage through the hill country of the warlike Kardouchoi, then turning under the eye of Orontes they traversed the northern tributaries of the Tigris until they entered Western Armenia. The satrap Tiribazos offered them unmolested passage and kept a watch on their flank until they raided his camp on suspicion that he intended to occupy the passes ahead of them. In due course they reached the Black Sea and were able to return to the Straits.[12]

The return of the Ten Thousand – or, as they came to be known, the 'Cyreans' – caused general embarrassment. Pharnabazos' cavalry repelled them from Bithynia, and when in desperation they captured Byzantium the Spartans tried to shoo them away. In the East Aegean the situation was one of conflict; for Tissaphernes could justly reproach the Spartans for supporting Cyrus and claim the tribute of the Greek cities, while the cities could equally justly demand that their Spartan liberators protect them. The Spartan authorities were trying to keep hostilities in a low key. But Pharnabazos, who was co-operating with them in 400 B.C., offended their retiring admiral; and a more aggressive policy was adopted the following winter, when the remnant of the seasoned Cyrean corps was incorporated in the Spartan expeditionary force in Asia Minor. Pharnabazos then paid the price for his first gaffe when Derkylidas, now Spartan commander-in-chief, took the army north and cut out his most westerly hyparchy. It was Tissaphernes, however, who was to pay the heaviest penalty; by using treachery against the Ten Thousand he had made himself detested, and by failing to stop them from returning home he had let it be seen that Greek troops were irresistible. He had one opportunity in 397 B.C. when the Spartans were surprised in the Maeander plain by the combined forces of the two satraps and their Ionic auxiliaries were starting to slip away in the deep corn. Pharnabazos wanted to fight, for with their powerful cavalry arm the Persians had their best chance ever of a victory. But Derkylidas' bluff and Tissaphernes' fear of the Cyreans carried the day, and the two armies went their separate ways.

Prior to this Pharnabazos had sensed the menace and travelled up to see the King; and though Ctesias claimed for himself the credit of being the principal intermediary, it was probably Pharnabazos who sold the new naval programme to Artaxerxes. On his way back before the campaigning season of 397 he called in at Cyprus to bring an admiral's commission to the Athenian expatriate Konon, funds for ship-building, and the order for the Cypriot kings to lay down 100 triremes. The dominant figure in the island was now Euagoras. Born in Cyprian Salamis when a Phoenician dynasty was ruling there after the Peace of Kallias, he had been compelled to seek exile when another Phoenician from Kition usurped the throne. But as a member of the old Greek royal family which claimed descent from Ajax' brother Teucer, Euagoras was able to seize the kingship about 411 B.C.; and he then set to work to make Salamis one of the great Greek cities, with a new harbour and fortifications and numerous Greek immigrants of the better class. He maintained especially good relations with the Athenians, whom he helped with corn supplies in their hour of need. He also in 405 B.C. welcomed the fugitive Athenian commander Konon who had been alert enough to get under way with a number of ships when Lysander destroyed the Athenian fleet. Before 398 Euagoras had been extending his rule to other cities of Cyprus and falling foul of the King. But now, as the patron of the leading Athenian admiral, he was restored to favour; he paid the tribute that was owing from him and in return obtained a free hand in Cyprus for the next half dozen years. Meanwhile crews were sent from Athens, and early in 396 Konon sailed with 40 ships to Caria in advance of the main fleet.

The next step was for Artaxerxes to re-inforce Tissaphernes on land. In 396 Sparta had sent a king, Agesilaos, to the front, and a conclusion to the hostilities seemed further away than ever. Tissaphernes began by agreeing to a truce. But when his army had risen to a figure that included ten thousand or more cavalry[13] he felt strong enough to order Agesilaos out of the country. He moved south to catch the Spartans in the Maeander plain again. But Agesilaos spent the summer plundering in the north. Next spring (395 B.C.) Agesilaos trailed his coat and surprised the Persian cavalry near Sardis, inflicting considerable loss on them and capturing their well-stocked camp; Tissaphernes' field force seems then to have disintegrated. There was now nobody to stop the Spartans moving at will through the King's territory, and Artaxerxes had to take action. According to Ctesias he was not able to stand up against his mother after she poisoned his wife Stateira, and Parysatis had not forgiven Tissaphernes for taking the King's side against Cyrus (and for deliberately encouraging the Ten Thousand to ravage her estates). No one had a good word to say for Tissaphernes, and so there was no protecting him now. Tithraustes the hazarapatish was sent to the West. Tissaphernes was summoned to Ariaios' fief at Kolossai, seized as he was taking a bath, and handed over for execution. Tithraustes appropriated his treasure, offered Agesilaos thirty talents to go north and harry Pharnabazos instead, and gave a much-needed 220 talents to Konon for the fleet. A sum said to be fifty talents had meanwhile been despatched to Greece to incite the cities there to make war on Sparta. Tithraustes then returned to his post at court, which he seems to have retained until late in Artaxerxes II's reign; but Ariaios may have felt his honour compromised if Xenophon speaks of him being in revolt at Sardis that winter (IV 1, 27, but perhaps referring back to 401 B.C.).

Agesilaos was accustomed to being economical and he had been bought off cheaply. But he was now having the time of his life. In his attempt to concert resistance Artaxerxes had sent for Otys, king of the Paphlagonians. But he was out of touch with the times; not unnaturally Otys refused to go. Now Agesilaos made an ally of him and so detached a nation from Persian suzerainty. Then he wintered at the satrapal centre of Daskyleion. Pharnabazos showed some fight but had his camp captured when he tried bivouacking at a large village. After that the two commanders met by appointment. According to Xenophon, Pharnabazos came with his carpet-bearers; but when he saw the Spartan king sitting on the grass he joined him, and as the elder of the two he was the first to speak.[14] He began by recounting all he had done to assist the Spartans in the past and reproached Agesilaos for driving him from his estates so that he had to live like the animals from what was left over. Agesilaos explained that that was what happened in war: his quarrel was with the King, and Pharnabazos was welcome to join forces with him. Pharnabazos answered that if the King sent down another commander to conduct the war he would do so, but if he were given the command by the King he would fight the Spartans with all his might. Agesilaos shook hands on this, and Pharnabazos rode away.

It may be that Pharnabazos did not yet know what was in store for him. In fact by this time Konon had been up to the court for money and had asked for him as his fellow-commander. In the meantime the King's gold was working in Greece, and Agesilaos had to return for a war at home. In August 394, before he had cut his way through to the Peloponnese, news reached him that the Spartan fleet had been destroyed in battle off Knidos. Pharnabazos became a hero overnight. He then sailed with Konon liberating the Greek cities from Spartan rule, and even set foot on the Spartan coast. 393 was a year of festivity. But Pharnabazos was then removed from the supreme command in the West, and at some stage he was recalled to court to become the King's son-in-law.[15] Tiribazos, who had looked after the King at Kounaxa and then gone to the West Armenia satrapy, was sent to Sardis to take control. Despite his defects Tiribazos was a realist. He saw that in the changed circumstances Sparta could help to enforce a settlement of the Greek question; he therefore negotiated with the Spartan emissary Antalkidas and went up to the King with new proposals. But Artaxerxes would have none of it – he hated the Spartans as bitterly as his father had hated the Athenians; and Tiribazos was not sent back. The war with the Spartans dragged on. In time, however, Artaxerxes came round. He had troubles in the Levant; and peace in the West would free his hands for an offensive there and open up the mercenary market. In 388 Tiribazos was despatched to Sardis again. The Spartans responded by sending out Antalkidas as admiral. He went up to court with Tiribazos and succeeded in charming the King. Then they put the screws on Athens by blocking the grain route through the Straits. This resulted in a permanent agreement (the King's Peace of 387–86 B.C.) by which the Greek cities of Asia and the island of Cyprus reverted to Persian rule.

It might seem that the clock had been put back 100 years. But it was quite a different world – one of strong men and hired armies – into which the Eastern Greeks were discharged; and though Athenian propagandists could claim that the Spartans had betrayed them, the cities may have been no worse off fending for themselves than being protected by a Greek hegemony. Certainly the period after the King's Peace was one of renewed urbanization in Ionia.

Konon was ostensibly a Persian admiral. But after the victory at Knidos he had shown himself more interested in restoring Athens' greatness. This did not fit Tiribazos' diplomacy in 393–92, and he was put in detention in Sardis. Thence he made his way to his old patron in Cyprus (above, p. 214). Thanks to Isocrates' sketch of him, Euagoras of Salamis stands out clearly, and his career does not have to be pieced together from scattered notices in different authors. Probably, along with Dionysios I of Syracuse, Mausolus of Caria, and perhaps Nektanebo I in Egypt, he should be recognized as one of the great figures of Artaxerxes II's era. Egypt had been out of the empire since before Kounaxa, and the King's pre-occupation was with its reconquest. Euagoras had no interest in seeing it under Persian rule again. He completed his conquest of Cyprus and become involved in war when the kings of the last remaining Phoenician cities appealed to Artaxerxes. In 390 the new satrap of Caria, Hekatomnos, together with Autophradates who is later known as the loyal satrap of Sardis, was ordered to attack Euagoras. He also had no incentive to fight against a fellow-despot; and Athenian sea-power, in alliance with Euagoras before the King's Peace, was once again a factor. In fact Artaxerxes had miscalculated. After that it was Akoris in Egypt who came under attack. Pharnabazos, who had sailed the Aegean in triumph, and Abrokomas who had preserved his army from Cyrus, together with Tithraustes the hazarapatish, who had disposed of Tissaphernes, struggled for three years to attack Egypt with a great army and fleet, and (Isocrates says) suffered worse injury than they inflicted; after which their enemies went over to the offensive, Akoris entering Palestine and Euagoras taking part of Phoenicia (including Tyre) and fostering revolt in Cilicia.

In the later eighties Artaxerxes commissioned another expedition, to attack Euagoras this time. Tiribazos was put in command of the fleet and Orontes, the King's son-in-law, of the land forces. Money was being freely spent on these and later expeditions to judge by the silver coins of Tiribazos, Pharnabazos, Datames, and others that turn up in hoards in south-eastern Anatolia; Tiribazos himself minted in Tarsus and Issos at least, with his name in Aramaic but with Greek lettering also.[16] At last the King had found a commander with some initiative, and the armada crossed to Cyprus.

Tiribazos preferred to stay on land because the fleet was under the command of his son-in-law Glos, son of Tamos of Memphis (who had been Cyrus' lieutenant and admiral in Ionia in 401 B.C. and was murdered when he landed in Egypt with Cyrus' treasure). Glos, like his father, seems to have been at home in the West, though he joined Cyrus in his march to Kounaxa. In 381 B.C. the fleet was brought from Kyme in Aeolis where Xerxes' fleet had wintered 100 years earlier; it would seem that the nucleus of Glos' fleet was East Aegean, perhaps being what Tiribazos and Ariobarzanes had put at the disposal of Antalkidas at the Straits six years earlier. There was evidently some naval tradition here. Euagoras had assembled over 200 Cyprian, Tyrian, and Egyptian ships; and a brush with the Persians' fleet off Kition began well. But he had underestimated his opponents. Glos rallied and won a great victory, and Euagoras was then besieged in Salamis. Next year (probably 380), despairing of sufficient help, Euagoras sued for peace. He agreed to two conditions: to confine himself to Salamis in future and to pay tribute as in the past. But his status was also in question. The statement that Tiribazos demanded that his obedience to the King should be that of a slave to his master and not of a king to a king is unsatisfying because Tiribazos was no pettifogger and, like his predecessors, Artaxerxes II styled himself 'King of Kings'. But whatever lay behind it, the settlement hung fire long enough for Orontes, who had no doubt felt slighted, to traduce Tiribazos to the King as a traitor. Tiribazos was arrested and brought to court to await trial; Glos took alarm, attempted to raise an anti-Persian coalition, and was murdered. In Cyprus the army was up in arms at Tiribazos' suspension, and Orontes had to make peace on the terms agreed by Euagoras.

The Kadousioi south-west of the Caspian Sea had now been in revolt for thirty years, and the King decided to take the field in person.[17] The campaign was a fiasco. The retreat showed that in his sixties Artaxerxes II had the makings of a soldier; when the horses had been eaten he is said to have led forced marches in full equipment at the head of his troops,[18] and on arriving safely at a royal chalet where the trees were sacrosanct he took the axe himself to fell timber to keep his men from freezing. But it was only the presence of his prisoner that had saved them. With his eye for the main chance Tiribazos had seen that the two enemy kings could be played off against one another and negotiated separately with each, thus successfully extricating his master. After this Artaxerxes referred the quarrel between Tiribazos and Orontes to judgement by three Persian nobles. Tiribazos was vindicated; and Orontes was in disgrace instead.

Artaxerxes then resumed the attack on Egypt. By now a septuagenarian, Pharnabazos seems to have been pressed into service again and spent years in laborious preparations. This is the occasion to which Theopompus referred (above, p. 110), when gold tents, embroidered and purple fabrics and bedding, couches, gem-encrusted gold and silver vessels, pack-animals, meat and seasonings, and bales of paper were contributed and stock-piled in huge dumps. At some point Datames comes on to the stage. He had distinguished himself on the Kadousian campaign, in which his father, Kamisares, lost his life; and after succeeding to the governorship in Cappadocia he had brought his Paphlagonian cousin Thus a captive to the King. He was then appointed to command the expedition against Egypt. Like Pharnabazos he minted quantities of silver coins in Tarsus; but before he could set out he was diverted to suppress an unruly chieftain in eastern Anatolia (Aspis in Kataonia), and soon afterwards he received warning of intrigues against him at court and withdrew to the safety of his satrapy. The attack that actually took place was under Pharnabazos. He had obtained from Athens the services of the veteran mercenary general Iphikrates who had been the inventor of new mobile light-infantry tactics; and in 374 or 373 the army began to crawl down the Palestinian coast from Acre. The Egyptian defences at Pelousion were too strong by this time; but the striking force with the fleet won control of the Mendesian mouth of the Nile and Iphikrates was poised for a dash upstream to take Memphis by surprise. Pharnabazos, however, could not approve such bold action without referring it to the King;[19] and meanwhile the defenders concentrated and the inundation duly came round. So ended another great expedition.

Pharnabazos' caution cannot have been simply a senility reflex. Too many Persian expeditions went like that; and on the other side Agesilaos was to go on campaigning resourcefully in Egypt till the age of eighty-four. We must suppose that Artaxerxes II, who always liked to take the credit for what his subordinates achieved, would not allow his commanders a free hand; it would be charitable to suggest that by appointing a plurality of them he also hoped to ensure they did nothing rash. It was said of him in retrospect that he was a gracious and courteous prince who cared for his people, but that in his later years he was too suspicious of those around him. He had now lost Datames. Earlier he had replaced Pharnabazos when he was triumphant in the Aegean, and then withdrawn Tiribazos when he was proving victorious in Cyprus and thereby lost Glos and his naval staff. Tiribazos of course was a 'prima donna'. The Greek writers speak of his 'kouphotes' – a word that, from the stories Plutarch tells of him, means 'vanity' in this case; he was too ebullient when in favour and insufferable when out of it. But his services to the accident-prone King were outstanding. Not only did he get him to the battlefield in 401 and lift him on to a horse when he was knocked down, but he is said at some time to have saved the King from a pair of lions which had killed his horses. In both war and diplomacy his policies had been rejected and later proved right. His great ambition was to be King's son-in-law. Artaxerxes, it was said, offered him his daughter Amestris but fell in love with her himself and reneged; and then he did the same with his daughter Atossa. In the end Tiribazos' patience ran out. He conspired with the crown prince to put an end to the aged King. The plot was betrayed and he went down fighting. No doubt Tiribazos' frustrations were largely due to his own over-insistence; but there was a necessary element of amour propre – if not panache – in the make-up of Persian nobles of vigour.

The impotence of the central power was by this time evident; and the history of the 360s and 350s is so different from what preceded it that it is worth pausing to try and take stock. Of the eastern half of the empire nothing is known. True, the Greek writers might not have been greatly interested in events there. But if Artaxerxes II had had major problems in the East, some word should have seeped through; his known campaigns form an unbroken sequence that leaves no gaps, and the upper satrapies stood firmly by the empire to judge by the gallantry with which their nobles supported Darius III a generation later. Despite the bias of our sources it is probably true that the Greeks formed the hinge on which the creaking gate swung. The question may therefore be asked 'Who won the "King's Peace"?' (above, p. 215). It is a commonplace that Artaxerxes was the winner. Some politicians in the Greek cities were virtually in the King's pay. Persian gold might at times start a war in Greece, and (as happened in the mid 370s and 340s) it could stop one if the King wanted a buyer's market for mercenaries. But in fact the special relationship with the Greeks did not help the Persians much in their efforts to strengthen their rule, so it is unlikely that much tribute often came the King's way from the West.

In fifth-century Greece the burning issues had been political. In the fourth century they were financial. The economy had not been expanding, and over-population was a problem. If at any given time 60,000 Greeks were being maintained by service in fleets or mercenary bands overseas, this in itself was a gain.[20] These men would return home with plunder and perhaps savings (Xenophon attributes the enthusiasm of the Spartans for foreign service at this time to their desire to enrich themselves); and as in the Greece of fifty or 100 years ago earnings from abroad were a major domestic asset. A new phenomenon of the times was the professional commander who could organize and lead expeditionary forces (Konon and Iphikrates were prime examples). As Pritchett has pointed out, though often engaged by satraps and despots they were not true 'condottieri' because they were normally elected generals by their cities.[21] It was a sort of militant venturing to which Athens was most addicted. The state would use up its meagre resources in equipping an expedition whose maintenance would then rest with the commander. The public chest might with luck profit from the proceeds of conquest and loot – Agesilaos spent his old age campaigning for the benefit of the Spartan exchequer; and the men came home better off.

At first, mercenary service could be dangerous. But it became an understood thing that Oriental troops ran away when faced with Greek mercenaries, to the extent that among the stratagems related are transvestite ones in which Orientals fled when confronted by natives who were got up as Greeks but fought against Greeks who were not. A certain cameraderie must have developed, so that unless the stakes were high (as in the first battle in the Delta in 343) one Greek mercenary corps would not wish to fight another unnecessarily and they were not averse to transferring their allegiance to a higher bidder.[22] The Greeks in fact owned a valuable commodity – the Greek 'man whose spear went forth far' – and they made the most of it. The obvious alternative that Isocrates preached, that the Greeks should unite to despoil the Persians, was not seriously contemplated because there were too many politicians who depended on the King's bounty. To that extent the King was the gainer, though some Persian paymasters got a poor return for the funds they disbursed. The Greeks, however, benefited from an access of funds that helped them to keep up a higher standard of living than their productivity warranted; and on balance the King's Peace might be reckoned a success for them.

Among those who benefited most were the high-power mercenary generals. Expecting rich rewards, and on rare occasions playing off one employer against another, they built up fortunes and acquired property abroad. They were mainly Athenians who after a while could not afford to live at home because of the crippling burdens on the wealthy; so they had their tax-havens in Cyprus, Lesbos, Thrace, and Egypt. Some of them, like Charidemos from Euboea and Chares, possessed themselves of towns in the King's territory. So also did other strong men such as the banker Euboulos in the Aeolis and Klearchos at Herakleia on the Black Sea, while greater despots like the Carian satraps and the Lycian dynast Perikles built up principalities. Not surprisingly, a high proportion of the ingenious stratagems collected by Polyaenus for Lucius Verus to study on his Parthian campaign date to this era.

Armies and fleets were costly to maintain, and the Persian Kings were notoriously bad paymasters.[23] Konon in 396–95 had been in a desperate plight trying to keep his fleet together; a commander with sufficient hold on his men might get through a bad patch by making them work for hire as labourers, and Datames was said to have got his troops to the Black Sea coast on the ground that there was no nearer mint where he could turn his silver into coin for them. The prime necessity was pay for buying food. These armies normally depended on private-enterprise markets which followed them around or sprang up en route. Xenophon speaks of Cyrus having wagons with reserve food stocks for the mercenaries at Kounaxa; but it sounds as if this was exceptional because there was in fact a Lydian travelling market in his train. Market ships sailed with Pharnabazos' and Artaxerxes III's expeditions to Egypt. But when Cyprus was invaded in 381–80 Euagoras unleashed privateers and prevented the merchants from bringing supplies to the camp, with the result that the troops mutinied and some officers were killed before the fleet was sent to escort a convoy from Cilicia.

At other times troops would do their own foraging to bring in supplies. Armies on the move had to have rest days; and marches had to be shortened, especially if precautions had to be taken against enemy or raiders. When – to take a modern instance – General Roberts 100 years ago sped from Kabul to the relief of Kandahar he is said in the outcome to have covered the 305 miles in twenty marching days; marches like this would break off in time for fodder to be sought and the officers to go and hunt game for the pot. Cyrus' march from Sardis to Kounaxa is reckoned as almost ninety marching days at an average of barely caravan speed and forty-five rest days (not counting halts of thirty and twenty days at Kelainai and Tarsus). There have of course been generals who organize supplies and march their armies hard. Edward IV of England, for instance, marched thirty-six miles to Tewkesbury the day before the battle in 1471; and Antigonus, who would have regarded Clausewitz as a joke, could keep up an average of that or more for a week or ten days on end.[24] Small bodies of unencumbered or mounted men can naturally exceed this; and on the other hand pack-camels slow down a march. Ancient military experts would perhaps have agreed with our nineteenth-century ones that marches of more than twenty miles a day, such as Artaxerxes II is said to have kept up on his retreat from the Kadousians' land,[25] were 'forced marches'.

The problem of supply was a serious one. If pay ran out, the troops could not easily be restrained from living by plunder, so that armies could be more formidable to their allies than to their enemies. After complaints in 400 B.C. the Spartan commanders maintained strict discipline to ensure that it was the King's land and not that of their allies that was ravaged. Persian armies on the march in the satrapies may normally have found dumps of food already requisitioned for them. But the King's subjects in Cilicia and Phoenicia must have suffered grievously when all the great expeditions were being mounted against Egypt and Cyprus; the resentment felt by the Sidonians proves this.

The 360s and in a lesser degree the 350s are marked by what are known as the Satraps' Revolts. Though Xenophon had lost touch with Persian affairs, a good deal of detail is know from other Greek sources of different kinds.[26] As regards Greece itself the period is marked by the recession of Spartan dominance on land under the growing challenge from Thebes during the 370s and by Athenian expansionism at sea which was no longer necessarily in conflict with Sparta. The latter blossomed into a second and less oppressive maritime confederacy that offered some stability in the Aegean until Mausolus administered a decisive blow to it in 357 B.C. By this time the city states were losing their momentum and the fringes of Greece becoming more important.

Datames had returned to his Cappadocian satrapy and was preparing to revolt. He seized the Greek cities of the Black Sea coast-line and minted coins there. But before he was ready his son Sysinas is said to have betrayed his plans (about 368 B.C.), and Autophradates, satrap of Sardis, was ordered to take the field against him. Almost immediately, however, a revolt was started further west by Ariobarzanes, who had held the Daskyleion satrapy while Artabazos, the son of Pharnabazos by the royal marriage, was growing up (above, p. 215). Autophradates was consequently occupied nearer home, and Artabazos is said to have taken over as the King's general in Cappadocia. It is related that having been on the defensive Datames turned an ugly situation into a major victory by embroiling his own defecting cavalry in battle with the King's army at night; and he is even spoken of as crossing the Euphrates into Mesopotamia. Meanwhile Ariobarzanes was subjected to a siege by Autophradates and Mausolus at Assos on the west coast; but a warning visit from the venerable Spartan king Agesilaos was sufficient to make the attackers desist. The rebels had in fact won through. By about 362 B.C. the western satraps appeared to be all in revolt (or·at least cohering in the prevailing anarchy), and the whole West – Asia Minor and Phoenicia as well as Egypt – was united in alliance against the King.

At this point disaster struck the confederates. The old miscreant Orontes who had married the King's daughter forty years earlier was now accepted by the satraps as their leader; and the true rebels were got rid of, Datames being murdered, and Ariobarzanes' mercenary commander being murdered while he himself was delivered into the King's hands. Orontes seems to have accepted the leadership in order to betray his colleagues. Cities, mercenary bands, and the war funds were turned over to the King's men. We are told that Orontes now confidently expected to be made viceroy in the West. Autophradates, however, reacted smartly. In the event he retained his satrapy, while Artabazos stepped into his own hereditary one of Daskyleion. The result seems to have been that Orontes was left holding a defused bomb. He may have gone south to join the insurgents in Syria; but in due course he made his peace with Artaxerxes' son and general, Okhos. Of the other belligerents the Egyptian Pharaoh Takhos, who had succeeded Nektanebo I, was betrayed by a palace revolution when he imprudently went with his army into Phoenicia; and he had to take refuge with the Persians while Agesilaos, whose warning he had disregarded, lingered in Egypt to establish his successor on the throne and then, laden with honour and gifts as befitted the greatest army-commander of the half-century, died on the voyage home to Sparta. Straton, King of Sidon, faced ruin and was despatched by his wife when he could not bring himself to commit suicide; and Cilicia became a normal satrapy. According to Trogus, when finally he died (in 358 or the end of 359) Artaxerxes II had no revolts on his hands.

Curiously, Trogus speaks of Orontes as the governor of Armenia when he rebelled. So it is possible that the satrapy that he had held for twenty years after Kounaxa had been given back to him; and certainly his descendants seem to have been established there later (above, p. 170). But if so it didn't suit him, because he was soon back in western Asia Minor causing trouble. His last stronghold was Pergamon in Mysia. Diodorus speaks of him as the satrap of Mysia at the time when he joined the great Satraps' Revolt; perhaps he was a fief-holder in that region.[27] It is a strange coincidence that in the period of Cyrus' viceroyship before 401 B.C. an Orontes was garrison commander on the King's behalf in Sardis, was disciplined by Cyrus, and went to Mysia to defy him. But this was the Orontes who was convicted of disloyalty to Cyrus before Kounaxa;[28] and though the story of his trial is peculiar (both in the publicity Cyrus gave to it in the camp and the fact that no one could discover what happened to him) and Orontes the King's Eye's son was of the stuff of double agents, Xenophon at least regarded them as two different people. Of Orontes' career in the period after Kounaxa we know of his royal marriage and appointment to Eastern Armenia, his command in the Cyprus expedition when he traduced Tiribazos, and his subsequent disgrace. The latest news of him is in an Athenian decree dated to 349. But it is not certain that the fragments naming him and giving the date go together, so there is some uncertainty about his last phase. But it has generally been believed that in the middle 350s he was in revolt against the new King, fighting against Autophradates, minting coins in the Greek cities of the coast, and allying himself with Athens. Possibly in the end he achieved his ambition of being the grandest Persian in the West before he handed Pergamon back to the King and died.

Artaxerxes II's reign lasted forty-six years. According to Plutarch, whose principal authority here was Dinon, he lived to the age of ninety-four, but this is vitiated by his statement that he reigned for sixty-two of them. Lucian has him die at eighty-six, which would put his birth about 444 B.C.[29] Since he had a daughter married forty-two years before he died this should not be very wide of the mark. His eldest son, Darius, whom he had made crown prince, conspired against him and was executed (above, p. 218). His other two legitimate sons were Ariaspes and Okhos. The former must have been of a nervous disposition if it is true that Okhos so alarmed him by false reports that he committed suicide. Old Artaxerxes then pinned his hopes on a bastard son Arsames and lost interest when he was murdered by Tiribazos' son. Effectively Okhos was commander of the King's armies from about 362 B.C. He came to the throne as Artaxerxes III. He is said to have been bloodthirsty and killed off his relatives who could have a place in the succession; and though his in-laws in the West safeguarded themselves by rebelling, he seems in the main to have been able to cow his opponents. The threat of the long-range murder weapon may have helped; but we find the Athenians and Idrieus of Caria also doing as they were bid. Under him the central power was eventually to become formidable again. But in 359 B.C., probably some months before he became King, a stronger man than he assumed power on the furthest limit of what had once been Darius' empire, at first as regent and then as king of Macedonia. This was Philip II. His country was needing a strong hand. The core of the Macedonian kingdom had been renovated culturally and economically by Archelaos half a century earlier, but the outlying principalities had remained barbarous and for a generation after him disorder prevailed. Philip had to bring the barons under control before he could become a conqueror; so to the Persians he was for a while no more than a small cloud on the horizon. Artaxerxes III had more pressing matters on hand.

At the new King's command the western satraps disbanded their private armies. But after that things went badly. Artabazos seems to have been pushed into revolt; and his good relations with Greek commanders resulted in the King's generals suffering heavy defeats at the hands of a few thousand Greek mercenaries. A Tithraustes bore the brunt of this war. Eventually Artabazos fell foul of his Theban commander and sought refuge in Macedonia, though as a man who commanded the respect of both Greeks and Persians he had an honourable career in front of him. Orontes on the other hand was a loner and probably becoming too old to be dangerous. If he really was alive still, Artaxerxes III seems to have let him be. In 352 at last the king had his hands free, and he had been building up armaments. The prize of course was Egypt. It is possible that before his accession he had been heading for there when Orontes created a diversion. Now he mounted a great expedition. There are problems with Diodorus here, with the result that it is not clear whether we are dealing with one campaign or more. But the outcome seems to have been so catastrophic as to incur universal ridicule; and it is at this point that the Levant revolted in earnest. The fifties ended disastrously.

Artaxerxes III had the virtue of perseverance. Preparations were resumed. Peace was bought in Greece and fresh contingents of mercenaries were hired. Phoenicia was the first to be attacked, by the satraps Belesys of Abarnahara and Mazaios of Cilicia who were repulsed,[30] and then in 345 B.C. by the King himself. Tennes, who had succeeded Straton as king of Sidon, took fright at the size of the attacking forces and endeavoured to save himself by betraying his city. But when they revolted a few years earlier Sidonians, whose patience must have been taxed to the limit by requisitioning, had burned the King's park and hay stocks and vented their hate on the officials of the Persian occupation forces who had given offence; and consequently Artaxerxes was determined, like Cyrus the Great at Akkad, to make an example of the place so that others would tremble and submit. In the end Tennes was put to death and the citizens committed themselves to the flames rather than surrender (a stray Babylonian tablet speaks of the arrival in Babylon and Susa of Sidonian captives and women for the palace in October 345). The Cypriot kings had revolted; but Idrieus, who had succeeded to the Carian satrapy and lacked his brother Mausolus' nerve, attacked them in company with an Athenian general and stifled the rising. Artaxerxes then turned against Egypt. He was better placed than previously. Himself apparently an incapable army commander, he had an able adjutant in Bagoas whom Diodorus calls a eunuch by sex, and among his generals was Mentor of Rhodes, who had been sent with troops to Sidon by the Pharaoh and switched his allegiance there along with Tennes.

Nektanebo II had ruled Egypt successfully for sixteen years since he supplanted Takhos. He is said to have had about 20,000 Greek mercenaries, an equal number of Libyans, and 60,000 Egyptian regular troops. His river fleet was very numerous, and the Pelousiac arm of the Nile bristled with fortifications. He had Greek commanders; but the failure of previous Persian assaults had made him self-confident and he assumed the command in person;[31] unfortunately generalship was needed this time. Artaxerxes divided his army into three columns and himself stayed at rear headquarters. A surprise landing by mercenaries of his led to an engagement in which a division of Pharaoh's Greek mercenaries was defeated; it may have been a localized break-out which could have been contained, but Nektanebo took alarm and fled back to Memphis. When this became known the Pelousion garrison came to terms, and the flying column under Mentor and Bagoas pressed on to Boubastis. The example of Sidon now took effect. City after city surrendered without a struggle; and Nektanebo fled south with what treasure he could carry. So Egypt was reconquered in the high summer of 343, and another Pherendates was appointed satrap until the last short-lived revolt (above, p. 207).

Bagoas and Mentor were the heroes. Bagoas was next sent to put the upper satrapies in order. Some fighting with Saka has been inferred from a royal seal. But the one thing we are told is that at some stage the Kadousioi, who had been in revolt since Darius II's reign, were brought to heel (they are later found in Darius III's army) in this campaign a cousin of the King, Kodomannos, won fame by killing an enemy champion and was made satrap in Armenia – he is later to re-appear as Darius III. Mentor was sent to the West as generalissimo of the coast. Being linked to him by marriage ties he reconciled the refugee satrap Artabazos and his eleven sons to the King, and he did the same for his own brother Memnon. Mentor served his master well, cutting out at least one independent despot (the philosopher Hermeias who had succeeded the banker Euboulos) and probably restraining the ambition of the rulers of Caria as well as expediting the supply of mercenaries. When he died he was succeeded in his military command by Memnon. At court Bagoas was virtually regent – if he was a son of Stateira, who had a daughter married in 401 B.C., Artaxerxes III must now have been advanced in years.

Meanwhile Philip of Macedon was closing in. He was not yet ready to invade Asia; and for the time being a non-aggression pact with the Persian King suited his strategy. Artaxerxes was probably glad to make an alliance and, like Stalin in 1939 with Hitler, hope that it would last. But when in 340 Philip attacked Perinthos and was clearly aiming at control of the whole length of the Straits, he ordered his satraps to help with its defence, and for the moment he seemed to have staved the Macedonians off. He must have lived to hear the news of the battle of Chaeronea which made Philip master of Greece, but almost certainly not of the session of the congress in Corinth at which

Philip proclaimed the forthcoming crusade against Persia. About the end of 338 he was murdered with his sons by Bagoas. One son, Arses, was spared to be a puppet king, probably under the throne-name Artaxerxes. Appalled by his viciousness, Arses planned too late to remove Bagoas; and he and his sons went the way of his father. Despite the purges there remained a man claimed as a descendant of Darius II in the legitimate male line, Kodomannos.[32] Offered the Kingship he walked into the parlour, but under no illusions, and being forewarned he forced the poisoned cup on Bagoas.

Philip had already started the war in 336 when he sent three of his generals over to Asia to make a deep penetration across the Straits. But in July of that year he was murdered.[33] For the accession of Kodomannos (Darius III) Diodorus may have had more than one source, because he seems to mention that he came to the throne after Philip's death but then goes on to say that he was relieved of his anxieties about the Macedonian invasion by the news of his murder. In all probability Darius came to the throne when the year 336 was well advanced. The Persians hoped that with Philip's death it was a bubble that had burst; but it was a storm-cloud. It soon became clear that Alexander held undisputed possession of his father's throne and was quelling incipient revolts in Greece and the North in a series of lightning campaigns; and though dissension and the lack of a follow-up caused his forces in Asia Minor to lose ground to Darius' commander Memnon, a foothold was retained across the Dardanelles until Alexander was ready to invade Asia.

Unlike his great namesake, Darius III lived on in Iranian legend as Daras; and in a hardly less mythical tradition he is Dryden's 'Darius great and good'. According to Plutarch he had once been a King's courier; we are also asked to believe that he understood Greek. He did not have time to show his capacity to rule; but Mary Renault in her well-informed novel 'Persian Boy' gives an impression of him that once read remains indelible. After the reign of terror there must have been high hopes of benevolent rule, and they might have been fulfilled. But Darius III lacked a sense of purpose; and when the moment of trial came he failed.

Despite the figures that the Greek writers give, huge armies were probably on the way out; whatever forces Artaxerxes III may have held in the rear, it was a small number of shock troops that overran Egypt in 343 B.C. The army with which Alexander crossed into Asia was Philip's creation, and the senior commanders had been Philip's men. Here for the first time in Europe a powerful force of heavily armed cavalry was developed, the nucleus of this in Alexander's army being the 2,000 Companions; he had of course allied cavalry in considerably larger numbers. The core of the infantry was 12,000 Macedonians – the phalanx 9,000 strong with long pikes, and so inflexible, and 3,000 hypaspists; there was a like number of Greek heavy infantry. Diversity was achieved for tactical purposes by the addition of light-armed contingents of archers, slingers, and javelin-throwers as well as a modern siege-train. The phalanx was a porcupine; the striking force was the Companions, whom Alexander posted on its right. By 331 B.C. Alexander had raised his numbers to about 40,000 infantry and 7,000 cavalry. On the Persian side the cavalry was numerous and full of dash, but in the main they were less heavily armoured and used javelin and scimitar rather than long spears; in close fighting the Macedonians with their heavier armour had the advantage. As regards infantry, in 343 B.C. Bagoas had Orientals who kept pace wth Mentor's Greeks in the Delta. The old-fashioned Persian line infantry of archer-spearmen may have become extinct, except perhaps for the royal guards; and these troops who accompanied Bagoas could have been 'kardakes', who are mentioned in the first two battles against Alexander but played no conspicuous part in them; whether they were the young Persians in training is not clear. So far as can be seen, the hard core of the Persian infantry was the Greek mercenaries, for whom a total figure of 50,000 is given. Financially the King was well provided for; that Alexander was deeply in debt made no odds.

The first battle after Alexander's crossing of the Dardanelles was crucial. It was fought on the R. Graneikos, fifty miles to the east. From the steep bank the Persian cavalry opposed the passage; and Alexander, who was conspicuous when he charged, was the target the high nobles converged on. He was struck on the helmet by one satrap from the Seven Families and then saved by his Companion-leader Kleitos who hacked off the arm of another as he swung at him from behind. The risks Alexander took were a hazard, but by taking them he became a legend to his enemies – Arrian says he was 'insatiable of praise'. In the end the Persians gave way. The flower of their western chivalry lay on the field. The Daskyleion satrap, Arsites, had vetoed Memnon's plan to withdraw and scorch the earth because he would not allow the King's land in his satrapy to be ravaged; and he may have been responsible for the failure to throw the Greek mercenary corps into the fight. He committed suicide after the battle rather than face his master; his son Mithropastes was picked up by Nearchus in 324 B.C. on an island by the mouth of the Persian Gulf where he had taken refuge from Darius III.[34]

Sardis was surrendered to Alexander. But Halikarnassos baffled him. Memnon had retired there and with the Carian satrap – now a Persian who had newly married into the dynastic family – he set the defences in order. Alexander was confronted by a professional. At one point he was repulsed by a counter-attack and his father's veterans in the reserve restored the situation – the one incident that with his love-hate relationship with his father Alexander could not bear to be reminded of. Leaving troops to blockade the fortresses after the town fell, he spent the winter in Lycia campaigning against the mountain folk who could not stay on the heights at that season; and after that he made his way through Phrygia to Cilicia. Darius had mobilized and moved west to meet him. His ground was well chosen. To pass from Cilicia to Syria Alexander must cross the Amanos; and the rift valley where the R. Orontes makes a U-turn seaward had to be traversed. The plain is several miles across, and Darius waited there. By chance Alexander had caught a chill and was delayed in Cilicia. Darius let himself be persuaded that Alexander dared not confront him; so he crossed the mountain by the Amanid Gates to look for him and descended to the Mediterranean. Alexander had meanwhile moved on to take the lower southerly crossing (see Chap. XVIII n.10), and consequently Darius landed in his rear; and though lines of communication meant little to him at that stage Alexander lost his sick-bay at Issos. Both commanders were equally surprised. Alexander must have been glad to turn back and fight the battle in the coastal strip where he could not easily be outflanked. The battle of Issos in the autumn of 333 was an inglorious one. Alexander again led the cavalry charge and Darius fled while the issue hung in the balance. As Darius hurried back to Babylon the royal family and women-folk of his nobles were captured, and the war chest and valuables which he had sent to Damascus for safety fell to Alexander. Darius wrote to him offering a ransom for his family and all Asia Minor west of the R. Halys but received a dusty answer.

Alexander went down through Syria receiving the submission of Abar-nahara. The struggle with semi-independent satraps in the east of Anatolia could be left in the hands of his experienced general Antigonus. But despite the capture of the Halikarnassos fortresses and Memnon's death the war conducted by Artabazos' son Pharnabazos in the Aegean still posed a threat which would only wither away when there were no Persian fleet bases left. Byblos and Sidon accepted Alexander – the Sidonians will hardly have recovered from what the Persians did to them a dozen years earlier. But the Tyrians reckoned their island impregnable and underestimated Alexander's persistence. It took him seven months to capture Tyre; and as he had trouble with Gaza and then had Egypt to organize under his rule, it was not until the summer of 331 that he returned to confront Darius. While at Tyre Alexander received a second overture from the King, with the offer of 10,000 talents ransom-money and all the territory west of the Euphrates. He is said to have questioned his senior commander Parmenion; and when he said that if were Alexander he would accept it, Alexander replied that he would do the same if he were Parmenion. In fact his mind had been made up when he claimed the Kingship of Asia in his first reply to Darius.

Darius III had now had almost two years respite. Larger levies had been assembled (Arrian enumerates twenty-five different peoples); the cavalry, which constituted his strength, was re-equipped with longer spears, elephants had been fetched, and a regiment of scythed chariots trained. Fording the Tigris east of Nisibis Alexander found Darius waiting for him on a levelled battle-pitch at Gaugamela near Arbela. The warlike Eastern Iranian cavalry was stationed on his left wing to face Alexander. Arrian has the Persians stand to all night while Alexander let his army sleep (III 10–11, 2); the passage implies that they were nervous in the dark.[35] The battle, on 1 October 331, seems to have been conducted with tactical grasp on both sides. The weak Macedonian left wing under Parmenion was soon hard pressed. But as the Persian centre moved forward, a gap opened and Alexander plunged in with his Companions. The cavalry of the Persian right under Mazaios made a corresponding break-through which could have been decisive if they hadn't ridden on to the camp in the hope of freeing the royal ladies.[36] But meanwhile at the approach of Alexander Darius fled again, and in the end his cavalry rode off the field with a share of the battle honours. The Eastern Iranians followed Darius up into Media; but the Persian army was no longer in being, and Mazaios rode to Babylon to prepare for its surrender. Alexander went on to capture the Persian capitals. The treasure he acquired was reckoned at 180,000 talents (over £40 million gold) apart from valuable objects of gold and silver. This may well be less than there had been before all the costly expeditions and the satraps' revolts. But it was enough to unbalance the economy of Alexander's world as it was released into circulation.

There remained the pursuit of Darius, who was now watching events from the old palace up at Agbatana. As long as the snows lasted he was secure there. But when Alexander left Persepolis he set off eastwards to find refuge in the upper satrapies. Alexander turned in pursuit of him. The royal equipage was not travelling fast, and after passing Rhagai and the Caspian Gates Alexander picked up his trail. With Darius were eminent nobles – the former Daskyleion satrap Artabazos and his sons, who with 2,000 Greek mercenaries remained unshaken in their allegiance to the King, the hazarapatish Nabarzanes, and three satraps capable of raising armies in the East, of whom the greatest was the King's kinsman Bessos. They had not by any means been defeated in the battle, and as governor of Baktria and Sogdiana Bessos believed there was still an Iranian realm to hold. Darius' apathy grew into unwillingness to flee any further. He refused to accept protection from those who were most loyal to him; and as Alexander came nearer the exasperated eastern satraps made him a prisoner and hurried him along in a covered wagon. Finally, when the dust began to spurt on the horizon behind them, they stabbed him, killed the coachmen, and then rode away leaving the King to die as the wounded draught-animals trundled the wagon off the road to a spring. It appears that the was no longer alive when Alexander reached him. He is said to have been about fifty when he died in the summer of 330. As his successor Alexander gave him royal burial.

The war-minded nobles were now clear both of pursuit and of the shackles of allegiance; they had borne with their King too long.[37] Bessos now proclaimed himself King (Artaxerxes). But Alexander advanced fast enough to prevent the nearer satraps from raising new divisions. The next spring, after a 1,500-mile march round by the south, he crossed the Hindukush into Baktria, compelled Bessos to retire beyond the Oxus, and finally had him brought back as a captive and executed in the same gruesome way that Darius I had treated the kings of Lie. So died the last of the line to raise his tiara as an Achaemenid King. Achaemenids of course lived on. Some, like Artabazos, were to serve Alexander as they had served his predecessors. Descendants of the old houses continued as satraps and independent rulers in eastern Asia Minor and Armenia at least; and a family tree leading back to Darius I or the Seven Persians was a source of pride. But the name Achaemenid became extinct in the way that that of Ottoman has done in our own life-span.

Epilogue

An empire the size of the Achaemenid one presents opportunities. Darius I, who had time after the conquests to sit back and think about the empire as a whole, was conscious of the advantages of scale. He transported skilled workers over great distances and had materials brought from many lands, he encouraged the transplantation of fruit trees and probably ordered the construction of underground water channels (and perhaps dams) to further agriculture. He was interested in opening up shipping routes, and it seems likely that he was concerned to promote commerce and the economic well-being of the empire. Unfortunately, his successors do not seem to have paid the same personal attention to provincial affairs as he did. As their coin-types, royal inscriptions, and details of their tomb facades show, they regarded the heritage of Darius as something to be rigidly conserved, with forms to be almost slavishly copied.

Achaemenid rule gave Western Asia 200 years of peace. The militancy of the Greeks and the resurgence of Egypt involved frequent struggles in the West. For the rest, however, frontiers were guarded against invaders, in the Caucasus and the Central Asiatic steppes, in Arabia, and for much of the time in Nubia. The Persians were not themselves city-dwellers by choice. Unlike the Greeks they did not feel the need of foci of civic activity such as markets, law courts, council chambers, or fortifications to protect an urban population. But they accepted existing cities as focal points in the more developed countries and created conditions which may have been conducive to the growth of cities in the less advanced ones. There can be little doubt that the Egyptians felt themselves oppressed and the Babylonians suffered from exploitation, while the Greeks of the East Aegean and Cyprus resented alien domination. But there is no evidence that the rest of the empire normally found Persian rule oppressive; and the loyalty shown to the King by the contingents from the upper satrapies indicates that a sense of unity pervaded the Iranian lands (Ariane). In the West barriers were being broken by the mixing of different races and religious beliefs, notably in Babylonia.

As regards officialdom, there may be indications in the Persepolis tablets of individuals gaining promotion. But the high positions at court and in the satrapies seem normally to have been filled by Persians of standing, and royal kinsmen were often given important commands when they were still quite young. Certainly there was not the sort of graded career structure that prevailed in the Roman empire and provided training for high office. A perplexing question is the role assigned to non-Persians in the imperial service. Under Cyrus the Great and Cambyses non-Persians could hold high commands; and they could be powerful at court also if we believe Ctesias on the Hyrkanian Artasyras and his son. But the bulk of the evidence goes to suggest that once Darius was firmly established on the throne hardly any new non-Persian families were admitted to the hierarchy. It is often said that Medes had equal standing with Persians in the royal circle. This depends on the assumption that of the two quite different forms of dress which courtiers and men-at-arms wear on the Persepolis friezes, the one with the flowing robe is worn by Persians, while the other (the trouser-suit with round felt cap) is worn by Medes. This established belief is now being questioned.[1] There are two conclusive arguments to oppose to it. First, Darius I's bow-bearer, Aspachana, is actually named at Naksh-i Rustam and he is depicted in the 'Median' costume;[2] but he seems almost certainly to have been the son of the high-ranking Persian Prexaspes (above, pp. 19 and 52). Secondly, the rankers of the Median 'delegation' on the Apadana staircases do not wear the usual round cap but one with a triple peak forward, and this special cap does appear – but with extreme rarity – on the Tripylon friezes. The implication would be that Medes were extremely rare in court circles, which fits with the literary evidence that we possess. The governing class, then will have consisted almost exclusively of Persians. Amateurs though they were, these Persians seem on the whole to have proved themselves responsible officials. Alexander the Great recognized their capacity and proceeded to use them freely in high positions.

Plate 19

Plate 21

As regards the qualities of the Persians we are in the main dependent on Greek sources. Clearly they were not a people that we should call intellectual. They do not themselves seem to have had an inclination towards literature, medicine, or philosophical and scientific speculation. They were probably most at ease when living as country gentlemen. Despite the uncompromising black and white of their religious creed as expressed by Darius, there is no trace of fanaticism in them, and in general they would seem to have been tolerant. They liked to live in pleasant surroundings; coming from a country in which cultivation is restricted to fertile patches of watered land they may have been rather narrowly 'oasis-minded'. Luxury appealed to them. Herodotus was already aware of the harmful effect that luxurious living and lack of self-discipline had on the Persians, though he also found things to admire in them. After 400 B.C. the Greek writers are more severe in their strictures, notably Xenophon, who fought against them, and Isocrates, who was trying to unite the Greeks against them. The charge of bad faith or treachery does not seem to be justified; it was directed mainly against Tissaphernes, and even with him it could be regarded as the reverse side of his loyalty to the King. Canon Rawlinson went so far as to remark of the Achaemenids that 'foreign powers never had to complain that the terms of a treaty were departed from'. The more serious charge was that luxury induced a lack of manliness and of physical toughness with the result that they were no match for Greeks in the field, and that there went with it a lack of courage and the mentality of people who were slaves rather than free men.[3]

There was no doubt some truth in this criticism of the King's armed forces. Yet the Persian nobles that we encounter, even in the death-throes of the empire, were by no means lacking in courage and vigour. Lewis has observed that status with the King took precedence over nearly all other motives with a Persian nobleman. In the lower social strata a similar allegiance to a superior no doubt operated, so that within a recognized hierarchy people were bound together by ties of service on the one hand and protection on the other. In these conditions prestige was all-important to a high-ranking Persian. Thus Intaphernes cut off the ears of the palace attendants because they refused him entry. Xerxes was in honour bound to march against the Athenians whom his father had failed to punish. Megabyxos had to worst the King's generals in order to recover his self-respect. The stories of Pharnabazos and Tiribazos show that there was a limit beyond which personal honour could not be pressed; and in 334 B.C. Arsites insisted on fighting at the Graneikos rather than allow the King's land in his satrapy to be ravaged. Finally there is no better indication of the courage and loyalty of Persian nobles than the number of those who gave their lives in many battles in Asia, Cyprus, Egypt, and Greece, leading their troops as the King's commanders in the field.

The fact that so much of our information comes through the Greeks has one disadvantage. The Greeks judged the Persians by comparison with themselves; and historians in modern times have tended to follow them, with the result that too little attention has been paid to comparisons with other oriental empires which have faced similar problems through the ages. Some parallels have been drawn in this book, but mainly in matters of relatively little consequence. The study of continuity in the customs and institutions of Iran itself is also capable of being instructive. In his *Cyropaedia* Xenophon often referred to practices which had survived from Cyrus the Great's time to his own. In this book we have met quite a number that survived ten times as long; and others could be added. For instance, Sir John Malcolm's talk of the use of animal fables as a way of addressing superiors without the dangers of plain language takes us back to the stories of Cyrus' origins (above, p. 27), Herodotus' mention of kingdoms given to the sons of fathers who had revolted (III 15) is echoed by Chardin in the seventeenth century (III 310); and the camps of Xerxes and Darius III are matched in Pietro della Valle's letter V, where he says that the number of the Shah's army is swollen because the officers and principal persons take their servants and family with them but nevertheless such abundance reigns during the march as to give rise to a saying that the King's army is one of the finest and best provided cities in Persia. Despotisms come and go, but there is a stability as old as the Achaemenids underlying the continuity in Persian history.

Notes

I The Emergence of Medes and Persians

1 The Great Khorasan Road is that leading from Baghdad (or Babylon) over the Zagros Gates to the Behistun valley and up to Hamadan (Agbatana), thence to the Caspian Gates and Khorasan.

2 For the view that it was Mt Elvend above Hamadan see L.D. Levine, *Iran* XII (1974) 118–19. Recent studies relevant to the positions and movements of these peoples.are T.C. Young, *Iran* V (1967) 11–34, D. Stronach, *Iran* VII (1969) 2–8, and *Iraq* XXXVI (1974) 239–48, C. Burney and D.M. Lang, *Peoples of the Hills* (1971) 116ff., R. Ghirshman, *CRAI* 1973, 210–21.

3 E. Benveniste in *La Persia e il mondo greco-romano* (1966) 479–85.

4 This argument of course depends on the assumption that the Cyrus of about 640 B.C. was Cyrus the Great's grandfather, which is discussed at the end of this chapter.

5 R. Ghirshman, *L'Iran et la migration des indo-aryens et des iraniens* (1977) 46–59.

6 Stronach in *Iraq* (above, n.2).

7 Astuages is the form used in Greek. Scholars have taken the name to be Arshtiwaiga ('spear-hurler'), for which compare perhaps a name Irishtiwanka in a Persepolis tablet. But both the Akkadian and Greek forms lack the initial vowel r.

8 For problems of the Lydo-Median war see, for instance, G.L. Huxley, *Greek, Roman and Byzantine Studies* VI (1965) 201–6.

9 Before the Babylonian Chronicle became known the fall of Nineveh was dated 606 B.C., which was then considered to be the earliest possible date according to Herodotus and the latest compatible with the testimony of the prophet Jeremiah. The story of the capture of Nineveh by the Mede Arbakes in Diodorus II 24–8 is contrary to all known evidence; Arphaxad, the king of the Medes overthrown by Nebuchadnezzar in the book of Judith 1, is apocryphal (G. Rawlinson suggested that he was the Khshathrita whom Darius I put down, and others have tried to identify him and Arbakes with Herodotus' Harpagos).

10 P.R.S. Moorey, *Iran* XIII (1975) 20; cf. T.C. Young, *Iran* V (1967) 33–4; C. Goff, *Iran* VI (1968) 132 would suggest a date late in the century. A cautious appraisal of the build-up of the Median realm now by P.R. Helm, *Iran* XIX (1981) 85–90 (with references).

11 Cha(h)ishpish according to Justi and more recently Hinz; the Elamite and Akkadian forms do not seem to lend support, and Greek is in such difficulties with the sound ch that it is no guide.

12 E. Cavaignac, *Journal asiatique* 239 (1951) 361–4; W. Eilers, *Acta Iranica* III (1974) 3, P. Calmeyer, *AMI* VII (1974) 49 n.3.

13 E.g. in Ghirshman and Porada. Hinz more cautiously gives a date about

590 B.C. and remarks on the longevity of these Achaemenids; but it is a question of the age at which they begot their successors.

14   *Old Persian* (1953) 159.

15   This could not be known to Cavaignac, who therefore only half-believed Herodotus and dressed two lines of kings with a Teispes in each.

16   If Hidalu is in the region of Fahlian (see p. 88), Cyrus I was in Persis.

II   The Sources

1   For a recent survey of these texts see J.C. Greenfield, *JAOS* XCVI (1976) 131–5.

2   This banking house, of Egibi, was of long standing, and the name may be the same as Jacob. But the suggestion that the family was therefore Jewish is questionable since the name is a pre-Hebrew one attested in High Mesopotamia as early as the eighteenth century B.C. See also p. 88f.

3   Cf. for instance D. Metzler, *Klio* LVII (1975) 443–59.

4   Herodotus in III 61 gives the second 'Magus' the name Patizeithes, which would make sense as a Persian title, while Dionysios' Panxouthes makes none; the Behistun inscription confirms Herodotus on Cambyses' one brother and Intaphernes, whereas Hellanicus seems rather to be adapting Aeschylus on this. Two or three other statements are attributed to Hellanicus which are not mentioned by Herodotus, but they appear false or suspect. What is clear is that neither he nor Herodotus knew the other's work.

5   For a recent discussion of this G.L. Huxley, *Greek, Roman, and Byzantine Studies* VI (1965) 207–12.

6   Herodotus says of Dikaios that he was in high repute among the 'Medes'; but this no doubt means Persians.

7   Hdt VI 28 and 30 (there admittedly called a Persian).

8   This is in sharp contrast to Darius I's tomb inscription, from which Alexander's companion Onesikritos quoted in free translation about his martial prowess and Plutarch on his claim to be able to keep his head in battle and emergencies (*Apophthegmata* 172 F); so a copy of this inscription, perhaps in Aramaic, must have been available in the royal archives. The proof that Herodotus never saw the Behistun text in Greek is his almost total ignorance of the revolts that occupy most of the inscription.

9   I 13, 6 on a naval war with Cyrus and the dating of Polycrates by Cambyses only, both of which have bedevilled scholarship (the latter probably in ancient times also). It is particularly strange that the most critical of historians accepted without question versions of the incriminating correspondence between Pausanias and Xerxes (see recently A. Blamire, *Greek, Roman and Byzantine Studies* XI (1970) 295–305) and Artaxerxes I's missive to the Spartans (see p. 129), in both of which cases his translation reads like an anti-Spartan distortion. He also seems to be wrong about Cyrus the Younger's arrival (below, Chap. XVIII n.5) and can not be regarded as reliable on matters that to him were peripheral.

10   For a recent discussion of Ctesias' career see T.S. Brown, *Historia* XXVII (1978) 1–19.

11   Dareiaios for Dareios is nearer to the Old Persian form; Akkadian yields Dariawush, but Lycian gives Ñtariyeus and the Egyptian is similar; apart from this Ctesias tends to be worse than Herodotus.

12   Diod. II 13 (Behistun), Phot. 15 (Bekker 38 A–B) for the tomb.

13   R. Drews, *JNES* XXXIII (1974) 387–93; cf. R.N. Frye, *Iranica Antiqua* IV (1964) 41 f.

14   C. Müller, *Geographi Graeci Minores* I (1855). Isidorus' eastern limit was Kandahar. The revolutionary re-routing proposed in *Iranica Antiqua* XII (1977) 117–65 suffers from unawareness of Alexander the Great's journey to the East and results in a displacement of the upper satrapies. Unfortunately, the work of the Greek writer known as 'Trogus' source', who probably wrote in Parthia in the early first century B.C. and knew the history of Greco-Baktrian rule, has left virtually no trace in the ancient historical tradition.

15   R. Drews, *Iraq* XXXVII (1975) 50.

III   The Deeds of Cyrus the Great

1   For recent attempts to find authentic sixth-century history in the Book of Daniel see, for instance, P.-R. Berger in *ZfA* LXIV (1975) 192–234. In spite of – or rather thanks to – Josephus in his *Ant. Jud.* book 10 it seems clear that Daniel can not be related to Achaemenid history.

2   In Herodotus' Persian stories significant dreams determine human destinies in the same way as oracles in his Greek stories. But Ctesias and other writers also introduced dreams (as well as portents and warning by allegory in song).

3   This is clearly not a post-eventum prophecy; and the date given in the middle 590s could fit with the precise circumstances of the ten years round 600 B.C., though Jeremiah's authorship of this chapter is commonly called into question.

4   F. Jacoby, *FGH* IIA, no. 90, fr.66.

5   R. Drews, *JNES* XXXIII (1974) 387–93. Sargon of Akkad was a historical king 1750 years before Cyrus.

6   For the Chronicle see S.S. Smith, *Babylonian Historical Texts* (1924) 114; J.B. Pritchard, *Ancient Near Eastern Texts* (1955) 305–7; and now for the Babylonian chronicles A.K. Grayson, *Assyrian and Babylonian Chronicles* (1975). P. Sacchi has argued vehemently for a dating in 554 or even earlier, claiming that Smith's 'prophetic perfect' didn't exist in Akkadian (*Parola del Passato* XX (1965) 223–33); but the dating in the Chronicle seems inescapable.

7   For up-to-date references for Nabunaid's activities and alleged seven-year illness see Joan Oates, *Babylon* (1979) 131–5.

8   Xenophon gives a lengthy account of this campaign in his *Cyropaedia*, but it could be altogether fictitious.

9   *Hist. Ind.* I 3. For a recent collection of material on Semiramis see W. Eilers in *Sb. Öst. Akad.* no. 274, 1971, 83 pages. Pliny speaks of a city founded by her apparently on the Kabul River.

10   For the Eastern satrapies see Chap. XVII.

11   Diod. XVII 81, Arrian *Anab.* IV 6, 6 and III 27, 4–5.

12   H. Pottinger, *Travels in Beloochistan and Sinde* (1816) 106.

13   Xenophon's Gobryas. Ugbaru was presumably a veteran in the royal Babylonian service, and in fact he seems to have died a week after Cyrus entered Babylon.

14   G.G. Cameron, *Acta Iranica* (1974) I 45–8; on the story cf. E. Herzfeld, *The Persian Empire* (1968) 7 n.3.

15   *NH* VI 120; Pliny calls it Narmalchan ('royal river').

16   M.A. Dandamaev, *Persian unter den ersten Achämeniden* (1976) 97–8. B. Skladanek sees it rather as a matter of dividing the merchant class against their rulers (*Acta Iranica* (1974) I 117–23).

17   D.B. Weisberg, *Guild Structure and Political Allegiance in Early Achaemenid Mesopotamia* (1967).

18   Cf. D. Stronach, 'Cyrus the Great', *Bastan Chenasi va Honar-e Iran* VII–VIII (1971), 16.

19   *ZfA* LXIV (1975) 218.

20   For the references to this contretemps see W. Hinz, *Darius und die Perser* (1976) 111–13; for a brief account of the ritual, Joan Oates, *Babylon* (1979) 175–6.

21   For the evidence on Cambyses' kingship of Babylon see Dandamaev, *Persien unter den ersten Achämeniden* (1976) 100–2.

22   For a recent discussion of this see R. Zadok, *Iran* XIV (1976) 62; and p. 158.

23   Nearchus in Arrian, *Hist. Ind.* XXXIX 3, cf. Strabo XV 728. P.J. Junge, *Dareios I* (1944) 192–3.

24   A. Godard, *The Art of Iran* (1965; in French, 1962) 108–9.

25   I. Gershevitch, *TPS* 1969, 179, and W. Hinz, *Orientalia* XXXIX (1970) 425, both arrived independently at this identification from study of the Persepolis tablets; the identical name Kuh-i Nifisht seems to have belonged here in Arab times. Hallock has, however, found reason to believe that Nupishtash lay some days' journey to the west.

26   Phot. 15 (38 A–B), with a single object to both verbs; in one manuscript a later hand has added 'snakes' as the object of the verb 'saw', which could equally well be an authorititative correction or a reader's guess.

27   Stephanus Byzantius s.v. Passargadai, citing at second hand Anaximenes in his Demises of Kings. The second component would then be as in Kurushkata (see p. 37) rather than 'city' as in Gulashkird and Tigranocerta. For the name see now D. Stronach, *Pasargadae* (1978) 280–2.

28   Diod. XIX 24–44. At a guess, Gav-khuni, where the river of Isfahan now gives out, might with suitable irrigation have been the centre of a prosperous region which would fit with the historical data.

29   See below, Chap. V n.1.

30   A. Demandt, *AA* 1968, 520–40. This is not of course the first time that the Zendan has been claimed as the tomb of Cyrus. For these towers see p. 151ff. For the Takht-i Rustam see W. Kleiss, *AA* 1971, 157–62, D. Stronach, *Pasargadae*, (1978) 300–4. A detailed discussion of the candidates for the tomb of Cyrus in E.F. Schmidt, *Persepolis* III (1970) 41–4.

31   Strabo XV 730, Arrian *Anab.* VI 29, 4–10.

32   F. Altheim and R. Stiehl, *Geschichte Mittelasiens im Altertum* (1970) 127–8, give Iranian derivations for Tomyris (tahma-rayish) and Spargapises; on the other hand, as Nöldeke perceived (but didn't sustain), the name given by an Alexander historian for the brother of the Saka king beyond the Jaxartes, Carthasis, fits perfectly with Turcic (Kardashi = brother-of-him).

33   E. Benveniste, *Journal asiatique* 234 (1943–45) 163–6; explorations by a Soviet team at Ura-Tübe in 1959 seem to support the theory.

34   For an example of lawlessness when the new Shah had not shown the flag in Baluchistan a year after Nasreddin's death in 1896 see P.M. Sykes, *Ten Thousand Miles in Persia* (1902) 274–5.

IV   Cyrus' Rule

1   See R. Ghirshman, *CRAI* 1973, 210–21; W. Hinz in *Festschrift für W. Eilers* (1967) 85–98.

2   Strictly speaking, he says 'some' did, but from what follows it is clear that he means the three principal ones.

3   W. Tomaschek, 'Zur historischen Topographie von Persien', *SB Öst. Akad.* 102 (1883) 175 ff. for this route. K. Miller in his *Itineraria Romana* (1916) puts it south-east of Sirjan, but his knowledge is much inferior. E. Herzfeld preferred an identification of Panthialaioi with the modern place-name Fahlian in western Persis. He also interpreted Dērousiaioi as 'long-lived', but the form fits modern Persian and ancient Greek better than Old Persian; a connection with the place Darab in the east of Fars is possible.

4   H. von Gall, *AMI* V (1972) 261–83. The widely accepted recognition of Elamite guardsmen on Achaemenid reliefs presents similar problems that will persist as long as Herodotus' statement that the Immortals were all Persians is disregarded.

5   P. Calmeyer believes that the Elamite script was in use at the Median court before Cyrus (*Proc. II Ann. Symposium* (1974) 112–27); there is no more evidence against this theory than there is in favour of it. Elamite, like Sumerian and Hurrian, is a linguistic waif; it is thought to be related to the Brahui of Makran (see p. 183).

6   For the 'charisma' of kingship in ancient Iran cf. R.N. Frye, *Iranica Antiqua* IV (1964) 36–54.

7   For recent study of the influences on Persian culture and institutions see especially W. Hinz, *Altiranische Funde und Forschungen* (1969) 66–93; also in R.N. Frye, *Iranica Antiqua* IV (1964) 36 ff. and elsewhere, R. Ghirshman, *Mem. Volume V Int. Congress* (1972) 83–91, G. Gnoli, *Acta Iranica* (1974) II 165, M.A. Dandamaev, *Persien unter den ersten Achämeniden* (1976).

8   See especially M.A. Dandamayev in *Festschrift für W. Eilers* (1967) 37–42.

9   For Cyrus' religious beliefs see D. Stronach, *Cyrus the Great* (above, Chap. III n.18) 16–21.

10   So R. Ghirshman, *Mem. Volume V Int. Congress* (1972) 84; Urartian and Median influence is difficult to assess.

11   W. Hinz, *Darius und die Perser* (1976) 116–20. See A. Farkas, *Achaemenid Sculpture* (1974) 7–28 (the bovine legs there remarked as Babylonian rather than Assyrian).

12   Cf. P.J. Junge, *Dareios I, König der Perser* (1944) 19 f.

V   The Critical Decade

1   Aeschylus is of course no sure guide (he gives Ekbatăna for Ha(n)gmatăna), but the Persian texts do seem to indicate a long vowel; Lewis remarks that vav in the Masoretic text implies a long vowel in the Hebrew form Koresh. Strabo says Cyrus took his name from the R. Kuros (XV 729), whereas Ctesias had it mean 'sun'. For possible interpretations see most recently W. Eilers, *Acta Iranica* III

(1974) 3–9, W. Hinz, *Darius und die Perser* (1976) 53–4, and references in R. Zadok, *Iran* XIV (1976) 63.

2   With vowel r; in the first syllable the a is inherent in the consonant. The current normal transcription of Old Persian is inevitably inconsistent, e.g. Bardiya (not Brdya) but Zra(n)ka (not Zara(n)ka); see Kent pp. 15–16. Rta- for Arta- may be philologically correct; but though Elamite gives Irda-, the vowel a is the first sign in the Old Persian spelling of these words.

3   *Moralia*, Apophthegmata Cyri 1; also in Sextus Empiricus, *adversus Mathematicos* XI 43.

4   Mardu, son of Kurash, named as a witness in a promissory note of 541/40 at Babylon is presumably not the name Bardiya; but there are forms in Akkadian tablets which may be identical, e.g. Banushtanu and Manushtanu (Menostanes in Ctesias).

5   *In Studia classica et medievalia A. Pagliaro oblata* (1969) II 171–3. The standard work on the names is M. Mayrhofer, *Onomastica Persepolitana* (1973). Lewis in particular is making attractive rapprochements between personal names in the Elamite and people mentioned by Herodotus.

6   This may have come about through attraction to the existing Greek names Smerdes and Smerdios. Herodotus also names a marshal in Xerxes' army Smerdomenes (perhaps barda-manish = 'high-minded'). In the name Bardiya the second component is lost through diminution.

7   Herodotus III 30 (the bow brought by the Fish-eaters).

8   For these Uruk tablets see M. San Nicolò, *Archiv Orientalni* XVII 2 (1949) 323–30. He did not take parnakka as a name, and the word has no name-determinative (as Lewis points out to me).

9   For 'doryphoros' meaning simply a member of the bodyguard in high Persian contexts cf. Hdt VIII 101, IX 107. The story he is telling (of Syloson of Samos giving his cloak away on impulse) is better pointed if the Persian spear-bearer he gave it to was a nobody at the time.

10   G. Posener, *La première domination perse en Égypte* (1936).

11   The historical narrative that in the main we have to follow for Cambyses' expedition and doings is that in Herodotus book III.

12   For Cambyses' behaviour towards the Egyptians and the problem of the Apis bulls see K.M.T. Atkinson, *JAOS* 76 (1956) 167–77.

13   E.g. Batanaea (Bashan), Pliny's Ecbatana at Mt Carmel, and Emmaus (Hamata), which are in unlikely positions for the army's route. Nicholas of Damascus and Flavius Josephus have Cambyses die in Damascus, so they knew no very obvious claimant to the name.

14   The earliest tablet dated by Bardiya is of April; but the document was written in Persis and may refer to the pretender Wahyazdata in 521 B.C. See R. Zadok, *Iran* XIV (1976) 74–6.

15   Indicated as a region in the Akkadian; Wahyazdata also collected reinforcements there in the early summer of 521.

16   From both the East and the West, he says, so perhaps not referring solely to Cambyses' army.

17   The broad vale of Borujerd (Silakhur) and those which connect with it would perhaps fit best. Borujerd is just over ninety miles from Agbatana by road, and the species of clover known as 'Median grass' can be found near Jowkar at least.   *Plate 37*

18   J. Marquart, *Untersuchungen zur Geschichte von Eran II* (1905) 161 for
      Intaphernes and for the assumed Mithra festival. Aeschylus has Mardos (Smer-
      dis) killed by 'noble Artaphrenes', on which a scholiast remarked that Hel-
      lanicus called the latter Daphernes (in Ctesias the name is Ataphernes); in
      Aeschylus Mardos is called a disgrace but he ranked as a legitimate ruler.

19   Ctesias (Phot.) 14–15 (38a). He has the Hyrkanian Artasyras and the holder of
      the palace keys, Bagapates, join the plot from inside and remain trusted servants
      of Darius until his death; he also speaks only of a single Magus, who was in bed
      with a Babylonian concubine when the Seven broke in but put up a stout fight
      with a chair leg.

20   H.H. von Osten, *Die Welt der Perser* (1956) 69–70; G. Widengren, *Acta
      Iranica* I (1974) 85; G. Gnoli, ibid. 161; M.A. Dandamaev, *Persien unter den
      ersten Achämeniden* (1976) 166.

21   Hallock has now published a tablet of the twenty-second year of Darius' reign
      (PFa 31, *Cahiers DAFI* VIII (1978) 115), in which there is mention of 'girls,
      daughters of Hystaspes', from which he infers that Hystaspes was still begetting
      children for some time after his son Darius became King. A new study is
      J. Wieschöfer, *Der Aufstand Gaumatas und die Anfänge Dareios I* (1978).

22   Dandamayev, op. cit. 182–3, where the point is well made.

23   It is not clear how far the situation resembled that confronting Shah Abbas on
      his accession, when the realm was splitting into independent khanates.

24   These figures therefore appear at Behistun in the Akkadian version only, but the
      Aramaic copy from Elephantine gives some countercheck, greatly confusing the
      issue at Kundurush but completing the figure of 55, 2.3 read at Behistun for
      those killed in Margush (and now also E.N. von Voigtlander's study of the
      fragment from Babylon, *Corpus Inscriptionum Iranicarum*, Part I Vol. II,
      1978). The literature of Darius' accession wars is considerable; for the essential
      facts and theories about the 'one year' see, for instance, A.S. Shahbazi, *BSOAS*
      XXXV (1972) 609–14. In general I have followed Hinz' dates, which are based
      on Hallock's arrangement.

25   Old Persian ba(n)daka, English 'bondsman'.

26   This deliberate self-elevation was already visible in the differences of scale in the
      Behistun relief. When taken in conjunction with the one-to-one relationship
      Darius claimed with Ahuramazda (below, p. 147) it leaves no room for a 'third
      person' to make up a trinity; so the concept of a 'royal hero' functioning in his
      likeness on reliefs and glyptic is one to be treated with reserve (especially as
      regards his coins).

VI   Darius' Conquests

1   On the use of the word 'dahyawa' (lands) see most recently G.G. Cameron,
      JNES XXXII (1973) 47–50. In general they correspond to people on the reliefs,
      but they are territorial entities.

2   This is based on the identification of Naksh-i Rustam with the Nupishtash of
      the Persepolis tablets. This seems now to be rejected by Hallock (above, p. 34),
      but the dating of the list there after 494 B.C. in any case seems certain.

3   Karka were active in Babylonia and are named along with Yauna as transport-
      ing roof timber of Lebanon from Babylon to Susa for Darius I's palace. W.
      Eilers' identification of them as Carians (*OLZ* XXXVIII (1935) 201–13) has
      been widely accepted in spite of the intrusive second k, and it is now confirmed
      by Krk for Caria in the Aramaic text of the trilingual inscription found at

Xanthos in Lycia in 1973 (below, p. 148). All other suggestions (Cilicians, Colchians, Carthaginians, Phoenicians, and the place Charax) now run into insuperable objections. For the texts of Darius' lists in Egypt see now *Journal asiatique* 260 (1972) 235–66, *Cahiers DAFI* IV (1974) for the statue and its inscribed base, with M. Roaf on the subject peoples pp. 73–160; for the date of the completion of the canal W. Hinz, *AMI* VIII (1975) 115–21 (498–97 B.C.).

4　See for instance A.R. Burn, *Persia and the Greeks* (1962) 128 n.4.

5　Olmstead claimed that 'Beyond the Sea' means the Daskyleion satrapy (*AJSL* XLIX (1932–3) 158), and so also R. Schmitt, *Historia* XXI (1972) 522–7; but the letter of Xerxes that Olmstead cited (below, Chap. IX n.6) cannot carry such a meaning. On these people see below, Chap. VII n.7.

6　Strictly, between 23 March 519 and 12 March 518, which was Darius' third year.

7　The Old Persian texts give Saka; and Herodotus uses the name Sakai in connection with the Persian empire in Asia, saying that it is the Persians' name for all Scythians (Skuthai). The name used by Near Eastern peoples had a stem like -s(h)kuz-.

8　W. Hinz, *AMI* V (1972) 243–51; for Kent's reading see *JAOS* LXXII (1952) 17–18. It seems clear that in the Old Persian inscriptions the word used here (draya) did not mean river (as darya does now) but sea, while the word used for a river (the Nile) is rauta (modern rud). Open water would therefore seem to be meant here. It is certain that the Oxus has linked up with the Caspian Sea in historical times, but it is impossible to determine its course in 519 B.C. The Caspian was higher then and a sheet of water on the edge of the Kara Kum desert cannot be ruled out.

　　The old belief that Herzfeld held to, that the Saka of Skunkha were the Scythians beyond the Danube and that the Bosporus bridge is referred to, was overtaken by the dating of the campaign to Darius' third year. The objections to making this Darius' Scythian expedition are now insuperable: the dating twelve years after Cambyses' conquest of Egypt in the Capitoline Annals; the order of citation (after India) in Herodotus; the later date of the appearance of Saka Beyond the Sea in Darius' lists, coupled with the fact that Darius clearly classes Skunkha's Saka as 'Pointed-cap' Saka (the Tigrakhauda of his lists); the fact that Herodotus names the three kings of the Scythians at the time and Skunkha is not among them; general historical probability, and the limits that can be set to the mendacity even of Darius.

9　Hdt III 120–9.

10　Hdt III 139–49.

11　So K.M.T. Atkinson, *JAOS* LXXVI (1956) 171.

12　Cf. later Hapta Hindu (Sapta Sindhavas of the Rig Veda). The d in Herodotus' Sattagydai and the Egyptian form (sdgwδ) remains unexplained.

13　Irmuziya for forty-three people in an Elamite tablet from Persepolis, in Greek Harmoza, Harmouza, and the like.

14　Hdt III 38, 98–106. For the voyage and Darius' use of this sea see H. Schwirek, *Bonner Jahrbücher* 162 (1962) 4–20.

15　Strabo XV 686–9.

16　Phot. 16–17 (38B).

17　Hdt IV 87–8.

18   *JRGS* XXIV (1854) 43–4. His host at Pinarhisar seems to have agreed that there had been a stone with letters 'like nails', but leading questions had evidently been put to him first. E. Unger has identified the springs (*AA* 1915, 3–17, with details of the bedding of the stele).

19   Hdt IV 134–5, Ctes. (Phot.) 17 (38B).

20   P.J. Junge, *Dareios I* (1944) 188 n.15, argued that the name should be Megabyzos.

21   For the range of conjectures see E. Herzfeld, *The Persian Empire* (1968) 348–9. The name suggests Scythians, in which case the usage would be comparable to ours in Britain when we speak of the inhabitants of Deutschland as Germans and those of Holland as Dutch.

22   Hdt IV 165–7, 200-end.

23   Nothing is known of these coins, and modern conjectures are not convincing.

24   Hdt VI 20, about 493 B.C.

25   W. Eilers, *ZDMG* 94 (1940) 225 ff., with Weissbach's ingenious suggestion of Hipponesos; E. Herzfeld, *The Persian Empire* (1968) 9, 43–4, 310.

26   Strabo XVI 741.

27   For the canal see W. Hinz, *AMI* VIII (1975) 115–21; and with reference particularly to Necho and his nautical aims A.B. Lloyd, *JEA* LXIII (1977) 142–55.

VII   The Character of Darius' Rule

1   G. Le Strange, *The Lands of the Eastern Caliphate* (1905) 188; the equation Sumayrah-Semiramis is self-evident, though complicated by an association of a Sumaira with the Prophet. For a view of the 'tooth' see for instance *AMI* I (1968) pl. 25, 1, and S.A. Matheson, *Persia* (1972) pl. 27 (25 in the 1976 ed.), with the cliff of Behistun on the left. Herzfeld also connected the name with the Simirria of Sargon II's eighth campaign. The altitude at the mountain foot is about 4,250 ft and the summits seem to be 10–11,000 ft. Ctesias (in Diodorus) spoke of the mountain as sacred to Zeus (i.e. Ahuramazda).

2   On Behistun and Darius' monument generally M.A. Dandamaev, *Persien unter den ersten Achämeniden* (1976) 1–90; H. Luschey, *AMI* I (1968) 63–94, with a series of excellent photographs taken from scaffolding erected for the Shah-in-Shah's visit.

3   L. Trümpelmann, *AA* 1967, 281–98.

4   The Sar-i Pol relief illustrated *AMI* I (1968) p. 69 (from E. Herzfeld, *Tor von Asien*), S.A. Matheson, *Persia* 135.

5   Recent arguments in favour of Darius are to be found in various works of, for instance, W. Hinz (and R. Borger), H. Luschey, C. Nylander, A. Farkas, D. Stronach, and Dandamaev (as above). Against, Struve and Diakonoff, Eilers, and recently R.T. Hallock, *JNES* XXIX (1970) 52–5, I. Gershevitch in Hallock, 'The Evidence of the Persepolis Tablets' (*Cambridge History of Iran*, 1971) 7–8, and groping for a compromise P. Lecoq, *Acta Iranica* (1974) III 25–107.

6   P. Calmeyer would have Elamite used by the Medes on the evidence of a cylinder seal that Herzfeld acquired in Hamadan (above, Chap. IV n.5).

7   Its greatest weakness is that a consonant cannot be shown without a following inherent vowel, and of these syllabic signs 22 represent consonant + a, 7

consonant + u, and only 4 consonant + i. Thus the name Ka(m)bujiya (Cambyses) is written Ka-ba-u-ji-i-ya and Hi(n)dush Ha-i-du-u-sha.

8   Kent's SDa, found at Egyptian Thebes. At least one scholar has claimed it for Darius II; but E. Porada has pointed out that the design of the wing-tips of the god fits with Darius I's monuments and not the more elegant forms of his successors and Dalton remarked on the form of the chariot as early Achaemenid.   *Plates 5 & 7 Plate 10*

9   G.G. Cameron, *JNES* XXXII (1973) 51–4, and D.M. Lewis, *Sparta and Persia* (1977) 2 n.3. Old Persian was also used in the sealings of documents excavated at Daskyleion (K. Balkan, *Anatolia* IV (1959) 123–28); for the range of objects with Old Persian inscriptions cf. M.A. Dandamaev, *Persien unter den ersten Achämeniden* (1976) 35–6. For additions to Kent's list of the inscriptions see W. Hinz, *Historia Einzelschrift* 18 (1972) 123–8, M. Mayrhofer, *Supplement zur Sammlung der altpersischen Inschriften* and *Nachlese altpersischen Inschriften* (1978).

10   Cf. G. Windfuhr, *Indo-Iranian Journal* XII (1970) 121–5, and Cameron (as above); cf. J.J. Jensen, *ZDMG* 125 (1975) 294–300.

11   The Greek noun 'stater' has also been claimed as Babylonian ('heads of Ishtar'); but the uses of the word are against this.

12   For Darius' coinage see generally C.M. Kraay and M. Hirmer, *Greek Coins* (1966) 358. For silver as currency A.D.H. Bivar, *Iran* IX (1971) 97–107, with references.

13   A recent parallel is that of Count Pahlen in Turkestan in 1908–9; he had Islamic law collected from French codifications in Tunis and Algeria and digests of case-law in British India and written down both in Russian and the relevant local language (K.K. Pahlen, *Mission to Turkestan* (1922, published 1964) 81 f.).

14   A.H. Gardiner, *JEA* XXIV (1938) 157–79.

15   *SB Berl.* 1928, 604–14.

16   R. Meiggs and D.M. Lewis, *A Selection of Greek Historical Inscriptions* (1969) no.12.

17   Aristotle, *Hist. Animalium* 580 B. Darius was of course not the first Oriental monarch to encourage such transplantation.

18   A.T. Olmstead, *AJSL* LI (1934–35) 247–9, *History of the Persian Empire* (1948) 119–34.

19   See most recently E. Haerinck, *Iranica Antiqua* X (1973) 108–32.

20   For a recent claim that it fell at the summer solstice to fit the supposed function of Persepolis as an observatory, *ZDMG* 121 (1971) and *Mem. Volume V Int. Congress I* (1972) 289–90; and playing down the New Year festival and ceremonies P. Calmeyer, *Iran* XVIII (1980) 55–6.

21   Hinz takes her name to be Hutautha ('with beautiful thigh').

22   So D.M. Lewis, *Sparta and Persia* (1977) 22.

23   It is at this juncture that Herodotus remarks 'Atossa had all the power'. Plutarch three times names Darius' eldest son Ariamenes, and he has him claim the throne peacefully, submitting to arbitration by Artabanos and thereafter loyally supporting Xerxes until he met his end as admiral at Salamis (*Apophthegmata* 173 B–C, *de fraterno Amore* 488 D–E, *Vita Themist.* 14). See below, Chap. XI, n.6, and cf. Lewis, *Sparta and Persia* 15 n.70.

24   For dating problems involving these sculptures see A. Farkas, *Achaemenid Sculpture* (1974) 38 ff. and 117–19, with discussion and references to the Tilias' recent discoveries; von Gall has however stressed that the King here does not wear the mural crown worn by Darius on his reliefs, and A.B. Tilia now argues that the King must be Xerxes (*AJA* LXXXI (1977) 69). The Tilias seem to have established beyond doubt that the two reliefs were carved for the Apadana stairs (each with the King facing the on-coming subject peoples).

25   Strabo XV 735, where the same author is quoted on the hoarding of bullion (see p. 137). Following Müller, scholars refer the passage to the geographer Poly-kleitos of Larisa (hence F. Jacoby, *FGH* IIB 128 fr. 3). Plutarch says that Artaxerxes I had the right arm longer than the left (*Vita Artax.* 1), but see below, Chap XII n.4.

26   W. Hinz, *Darius und die Perser* (1976) 221.

27   Hdt III 159.

28   Hdt VII 194 (Sandokes).

29   Hdt VI 30. Darius also thought the world of Zopyros and Megabazos.

30   P.J. Junge, *Dareios I, König der Perser* (1944).

31   H.H. Schaeder, *Das persische Weltreich* (1940/41) 11, 26–7.

32   A.J. Toynbee, *A Study of History* VII (1954) 611 ff.

VIII   The Organization of the Provinces

1   'Khshathrapan' or the like (Protector of the Realm). The form appears to be Median (in Old Persian it is written khshaśapawan); normally satrapēs in Greek, but (as also in Lycian) forms closer to the Median are found. Cf. M. Mayrhofer, *Anz. Öst. Akad.* 112 (1975) So. 10, 274–82, and J. Teixidor, *JNES* XXXVII (1978) 181–5.

2   Hdt VI 42. The Chronikon Paschale gives 'Darius first fixed tribute from the subjects' under the year 518 B.C. but probably had no better authority than Herodotus. There seems to be no proof that Abarnahara became a separate satrapy before the revolts in Babylon early in Xerxes' reign.

3   G. in the Old Persian, P. in the parallel Akkadian and Elamite texts. See below, p. 191.

4   XPh. Akaufaka (the equivalent of modern Kohistan) is unidentifiable with so many mountain masses on the borders of the empire.

5   The assessment for silver ('nomoi' 1–19) was in Babylonian talents, which were heavier than the Euboic: hence the discrepancy in the addition.

6   Dalbergia sissoo Roxb., a hard brown wood used by preference for door frames in East Iran (I. Gershevitch, *BSOAS* XIX (1957) 317–20). The main source cited is Gandara (DSz says 'also from Karmana', while DSaa omits the name). Gandara is rich in deodars; but Darius' name for the wood is 'yaka' (in DSaa 'makan/wakan'), so it should be a different tree from the 'timber of the gods'.

7   'Those at/in the Sea' in the Behistun list seem by their position to be western and could refer to Cyprus, but hardly to the Daskyleion satrapy, which was on the Asiatic mainland ('ushka') in Darius' terms (DPe) and contained only a sprinkl-ing of Greeks along the coast.

8   So, recently, F. Altheim and R. Stiehl, and J. Ölsner.

9   O. Leuze listed twenty-two objections on pp. 166 ff. of the separate pagination of his massive article on the organization of the western satrapies, 'Die Sat-

rapieneinteilung in Syrien und im Zweistromlande von 520–320' (1935), *Schriften der Königsberger Gelehrten Gesellschaft XI, Geistesgewiss. Klasse 4,* 157–476.

10　See D.M. Lewis, *Sparta and Persia* (1977) 78 n.184, with A.T. Olmstead, *History of the Persian Empire* (1948) 293 n.21 (which Lewis kindly tells me Professor O.R. Gurney and he would assign to Artaxerxes II, thus giving 402 instead of 462 B.C.).

11　For tribute before 522 B.C. see Hdt III 13 and IV 165 (fixed tribute of Libyans and of Cyrenaeans), III 67 (Smerdis remitting the tribute); his statement that before Darius the subject peoples contributed gifts rather than fixed tribute III 89.

12　Probably 'hamspah' in Persian, G. Widengren, *Orientalia Suecana* V (1956) 153–5.

13　A. Christensen, *L'Iran sous les Sassanides* (1936) 20, 95 ff.

14　M. Ehtécham, *L'Iran sous les Achéménides* (1946) 72. His Iran-India satrapy would in fact comprise most of the Sassanian empire.

15　P.J. Junge, *Klio* XXXIV (1942) 5, *Darius I, König der Perser* (1944) 94 f.

16　A.J. Toynbee, *A Study of History* VII (1954) 583 ff., 683.

17　*Anab.* I 9, 7, *Hell.* I 4, 3; *Cyrop.* VI 2, 11. Widengren (above, n.12) places Xenophon's Thymbrara in Syria; but his use of the last passage is misleading (either the meaning is 'the barbarians (i.e. Persians and such) below Cappadocia (i.e. west of the Halys)', or the editors have done the right thing in removing the word Syria from the text.

18　For Ur see Widengren 153 n.4.

19　Thuc. VIII 58; *Tituli Asiae Minoris* I 44 (unfortunately in Lycian only and so of unknown content).

20　Hell. II 1, 8–9, possibly from Ctesias, in whom it would seem more in place (D.M. Lewis, *Sparta and Persia* (1977) 104). Cf. Chap XVIII n.7. In this connection the belief of Soviet scholars that even satraps were under the eye of 'secret police' seems to be an artifact of their dogma.

21　For Aramaic as the principal medium of official communications throughout the empire see most recently J.A. Delaunay, *Acta Iranica* (1974) II 219–36, M.A. Dandamaev, *Persien unter den ersten Achämeniden* (1976) 42 ff. This does not mean that the existing media disappeared in the more developed parts of the empire; in Egypt, for instance, satrapal correspondence was conducted in demotic also and documents were attested both by a royal secretary and by a native scribe.

22　As above, p. 185. Von Gall now suggests that only these three 'clans' were Iranian; but Herodotus for instance says the Sagartians spoke Persian (VII 85), and the Persepolis tablets show a high proportion of Persian-sounding names in the different regions of Parsa (I. Gershevitch, *Studia classica et orientalia A. Pagliaro oblata* (1969) II 167–70, finding a much greater number than E. Benveniste in his *Titres et noms propres* (1966) 97 – the one was looking for Iranian names and the other for Elamite).

23　R.T. Hallock, *Persepolis Fortification Tablets* (1969). 33 more selected tablets (PFa) are published by Hallock in *Cahiers DAFI* VIII (1978) 109–36. The term 'Fortification' is explained by the position in which they were found at the north end of the great terrace.

24　G.G. Cameron, *Persepolis Treasury Tablets* (1948), with supplementary material *JNES* XVII (1958) 172–6, XXIV (1965) 170–85; R.T. Hallock, *JNES* XIX (1960) 90–100.

25   Cf. Hallock, 'The Evidence of the Persepolis Tablets', *CHI* fasc. (1971) 15.

26   For the way Elamite was used see I. Gershevitch in the introduction to Hallock's *CHI* fasc. (1971), with the pertinent observations of Cameron in *JNES* XXXII (1973) 47–56.

27   See for instance M.A. Dandamayev, *Historia Einzelschrift* 18 (1972) 33–42 on slavery, and R.N. Frye, ibid. 86; Dandamayev, *Altorientalische Forschungen* II (1975) 74–8, where useful statistics are given.

28   For Greeks cf. G.P. Carratelli, *East and West* XVI (1966) 31–6, G. Gullini, *Parola del Passato* 142–4 (1972) 13–39. Groups of Yauna workers are rare and not large (though we may allow for Greeks among those sent up from Sardis and perhaps among the Karka); as individuals they are the opposite of ubiquitous in the tablets (Yauna as the assistant of Parnaka in 499–98 B.C. and of Artatakhma in 481). The evidence is in D.M. Lewis, *Sparta and Persia* 12–14; see below, Chap. XV n.8 for sculptors.

29   Herzfeld's identification of Skudra in the lists of lands with Socotra is less convincing because of their wintry dress in the reliefs.

30   See his *CHI* fasc. (1971) 17–20. For the numbers employed at the different centres see Dandamayev's statistics (above n.27). Since then Hallock has enlarged on the topographical implications of the tablets and seals (*Bibliotheca Mesopotamica* VI (1977) 127–33, *Cahiers DAFI* VIII (1978) 109–16), altering the areas he had defined and making some locations seem more hazardous; granted that Bairsha (Parsa) is Persepolis, it would now appear that at least two of the following equations must be erroneous: Matezza = Humadeshu, Rakkan = Arrajan, Badrakatash = Pasargadai, Nupishtash = Naksh-i Rustam, Narezzash = Neyriz, Tamukkan = Taoke.

31   *CRAI* 1973, 211. For references for Hidalu and Madaktu see for instance D.D. Luckenbill, *Ancient Records of Assyria and Babylonia* II no.878, and for Susa II no. 809.

32   *CHI* fasc. (1971) 17–18; *Bibliotheca Mesopotamica* VI (1977) 130.

33   See R. Zadok, *Iran* XIV (1976) 67–78.

34   Neither Babylon nor Susa has been a courier or caravan terminal in modern times, so stage figures are not to hand; Alexander's army took twenty days, Antigonus twenty-two with baggage and treasure. Naturally a horseman could travel much faster than an army; Babylon-Susa is barely 200 miles as the crow flies, but Susa-Persepolis would not be much under 400 miles by road.
    For the firm of Egibi see above, p. 13 and Chap. II n.2. It had dealings with the household of Cambyses before Cyrus' death, and in 521 B.C. a member of the family was administrator of the temple of Eanna at Uruk (for whose connection with Cambyses' court see above, p. 46).

35   *ZfA* (1971) 260–311.

36   For a study of the sheep-farming P. Briant, *Journal of Econ. and Soc. History of the Orient* XXII (1979) 136–61. There are several recent articles in Russian by Dandamayev on matters relating to the tablets.

IX   Darius' Feud with the Athenians

1   Hdt V 12.

2   Curtius Rufus V 2, 19. In Hdt IX 109 Amestris, the wife of Xerxes, is spoken of

as having woven a robe for her husband, but presumably her women worked the loom.

3 The main source of narrative now is Herodotus book V.

4 Hdt VII 59 (from the time of Darius' Scythian expedition).

5 Plutarch, in order to fault Herodotus, has the Greeks return to Miletus, which would have been impossible by land at that time without a troublesome detour through the mountains of Caria.

6 Cf. Darius I's tomb inscription (DNa): 'Me may Ahuramazda protect from harm, and my royal house, and this land: this I pray of Ahuramazda, this may Ahuramazda give to me' (Kent). For the Persian phrases in Hdt V cf. the letter of Xerxes to Pausanias in Thucydides I 129 (Olmstead, *AJSL* XLIX (1932–3) 154–61).

7 Herodotus' account of it V 99–VI 33. For the war see now P. Tozzi, *La Rivolta ionica* (1978).

8 See A.R. Burn, *Persia and the Greeks* (1962) 203–5; K. Nicolaou in *Princeton Encyclopedia of Classical Sites* (1976) 675–6 with references. For the possibility that some form of catapult was used cf. *JHS* XCIX (1979) 206 referring to the publication of finds from Paphos; A.W. Lawrence, *Greek Aims in Fortification* (1979) 46 and 476.

9 Book VI of Herodotus now begins.

10 Herodotus (VI 43) says Mardonios was then newly married to Artozostre; but a Persepolis tablet speaks of the 'wife of Mardonios, daughter of the King' in early 498 B.C. (R.T. Hallock, *Bibliotheca Mesopotamica* VI (1977) 129 and *Cahiers DAFI* VIII (1978) 110, 118) and since she was then travelling with Mardonios' father, Gobryas, in Persis there can be little doubt about the identity of this Mardonios.

11 Herodotus was not in the habit of making qualitative judgements on people in the way modern writers do. But talking as he did to people who lived through those times he had the feel of things. It is therefore relevant that he twice refers to Mardonios' obstinacy in refusing to listen to advice (IX 3 and 41).

12 This can be thought of as half a fleet conventionally estimated at 600.

13 A. Raubitschek in *Charites* (ed. K. Schauenburg, 1957) 234–42.

14 See D.M. Lewis, *JHS* C (1980) 194–5.

15 *SB Berl.* 1928, 614–22.

16 Diod. I 46.

17 The year when Xerxes was in Greece is securely fixed as 480 by the Athenian archon Kalliades, an eclipse in the autumn, and the fact that it was the year of the quadrennial Olympia festival. It is generally accepted that the year of Marathon is 490 but not absolutely certain.

18 An expedition to Central Africa under Xerxes has been postulated by L.S. de Camp on the strength of the pygmy-like delegates and okapi in the procession *Plate 29* frieze of the Persepolis Apadana (*Isis* LIV (1963) 123–5, which I have not seen). Kush was of course in the lists under Darius. The claim in *Iran* XVIII (1980) 156–7 that the okapi is really a nilgai is perplexing.

19 The account of the Babylonian risings given here follows F.M. de Liagre Böhl, *Bibliotheca Orientalis* XIX (1962) 110–14.

20　Josephus is badly at fault in placing Ezra's and Nehemiah's missions in the reign of Xerxes, and Esther in the time of his son Artaxerxes. But he was trying to rectify a hopelessly confused Biblical tradition. Agatha Christie in one of her novels might seem to support him in identifying Ahasuerus with Artaxerxes; but she was not purporting to write history.

X　The Armed Forces and Communications

1　Hdt VII 83. Some scholars have suggested that the Greek name for them rests on a misunderstanding of a Persian word; but no convincing explanation has been offered, and Herodotus uses the word with the same meaning in another context (p. 142).

2　See especially G. Widengren, *Orientalia Suecana* V (1956) 160–8. For Xenophon's reconstruction of Cyrus' army see especially *Cyropaedia* I 5, 5 and II 1. Widengren's contentions wear thin when he has to make his second-rank javelin-throwers = spear-bearers = slingers; armies with the regular formations of 10,000 that he presupposes will hardly have been restricted to three ranks one deep.

3　For these fiefs see below, p. 203, and especially the book by Cardascia cited there.

4　Since in Herodotus only infantry was provided by the Babylonians ('Assyrians') they may have joined the Iranian cavalry contingents. In early Achaemenid times chariots seem to be drawn by two horses, not four.

5　Hdt IV 84 (Darius), VII 38–39 (Xerxes).

6　Athenaeus XIII 608.

7　For these warships and their handling the most authoritative work is J.S. Morrison and R.T. Williams, *Greek Oared Ships 900–322 B.C.* (1968).

8　Cf. A.R. Burn, *Persia and the Greeks* (1962) 364–77. There is a copious literature on this topic.

9　Hdt VII 32, 131–3; cf. Burn *Persia and the Greeks* 343.

10　W. Leaf, *Geographical Journal* XL (1912) 39–40; cf. J.M. Cook, *The Troad* (1973) 306 n.1, 392–3.

11　The Sangbur (Tang-i Bulaghi), M. Aurel Stein, *Iraq* III (1936) 220, now D. Stronach, *Pasargadae* (1978) 166–7. The cutting is 270 yards long and five-and-a-half ft wide (so able to take a loaded pack-animal).

12　Stein, *Old Routes of Western Iran* (1940) 18–27. Cf. H.L. Wells, *Proc. RGS* V (1883) 161–62.

13　For discussions of disputed sections of the route see D. Magie, *Roman Rule in Asia Minor* (1950) II 786–9 for Anatolia, and L. Dillemann, *La haute Mésopotamie orientale* (1962) 147–55 for the Armenian sector. This is distinct from the 'southern highway', which can be pin-pointed at the Cilician Gates above Tarsus, Issos, and the 'Syrian Gates', and crossed the Euphrates at Thapsakos.

14　R.S. Young, *AJA* LX (1956) 266.

15　Most scholars take Herodotus to mean at every courier's day's journey, which might fit with *Cyropaedia* VIII 6, 17–18 (Cyrus the Great's posts working in day and night shifts); but there would have been nothing noteworthy in that. For references D.M. Lewis, *Sparta and Persia* (1977) 56–7. The word for the courier service in the Persepolis tablets is 'pirradazzish'.

16   Hdt VII 33–6, 54–6. For the topography W. Leaf, *Strabo on the Troad* (1923) 116–25.

17   For these preparations in Thrace Hdt VII 22–5.

18   F. Jacoby, *FGH* II B, 115 fr.263. See p. 217.

19   For Deve Höyük, where there were Iranian troops both cavalry and infantry in the fifth century, and the garrisoning of the region of the Euphrates crossing see P.R.S. Moorey, *Levant* VII (1975) 108–17 and his work mentioned in Chap. XV, n.15.

20   Hdt III 91.

21   For garrisons in Egypt see E. Bresciani, 'La satrapia d'Egitto' (*Studi classici ed orientali* VII, 1958) 147–53.

XI   Xerxes' Great Expedition

1   The literature of the Persian Wars is large. Recent surveys in English are A.R. Burn, *Persia and the Greeks* (1962), and C. Hignett, *Xerxes' Invasion of Greece* (1963).

2   The main point is the water-retaining capacity of the slopes. If a figure is given for the size of a marching force that could now be watered on a particular stretch, it is anybody's guess whether it should be multiplied by two or five for 480 B.C.

3   This point usually passes unnoticed. Beloch was aware of it and took the bull by the horns, declaring that there were not two bridges (Plutarch, *Vita Themist.* 16, tells an anecdote that implies that there was only one). It is impossible to calculate for the baggage trains. But – barring accidents – the fighting troops, who according to Herodotus used the upstream bridge, might have crossed at the rate of 9,000 an hour – so a million and a half in a full week, or 400–500,000 if Xerxes' place was in the middle (see, p. 117).

4   In the prevailing controversies about Aeschylus' plays the authenticity and dating of the *Persae* do not seem to have been impugned.

5   VII 89, where he includes 'Syrians in Palestine' with the Phoenicians (there appear to be no land forces from Abarnahara).

6   Diod. XI 57 for Mandane and her sons. The Ariamenes whom Plutarch makes Xerxes' eldest brother and lost in command of the fleet at Salamis (see Chap. VII n.23) could be Herodotus' Ariabignes, though as the eldest son he should be his Artobazanes. Plutarch also has three sons of another of Darius' daughters, Sandauke, captured on the islet and sacrificed (*Vita Themist.* 13, *Vita Aristid.* 9). For the twelve sons of Darius named by Herodotus (and their mothers), which G. Rawlinson and F. Jacoby underestimated, see A.R. Burn, *Persia and the Greeks* (1962) 333–4 (the only uncertainty being whether Arsamenes was son of Gobryas' daughter or of Phaidyme); possible additions to his list of members of the royal family on active service in 480–79 are Pharandates (son of Teaspes) and Artabazos. On Plutarch's reliability here see Burn 474–5.

XII   Narrative of Middle Achaemenid History

1   The two commanders were so named by Ephorus; Callisthenes, however, named Ariomandes, son of Gobryas (and so perhaps grandson of Darius and Artystone), as overall commander (Plutarch, *Vita Cim.* 12). As regards people with the name Farnadata, the one who had the Coan concubine may have been the son of a sister of Darius I, but presumably he had perished at Plataea (above, p. 105).

2   Charon of Lampsakos and Thucydides both said Artaxerxes, but the fourth-century writers with knowledge of the Persian court all said Xerxes. Most scholars follow Thucydides.

3   See p. 143. For a discussion of Artabanos in this context see D.M. Lewis, *Sparta and Persia* (1977) 19 n.96.

4   For events in which the Greeks were not primarily concerned our main source is Ctesias in Photios' chrestomathy and Diodorus, whose annalistic arrangement spreads the narrative over books XI to XIV, with Plutarch's Lives of Themistocles and Artaxerxes (II). For the name 'Long-arm' cf. above, p. 75. P.M. Sykes, however, explained its significance by reference to Yasht XVII:

> Beauteous art thou, Zarathustra,
> Shapely art thou, O Spitama;
> Fair of limb and long in the arm thou,
> Glory to thy body is given

Plate 9

(*History of Persia* (1915) I 214); here the authority of the Avesta may seem preferable to that of the ancient and modern scholars. As regards Artaxerxes I's age the clues are slight. His father Xerxes was presumably nudging his middle thirties when he came to the throne. He had children with him in Greece in 480; but in fact Herodotus spoke of them as illegitimate ones. If, however, the Treasury reliefs show Xerxes and not Darius as King (above, p. 75), he presumably had legitimate sons before his accession. In any case Artaxeres I seems to have had a grandson about twenty years before he died (below, p. 222); so he should have lived well into his sixties.

5   VI 98, where in a punning passage the name Xerxes is mistakenly translated 'warlike' and Artaxerxes 'great warlike'.

6   Hdt VII 151, Diod. XII 4. Some scholars prefer to have an earlier embassy of Kallias to Susa and date the Argive mission then.

7   *Vita Pericl.* 24; A.T. Olmstead, *History of the Persian Empire* 346. This all seems very nebulous.

8   When Herodotus speaks of 'Assyrian letters' on the marble set up by Darius at the Bosporus (one slab which he saw being full of them) the probability is that the three cuneiform scripts were used (IV 87).

9   The date, together with the accession and early struggles of Darius II, is fully discussed by Lewis, *Sparta and Persia* 70–82. Our text of Ctesias says that Damaspia died on the same day as Xerxes, but Artaxerxes must be meant.

10   If this was at the Mithra festival when the King was expected to get drunk, Artaxerxes would have died about mid August 424; curiously, a Babylonian tablet apparently of 16 August 424 is dated already by Darius (Lewis, *Sparta and Persia* 71–2, but Lewis tells me that M.W. Stolper thinks the date is erroneous). Sogdianos' throne name is unknown.

11   Photios here (47 = 42 A) calls this satrap Arxanes; his true name was Arshama (Greek Arsames), known as a royal kinsman and satrap of Egypt from records of 428 B.C. onward. In 35 (40 B) the name Sarsamas seems to be given to the satrap who was appointed after the Egyptian revolt of the 450s. Assuming Sarsamas and Arxanes are the same man and that Ctesias must have known the name, we can convict Photios' scribe of carelessness and infer that Diodorus is likely to be the more reliable of the two when he is following Ctesias.

12   A discussion in Lewis, *Sparta and Persia* 24 n.32, 79–81, casting doubt on the identification.

13   Probably the satrapy that included Zranka (Seistan) because a city of Zaris is mentioned (see below, p. 188).

14   He is said to have loved his own half-sister, who could hunt with the best, and arranged to do away with his unwanted royal bride.

15   Xenophon, *Anab.* I 2, 7–9. In one of his anecdotes Plutarch speaks as though there were a satrap in Sardis in the mid 460s (*Vita Themist.* 31), but this could be simply an assumption.

16   For the aid to Samos and talk of a Phoenician fleet (440 B.C.) see Lewis, *Sparta and Persia* 59–62. Modern scholars disagree considerably, but not so much on the facts as on the question whether they constituted infringements of the treaty terms.

17   Megabyxos also had Greek mercenaries on his hands after 454 B.C. It is not clear whether he actually used them in battle, but Ctesias speaks of his son having Greek mercenaries later. (See also p. 169).

XIII   King and Court

1   *Agesilaus* 9, 1–2, where a contrast is being drawn with the Spartan king. Plutarch, however, makes Artaxerxes II a notable exception, saying that he not only let his subjects have free access to him but even encouraged his wife to draw the curtains of her carriage so that people could speak to her on the road (*Apophthegmata* 173 F and *Vita Artax.* 5 and 27. Cf. *Vita Themist.* 26 for the protection of Persian ladies from the public gaze – a habit that dies hard in the East).

2   Plutarch (*Apophth.* 173 D) says Artaxerxes I waived this rule; but the recorded instance of its application is Ctesias' statement that Megabyxos was condemned to death (and then exiled to the Deportee Islands) for anticipating him, and the waiving of the rule would fit better with Artaxerxes II who is represented as being not ungrateful to Tiribazos for saving him from a couple of lions. For the King on a lion-hunt see Plate 33, notionally perhaps in a river plain of Elam to judge by the palm trees.

3   The Greeks used the word 'doulos' (slave) frequently in this context (e.g. of a governor in the Gadatas letter, of Cyrus the Younger in relation to his brother the King in Xenophon, and humorously of Pelops as the slave of Xerxes' ancestors in Herodotus). Darius uses the word 'bandaka' (bondsman) of his generals and satraps. The treaty with Euagoras of Salamis in about 380 B.C. turned on the question whether he was to be called the slave of Artaxerxes II or a king vis-à-vis his suzerain (see p. 216f.). In the Orient there is nothing unusual in this attitude; it was remarked by the European travellers that courtiers and nobles under the Safavids were happy to call themselves slaves of the king.

4   *Persae* 156.

5   It is difficult to gainsay Ctesias when he claims to have the authority of the queen-mother Parysatis for the statement that Cyrus was born after his father's accession; but since he assigned Darius II a reign of thirty-five years he will not have realized that Cyrus would hardly have been sixteen when he was appointed to command in the West. See p. 210.

6   For a discussion of the Achaemenid succession see G. Widengren, *Der Feudalismus im alten Iran* (1969) 102–8.

7   According to Ctesias, Megabyxos had cause to complain of his wife Amytis' lapses from chastity (though she seems nevertheless to have loved him), and Teritoukhmes tried to make away with his wife (the younger Amestris). Phar-

nabazos was brought back to court to marry a daughter of the King after a long career in his hereditary satrapy of Daskyleion; he had reached a stage where his loyalty to the King had been under severe strain. Royal brides were conferred on men who were already married: there are also instances of nobles having more than one wife.

8　Hdt III 84.

9　We should expect this to be the paladin Otanes, but Herodotus (VII 61) speaks of him as commanding the Persian infantry division in 480 B.C. (see p. 170).

10　Hdt II 98 (Anthylla), cf. Athen. I 33 F. Xen. *Anab.* II 4, 27, I 4, 9, and G. Cardascia, *Les archives de Murašû* (1951) for Parysatis. Plato, *Alcib.* I 123 B (assuming that, unlike II, Alcibiades I is genuine).

11　See D.M. Lewis, *Sparta and Persia* (1977) 20–1.

12　We know too little of the parentage of Persian grandees in the provinces, but Okhos (Darius II) is the only royal bastard heard of as a satrap (in a minor satrapy) and Tithraustes the only one as an army commander (see p. 126).

13　For the Persian robe see recently B. Goldman, *Iranica Antiqua IV* (1964) 133–52, G. Thompson, *Iran* III (1965) 121–6, W. Hinz, *Altiranische Funde und Forschungen* (1969) 70–4, P. Beck, *Iranica Antiqua* IX (1972) 116–22, A. Farkas, *Achaemenid Scuplture* (1974) 33–5. Elamite influence is as usual possible; but what Herodotus says is that the Persian costumes, both civil and military, were Median dress.

14　For the royal headgear cf. H. von Gall, *AMI* VII (1974) 145–61. The zigzag-topped crown seen on small-scale works like seals is not in fact confined to Kings.

15　Such figures are of course very misleading because subsistence levels are so much higher in the modern Western world.

16　But see J. Hofstetter, *Historia Einzelschrift* 18 (1972) 106–7. A discussion of 'proskynesis' generally by E.J. Bickerman, *Parola del Passato* XVIII (1963) 241–55; cf. R. Lane Fox. *Alexander the Great* (1973) 535–36.

17　Cf. J. Boardman, *Antiquity* 1970, 143, C.H. Greenewalt and L. Majewski in K. de Vries ed., *From Athens to Gordion* (1980) 133–40; for Greek literary references K. Holeschovsky, *Wiener Studien* III (1969) 166–80; for cloth with animals in fast dyes produced in the Caucasus Hdt I 203, and for covers H. Kyrieleis, *JdI Erg.-Heft* XXIV (1969) 148–9. For luxuries of this sort *Athenaeus* XII 513–15 is a substantial source.

18　A more appropriate example of royal fortitude was set by Sennacherib in Kurdistan: he pursued the enemy across gullies, torrents, and cliffs in his sedan chair, then climbed the mountain peaks like a young gazelle, stopping to drink cold water from the skin whenever his knees gave way (D.D. Luckenbill, *Ancient Records of Assyria and Babylonia* II no. 244).

19　It is not clear how precisely Herakleides distinguished breakfast ('ariston') from dinner ('deipnon').

20　This is presumably how the queen came to be present when Nehemiah received his permission to go to Judah. We are told that Artaxerxes II had his younger brothers Ostanes and Oxathres dine with him.

21　Cf. p. 110. The polite way of justifying such appropriation was known to Sir R. Sherley who, when entertained by the Duke of Shiraz, put the gold cup in his pocket remarking that 'after so unworthy a person had breathed in it it was some indignity to return it'. Xenophon speaks of it as being no shame among the Persians to have come by such cups dishonestly.

22 Thuc. I 138, 5, with additions for bedding and plaids in Plutarch, *Vita Themist.* 29, 11.

23 D.M. Lewis, *Sparta and Persia* (1977) 4–5.

24 Hdt I 188. This is not unusual. Layard in this connection says not only that Mahomet Ali had Nile water sent to him when he campaigned in central Arabia, but that in his time the water of the Kerkha was highly esteemed in Persia and sent to persons of high rank (the Kerkha, however, which is golden in colour, is the other river of Susa (the Eulaios) if (*pace* Strabo) the Choaspes is to be identified as the Shaour, cf. J. Hansman, *Iranica Antiqua* VII (1967) 21–58). Ctesias is also said to have spoken of the 'golden water' as being light and sweet.

25 Strangely enough a late source tells us that Ctesias referred to pepper as coming from troglodytic pygmies who lived in the vicinity of Azoumes (Aksum?), Ctes. Fr. 63 Jac. It was of course a novelty barely know to the Greeks in his day.

26 The earliest mention is of an Egyptian eye specialist whom Pharaoh Amasis sent on request to Cyrus before 530 B.C. (Hdt III 1); for their specialization II 84.

27 Hdt III 129–33; see p. 17.

28 W. Hinz, *Darius und die Perser* (1976) 226. In Hallock (PF 1853) he is said to have been mustered to the King as an 'irrigation-maker (?)', and there is nothing to suggest he was a person of importance.

29 Athenaeus X 434 E–F (from Douris of Samos); the Persikon is described in Xenophon, *Anab.* VI 1, 10 (squatting and jumping up again while clashing the shields).

30 Strabo XV 733, XVI 742 (where the uses of the palm are described). On the oral traditions of Iranian minstrelsy M. Boyce, *JRAS* 1957, 10–45.

31 Holes for planting trees have been remarked on the platform there; and there seems to be mention in a tablet of very large numbers of seedlings for planting, presumably in orchards.

32 H.H. Schaeder, *Iranica* I (Berlin 1934), Abh. Göttingen no.10, where full references are given.

33 Photius' text of Ctesias in fact reads 'azabarites', but the error will hardly be Ctesias'.

34 *Themist.* 27, 2 and 29, 2. Diodorus also says this Artabanos had the greatest power under Xerxes at the end of his reign and was commander of the guardsmen (XI 69). According to Ctesias he was a Hyrkanian, his father having had a leading place at court under Cambyses and Darius.

35 It has been suggested that the chiliarch had command of the select 1,000 cavalry; but we are presumably dealing with a palace guard rather than a sovereign's escort.

36 Nepos, *Conon* 3, 2–3, says in reference to this that Tithraustes was chiliarch and held the second position in the empire.

37 Diod. XVI 47. Ctesias also mentions Menostanes as becoming the hazarapatish of the first usurper in 424 B.C.

38 Orontopates (Jacoby FGH no. 3, fr. 174); he is made to be the interpreter of the Scythian gifts in place of Herodotus' Gobryas. Ctesias names one of the Seven Norondabates.

39 P.J. Junge, *Klio* XXXIII (1940) 13–38. If Junge goes too far in assigning functions to the hazarapatish, M. Ehtécham goes too far in naming holders of

the office in his *L'Iran sous les Achéménides* (1946). More negative assessments are given by Frye and by Lewis, *Sparta and Persia* (1977) 16–19 (where references are given).

40   Xenophon, *Anab.* I 6. (see pp. 222).

41   For Cyrus there Hdt I 153, Ezra 6, 2, and Itti-Marduk-balatu's visit (see p. 89); for Cambyses Hdt III 64 and 74.

42   Eumenes with his army in 317 B.C. took twenty-four days from the Pasitigris (Karun) crossing to Persepolis, which would make twenty-eight days from Susa; but he had impedimenta and was enjoying a leisurely progress. If Darius I used Kinneir's and Aurel Stein's shorter route by the Tang-i Khas (see p. 107), we might expect the journey to comprise about twenty daily stages; but riders travelling light and not retarded by baggage-camels might cut the time by half. By the later Achaemenid chaussée that Parmenion followed in 331 B.C. the journey would be several days longer.

43   Hdt III 117. Also picketing by people who came petitioning the King, like Intaphernes' wife (III 119), Syloson (III 140), and Mordecai in the Book of Esther.

XIV   Old Persian Religion

1   The word for god here is 'baga', not 'daiwa' (which in Xerxes' inscription XPh has the meaning of false gods or demons). In DPd Weissbach's translation 'all the gods' sounds more in keeping than 'the gods of the royal house' (cf. Kent 208 vitha-). M. Mayrhofer has in fact now claimed it as the correct reading.

2   Besides the Persepolis copies in Kent there is a new one from Pasargadai (*Iran* III (1965) 19–20, pl. 5); this distribution shows that Xerxes set some store by his action.

3   Hdt V 102.

4   Hdt I 131. Alilat is the same goddess as the Hanilat to whom Qainu the Kedarite made dedications (see Chap. XVI n.22).

5   Thuc. VIII 109.

6   Xenophon, *Hell.* I 2, 6.

7   Herodotus (VII 43) has Xerxes sacrifice 1,000 oxen to Athena at Ilion (Troy) and the Magi pour libations to the heroes there. As with Datis' dedications to Athena at Lindos, the purpose was no doubt conciliatory. Plutarch speaks of the goddess worshipped at Pasargadai as warlike and equates her with Athena (*Vita Artax.* 3).

8   *CRAI* 1974, 145–7. Cf. M. Mayrhofer, *Anz. Öst. Akad.* 112 (1975) 279 and his further contribution in *Fouilles de Xanthos* VI (1979) 184–5; also J. Teixidor, *JNES* XXXVII (1978) 181–5. Surprisingly, the Lycian text by implication renders Apollo as Natr-; and a recently published head-vase of similar date with a scene of the Judgement of Paris in relief and names appended shows that Aphrodite and Alexandros (Paris) were given their Greek names (Pedreta and Alekssa-) but Athena was known by the old Asianic name Maliya (R.D. Barnett, *Mélanges Mansel* (1974) 893–903). Clearly syncretism was well advanced before the end of the Persian empire.

9   Cf. A.T. Olmstead, *History of the Persian Empire* (1948) 461–3, M.A. Dandamayev, *Historia Einzelschrift* 18 (1972) 57–8. For a couple of examples of such crossing in dedications to Arabian deities in Tema and the eastern Delta see I. Rabinowitz, *JNES* XV (1956) 5.

10 Asura (Ahura, written Aura in Old Persian, Ura in Elamite and Ōro- in Greek) was the title given to Indo-Aryan remoter deities, whereas daēva (daiwa) were originally those in closer contact with mankind.

11 Xen., *Anab.* I 10, 12 (at Kounaxa), *Cyrop.* VII 1, 4 (Cyrus the Great and his successors). Curtius Rufus has the gold eagle mounted on the chariot yoke (III 3, 16) and a solar disk over the King's tent (III 3, 8) which reminds us of the disk recently detected by Stronach above the doorway of the Tomb of Cyrus at Pasargadai.

12 Recently A.S. Shahbazi, *AMI* VII (1974) 135–44, P.R.S. Moorey, *Iran* XV (1977) 145–6, XVI (1978) 146–8; a detailed discussion of the figure at Behistun by H. Luschey, *AMI* I (1968) 80–3.

13 There is new evidence of what may have been a fairly exclusive cult of Ahuramazda, set up with a statue, in Sardis (L. Robert, *CRAI* 1975, 306–30, the god being called Zeus); see also *Archaeological Reports* 1978–9, 70. The mention of an altar of Artemis at which in the Greek account Cyrus the Younger made his relative Orontes swear (Xen., *Anab.* I 6, 7) implies a cult of Anahita there.

14 Anaitis had her own triad in Zela, including the attribute Vohu Manah (Right Thought). References for these cults are J. Keil, *Anatolian Studies Ramsay* (1923) 250 f., and generally in S. Wikander, *Feuerpriester in Kleinasien und Iran* (1946); also P. Herrmann, *Ergebnisse einer Reise in Nordostlydien* (1962) 35, L. Robert, *Monnaies grecques* (1967) 74–5, *Hellénica* VI (1948) 108–9 and X (1955) 163, R.P. Harper, *Anat. Studies* XVII (1967) 193; cf. L. Robert, *Annuaire de l'école des hautes études* 1968–9, 166 ff., 193. In late Roman times temples of Anahita are said to have been destroyed in Armenia at Artaxata and what are now Erzinjan and Mush.

15 Cf. *Orientalia* XXXIX (1970) 428, where either 'the god Mithra' (Gershevitch) or 'all the gods' (Hinz) may be read on a tablet. The association of inscribed chert vessels excavated at Persepolis with a haoma-cult (R.A. Bowman, *Aramaic Ritual Texts from Persepolis*) has not won general assent; see for instance J.A. Delaunay, *Acta Iranica* (1974) II 193–217 (with further reference) and I. Gershevitch, *Mémorial J. de Menasce* (1974) 52–4.

16 Strabo XI 530.

17 In his account of their customs (I 131–40). On the deities he is confusing because he does not speak of Anahita and makes Mithra a goddess instead. Xenophon however knew Mithres as a male god of oaths.

18 XV 732–3. On the detail concerning sacrifices and the rituals practised by the Magi of Cappadocia in his own day he speaks with authority. Cf. R.C. Zaehner, *The Dawn and Twilight of Zoroastrianism* (1961) 168–9.

19 W. Hinz, *Orientalia* XXXIX (1970) 427–30. Herodotus has Xerxes pray to the sun at the Hellespont before crossing to Europe.

20 DB I 63–4. In the context they seem to have belonged to the Persian nobility whom Darius was concerned to vindicate; so the recurring suggestion that they were Elamite is implausible. There is now a strongly held notion that the ruined Zendan at Pasargadai is referred to; but its ruined state is not to be attributed to Gaumata since Darius claimed that he had restored the ayadana, and Hinz' argument that Darius built the Kaaba at Naksh-i Rustam as a replacement for it is countered by Stronach's observation that the socle of the Zendan at some time underwent repair. *Fig. 9*

21 Above them on the hillside are two more pairs and three single stone altars, but they are definitely thought to be of later date. Fire altars appear also on Median

rock tomb-reliefs (von Gall in the article n.24) and Achaemenid seals (cf. *Iran* XVI (1978) 149 f.).

22　Possibly also one of Achaemenid date at Pasargadai; but the great terrace at Tureng Tappeh in Hyrkania is now dated much earlier, and that at Firuzabad south of Shiraz seems to be post-Achaemenid. A terrace dated to Achaemend times has however been reported in the Surkhan valley north of the Oxus. Ghirshman, to whom our knowledge of the terraces in the Bakhtiari country is due, believes that they date to a time when Persians first established themselves there about 700 B.C. and that they carried an open-air altar on a podium for the fire ceremonies, thus constituting the 'ayadanas' of which Darius speaks at Behistun.

23　Principal recent references for fire cult installations are S. Wikander, *Feuerpriester in Kleinasien und Iran* (1946); A. Godard, *The Art of Iran* (1965) 142–52; U. Scerrato, *East and West* XVI (1966) nos. 1–2 (Dahan-i Gulaman); W. Hinz, *Orientalia* XXXIX (1970) 427–30 (Persepolis tablets); D.M. Stronach, current reports in recent issues of *Iran* (Nush-i Jan) and his *Pasargadae* (1978); K. Schippman, *Die iranischen Feuerheiligtümer* (1971), which is the substantial work on fire sanctuaries, and in *ZDMG* XVII suppl. I 3 (1969) 1021–31 and *Mem. Volume V Int. Congress* (1972) I 353–62; R. Ghirshman, *Mem. Volume* I 84–87, Terrasses sacrées de Bard-e Nechandeh et de Masjid-i Solaiman, *Mém. DAFI* XLV (1976), and in *Le plateau iranien et l'Asie centrale des origines à la conquête islamique* (1977) 343–48.

24　Cf. for instance H. von Gall, *IInd Annual Symposium on Archaeological Research in Iran* (1974) 139–41 for such tombs with figs 1–6.

25　XXIII 6, 27–32 (a passage in which the mention of Magi seems to be a device to introduce the subject of magic).

26　*Iranica Antiqua* IV (1964) 45.

27　Eudemos ap. Damascius, *de Princip.* 125 bis (Ruelle).

28　Cameron does, however, note 'the Carian' of a Magus called Kurka in *Persepolis Treasury Tablets* (1948) p. 7.

29　Plutarch, *Vita Artax.* 3. Cicero and Plato in *Alcibiades* I seem to have thought of the Magi as teachers of the Kings.

30　Cf. Amm. Marcellinus XXIII 6, 32, where Hystaspes is spoken of as the next great contributor to the art of magic after Zoroaster!

31　Diogenes Laertius init.; modern editors prefer 6,000 (as against 600 in some manuscripts that are classed as inferior); it is of course conceivable, as A.S. Shahbazi contends (*BSOAS* XL (1977) 25–35), that 6,000 is a scribal interpolation to harmonize with other writers on the subject and that 600 should be preferred. In a lengthy passage on Zoroastrianism Pliny, *Nat. Hist.* XXX init., speaks of the knowledge of it being brought to the Greeks by a Persian Ostanes when Xerxes invaded Greece. Plato in *Alcibiades* I makes Zoroaster the son of Oromazes (Ahuramazda)!

32　The word 'ushtra' in the prophet's name means camel. For anyone who felt inclined to give credence to the Greek writers this would at present be a serious objection to a dating around 6000 B.C. when the first irrigation cultures were providing a suitable ecological setting for Zoroaster on the borders of Turkestan. If conditions could be regarded as comparable, he would seem to have been culturally more advanced than Abraham.

33　Arta is an attribute which was one of six Amesha Spentas ('archangels') in the Zoroastrian scriptures. The belief that in Xerxes' text 'arta' is a noun coupled with Ahuramazda has been questioned, but he three times uses the word 'artawan' (= blessed in the hereafter).

34 For recent views on the question whether the Achaemenids were Zoroastrians see J. Duchesne-Guillemin's critical survey in *Historia Einzelschrift* 18 (1972) 59–82 with bibliography.

35 E. Benveniste, *Titres et noms propres en Iranien ancien* (1966) 97–8. Gershevitch avoids committing himself on the absence of Zoroastrian names at Persepolis.

36 See the article cited in n.34, pp. 78–80.

XV   Palaces and Art

1 For Susa see recent reports in issues of *Cahiers DAFI*, Studia Iranica, and Syria for the 1970s. For Persepolis, apart from E.F. Schmidt's *Persepolis*, reference may be made to A. Godard, *The Art of Iran* (1965), D.N. Wilber, *Persepolis, the Archaeology of Parsa* (1969), A.B. Tilia, 'Studies and Restorations at Persepolis' (Reports and Memoirs *IsMEO* XVI, 1972) and *AJA* LXXXI (1977) 66–77, S.A. Matheson, *Persia* (1976) 225–34; W. Culican, *Imperial Cities of Persia* (1970) is also cited. For reconstructions F. Krefter, *Persepolis, Rekonstruktionen* (1971).

2 C. Nylander, *Ionians at Pasargadae* (1970).

3 This has been disputed on the ground that a Cypriot coin found in the deposit can be claimed as early fifth-century (cf. M. Roaf, *Cahiers DAFI* IV (1974) 90 n.62).

4 *JNES* XXXIII (1974) 383–6.

5 See now A. Farkas, *Achaemenid Sculpture* (1974). For Achaemenid art reference may be made to A.U. Pope, *A Survey of Persian Art* (1938), E.F. Schmidt's *Persepolis*, R. Ghirshman, *Persia* (1964), A. Godard, *The Art of Iran* (1965), E. Porada, *Ancient Iran* (1965), W. Culican, *The Medes and Persians* (1965).

6 D.M. Stronach, *Journal asiatique* 260 (1972) 235–66, and *Cahiers DAFI* IV (1974); above, pp. 58, 99. Other fragments from Susa are mentioned.

7 For the Behistun style see H. Luschey, *AMI* I (1968) 84–90, and Farkas pp. 30–7. For Assyrian subject matter and renderings in Darius' reliefs and the problems of transmission Farkas pp. 55–8.

8 The question is discussed in detail in Farkas chapter 4, where a position is reached that Persian art under Darius was shaped by the trends in Greek art and that 'the sources of continuity would lie in Greek artistic traditions and not in a native school of artists attached to the Persian court' (which is fully argued though perhaps overstated), but at the same time that Greek elements in the art will not have overwhelmed the Persian ones. The argument for a new impulse from Greek art at Susa in the later fifth century (her pp. 76–82) is difficult to judge; as regards Telephanes, the mention of Xerxes' and Darius' workshops cannot be brought down to that period because Xerxes II did not have time to establish his rule (above, p. 129). J.P. Guepin's theory that workers mentioned in Treasury tablets as sent by Farnadata in the last two years of Xerxes' reign were Greek artisans captured by the general Pherendates at the time of the Eurymedon campaign (above, p. 126) is quite speculative (*Persica* I (1963–64) 34–52) cf. Chap. VIII n.28. The evidence about sculptors at Persepolis is now assembled by M. Roaf, *Iran* XVIII (1980) 65–74.

9 Of the 'delegations' depicted in the Apadana reliefs half can not be named with certainty. A royal tomb at Persepolis labels thirty 'throne-bearers' (see *Persepolis*

III for all these series); but the renderings are not distinctive enough to allow closely similar parties from the upper satrapies or from west of the Euphrates to be identified on the Apadana panels. For new photographs and discussion see G. Walser, *Die Völkerschaften auf den Reliefs von Persepolis* (1966), and for a more recent discussion with references M. Roaf, *Cahiers DAFI* IV (1974) 73–160. For the dating of the north and east staircase sculptures and advances in the latter see Farkas chapter 3.

10   Later reliefs at Persepolis, such as the jambs of the Hall of 100 Columns and the staircase of Palace H with no less than thirty 'delegations' depicted, seem to add marginally to the graphic repertory but not to show an advance in technique or style.

11   Athenaeus XIII 575.

12   Three or four possible instances in the minor arts are cited by P. Calmeyer, *Iran* XVIII (1980) 60–1, but the motif of man greeting woman is not only unspecific but obviously a rare one in the art of the Achaemenid raj. A medium, however, that we know next to nothing about is wall-tapestries.

Plates 33, 34 & 36

13   See J. Boardman, *Iran* VIII (1970) 19–45 with many illustrations of stamp seals. The Achaemenid cylinder seals, of an old-fashioned Mesopotamian type, seem to be more closely associated with the royal court. For seals see also C.G. Starr in the article mentioned in the following note.

14   From the study of satrapal coinages of the Levant in particular C.G. Starr has reached the view that the Greeks were becoming less dominant artistically at this time (in the second of his two important articles on Greeks and Persians in the fourth century, *Iranica Antiqua* XII (1977) 49–115). At the same time Hanfmann has stressed that Sardis was becoming increasingly hellenized in the Persian era.

15   O.M. Dalton, *The Treasure of the Oxus*[2] (1926). The Oxus treasure, apparently found near the north bank of the river opposite Kunduz, had become loot before it attracted the attention of antiquarians; it seems to have been a buried sanctuary deposit with objects dating from the early fifth century to as late as 200 B.C., but the bulk of what is preserved is thought to be of the fifth and fourth centuries. A recent stylistic analysis is by E.E. Kuzmina, *Le plateau iranien et l'Asie centrale* (1977) 201–14. For the distribution of works of minor art of Achaemenid stamp see now P.R.S. Moorey, *British Archaeological Reports, International Series* 87 (1980) 128–42.

XVI   Satraps, Hyparchs and Fief-holders

1   Tritantaikhmes, son of Artabanos, who was a marshal in 480 (Hdt VII 82), would be the satrap of that name in I 192 if Artabanos should be read instead of Artabazos.

2   The issue is complicated by the fact that Diodorus gives the name Artabazos to the Persian commander in Cyprus in 450/49 B.C. (XII 3–4), which might seem surprising if he were a first cousin of Darius I.

3   See p. 130. Since, according to Ctesias, his daughter Stateira married Artaxerxes II and his son was given a daughter of Darius II as wife, he ought to belong to one of the Seven families; but of course he could have been descended from one of Darius I's many sons.

4   According to the *Reallexikon der Assyriologie*, s.v. 'Gubaru', Gobryas had properties at Nippur and business interests at Sippar, and also a son named Nabugu.

5   Diod. XXXI fr.19, where his family's hereditary rule in Cappadocia is spoken of. Confusion in Otanes' family may have arisen from the great difference in age between his children by his first wife and those by Darius' sister.

6   A recent discussion of holders of the name in D.M. Lewis, *Sparta and Persia* (1977) 83–5.

7   Herodotus calls him simply 'Hydarnes, son of Hydarnes', but that seems sufficient warrant.

8   Polybius V 43, 2 for Darius' gift of land near the Black Sea; Strabo XII 547 for an old palace at Gazioura. See above on Anaphes.

9   The references for these royal lines were collected and discussed by Ed. Meyer in his *Geschichte des Königreichs Pontos* (1879). Descent from Cyrus would have to be through one of the three princesses of the blood whom Darius married.

10 Strabo XI 531.

11 Trogus also seems to speak of him as 'prefect' of Armenia 40 years later. Orontes (Aroandas) was a particularly common name in high circles, but this one (the 'Baktrian') seems identifiable as a tempestuous figure in Persian history for half a century. See below, pp. 170, 221f.

12 W. Dittenberger, *Orientis Graeci Inscriptiones Selectae* (1903–5) nos. 388–9.

13 Diod. XI 71.

14 Xen. *Hell.* IV 1, 39–40. Xenophon had presumably forgotten the boy's name; he speaks of him as the son of Parapita, which distinguishes his mother from the King's daughter Apame. He was evidently a legitimate son and successor since he is said to have been 'deprived' of the satrapy when his father went away. Xenophon elsewhere speaks of Pharnabazos as having wanted to take the daughter of the high noble Spithridates not as wife but as a concubine (Agesilaus 3, 3) about 395 B.C. before his royal marriage. The two passages are tantalizing. Pharnabazos had a brother, Bagaios, who was illegitimate. At this level it seems as though bastards might enjoy high standing but not expect to succeed their fathers if there were legitimate sons. Possibly, despite Xenophon's silence, the brother was Ariobarzanes.

15 Hdt III 14–15.

16 For the combination of Parthia and Hyrkania in Achaemenid and Macedonian times cf. also Strabo XI 514.

17 Strabo speaks of Cappadocia as having been divided into two satrapies by the Persians (XII 534); this might relate to a period after Datames, to judge by Diod. XXXI 19, 2.

18 Hdt IX 107, as a reward for stopping a fight between two Persian high commanders. But since a daughter of a Syennesis had been married to a leading Carian of Kindya about a generation earlier (V 118) there may have been a family connection (Kindya being in the hinterland of Halikarnassos). It has been suggested that Lycia should be read in place of Cilicia in IX 107, but there is nothing in the history of Lycia to suggest that it was unified.

19 D.M. Lewis, *Sparta and Persia* (1977) 78 n.184. Tattenai (above, p. 61), governor of Abarnahara under the Babylon satrap in 520/19 B.C., was presumably non-Iranian since he re-appears as Tatannu in a tablet of nineteen years later (this put an end to the belief that he was the same person as Hystanes, see A.T. Olmstead, *JNES* III (1944) 46).

20 E. Bresciani, *Studi classici ed orientali* VII (1958) 139. Tamos of Memphis and his son Glos have belonged to another such family.

21   For a possible governor's residence at Paphos in Cyprus see J. Schäfer, *Opuscula Atheniensia* III (1960) 155–75; the plan shows some resemblance to Achaemenid palace buildings and it was standing in Achaemenid times, but the city had its Cypriot Greek ruler in the fifth century and there are no finds of a Persian character. In contrast Samaria, where Sanballat resided, has yielded a couple of lion-paw legs from a throne evidently of Achaemenid type (*Israel Exploration Journal* XXIV (1974) 37–43).

22   For Geshem and his son Qainu and their dating see I. Rabinowitz, *JNES* XV (1956) 5–9, where a silver bowl, dedicated by Qainu and almost certainly found at Tell el-Maskhuta in the eastern Delta, is published. The first mention of an Arab king as a possible trouble-maker (Diod. XIII 46, of 411 B.C.) is very obscure, and perhaps not certain.

23   The dating of Nehemiah's appointment, in the twentieth year of an Artaxerxes, is fixed with near-certainty to the reign of Artaxerxes I by the synchronism of Sanballat and Geshem and the sequence of high priests. Ezra, in the seventh year of Artaxerxes, is placed before Nehemiah by the Chronicler. But most scholars are now agreed that the narrative of Nehemiah's governorship presupposes that there had not already been a successful mission to establish the Law, and they therefore date Ezra either to the seventh year of Artaxerxes II (398 B.C.) or to the thirty-seventh of Artaxerxes I (which is the one plausible emendation).

24   Bagohi was in a position of authority in the late fifth century when the Jews of Yeb were seeking permission from Palestine for the rebuilding of their temple. The name (Bigvai) could be borne by Jews; but if he is the same person as the Bagoses of Josephus, who is admittedly at his most unreliable here, Bagohi was probably not Jewish. Darius II actually sent a rescript to Arsames in Egypt about the keeping of the Jewish Passover at Yeb.

25   *Anab.* VII 8.

26   Xen., *Hell.* III 1, 6, names other places in the vicinity as belonging to the Gongylids.

27   L. Robert, *CRAI* 1953, 410–11.

28   See especially P. Bernard, *Syria* XLI (1964) 209–12; L. Robert, *Documents de l'Asie mineure méridionale* (1966) 31–2. For fifth-century Achaemenid rule in Lycia see O. Mørkholm and J. Zahle in *Acta Archaeologica* 1972.

29   L. Zgusta, *Charisteria Orientalia Rypka* (1956) 397–400, has argued a case for Persian names being adopted in Lydian families; but the evidence tends to be insufficient.

30   Xenophon, *Hell.* III 1.

31   Some random references for such names are P. Bernard, *Syria* XLI (1964) 209–12; L. Robert, *Noms indigènes dans l'Asie mineure* (1963) index s.v. 'Perses', *Hellénica* XIII (1965) 94, (in J. des Gagniers) *Laodicée du Lycos* (1969) 333–34; R. Schmitt, *Die Sprache* XVII (1971) 177–80 and (taking in Egyptian papyri) *Zeitschrift für Papyrologie und Epigraphik* XVII (1975) 15–24. Cf. references in R. Lane Fox, *Alexander the Great* (1973) 515–17.

32   Sample references for these monuments and reliefs are H. Metzger, *Rev. arch* 1967, 355–60, *Antiquité classique* XL (1971) 505–25, *Rev. arch.* 1975, 209–20; P. Bernard, *Rev. arch.* 1969, 17–28; J.M. Dentzer, ibid. 195–224; J. Borchhardt, *Ist.Mitt.* XVIII (1968) 161–211; J.M. Cook and D.J. Blackman, *Archaeological Reports* 1970–1, 59–61; S. Mitchell, *Arch. Reports* 1978–79, 65 and 86; M. Mellink in recent issues of *AJA*, in *Rev. arch.* 1976, 45–54, and *CRAI* 1979, 476–96 (Elmali); B. Tezcan, *VIII Türk Tarih Kongresi* (1979)

391–97 (Ikiztepe). There is much that is relevant in C.G. Starr, *Iranica Antiqua* XII (1977) 49–115. See now Moorey's work referred to in Chap. XV, n.15.

33　*Anab.* I 2, 7–8, *Hell.* IV 1, 15. The Bünyan relief E. Akurgal, *Die Kunst Anatoliens* (1961) 173 fig. 120.

XVII　The Extent of the Empire

1　Arrian, *Indica* 40; Strabo XV 727, 729; Diodorus XIX 21.

2　The castle of the Median kings seems to have continued to be used as a royal palace. The satrap's seat may have been the palace at which Antigonus wintered in 316 B.C. at a village in the countryside (Diod. XIX 44); from Isidorus we may perhaps infer that it was in the sheltered plain of Asadabad at the foot of the declivity of Mt Elvend, which is separated from Hamadan by the 7,300 ft Shah pass but has easy access westward.

3　*I?aq* XXXVI (1974) 239–48. Luristan surveys have mostly been reported on in annual issues of the journal *Iran*.

4　Cf. Strabo XI 524 (quoting Nearchus). For Alexander's campaign against the Kossaioi Arrian, *Anab.* VII 15, Diod. XVII 111.

5　Works that are of especial value on the Iranian lands generally are G.N. Curzon, *Persia and the Persian Question* (1892), G.Le Strange, *The Lands of the Eastern Caliphate* (1905), W.W. Tarn, *The Greeks in Bactria and India* (1938), F. Altheim and R. Stiehl, *Geschichte Mittelasiens im Altertum* (1970), R. Lane Fox, *Alexander the Great* (1973) with notes, and various works of P.M. Sykes, E. Herzfeld, and M. Aurel Stein. Though 120 years old, Canon G. Rawlinson's *Five Great Monarchies* can be read with profit. For topography and ancient remains within the boundaries of modern Iran, L. van den Berghe, *Archéologie d l'Iran ancien* (1966), S.A. *Matheson, Persia, an Archaeological Guide* (1972 and 1976); for Afghanistan N.H. Dupree, *An Historical Guide to Afghanistan* (1971) and for routes in western Afghanistan J.P. Ferrier, *Caravan Journeys and Wanderings* (1857). The volumes of L.W. Adamec's *Historical and Political Gazetteer of Afghanistan* (1972–) and *Historical Gazetteer of Iran* (1976–) are in process of appearing. See also F.R. Allchin and N. Hammond, *The Archaeology of Afghanistan from earliest times to the Timurid period* (1978).

6　The 'Parabeste' of Pliny is by its position unquestionably Bist, the 'para' resulting from his misunderstanding of a Greek idiom; the text of Isidorus has 'Biut' here. The 'Bestia deselutia' of the Tabula Peutingeriana is read as 'desolata'; but possibly it could be evidence of a Seleucid city (e.g. 'Best, ide(m) Seleucia'). Despite the intense glare and heat of the sun Bist seems to have a less dehumanising climate than Seistan.

7　If, as is widely believed, he chose the hazardous route deliberately in order to make preparations for the fleet, he would hardly have come with the bulk of his forces including women, children, and baggage train; they could have gone with Krateros' column.

8　The army that the Caliphs of Baghdad sent to Sind kept to the seashore so as to be certain of obtaining water by digging on the beach.

9　Strabo's Persian ode on the 360 uses the palm (above, p. 142) seems to have referred to date palms which of course present many possibilities for food and drink. If we include the ubiquitous dwarf palm, a considerable list of other uses can be gleaned from the accounts of recent travellers in Baluchistan: shoes and sandals, caps, huts, ceiling slats and thatching, bedding, mats and baskets, saddlery, ropes, torches, tinder and fuel, cups, hookahs or pipes, sword-belts and gun-slings.

10   Fahraj, the Persian stronghold since the annexation in the middle of the last century, has generally been preferred by modern scholars (though not by Aurel

Plate 38

Stein) on grounds that are presumably philological. But no site seems to be known there, whereas Bampur has the great mud-fortress mound which shows extensive occupation in prehistoric and early Islamic times but also yields the odd Achaemenid sherd.

11   This word has been brought into relationship with Avestan Upairisaena ('higher than the eagle'), referring to the Hindukush.

   To the Greeks Paropamisos was the name of the Hindukush here. The name Hindukush (supposedly = 'Hindu-killer') is relatively recent.

12   The Pyanj, which rises in Little Pamir, is the longer arm and now recognized as the main source of the Amu Darya; but it is the Waksh which still bears the name Oxus.

13   A.K. Narain, *The Indo-Greeks* (1957) 6. A number of important colloquium articles on aspects of Eastern Iranian culture are now printed in *Le plateau iranien et l'Asie centrale des origines à la conquête islamique* (1977); for the archaeology of Russian Turkestan generally see G. Frumkin, 'Archaeology in Soviet Central Asia,' in *Handbuch der Orientalistik* VII iii, 1 (1970), and E. Knobloch, *Beyond the Oxus* (1972).

14   Also mistakenly recognized as the Tanais (Don) in Alexander's time.

15   The list of anomalies is a substantial proportion of the whole. Egypt does not produce silver (though of course the Greeks traded there with their coin); Baktria has virtually no gold, and Siberian gold should rather have come through Sogdiana; ivory from Arachosia has perplexed scholars (above, p. 188); and the semi-precious blue stone taken to be lapis lazuli comes from mines high up the Kokcha valley in Baktria (Badakhshan), not from Sogdiana. The text known as DSf is composite. Two well-preserved marble plaques were more recently found together on the Apadana tell at Susa (F. Vallat, *Syria* XLVIII (1971) 53–9), one in Elamite (DSz) and the other Akkadian (DSaa). Prima facie they should relate to the same construction as DSf; but DSaa, which is briefer and lists lands without mentioning what materials came from each, shows surprising differences (Sind, Karmania, and Ethiopia (Kush) are omitted, and Persis, Yauna, Armenia (Urartu), Cappadocia, Parthia, Drangiana, Areia, Sattagydia, Saka (Cimmerians), and apparently Maka are added).

16   See now R. Rolle, *Praehistorische Zeitschrift* XLVII (1972) 76–7 on Saka burials in Central Asia with remains of a pointed cap which was twenty ins high and decorated in animal forms in gold leaf on wood.

17   If 'haumawarga' really is connected with haoma, Ctesias' fraudulence stands revealed when he applies the name to a Saka king Homarges or Amorges and recounts the history of his exploits with Cyrus. But Hellanicus mentioned a plain of the Sakai named Amyrgion, which fits with Herodotus' Amyrgioi and causes a niggling doubt about the haoma derivation. On the name see now I. Gershevitch, *Mémorial J. de Menasce* (1974) 54–6.

18   In general the name Caspian in the ancient writers referred primarily to the Caucasus (Caspian Mount and Way, and Caspian Gates = Dariel Pass); the sea on the east was commonly called Hyrkanian (though Caspian in Herodotus). Alexander the Great's Caspian Gates south of the Elburz entered the literature and can be identified; but the name may have been a misnomer.

19   This is a matter of fact and not of supposition; so it is to no purpose that scholars recognize Atropatene as the Antirpattianu of Sargon II's annals or derive it from a word relating to fire-worship.

20 For Armenia and Asia Minor books of substance are H.B.F. Lynch, *Armenia* (1901), C.F. Lehmann-Haupt, *Armenien Einst und Jetzt* (1910–31), D. Magie, *Roman Rule in Asia Minor* (1950), C. Burney und D.M. Lang, *The Peoples of the Hills: Ancient Ararat and Caucasus* (1971). For the western and southern coastlands see the four volumes of the series of Archaeological Guides by G.E. Bean; for Caria and much more, S. Hornblower, *Mausolus* (1982).

21 It has been suggested that the lack of tablets concerned with long-range trade may be explained by the carrying trade being in the hands of Aramaeans who would not have used cuneiform. For the Babylonian economy in Achaemenid times G. Cardascia, *Les archives des Murašû* (1951) is basic; useful recent essays and surveys include M. Meuleau in H. Bengtson, *The Greeks and the Persians* (1969) 354–85, M.A. Dandamayev, a summary of two articles in Russian in *Ancient Mesopotamia* (Moscow 1969) 296–311, and articles in *Festschrift W. Eilers* (1967) 37 ff., *Historia Einzelschrift* XVIII (1972) 15–58 and *Mem. Volume V Int. Congress I* (1972) 258–64, M.W. Stolper, *Management and Politics in Later Achaemenid Babylonia* (1974). On Babylonia more generally see A.L. Oppenheim, *Ancient Mesopotamia* (1964 and later) and J. Oates, *Babylon* (1979).

22 Nothing seems to be known about the chariot fiefs; for a cavalryman's fief see above, p. 102, and most recently P.A. Rahe, *AJP* 101 (1980) 79–96.

23 A book in English by E. Stern on the Material Culture of the Land of the Bible in the Persian Period has been announced. For finds of Achaemenid type in Abarnahara and Egypt, see Moorey's work referred to in Chap. XV, n.15.

24 For these expeditions against Egypt see Chapter XVIII.

XVIII Narrative of Later Achaemenid History

1 G. Rawlinson, *The Five Great Monarchies* IV (1867) 430.

2 Cf. p. 130. The possibility of omitting the conjunction 'and' in *Anab.* II 3, 17, which would make Tissaphernes the brother of Stateira, is ruled out by II 3, 28, where it is clear that Stateira's brother was a different person. According to Ctesias (Phot. 56 = 43a) Teritouchmes' two brothers, Mitrostes and Helikos, with two sisters, had been put to death and only Stateira survived. The Lycian Xanthos stele (above, p. 85) is the authority for Tissaphernes' father's name.

3 *Anab.* II 5, 35 (with Tissaphernes and others east of the Tigris).

4 This may sound cynical. But if a Levantine fleet could have been trusted to fight against the Athenians, Cyrus should have brought it into play when he wanted a speedy end to the war. Diodorus curiously mentions (XIII 46) that the fleet was withdrawn because of trouble caused by the 'king of the Arabs and the (king) of the Egyptians'(!) (in 411 B.C.); and D.M. Lewis has made a case for an abortive rising in Egypt then (*Historia* VII (1958) 392–7); but this should not account for it being stood down permanently. It seems that this Phoenician fleet was not used to prevent Euagoras from setting up Greek rule in Cyprian Salamis about 411 B.C.

5 If he really meant to say that the Athenians stood up to their existing enemies for three years and then to Cyrus as well, Thucydides could be implying 410 or 409 as the year of Cyrus' arrival (II 65, 12). But Xenophon's narrative, though chronologically imperfect, is precise enough to rule out any date before spring 408.

6 On the assumption that Darius acceded in February 423 (Lewis, *Sparta and Persia* (1977) 70). Cyrus was in Phrygia on his way to Sardis in spring 407 (or possibly 408), and with officials and provincial matters to deal with west of the Euphrates he must by then have been several months on the road.

7   *Hell.* II 1, 8. Some editors, however, regard the passage as an interpolation, in
    which case Ctesias is the most likely authority (Lewis, *Sparta and Persia* 104).

8   The place where he lay ill is called Thamneria by Xenophon. Iron Age and
    Achaemenid levels have recently been found on a prehistoric mound near
    Sagzabad (a place named by the Arab geographers) thirty-five miles south of
    Qazvin. A likely spot for convalescence would be Abhar, forty miles west of
    there.

9   In the later stages of his march at least Cyrus had some wheeled transport. But
    at the Cilician Gates it is not likely to have been enough to cause serious delay in
    the passage, which seems to have been of about vehicle-width in the narrows.
Plate 41
    Scarping in Roman times made a roadway which has been widened more than
    once since. The defile is now named Gülek Boghazi.

10 The name Syrian Gates was given to the mountain crossing behind it in 333 B.C.
    The two crossings, at about 3,750 ft (Amanid Gates) and 2,450 ft (Belen or
    Topboghazi Pass) are nearly fifty miles apart.

11 His 400 Greek mercenaries stayed behind and joined Cyrus; so no doubt his
    force had been tampered with and he may have done well to keep clear of Cyrus.
    The position of Thapsakos is uncertain, but on balance it seems to have been
    below Carchemish. The Zeugma (boat bridge) by the modern Birecik, fifteen
    miles north of Carchemish, became the regular crossing in Seleucid times.

12 As regards the crossing of Armenia most scholars agree on an acute-angle
    detour to the north-east; but the different routes that have been proposed are all
    speculative because there is no means of telling whether Xenophon's Euphrates
    here is the northern (Firat) or eastern (Murad Su) arm of the river.

13 The number given by the Oxyrhynchus historian is incomplete but must be
    between 14,000 and 19,000. Diodorus has 10,000.

14 Xen., *Hell.* IV 1, 29–40. Pharnabazos cannot therefore have been born appreci-
    ably later than 450. Xenophon did not need to tell Greek readers that deference
    to elders was engrained in Spartans.

15 Xenophon speaks of him as though he was still in his old satrapy four years
    later; and the mention of his son by Parapita being deprived of his rule when
    Pharnabazos left (above, p. 171) would fit with this. Ariobarzanes, a grandee in
    the province who was serving Pharnabazos in 404 B.C. and appears to have
    been both a scion of the Seven Families and an old friend of Tiribazos, was
    acting as though he was satrap in 387 and certainly was so later (below, p. 221).

16 The payment of mercenaries and crews will have been a large element in the
    expenditure; but food supplies, horses, cloth, and livestock may have had to be
    purchased.

17 From Plutarch we might assume that this campaign came later than Phar-
    nabazos' second assault on Egypt. But the careers of Tiribazos and Datames fit
    better with an earlier dating.

18 In making Artaxerxes march not only with his armour but with 12,000 talents'
    worth of ornament on his person Plutarch cannot have calculated the load he
    was imposing on him.

19 Diodorus (XV 41) twice makes this point in connection with Pharnabazos'
    dilatoriness on this campaign; but as regards the dash for Memphis the sugges-
    tion is made that he wanted his main body there for fear that Iphikrates and the
    mercenaries might conquer Egypt for Athens instead of Persia!

20 In the mid fourth century Athens still had 283 triremes (and so berths for nearly
    60,000 men) though she had not the money to pay crews to man them all. In the

struggle between Artaxerxes III and Nektanebo II alone 34,000 Greek mercenaries are reported to have been engaged on land.

21 Chabrias went to assist Euagoras but was apparently withdrawn by Athens because of the King's Peace; he was withdrawn from Egypt later when Pharnabazos complained to Athens, and Chares was withdrawn from Phrygia when Artaxerxes III protested (thus enabling the Thebans to secure a profitable contract). Some satraps, as Ariobarzanes and Orontes, gained assistance by generous gifts to Athens, and of course they had the equivalent of 'slush funds' for securing the services of politicians like Demosthenes.

22 This was recognized behaviour from the outset (as with Pissouthnes and Megabyxos' son); Amorges' mercenaries were content to join the Spartans as volunteers and Abrokomas' joined Cyrus.

23 *Hell. Oxy.* 19, referring to Konon but making a generalization of it. Probably it was not so much that the King was worse than other paymasters as the feeling that he at least did have the money to pay.

24 The figure given for his seven-day march from south-western Cappadocia to Pisidia is 2,500 stades (short furlongs) (Diod. XVIII 44); to judge by the associated names the distance must have been 250 miles as the crow flies. Neither terminal of his march across the central salt desert of Iran (p. 186) is fixed; but it sounds a remarkable feat with the men carrying their supplies. Alexander's dash with a selected mobile force to Rhagai in pursuit of Darius III, with horses dying and men dropping from exhaustion, would of course be farcical if we followed Arrian in making Agbatana the starting-point (III 19–20): eleven days spent in covering a distance of about 190 miles (eight stages in Curzon and Ferrier) would rank as 'long' marches but not forced ones. Some scholars assume that the error in Arrian lies in making Rhagai and not Darius' death-place the terminal. But a better solution is that given by Curtius Rufus: on the road from Persepolis Alexander received news of Darius' flight and forked off with his mobile column, while the main body continued to Agbatana. If Alexander was in a class with Antigonus this happened far to the south (on the fairly direct modern road by Isfahan and Qom Rhagai is 540 miles from Persepolis), and in fact Arrian has Alexander learn of Darius' flight as he entered Media twelve days out from Persepolis. There have been two routes into Media (that by Pasargadai and the 'summer route'), but at twelve days' normal travelling from Persepolis they would no longer be far apart: and we might reckon a daily average of about thirty-four miles for the eleven-day dash to Rhagai. On some of Alexander's marching speeds cf. C. Neumann, *Historia* XX (1971) 196–8.

25 200 stades (twenty-two to twenty-three miles) a day. Alexander is said by Arrian to have marched from Pella to Sestos (a good 400 miles) in twenty days in 334 B.C.; this was of course through his own territory where supplies would have been ordered in advance. Cyrus the Younger seems to have raised his speed to perhaps twenty miles a day when he started to press on in the Syrian desert. The continuous march of Abbas Mirza's army in the Russian war, which Col H. Rawlinson shortly afterwards reckoned to be 2,500 miles at an average of twenty-one and a half miles a day, has been claimed as a unique feat in history.

26 Such direct narrative as there is comes in Diodorus; Attic orators, Plutarch's and Nepos' biographies, collections of stratagems, coins, and Greek inscriptions help to complicate the issue. The essential modern work remains W. Judeich, *Kleinasiatische Studien*, whose sixty pages of chronological tables and elaborate index present the detail as it was available in 1892.

27 Diod. XV 90. It is often claimed that he was made governor there as the subordinate of the Sardis satrap. But there was never a satrapy of Mysia, and it

is intrinsically more likely that when rusticated he returned to his country seat. Armenia has been read in place of Mysia, but wrongly because Diodorus is expressly speaking of the coastal lands. The ethnic 'Baktrian' given to Orontes is a problem on its own since his father, Artasyras, was a high dignitary at the King's court (above, p. 173); it is tempting to suggest that Artasyras' father was a royal kinsman who had held the Baktrian satrapy.

28   Xen., *Anab.* I 6. He was in contact with the King and accused of trying to defect to him with 1,000 of Cyrus' cavalry.

29   To Ctesias he would have been distinctly over thirty-five when he came to the throne. If he is right in making Cyrus the third of a brood of thirteen children by the one wife, the difference in age between the two brothers will hardly have been more than a few years; so Cyrus may have been in his thirties when he died.

30   After 345 B.C. Mazaios was satrap of both Cilicia and Abarnahara and struck coins in both provinces. He later served with distinction under Darius III.

31   A dream that helped to inspire him is related in an Egyptian popular tale which purports to account for the defeat on religious grounds (cf. A.T. Olmstead, *History of the Persian Empire* 438–40).

32   The purge may have been exaggerated because a brother of Kodomannos, Oxathres, is mentioned fighting heroically at Issos in 333. Similarly Bagoas' purge of Artaxerxes III's sons does not seem to have been complete (Arrian, *Anab.* III 19, 4).

33   In his correspondence with Darius III in 333 B.C. Alexander accused the Kings of procuring the murder of Philip among other misdeeds. But there is no reason to suppose that he believed it.

34   Strabo XVI 766–67.

35   For other suggestions of vulnerability in the dark cf. pp. 92 (Megabates), 95 (Daurises), 96f. (Mardonios), 121 (Salamis), 221 (Datames' victory). Against this we must set the long and arduous night march of the Immortals round the Thermopylae position in 480.

36   It is worth noting that the Persian cavalry were foiled at the camp by Alexander's reserve infantry; it would seem that in close work they were less effective than the Macedonian cavalry (Agesilaos' battle at Sardis in 395 as described by Xenophon actually shows his infantry charging the Persians' cavalry after his own cavalry had engaged them).

37   The fact that Alexander was willing to pardon those of them who subsequently submitted to him, including the satrap Satibarzanes who had stabbed Darius, shows that he didn't really consider them traitors.

Epilogue

1   E.g. M. Roaf, *Iran* XV (1977) 147, and in my chapter for *CHI* II. From Herodotus we would gather only that Persian dress both at court and in the field was of Median origin.

2   E.F. Schmidt, *Persepolis* III (1970) pl. 24.

3   For this see C.G. Starr, *Iranica Antiqua* XI (1975) 48–53.

Appendix 1
Select Table of Kings

Lydia	Media	Assyria	Babylonia	Egypt
Gyges c.682–c.644	Khshathrita?	Esarhaddon 680–		Psammetichus I 663–
Ardys	Phraortes c.647–	Ashurbanipal 668–627		
Sadyattes		Sinsharishkun		
Alyattes 617 or later –	Kyaxares c.625–		Nabopolassar 625–	
		FALL OF NINEVEH 612 B.C.		Necho 609–
	Astyages c.585–		Nebuchadnezzar 605–561	Psammetichus II 594–
				Apries 588–
				Amasis 568–
Croesus c.560			Nabunaid 555–	
	PERSIAN CONQUEST c.550 B.C.			Psammetichus III 526–
PERSIAN CONQUEST c.546 B.C.			PERSIAN CONQUEST 539 B.C.	PERSIAN CONQUEST 525 B.C.

Appendix 2
List of Achaemenid Kings

Cyrus the Great	560/59–530
Cambyses	530–522
Bardiya (Smerdis)	522
Darius I	522–486
Xerxes I	486–465
Artaxerxes I (Arshu ?)	465–424
Xerxes II	424
Sogdianos	424–423
Darius II (Ochos)	423–405/4
Artaxerxes II (Arsakes)	405/4–359/58
Artaxerxes III (Ochos)	359/58–338/37
Artaxerxes IV (Arses)	338/37–336
Darius III (Kodomannos)	336–330

For ancestors of Cyrus the Great and Darius, see pp. 8–10

Index

Abanu 46
Abarnahara ('Beyond the River') *see esp*. 32, 61, 73, 77, 79, 81–2, 100, 169, 171, 173–5, 204–7, 223, 227, 242, 247, 257, 261, 264
Abbamush 74
Abbas Mirza 263
Abhar 262
Abraham, Patriarch 24, 147, 254
Abrokomas 84, 212, 216, 263
Abydos (Egypt) 111
Abydos (Hellespont) 109
Achaemenes (ancestor) 1, 8–10, 40, 44–5, 52, 137, 149
Achaemenes, son of Darius I 99, 167–8, 171
Achaemenian Village' 3
Acre 217
Adramyttion 178
Aegina, Aeginetans 97, 121
Aeolis, Aeolians 78, 95, 173, 216, 219
Aeschylus 42, 44, 115–16, 121, 132, 143, 145, 233, 236, 238, 247
Afghans 186
Afridis 191
Agbatana (Ekbatana) *see esp*. 4–6, 8, 22, 26–7, 29, 33, 49–50, 54–5, 67, 79, 88–9, 107, 145, 150, 183, 185, 228, 263
Agesilaos 21, 70, 171, 178, 214–15, 218–19, 221, 264
Ahasuerus 45, 100, 145, 246
Ahmose 174
ahura 155, 253
Ahuramazda *see esp*. 43, 67–9, 75, 93, 102, 104, 133, 147–50, 155–7, 238, 240, 245, 253–5
Ahwaz iv, 109
Akanthos 96
Akaufachiya 78, 242
Akes, R. 195
Akkad 30–1, 42, 223
Akoris 216
Alabanda 178
Aladdin Keykobad 144
Alai Mts 192
Alarodioi 79, 197
Alcibiades 209
Aleppo 29, 32, 53, 174, 204
Aleuadai 119
Alexander the Great *see esp*. 14, 23, 36–7, 65, 103, 109, 133, 184, 189–90, 197, 202, 207, 225–8, 230, 263–4
Alexander historians *see esp*. 23, 29, 35–6, 133, 185, 190
Alexandria (by Egypt) 23
Alexandria Eskhate 37
Alexandropolis (Kandahar) 189
Alilat 66, 111, 148, 252
Alp Arslan 186

Altin Tepe 198
Alyattes 4
Amanid Gates, Mt Amanos 199, 204, 212, 226, 262
Amardoi 182
Amasis 46, 251
Amathous 93
Amestris, daughter of Otanes 135, 169–70, 244; *others of same name* 218, 249
Amman 175
Ammianus Marcellinus 23, 154, 187
Ammon, Oasis of 48, 141
Amorges (Homarges) 37–8, 260
Amorges, son of Pissouthnes 84, 130, 178, 208–9, 263
Ampe 65
Amu Darya *see* Oxus
Amyntas 178
Amyrgian, Amyrgion 196, 260
Amyrtaios 127, 169, 172
Amytis, daughter of Astyages (?) 33
Amytis, daughter of Xerxes 141, 168, 249
Amyzon 177
Anabasis of Cyrus 20, 130, 211–12
Anahita, Anaitis 69, 147–51, 180, 253
Anamis, R. 186
Anaphes 170, 257
Anatolia *see esp*. 11, 26, 102, 111, 117, 147, 166, 173, 180–2, 199
Anaxibios 210
Anaximenes 35
angaros 108
Anopaia 119–20
Anshan 2–3, 8–10, 27, 32–3, 35, 107
Antalkidas 215–16
Anthylla 135, 250
Antigonus 35, 186, 220, 227, 259, 263
Antilebanon 204
Antiochus III 186
Antitaurus Mts 180
Anubanini 67
Aornos 192
apadana *see esp*. 49, 75, 91, 142, 158–64, 230, 242, 255–6, 260
Apad(a)na 36
Apame 74, 171, 257
Aparytai 79, 191
Apasiakai 194–6
Aphrodite 148, 252
Apis 49, 60
Apollo 43, 148, 252
Apollonides 141, 168
Arab geographers 67, 88, 107, 188–9, 197
Arabah 206
Arabaya, Arabia 28, 30, 77, 79,

81–2, 172, 190, 206, 229, 252
'Arabian Gulf' (Red Sea) 64, 205
Arabian Sea 14, 64, 78
Arabitai 190
Arabs *see esp*. 46–8, 87, 103–4, 111, 140, 148, 172, 175, 203–7, 258, 261
Arachosia 29–30, 56, 61, 63, 71, 78, 81–2, 166, 173, 188, 260
Arachotos, R. 188
Arados 65
Aral Sea 69, 194
Aramaeans 175, 205, 261
Ararat, Mt 197
Araxes, R. (Aras) 197–8
Araxes, R. (Jaxartes?) 36, 194
Araxes, R. (Persis) 35
Arbakes 212, 232
Arbela 28, 73, 88, 185, 227
arche, archon 77, 82, 84, 172
Archelaos 223
Arderikka 73, 98
Ardumanish (?) 19, 54, 167
Areia 78–9, 83, 88, 173, 190, 195–6, 203, 260
Argandab, R. 188
Arginousai 210
Argos 97, 128, 248
Ariabignes 121, 247
Ariaios 178, 212, 214
Ariamenes 241, 247
Ariana, Ariane iii, 62, 193, 229
Ariaramnes, son of Teispes 8–9, 69; *others of same name* 62, 177
Ariaspai 29
Ariaspes 222
Ariobarzanes 171, 178, 216, 221, 257, 262–3
Arioi 80
Ariomandes 247
Arishittu *see* Arsites
Aristagoras 92–5
Aristazanes 144
Aristeides 97
Aristoboulos 36
Aristophanes 143
Aristotle 73
Ariya (Aryan) iii, 7, 40, 68, 76, 80, 149–50, 154
Ariyaramna *see* Ariaramnes
Ariyawrata 173
Arizantoi 7
Armenia, Armenians *see esp*. 11, 26, 30, 55–6, 73, 79, 82, 102, 108, 111, 115, 150, 170–1, 185, 197–8, 203, 213, 215, 222, 224, 253, 260–2, 264
Armina (Armenia) 78, 198
Aroandas (Orontes) 257
Arphaxad 232
Arrajan 88, 244
Arrian *see esp*. 23, 29